MW00330943

Yugoslavia and After

Yugoslavia and After

A Study in Fragmentation, Despair and Rebirth

edited by
DAVID A. DYKER and IVAN VEJVODA

Longman
London and New York

Pearson Education Limited
Edinburgh Gate
Harlow, Essex CM20 2JE, England
and Associated Companies throughout the world.

*Published in the United States of America
by Addison Wesley Longman Publishing, New York*

© Pearson Education Limited 1996

The right of David Dyker and Ivan Vejvoda to be identified
as the editors of this work has been asserted by them in
accordance with the Copyright, Designs and Patents Act 1988.

All rights reserved; no part of this publication may be
reproduced, stored in a retrieval system, or transmitted
in any form or by any means, electronic, mechanical,
photocopying, recording, or otherwise without either the
prior written permission of the Publishers or a licence
permitting restricted copying in the United Kingdom issued
by the Copyright Licensing Agency Ltd.,
90 Tottenham Court Road, London W1P 0LP.

First published 1996
Second impression 1999

ISBN 0 582 24637-7 PPR

British Library Cataloguing-in-Publication Data

A catalogue record for this book is
available from the British Library

Library of Congress Cataloging-in-Publication Data

A catalogue record for this book is available from the Library of Congress

.

Set by 8 in 10/12 Times
Produced by Pearson Education Asia (Pte) Ltd.
Printed in Singapore

Contents

List of Contributors   ix
Preface   xi

Chapter one **Introduction, *David A. Dyker***   **1**

PART I: THE ANATOMY OF COLLAPSE

Chapter two **Yugoslavia 1945–91 – from Decentralisation Without
Democracy to Dissolution, *Ivan Vejvoda***   **9**
  An historical sketch   10
  The Yugoslav communist experiment   11
  The legacy of communism – from hard to soft totalitarianism   13
  Constitutional experiment – decentralisation without
    democratisation   15
  Demise of the federal state – rise of the proto-states   16
  The ethnification of politics   17
  Society and citizens – privacy without democracy   21
  Of constitutions and electoral laws   22
  Conclusion   23

Chapter three **The Disintegration of Yugoslavia: Causes and
Consequences of Dynamic Inefficiency in Semi-command
Economies, *Vesna Bojičić***   **28**
  Introduction   28
  Development strategy, economic system and economic
    efficiency in postwar Yugoslavia: factors of disintegration   29
  Investment, technological development and structural change   35
  Regional development   40
  The supremacy of politics over economics   44
  Concluding remarks   45

Chapter four **The Degeneration of the Yugoslav Communist Party as a Managing Elite – a Familiar East European Story?** *David A. Dyker* **48**

  Introduction 48
  The Soviet Communist Party – model of control, model of
    decline? 50
  The Yugoslav communist system – evolution and degeneration 53
  How familiar is the story? 60
  How much difference does it make? 61

Chapter five **The Collapse of Yugoslavia – Between Chance and Necessity,** *Slavo Radošević* **65**

  Introduction 65
  Technico-economic factors of the disintegration of
    Yugoslavia, and the structural schlerosis of the 1980s 67
  The socialist political elite and the victory of national
    liberalism 74
  Collective memories, identity and ontological insecurity in
    the dynamics of collapse 77
  The limits of irrationality and the re-emergence of economics? 80

PART II: IN THE EYE OF THE STORM

Chapter six **Bosnia and Hercegovina – State and Communitarianism,** *Xavier Bougarel* **87**

  State and communitarianism in Bosnia: from *millets* to nations 88
  The resurgence of communitarian politics and nationalist
    ideologies in socialist Yugoslavia 93
  The tripartite coalition and the communitarian dismantling
    of the state 98
  From the dismantling of the state to the disintegration of
    the communities 103
  Return of the state, return of the communities? 108
  The Croat-Muslim Federation: one state or two? 110
  The Serb Republic in crisis 111
  Turnabouts and continuities 112

Chapter seven **The Yugoslav Army and the Post-Yugoslav Armies,** *Miloš Vasić* **116**

  Introduction 116
  Communism and Bonapartism 117
  The history: from heroism to paralysis 118
  Enter Milošević: the collapse of communism 121
  The arming of Croatia 122

Saving communism and Milošević   124
A history of failed coups   125
A Slovenian interlude   127
A war of expansion: Croatia   128
A time of purges   130
The loss of Bosnia   131
The three Serb armies   132
The VJ and Milošević's police today   134
Croatia: a new power in the Balkans   134
The Bosnian Army and the people's war   135
Conclusion   137

Chapter eight **The Albanian Movement in Kosova,**
Shkelzen Maliqi   **138**
   The social framework   138
   Harbingers of the Albanian movement – the demonstrations
     of 1968 and 1981   139
   The formation of a pluralised Albanian movement under the
     threat of war   141
   The roots of Albanian political organisation   143
   Political organisations and parties on the contemporary Kosova
     political scene   145
   The suspension of the autonomy of Kosova by Serbia 149
   The impact of the suspension of Kosova's autonomy on the
     process of democratisation   150
   The unofficial elections of 1992   151
   A path to the future?   152

Chapter nine **The West and the International Organisations,**
Susan L. Woodward   **155**
   Introduction   155
   Interdependence and transition: origins of the crisis 156
   International intervention   164
   Toward new frameworks?   172

PART III: THE SUCCESSOR STATES

Chapter ten **Neither War nor Peace: Serbia and Montenegro in
the First Half of the 1990s,** *Jovan Teokarević*   **179**
   Introduction   179
   From peace to war   179
   From war to peace   185
   Neither war nor peace   190

Chapter eleven **Croatia, *Christopher Cviić*** **196**
Introduction 196
In and out of empires 197
The Croats and Yugoslavia 200
The communist corset 202
'Croatia firstism' triumphs 205
Unfinished business 209

Chapter twelve **Slovenia: a Success Story – or Facing an Uncertain Future?** *Frane Adam* **213**
Political system: on the way to stability 213
Economic performance and problems 217
The new social portrait: winners and losers 224
Conclusion 229

Chapter thirteen **Macedonia – an Island on the Balkan Mainland, *Ferid Muhić*** **232**
Introduction 232
The trials of history and the imperative of identity 233
Historical disputes 235
Factors in the break-up of Yugoslavia 239
The 'Sinking of the Titanic' as a social and political paradigm 241
A beleaguered economic transition 245
Prospects for social peace 246
Leadership and security 246

Chapter fourteen **By Way of Conclusion: to Avoid the Extremes of Suffering ..., *Ivan Vejvoda*** **248**
Identity crisis, political crisis 250
Yugoslavia's unsuccessful 'revolt against Yalta' 252
The Great Fear 253
The consequences and costs of war and the 'high price of peace' 254
Of the role of individuals and states 256
Pax Daytoniana – ceasefire or peace? 257

Index 264

List of Contributors

Frane Adam: Professor at the Faculty of Social Sciences, University of Ljubljana. Frane Adam is editor of *Elections and Politics Slovenian Style* (1993).

Vesna Bojičić: formerly Lecturer in Economics at the University of Mostar, Bosnia and Hercegovina, Vesna Bojičić came to Britain after the outbreak of war in Bosnia. She is now Visiting Fellow at the Sussex European Institute, University of Sussex. She is the author of *The Political Economy of the War in Bosnia-Herzegovina* (1996).

Xavier Bougarel: collaborator of the *Centre d'Études et de Recherches Internationales* of the *Fondation Nationale des Sciences Politiques*, Paris, Xavier Bougarel is author of *Bosnie: Anatomie d'un Conflit* (1996).

Christoper Cviić: born in Croatia and educated at the Universities of Zagreb, London (London School of Economics) and Oxford (St Antony's College), Christopher Cviić has lived in Britain since 1954. He was a producer and editor with the BBC World Service in London until 1969. From 1969 to 1990 he was *The Economist's* East and Central Europe Correspondent. His book *Remaking the Balkans* was published in 1991. A second, updated edition came out in 1995.

David A. Dyker: Reader in Economics in the School of European Studies and co-director of the East Europe Programme of the Science Policy Research Unit, both at the University of Sussex, David Dyker has been researching and writing on Eastern Europe for more than twenty-five years, and lived in the former Yugoslavia for a number of extended periods. He is the author of *Yugoslavia: Socialism, Development and Debt* (1990).

Shkelzen Maliqi: philosopher, writer and politician from Prishtina, Kosova, Shkelzen Maliqi is the author of *Byzantine Iconoclasm* (1982), *Knot of Kosovo* (1990), *Albanian Ghandism* (1993) and *Albanians and Europe* (1994). He was a founder of the Social-Democratic Party of Kosova. He is the senior editor of the Prishtina journal *MM*.

Ferid Muhić: Professor at the Faculty of Philosophy, University of Skopje, Ferid Muhić is the author of *Motivation and Meditation* (1987), *Philosophy and Iconoclasm* (1988), *The Language of Philosophy* (1995), and *Macedonia: Catena Mundi* (1994).

Slavo Radošević: formerly Research Fellow at the Institute of Economics, Zagreb. Slavo Radošević is currently Leverhulme Research Fellow on the East Europe Programme of the Science Policy Research Unit, University of Sussex. He is the author of many articles on industrial and technology policy issues in transition countries.

Jovan Teokarević: Research Fellow at the Institute for European Studies, Belgrade. Jovan Teokarević is the editor of *Reforms – the Second Step: Hungary, Poland, Bulgaria* (1988), co-editor of *Departing from Socialism* (1990), and co-author, with S. Živanov, of *Reforms in Socialist Countries* (1990).

Miloš Vasić: a senior writer for the independent weekly magazine *Vreme*, Belgrade. Miloš Vasić is also a contributor to the *Guardian* and *Balkan War-report* (London).

Ivan Vejvoda: Research Fellow at the Sussex European Institute, University of Sussex, and at the Institute of European Studies, Belgrade, Ivan Vejvoda has edited the selected works of La Boetie, Robespierre and Saint-Just. He is also co-editor of *The French Revolution and the Present* (1990). He was one of the founders of the Democratic Forum in Belgrade (1989) and of the Belgrade Circle – Association of Independent Intellectuals (1992).

Susan L. Woodward: Senior Fellow in the Foreign Policy Studies Program at the Brookings Institution, Washington DC, Susan L.Woodward is author of *Socialist Unemployment: The Political Economy of Yugoslavia 1945–1990* (1995) and of *Balkan Tragedy: Chaos and Dissolution After the Cold War* (1995).

Preface

This book is the product of collaboration at the University of Sussex between the Science Policy Research Unit (SPRU), specifically its ESRC-financed STEEP programme, and the Sussex European Institute (SEI). The collaboration developed for two reasons, one fundamental and intellectual, the other happily accidental. On the one hand, the obvious interest of SEI in an important and volatile region of Europe converged with that of STEEP's East European sub-programme in the conditions and characteristics of economic and political transition. On the other, there happened to be, just at the time when the Yugoslav crisis was breaking, a remarkable concentration of expertise on the region in the two institutions. In assembling the roster of authors we were able to access not only that concentration of expertise, but also the wide-ranging network of contacts that clusters around it. The result is a book written largely by 'insiders' – but insiders with global perspectives. It would be difficult to name all the people who have helped with the preparation of the volume. We take this opportunity to thank them all. Responsibility for the final product does, of course, remain with us.

David A. Dyker and Ivan Vejvoda
April 1996

Chapter 1

Introduction

DAVID A. DYKER

Why study the former Yugoslavia? Four reasons spring immediately to mind:

1   Yugoslavia, in one form or another, was the political framework for the
    majority of South Slavs (Yugo-Slavs) for the greater part of the twentieth
    century. Thus the twentieth century history of the Slovenes, Croats, Serbs and
    Macedonians, not to mention the Montenegrins, Kosovo Albanians and
    Vojvodina Hungarians, has been played out on a Yugoslav stage. Anyone
    wishing to understand the dramas that have unfolded on that stage must
    understand the successive Yugoslav political frameworks, in all their
    imperfections and ultimate futility.
2   That imperfect and ultimately futile Yugoslavia played, in its second
    (communist) incarnation, a vital international role, both regional, in terms of
    the Balkans, and globally, in terms of the Cold War. Communist Yugoslavia
    was always the dominant power in the communist-dominated part of the
    peninsula in the postwar period, the only Balkan country to have a truly
    distinctive foreign policy stance, with Zhivkov's Bulgaria largely content to
    be the 'sixteenth republic' of the Soviet Union, and Romania and Albania
    tending, in the post-Stalin period, to fall into more or less bizarre forms of
    isolationism. If we want to understand the dynamics of the Cold War, and the
    way it affected an inherently unstable and painfully backward region of
    Europe, we have to be able to discern not only the key features of
    communist-Yugoslav foreign policy, but also *the internal factors that
    conditioned that policy.*
3   The successor states of Yugoslavia are, each one, worthy of detailed scholarly
    study in their own right, and there is no successor state that does not present
    critical policy-making issues for the European Union, the United States, the
    other OECD countries and Russia. Slovenia is an outstanding success story
    of economic transition, a country that seems to be able to tell other transition
    countries where to be conservative, where to be radical in relation to
    transformation policies. It is a country anxious to gain membership of the
    European Union, and with a strong case in terms of basic political and
    economic criteria – but until recently thwarted by a dispute with Italy over
    property rights which bore a baleful similarity to the kinds of disputes that

fuelled the Yugoslav wars. At the other end of the spectrum, both geographically and in terms of levels of economical development, stands Macedonia, a country which cannot, for the moment, pretend to be a serious candidate for European Union membership but which, like Slovenia up to mid-1996, is involved in an arcane dispute with an EU member – in this case Greece – over names and historical symbols, a dispute that has left Macedonia with the curious official (though temporary) title of 'Former Yugoslav Republic of Macedonia'.

Serbia/Montenegro, newly liberated from the burden of sanctions, has yet to be welcomed back into the global family. And with the Kosovo problem apparently insoluble, and Slobodan Milošević as secure in power as ever and tending to become, if anything, even more dictatorial, the immediate prospects of full normalisation of relations with the rest of the world are poor. This is a problem for the West, because Serbia/Montenegro, economically exhausted and militarily dispirited as she is, remains a major power in the Balkans. It is a major problem for Russia, because Russian public opinion demands that Moscow give more support to Belgrade than is consonant with Russia's own globalisation agenda. And therefore it is also a problem in relations between the West and Russia. Croatia is somewhere in between Slovenia and Serbia/Montenegro, with significant economic success to its credit, which has nevertheless yet to achieve critical transformational mass, but at the same time with a 'democratic deficit' almost as serious as the Serbian one. And because the West has been more prepared to support Croatia in its efforts towards economic and political transition, Croatian shortcomings are that much more embarrassing for the Western allies. Bosnia, finally, is, despite the Dayton agreement, still not really a state at all. It is rather a framework within which three communitarian, even sectarian politico-military constellations *may* be able to reconstruct a viable consociationalism in the future. It is a framework which is at its weakest in relation to the critical military dimension. And with the Army of Bosnia and Hercegovina now, by common consent, one of the finest fighting forces in Europe, and the Croatian forces in Bosnia equally formidable, the danger that the integument may burst, and the conflict reignite, cannot be dismissed from the council rooms of the West.

4   Each of the successor states shows a striking degree of continuity with one or more aspects of the old Yugoslavia, or in some cases with elements of society and polity that go back before the creation of the First Yugoslavia. Slovenia, it seems, is the legitimate heir of Yugoslav market socialism, able to enjoy the luxury of gradualism in transition policies because so much of the groundwork had been laid before transition officially started. Macedonia continues to be ruled on the basis of the kind of delicate ethnic consensus that Titoist Yugoslavia had seemed so good at (with the benefit of hindsight we can see that it flattered to deceive). Bosnia, by contrast, is faced with the daunting task of trying to build a more sophisticated form of the consociationalism it has practised for centuries, amidst the devastation of war and the spectres of ethnic cleansing. Milošević's Serbia is a classic case of

'*nomenklatura*[1] nationalism', with an old communist apparatchik, having completed a seamless transmogrification from Marxism-Leninism to nationalism, still in power, and still wielding power in an essentially communist way. Tudjman's Croatia, too, owes more to Titoist Yugoslav practice than the Croatian president would like to admit, while at the same time also reaching back to earlier incarnations of the Croatian state.

In this volume we have sought to address all these four points: to study Yugoslavia in the context of post-Yugoslav reality, to study the successor states, in their own right, and in the context of the Yugoslav and pre-Yugoslav background – and to fix all these firmly in the global context. In so doing, we have had to grapple with a whole range of methodological problems.

In Part I, 'The Anatomy of Collapse', we had originally thought in terms of a ·division of labour', with a political scientist treating the political side of the disintegration of Yugoslavia, a couple of economists presenting different aspects of the economic side of the break-up, and a political economist putting the whole story into the context of the general trends in Eastern Europe over the past few decades. It soon became clear that this division of labour would not hold. Anyone seeking to tell the story of the collapse of Yugoslavia, whatever their emphasis or disciplinary background, is bound to span the whole gamut of social-scientific methodologies, and is bound to situate their analysis within the context of the story of the decay and disintegration of communism across the whole East European region. So each of the four chapters of Part I tell essentially the same story – but in different ways and with different insights. This has inevitably meant a slight element of overlap, though even where there is overlap, it is enriching overlap, which helps to sharpen the focus through illumination from different angles. And it means that the chapters of Part I have to be taken together, read, as it were, 'simultaneously', rather than consecutively.

How to treat the *successor states*? The former Yugoslavia has not fallen apart neatly, like a ripe orange. Only one of the successor states – Slovenia – has managed to disentangle itself completely from the old constellation and achieve total redefinition as a Central-East European state with the same global aspirations as other Central-East European states like Hungary and Poland. Croatia aspires to the same status as Slovenia, but in practice to a great extent it is still locked into a peculiar, post-Yugoslav political economy in which relations with other successor states – and in particular Serbia/Montenegro – are still critical. Serbia/Montenegro itself remains unrecognised in the West and remains, even with the suspension of sanctions, something of a pariah state. Macedonia, formally as independent as any of them, has still to prove that it is viable as a wholly separate state. But the real problems start when we come to Bosnia. Recognised as a successor state by the international community, Bosnia in practice has been partitioned between three militarised, ethnically based political movements. It was still, at time of writing, quite unclear whether, or in what form, the baroque architecture of the Dayton agreement would actually deliver a system of state administration in this critical region. Even more difficult to handle is the case of Kosovo. Formally (for the world as well as for

---

[1] I have used the Serbo-Croat forms throughout for singular and plural, namely *nomenklatura* and *nomenklature* respectively.

Belgrade) Kosovo is simply a part of Serbia with a large Albanian populaton. In reality, it is an Albanian-Kosovar shadow state, with government, civil service, social services, etc.

As with so many aspects of the former Yugoslavia, then, the successor states present a spectrum rather than a series of neat categories. We decided to treat Slovenia, Croatia, Serbia/Montenegro and Macedonia as fully-fledged successor states, demanding treatment in terms of their own, individual institutions, policy preoccupations, etc. Bosnia and Kosovo, by contrast, have been treated as unsettled issues, pregnant with the possibility of future instability, even conflagration. In these cases we have, accordingly, placed primary emphasis on the unsettled issues, and the background to those issues, rather than on the structures, or parastructures of state and policy-making.

In Part II of the book, 'In the Eye of the Storm', the reader will find not only chapters on those two unsettled regions, but also chapters on their international and military dimensions. Here again, we faced methodological difficulties. Since every author in the book has had, perforce, to face up to the international dimensions of the particular story they are telling, why have a special chapter on the international dimension? Chapter 9 does, of course, speak for itself. But it may be in place to state, at this introductory stage, some of the underlying factors that have shaped our treatment of the international dimension. It is palpably not enough to look at the international relations of the individual successor states, or even to look at the international context of the former Yugoslavia from the point of view of this or that specific aspect of the internal political dynamics of that state. If the picture is to be complete, both Yugoslavia and the successor states have to be set firmly within the framework of the unique circumstances of a world globalising in conditions of Cold War, and of a successor world where continued globalisation without the trammels of the Cold War has served merely to highlight the fault-lines, the inherent tendencies to fragmentation, which were indeed largely concealed or patched up under conditions of geostrategic confrontation.

With the war now over, at least for the time being, it might seem inappropriate to include a chapter specifically on the military dimension. On reflection, however, we felt that peace had, if anything, strengthened the case for placing in perspective the military configurations of the region, past and present. As long as scholars try to understand communist Yugoslavia, they will have to try to understand the Yugoslav People's Army, the 'Seventh Republic'. And if scholars and policy-makers want to understand the contemporary political dynamics of the former Yugoslav region, they will have to take account of the unique, and potentially explosive, distribution of military potential of that region. They will have to consider the implications of the juxtaposition of small, lightly armed but efficient armies and large, heavily armed but inefficient ones; more particularly, they will have to consider the likely consequences, in case those small, efficient armies become increasingly heavily armed.

Finally, we had to address the issue of *personal colouring*. In choosing our team, we placed first priority on expertise – more specifically on 'hands-on' expertise. In that context it was only logical for us to ask a Slovene scholar to write the chapter on Slovenia, a Croat (though of British citizenship) to write on Croatia, a Serb on

Serbia/Montenegro and a citizen of Macedonia on the most southerly of the successor states. We extended that logic further in asking a Kosovo Albanian to write on Kosovo. We asked a young French scholar with intimate knowledge of Bosnia and Hercegovina to treat the epicentre of the conflict. Finally we engaged the leading specialist on the armed forces of the former Yugoslavia, a Serb, to write on the military dimension. For the more contextual chapters we put together a team of Western-based specialists, some of Yugoslav origin, some not, but all with an intimate knowledge of the area, of the East European region and of the global context.

In so doing, we did not ask Serbs to 'filter out' their Serbness, Croats their Croatness – or indeed Americans their Americanness. We believe there is nothing tendentious in any of the chapters that follow. But each specialist follows their own line of analysis, coloured by their personal experience, informed by their special insights, and shaped by their personal standpoint *vis-à-vis* the conflict. Inevitably, then, there are differences of perspective between authors. But these are differences of sentiment, rather than argument. Some of our authors regret the passing of the Second Yugoslavia, some do not. None see any prospect of the emergence of a Third Yugoslavia within the foreseeable future, and accordingly all insist that, for better or worse, the framework, or rather spectrum, of successor states will provide the institutional context of the South Slav area – for South Slavs, Kosovo Albanians, Vojvodina Hungarians and the international community alike – into the new millennium. And once the focus shifts to the successor states, there is a remarkable degree of consensus among the contributors:

1   All the successor states are, to a greater or lesser degree, 'unfinished states' – like the First and Second Yugoslavias; and Slovenia, for all its achievements and stability, is no exception.

2   All the successor states (Slovenia and Macedonia are genuine partial exceptions here) suffer from a problem of 'democratic deficit'.

3   The weight of traditional political culture weighs heavily on all the successor states apart from Slovenia. To a degree, this factor merely reinforces, or helps to explain, Factor 2, above. Presidents Tudjman, Milošević and Izetbegović are all *caudillos* in the Karadjordjević/Tito tradition. But there is another, more ambivalent side to the traditional political culture issue which is best exemplified by the cases of Bosnia and Macedonia. To the extent that these two countries have any tradition of civil society, of local self-government, it is a tradition of informal consociationalism, of 'good neighbourliness' (*komšiluk*). This is not the same thing as a tradition of democracy, but it is, nevertheless, an element of political culture which can hardly be ignored in any attempt to build democracy in these regions.

4   Though the war is ended, we should talk in terms of permanent truce, rather than of true peace. The former Yugoslavia is still littered with 'powder kegs': Eastern Slavonia, the Sandjak, Kosovo, the Albanian-majority areas of Macedonia. 'Soft' ethnic cleansing continues, and continues to corrode what is left of the social fabric in the regions affected. Serbia's refugee problem, already extremely serious, could grow to critical, destabilising proportions. The spirit of ethnic sectarianism still dominates in many places and at many

levels. The successor states are not disarming and there is far too much military hardware and far too many men under arms in the region for its own good. The Dayton political architecture for Bosnia, its overcomplexity apart, is unsound in the sense that it recognises the negative aspects of traditional culture without recognising the more positive ones.

5   With the exception of Slovenia, all the successor states face extremely uncertain economic prospects. Privatisation has hardly begun and there has been little restructuring with a view to addressing global markets. There has been restructuring, in the direction of militarised autarky, especially in the case of Serbia/Montenegro, and almost everywhere in terms of an expansion of the gangster economy which goes beyond anything experienced in the other transition economies. It goes without saying that this kind of restructuring can only make the job of genuine restructuring that much more difficult.

6   As with the Second Yugoslavia, the international community has played a deeply ambivalent role in relation to the successor states. Sanctions and continued isolation have weakened and impoverished Serbia/Montenegro. But the more positive Western attitude to Croatia has also created problems, with inflows of aid and multilateral military expenditure lending the Croatian balance of payments and the Croatian currency a false air of strength – and making life difficult for the Croatian firms that would conquer new international markets. Bosnia, in its post-Dayton incarnation, can only survive on international charity. Yet it is not clear exactly how, and in what amounts, that charity will flow. Macedonia can, perhaps, count on the support of distant friends. But her immediate 'Western' neighbour continues to view her with hostility and suspicion.

The sobering conclusion is that *most of the successor states suffer from exactly the same problems as the first two Yugoslavias suffered from.* That is not necessarily grounds for despair. But it does mean that the governments and peoples of these states, and the international community, will have to do much better in the future than they have done in the past, if the nightmares of the past are not to return.

Part One

The Anatomy of Collapse

Chapter 2

Yugoslavia 1945–91 – from Decentralisation Without Democracy to Dissolution

IVAN VEJVODA

If we want to be at home on this Earth, even at the price of being at home in this century, we must try to take part in the interminable dialogue with the essence of totalitarianism.

Hannah Arendt (1954)

Nationalism is … perhaps the most compelling of all motives that can lead men to abandon or scorn politics.

Bernard Crick (1962)

After existing for seventy years, Yugoslavia failed, in the aftermath of the 'year of revolutions' of 1989, in its attempt to recast its institutions and make the passage toward a democratic, multinational – and secular – polity. It would be fair to say that the collapse of the bipolar European architecture that had buttressed the 'independent' country of Yugoslavia suddenly exposed, in a broader arena, the unsettled state and weaknesses of the Yugoslav communist federation. With a delicate irony, Marx's idea of the 'withering away of the state' had by 1989, and in unorthodox fashion, come to fruition in Yugoslavia (at the federal level), even as new states arose within it.

If we are to understand the violent breakdown of a European country at the end of the twentieth century, when state frameworks on this continent at least seemed generally secure, we must go beyond simple explanations. The need for an approach which brings out the intricacy and many-sidedness of the political, social and economic dynamics of the situation is palpable. Former Yugoslavia cannot be understood outside the context of a complex approach, indeed 'it cannot be simplified … without being distorted out of all recognition' (Pavlowitch, 1971: 20). Only if painstakingly delineated in its historical, cultural, social-anthropological, political and social dynamics, can the narrative take on the forcefulness required to come to grips with the questions which present themselves: not just the why of the disintegration, but the how and especially the why of the extreme violence.

In a brief chapter, only a résumé of some of the key elements of a complicated picture can be offered. At the outset, it should be stressed that the absence of any meaningful democratic political culture, of a civil society, of representative political institutions, of democracy, combined with a legacy of 'surreal' (Puhovski, 1990: 32), unaccountable, instrumental and manipulative communist politics, in which citizens were intentionally kept away from decision-making processes, provided the worst possible basis for democratic transition. The only 'political' expression of a broader sort under the old system was collective and communitarian, in the first place through the Communist Party and, as that shell became increasingly void and meaningless and the search for renewed legitimation more and more urgent, through nationalist ideology. Against the background of power struggle among the governing elites for the political, social and economic inheritance of communist Yugoslavia, the challenge of peaceful, pluralist and democratic transformation proved to be a task beyond the reach of men and women who had come to power mainly through the negative selection patterns of obedience and loyalty to the party hierarchy. Their shared dissatisfaction with Yugoslavia and the distribution of power within it found no rational political expression. It succeeded only in generating a violent, belligerent competition for territories and new boundaries, in which the people in whose names these changes were being advocated suffered enormously.

An historical sketch

The Kingdom of the Serbs, Croats and Slovenes was born on 1 December 1918, in the aftermath of the First World War, of the subsequent breakdown of the Austro-Hungarian Empire, and of the final demise of the Ottoman Empire. It emerged as the result of an interaction between several cultured, national Slav elites, all aspiring to create a new, common state in which they could find shelter from the surrounding bigger nations, and consequently strength in togetherness, while at the same time fulfilling older aspirations. The Slovenes and Croats greatly improved on their previous status by entering the new country (whose name became Yugoslavia only in 1929), while the Serbs were able to unite ethnically within one state, having previously been scattered and divided. It is interesting to look back at a 1933 appraisal of the result:

> Yugoslavia ... inherited peoples from different jurisdictions: all of the former Kingdoms of Serbia and Montenegro; Croatia-Slavonia and part of the Banat from Hungary; Carniola, Dalmatia and parts of Istria and Carinthia from Austria; a part of Bulgaria; and the two imperial provinces of the former Dual Monarchy, Bosnia and Herzegovina. With the exception of a half million or so Germans and an equal number of Magyars, most of the peoples inhabiting these areas may be considered South Slavs; but Croat, Slovene and Serb are even further apart than Russian, Austrian and Prussian Poles. Cultural traditions, economic standards, religion, political temper, and even language separate them. If they are ever to be reconciled it will take more political imagination than Yugoslavia's present rulers appear to possess.
>
> (Zurcher, 1933: 274)

The short, twenty-three-year life-span of the first Yugoslavia was strewn with assassinations and failed attempts to create a viable parliamentary monarchy, a 'trione' Yugoslav nation (in terms of an effort to merge the three main constituent nations), to resolve problems of the mutual relations and aspirations of the recognised and unrecognised (Macedonians, Muslims and Albanians) ethnic groups. A revision of the centralist construction of the state in 1939, conceding autonomous status to Croatia in the form of a separate *banovina* (province), pointed in the right direction, but was too little, too late. And the first Yugoslavia disappeared in the course of the Second World War, having emerged from the First.

The institutionally centralised, monarchist construction of the state (1918–41) gave way, through a national liberation war and a concurrent civil war, to a (at first only nominally) federal communist reconstruction of the (party)state (1944–91), in which the whole architecture of the country was recast to give republic status to Slovenia, Croatia, Serbia, Bosnia and Hercegovina, Montenegro and Macedonia (running from north to south). The war had proved to be an extremely violent and traumatic experience. Yugoslavia had disappeared off the map of Europe, carved up by the Axis powers after the 6 April 1941 German bombing of Belgrade which initiated the war. Hitler had created a quisling state in Croatia, which engulfed Bosnia and persecuted Serbs, Jews and Gypsies. The war against the occupiers and the interethnic killing combined claimed over a million victims (Pavlowitch, 1988: 137–8; see also fn. 3 to Chapter 11 in this volume). Of the rival liberation forces, it was the partisans, under the leadership of the Communist Party of Yugoslavia and its chief, Josip Broz Tito (1892–1980), who came out as the winners, with an army of 800,000 strong by 1945 – but in a country that also had 350,000 fighting as quislings (Pavlowitch, 1988: 49).

Without wishing to deny the importance of the 'long waves' of history, or of particular historical watersheds such as the split of the Roman Empire into Western and Eastern halves, the rise and fall of various medieval and modern South Slav statehoods or the developments since the early nineteenth century when the 'Yugoslav idea' began to take shape, I shall focus in this study on the post-Second World War period, which lasted forty-six years and gave Yugoslavia a new regime, and a period twice as long as that vouchsafed to the First Yugoslavia to pursue state- and nation-building dynamics. Under the new communist leadership, within a period of one decade, the country managed to gain an international respectability, prestige and status unusual for such a relatively small – and communist – country.

The Yugoslav communist experiment

Yugoslav communism was not imported by Soviet Red Army tanks. It had a political tradition going back long before the Second World War. In the first elections of the First Yugoslavia in 1919, the Communist Party of Yugoslavia fared well, coming fourth with 12 per cent of the vote. The 1929 annulment of the 1921 constitution, and the associated banning of all political parties, forced the CP underground. It became a small, militant and well-organised Third Communist International (Comintern) Communist Party, to the leadership of which Tito succeeded in 1937. It was, among other things, that militant and well-organised base that permitted it to come through as the dominant political force in the wartime period.

This Communist Party, that was destined to lead the Yugoslav peoples victoriously in the struggle against Nazism and Fascism, and then into postwar reconstruction under the slogan of 'brotherhood and unity', fulfilled an ironic destiny in prematurely anticipating the much later tragic disaggregationary developments. The Leninist-Stalinist, Moscow-led Comintern considered the First Yugoslavia to be a

'Versailles-construction' of an imperialist kind, that was expected to benefit from future emancipation in the form of self-determination for its oppressed peoples, and thereby dissolution of the 'Versailles-created' country itself. In view of these expectations, and with the intention of getting a sufficiently secure foothold, the Comintern urged the formation of separate CPs among the different nations. Thus separate, autonomous CPs of Slovenia and Croatia were formed, in 1937 and 1938 respectively. The CPs of Serbia, and of the other republics, were to be formed only after the Second World War. This federalisation of the Communist Party of Yugoslavia, which reflected genuine national aspirations, presaged the future configuration of the Second Yugoslavia.

The legitimacy of this homegrown Yugoslav communism was reinforced by the victorious outcome of the Partisan struggle in the Second World War, and its message – that internecine strife must be overcome and a new Yugoslavia built – carried far. The still overwhelmingly agrarian population was ready to accept the imposition of a new regime and the turning of a new page. The dark past would be swept away by the emphatic promise of a bright future.

The Communist Party of Yugoslavia under Tito carried out an extensive postwar purge, eliminating physically or sidelining anyone they considered to be an obstacle to their project of creating a 'new man' on an historical *tabula rasa*, and of which they were going to be the grand architects. Faithful to Stalin and Stalinism to a fanatical degree, Tito and his party nevertheless became rapidly disillusioned with Stalin's attempt to satellise them. In 1948 they were expelled from the Cominform, as uncooperative partners and heretics. They then embarked on a grand political and social (communist) experiment which was to lead through a period of prosperity and development – punctuated by crises and tensions – to the break-up of Yugoslavia in 1991.

Having stood up successfully to Stalin, to the Communist Party of the Soviet Union and the Soviet Union itself (Soviet troops were stationed on Yugoslavia's eastern borders, poised for intervention, for several years after the Tito–Stalin split) Tito and his acolytes felt they could go their own (communist) way. And although the quarrel between Stalin and Tito was largely a conflict and power struggle between two bureaucracies (Castoriadis, 1988) it is nonetheless incontestable that the CP of Yugoslavia came out of the fraught showdown with the Soviet leadership with reinforced legitimacy and popularity.

Tito, with his main ideologist, the Slovenian Edvard Kardelj, the Croat Vladimir Bakarić (second fiddle to Kardelj), the fearsome Aleksandar Ranković (Serb) organisational secretary of the party and head of the secret police (until 1966), and the Montenegrin (and later arch-dissident) Milovan Djilas, together with several others, started to conceive of a 'third way' between Soviet Communism and Western Capitalism. After four constitutions (1946, 1953, 1964 and 1974), the invention of the regime of 'socialist self-management', which was to attract the attention of many leftists throughout the world, after the co-founding of the Non-Aligned Movement in 1961 (along with Nehru of India and Nasser of Egypt), after having become a cherished buffer state between the contesting blocs of the Cold War, and having attempted to solve the national question in a communist way, the society of the Second Yugoslavia ended up internally atomised, fragmented and *thus utterly unprepared and disabled in the face of the challenge of the end of communism.*

The legacy of communism – from hard to soft totalitarianism

The communists of Yugoslavia, like all the other communists in postwar Eastern Europe, operated under the assumption that they would be in power forever, and that they would accordingly remain in control of everything. They created a system ruled by the logic of totalitarianism (Lefort, 1986: 273–91). The two key aspects of the totalitarian project, inseparable from each other, are the abolition of the boundary lines between state and society, and of the contours of internal social division. The criteria of law and of knowledge remain a rigorously enforced monopoly of political power, and are defined and implemented by that power. So it was in Yugoslavia. The weak surviving elements of postwar civil society were destroyed or engulfed by the party-state, and there was a de-differentiation of the (weak) autonomous social spheres (economic, legal, educational, scientific). The party became ubiquitous, omniscient, omnipotent. Ideology and terror induced fear and crippled any potentially significant political opposition to the regime. The party *was* the state, and the secret police, army and transmission organisations (trades union, youth organisations, women's organisations, mass organisations) were all cast in the role of instruments of militarisation and politicisation – homogenising or, more precisely dissolving, the social fabric, destroying the horizontal and strengthening the vertical links.

The Yugoslav communist leaders, like their fellow communists in other Central and East European countries, had initially followed the Soviet model, with a strongly centralised state (though nominally a federation), wholly controlled by the party. After the break with Stalin, they became more adventurous, realising that they could stretch the model so as to create scope for a certain pluralism with respect to economic activity, and space for bounded liberties that would not endanger their uncontested leadership. Many an East European citizen, or even communist *apparatchik,* envied the Titoist, Yugoslav regime. By the mid-1960s, pressured by a deep economic crisis, the communist leaders decided to open the borders and issue passports to Yugoslavs, rather than face growing unemployment within the country. Those who plumped for the status of individuals 'temporarily working abroad' (*na privremenom radu u inostranstvu*), as they were officially called, became the pioneers of the still large community of *gastarbeiter* in Germany, France, Scandinavia and the Benelux countries.

Hand-in-hand with the opening-up of borders and the establishment of freedom of movement came the privilege of holding unlimited and untaxed foreign currency bank accounts. In the field of culture the 'modernist' current in literature and art emerged victorious from a harsh struggle in the mid-1950s against the socialist-realist and traditionalist currents. Artistic freedom became a fact of everyday life. University curricula in the humanities and social sciences were largely freed from the grip of Marxism, and James Joyce and Stephane Malarmé, Pablo Picasso and

Henry Moore, Herbert Marcuse and Martin Heidegger became part and parcel of higher education.

Of course there were still clear-cut taboos and off-limit areas. Compulsory classes in Marxism and 'socialist self-management' were run in all schools and universitiy faculties. Much 'anti-communist bourgeois' social science (e.g. Karl Popper) was not translated (Indjić, 1994). The logic of totalitarianism was still pervasive and functional. If at any moment the regime felt endangered or threatened – perhaps by as little as a minor negative reference to its core values – its thunderbolts struck without pity. Certainly, once the Yugoslav 'Gulag' period (featuring the Goli Otok camp for supporters of Stalin and the Soviet Union and other, innocent victims caught in the 'crossfire' of the Tito–Stalin split) had passed, political prisoners were not killed, but rather sentenced to terms in prison. Milovan Djilas spent many years in jail. In the later period purged Yugoslav communist leaders were simply sidelined and given retirement pensions (Aleksandar Ranković in 1966, the Croat and Serb Communist Party leaderships in 1971–72). Those not in ranking party positions still ended up in gaol, especially if they were considered to be nationalists. Those who dared in any way to argue with or criticise Tito or the Communist Party or 'socialist self-management' were ostracised and condemned. University professors were ousted from their jobs (eight university professors and lecturers from the Praxis group in Belgrade in 1975), films were banned (the 'Black Wave' in 1969–70), and a young film director (L. Stojanović) was sentenced to a term in prison. Some books were banned and burnt, some politically slanted art exhibits censored. The party's vigilant eyes and ears were always alert.

Communist modernisation without democracy

Great strides were made in industrialisation and economic growth. A largely poor agrarian country was transformed into a middle ranking 'Second World' country in record time. The standard of living rose, and Yugoslavs were progressively introduced, from the late 1960s, to the world of Western consumerism. *But it was modernisation without the key institutions of modernity* – an opening into the world of consumer goods, foreign travel and media entertainment *within the logic of totalitarianism*. People were politicised (more and more ritually as time passed) via the party and its transmissions, drawn into the system to swell its ranks and reinforce its legitimacy. The country prospered – its own efforts apart – thanks to large financial injections from the Western powers to bolster and strengthen Yugoslavia's position as a buffer against the Soviet Union.

The 'success story' of Yugoslav market socialism in the 1960s and 1970s gave the communist leaders the illusion that they had solved all political, social and national problems, and that they had managed to create a 'haven of peace in Europe' (a favourite regime slogan) at a time when ETA, IRA, Baader-Meinhof and Brigate Rosse terrorism was rife in the rest of Europe. The illusion was, in historical terms, short-lived. In terms of individual experience, it gave Yugoslavia's population of twenty-four million a decade more of peace (or of ceasefire, as some would say) to live through, before entering the inferno and suffering loss, despair, further fragmentation – and in many cases death.

Constitutional experiment – decentralisation without democratisation

In the wake of the Slovene 'road-building crisis' in 1969,[1] the upsurge of national grievances in Croatia in 1971 (see Chapter 11), and of the reformist strain within the League of Communists of Serbia (Burg, 1983: 83–187) – all, in their own way, demanding deep-seated reforms – Tito and Kardelj finally decided to embark on (what was to prove to be) their final experiment: the 1974 constitution. In response to the pressures, dissatisfactions and vocal grievances coming from some of the republics, they decided to devolve administrative, economic, social and some political cal power. While retaining all decision-making over foreign, military and key external nal trade affairs in their own hands, they handed the rest down to the republics and autonomous provinces, thus producing a *de facto* confederalisation of the country. More precisely, the six republics were defined in Article 3 of the 1974 constitution as 'states based on popular sovereignty'. In addition, Articles 398, 400 and 402 predicated that any change in the constitution required the consensus between all federal units: the six republics *and* the autonomous provinces (Vojvodina and Kosovo). The confederal character of the constitution was further evidenced by the parity of all federal units established within the collective state presidency, and by the principle that members of the collective state executive should be delegated by the federal units, rather than elected by the Federal Assembly (Article 321).

Apart from being one of the longest constitutions ever written anywhere in the world and having the exclusive curiosity (and institutional monstrosity) of an article bearing the name of an individual (the one that stipulated that Tito was to be President of the Socialist Federative Republic of Yugoslavia for life), the 1974 constitution did take the devolution of power and empowerment of federal units to unparalleled heights. All federal units were empowered to vote their own constitutions, all were empowered to have presidents, collective presidencies, parliaments, ministries (including of foreign affairs), and wide competences in economic policy, social welfare and education.

The Socialist Republic of Serbia was unique among the six republics in having within itself two autonomous provinces. A constitutional anomaly arose here, in that the Assembly of Serbia could only change its own constitution with the assent of the Assemblies of the autonomous provinces (which thus had the power of veto), while the autonomous provinces could change their own constitutions without out the Republic's consent (Goati, 1989: 47–53). This was to have a critical bearing on subsequent developments (see Chapter 8). The result of this *de facto* confederalisation was a weakening of central federal power. More insidiously, Yugoslavia also disappeared *de facto* from the constitutional order of the country,

---

[1] In 1968–69 each republic and province was asked to submit proposals for road construction to the Federal Executive Council (Federal Government). These were, after deliberation by the FEC, to be included in the new Yugoslav funding application to the World Bank. Some of the projects proposed by Slovenia were not included in the definitive version of the application. This sparked off vehement protests on the part of the Slovenian authorities and public.

in that 'Yugoslavia' was now only what the federal units decided, by consensus, it would be.

Tito and the other communist leaders were still functioning under the logic of totalitarianism and thus did not need to burden themselves with the technicalities of the 'paper' constitution of 1974. They continued to make all the key decisions, and to exercise absolute discretion in relation to the handling of (*nomenklatura*) human resources. To satisfy republic appetites for a greater say in their own internal affairs, however, the League of Communists itself underwent further (con)federalisation. As long as the supreme arbiter was there as the 'only effectively functioning institution' (Tepavac, 1995: 68), this had no great importance, because Tito could always cut through any Gordian knot of Yugoslav (communist) political life, and resolve any internecine conflict without cavil or quibble. The problem would arise after his death in 1980, when his heirs were left with consensual procedures and (con)federalised structures of state *and* party which were wide open to communitarianisation (see Chapter 4).

Demise of the federal state – rise of the proto-states

The 1974 constitution, which represented the culmination of Edvard Kardelj's institutional engineering, was based on a patchwork of socialist theoretical and practical writings and experiences – mainly Pierre-Joseph Proudhon's ideas of federalism, plus the experience of the Paris Commune of 1871 and Marx's interpretation thereof. The distillation that resulted was what Kardelj called the 'system of delegation' and the major innovation involved a new kind of non-party pluralism: the pluralism of 'self-managed interests'. The long and the short of the 1974 constitution is that, just as the logic of (soft) totalitarianism destroyed social bonds and, through the 'micro-physics of power' (Foucault, 1984), penetrated into the smallest pores of society, it set in motion a progressive dismantling of what Yugoslavia had had – even under communism – up till then. Self-management *had* given workers some meagre degree of empowerment at the workplace level. But self-management was ultimately a façade, a veil for the real decision-making going on at the highest levels of communist power, and by the early 1970s it was ridden with problems and conflicts (Meister, 1972).

The Yugoslav communist leaders knew that they had to give more freedom to political actors, so as to respond to grievances and prolong the life of the (communist) party-state. But they did so by empowering collective actors – the regional (republic and autonomous province) *nomenklature*, i.e. by reinforcing the tendency to articulation of proto-states (republics). Meanwhile the federal state weakened and withered, and the individual Yugoslav citizen, with no say whatsoever in effective decision-making, was further disenfranchised. The communist rulers were out of reach of popular control, there was no true interest representation, and no effort whatsoever was made to give greater political freedom to individual citizens. Communist power was completely unaccountable – just as in any other Soviet-type regime.

The phenomenology of this process of disaggregation of Yugoslavia was visible in every area and walk of life. The republic *nomenklature* became increasingly uncompromising in their assertions of their sectional interests in mutual bargaining, and the deadlocks multiplied and mutual mistrust grew. The federal state and party institutions sunk more and more to the status of (indisciplined) talking-shops. In areas such as education, transport and the media, the centrifugal forces became stronger and stronger. Educational authorities haggled endlessly as they tried to come to an agreement on what should be the common elementary and secondary core-curriculum in literature and history for the whole country. But there was no Yugoslav Jules Ferry.[2] In transport and road infrastructure it is curious to note that the highway/motorway between Yugoslavia's two biggest cities, Belgrade and Zagreb, was never finally completed, while motorways (admittedly shorter in distance) linking main cities within each republic were built (Ljubljana–Kranj, Zagreb–Karlovac, Belgrade–Niš, Skopje–Greek border). Each republic and autonomous province had its own TV and radio station, and there was no national TV or radio station (in the US sense). During the 1970s and 1980s, the Slovenes, Macedonians and Albanians joined in the commom Serbo-Croat language TV programmes only on very rare occasions. What was separate even for the Serbo-Croat-speaking groups were the news programmes. There was a common one on Sunday evenings on the first channel, by rotation among Zagreb, Novi Sad, Belgrade, Sarajevo and (latterly) Titograd, although one could see the news from other republics and autonomous provinces (again by rotation) on the second channel. All these divisions would prove only too easy to exacerbate when a real crisis of conflict of interest arose between the republics.

The ethnification of politics

As we have seen, the state and party had been decentralised and (con)federalised by the decisions taken by the political leadership in the early 1970s. The intended or unintended consequences of these decisions were that the six republics and two autonomous provinces (*de facto* republics) began to develop largely within their own particularist frameworks, following their own general 'national' interests, becoming more and more self-centred and less and less willing to work in the interests of the country as a whole. The task of guarding the Yugoslav national interest was left to the apex of the party-state apparatus, concentrated around an ageing president Tito (who always combined the functions of president of Yugoslavia and president of the Yugoslav Communist Party, thus epitomising the (modified) adage '*l'Etat et le parti, c'est moi*').

Within this developing, centrifugal dynamic there was one exception. The Yugoslav People's Army (JNA), often labelled Tito's Praetorian guard, greatly privileged in terms of the high level of investment into all its various activites and the standard of living of its members, was in effect a seventh 'invisible' republic in its own right. The army developed in a detached manner, not only because of the

---

[2] The great French educational reformer of the Third Republic, who created the unified system of compulsory, lay and free state education in France.

particular communist mind-set of the regime, but also because it was linked much more to what remained of the central authority than to the authority of the republic leaderships which were in sense going their own way. Certainly, the exception was by no means complete. The JNA was in fact itself subject to progressive 'intrusion' by the principle of the 'federal key', which predicated how the different nationalities should be represented among the top brass in the General Staff, and in the Army Corps. In addition to this, the Territorial Defence units formed with the switch to a 'Generalised Popular Defence' system after the invasion of Czechoslovakia by the Warsaw Pact troops in 1968 not only redeployed the bulk of the army to the eastern borders of the country, but located them within a command and control system nested in the republics. These Territorial Defence units proved, in 1990–91, to be ideal for the development of the armies of the proto-successor-states.

The republics had become 'sovereign states' by the provisions of the 1974 constitution, and through the interpretation of the ideology of self-managing socialism. There was a clause in the constitution defining six constituent nations of Yugoslavia: (from north to south) Slovenes, Croats, Serbs, (Ethnic) Muslims, Montenegrins and Macedonians. This produced a congruence between republic/ state and majority nation in all the republics except Bosnia-Hercegovina. There, there was a delicate balance of three constituent nations (Muslims 43.7 per cent, Serbs 31.3 per cent and Croats 17.3 per cent). Bosnia-Hercegovina was in fact a mini-Yugoslavia which functioned politically, even under communist rule, on a strict parity – effectively consociational – basis, with rotation of representatives of the main nations in the leading seats of political power, and also in the top jobs in industry and administration (see Chapter 6).

The 1974 constitution was a document characterised by confusion of principles and overlapping rights. This was a direct result of Kardelj's wish to accommodate the diverse reality and mixture of nations and cultures that was Yugoslavia – but also of his megalomaniac desire to codify every conceivable aspect of social and political life. Thus, for example, both the constituent nations and the republics had national rights by the letter of the constitution. That incongruity was of no great importance as long as the monopolistic political rule of the communists prevailed and all the republic leaderships/*nomenklature* obeyed, and were loyal to, the supreme leader, Tito. It was therefore the latter, not the constitution, that was the guarantor of the unity of the country. But the 'paper' constitution of 1974 did, nevertheless, have a certain social, political and economic reality, in that it induced a centrifugal dynamic; more importantly, it became the legal text with which all the main political actors on the Yugoslav stage had to reckon when putting forward proposals for reform and changes of regime, once communism had collapsed in Europe.

The consensus rule meant that any change in the constitution, and therefore any recasting of the federation, would be a long and complicated process. One particularly important obstacle to the creation of a Third, democratic Yugoslavia was the issue of federal elections. Any major political change would clearly have involved free elections, with a multiplicity of political parties founded on the basis of freedom of association (what the communists had been deliberately avoiding for forty-six years), to make possible the convening of a constituent assembly, representative of the electoral body on a one-man-one-vote-basis, and of a second chamber representing the rights of national majorities and minorities. This in the end proved an impossible task. Every proposal for holding elections at the federal level put forward by the last federal government was systematically obstructed by Slovenia and and Serbia, and most of the time by Croatia also.

It became apparent that the effective power resting at the level of the republics was so strong that the parts were able to dictate the rules to the whole. *The federal units in effect blocked off any possibility for the central authorities (in which all the units were equally represented, on a parity basis) to relegitimise themselves democratically.* The federal centre had been weakened by years of centrifugal development and haggling between the republics, becoming nothing more than a political stock-exchange, where deals were brokered. That might have seemed a good omen, since it might have been expected that such an exercise in compromise and negotiation would constitute a learning process in peaceful resolution of interest conflict. *The Yugoslav case proves that in the business of conflict resolution, nothing can substitute for democracy and democratic institutions.*

Having successfully stopped the federation from relegitimising itself through federal elections (Linz and Stepan, 1992), the republics then proceeded to reinforce their own legitimacy by holding republic-level elections (remember that under the 1974 constitution these were states based on popular sovereignty with the right to self-determination). The political identity of the republics was reinforced in each case through identification with the majority nation. This resulted in a 'constitutional nationalism' (Hayden, 1992), and completed the process of 'ethnification' of communist politics (Offe, 1993) which had started in the 1970s.

Let us pause to reflect on the factors underlying this process of transformation. The national question was a constant feature and political issue throughout the whole of the history of Yugoslavia, from its inception until its dramatic downfall. Ethnic/national groups had already had a distinct identity even before the creation of Yugoslavia. They had all been touched by some form of nation-building process, and this process had been reinforced in both the First and Second Yugoslavias. The socialist 'statehood' conferred on the Yugoslav republics by the 1974 constitution consolidated the process further. A pattern of growing ethnic homogenisation around the core nation of each republic emerged, with progressive redefinition of other nationalities (bigger or smaller) within the borders of the republics as minorities with respect to the majority nation (whatever their constitutional status might be, and even if they were 'constituent nations' of Yugoslavia). For Bosnia and Hercegovina, with its ethnic patchwork, this process was redolent of future disaster. The drive to constitute fully blown nation-states on the basis of the republics (proto-states) became the key federation-breaking factor. Underpinning it and driving it on was the power struggle unleashed by the impending need to reformulate and recast political power within the federation. Powerful and deeply vested material and political interests were at stake. Each republic party-state leadership was threatened by this process of possible recasting. Each tried to hang on to as many political and economic privileges as possible.

The obvious political tool for the regional political leaderships, as they strove to muster support, was national sentiment – the ideology of nationalism. As Slavo Radošević argues in Chapter 5 in this volume, atomised individuals in a disabled society were confronted with loss of existential certainty and ejection from the socialist welfare cocoon in which they had been living. The new certainty being offered them was another safe haven of security: that of national homogeneity. The structural set-up of latter-day Yugoslavia was in a sense ideal for this kind of political strategy. Blame for hardship could be cast at the door of the neighbouring republic. A whirlwind of mutual recriminations for exploitation and hardship between the leaderships of the respective republics was unleashed. Nationalist intellectuals who had long been waiting on the sidelines brought forth their narratives of suffering of their peoples, and explained why a parting of the ways was better for everyone. The media provided the major technical tool by which these messages were, at first cautiously and then forcefully, imposed on listeners and viewers of the endgame (Pejić, 1992; Thompson, 1994).

But why was the breakdown so violent? There have been diverse and complex reasonings on this topic (Bowman, 1994; Schierup, 1994). The fact that the federal state had collapsed, and with it central political authority, meant that the bodies ultimately defining civil and political order disappeared. The proto-states were aspiring nation-states, but had not yet been recognised by the international community. Accountability for law and order still rested on the state of Yugoslavia; when it disappeared a vacuum appeared, bringing with it legal void and anomie. The republics were unaccountable with respect to the international community, and thus in a certain sense free of responsibility. In a context where the monopoly of the legitimate use of force is no longer vested in a 'legal' state, violence is no longer constrained. It could be said that an 'anything goes' situation arose, in which the different leaderships, buttressed by the support they had managed to get from their majority nations, tried to maximise their immediate gains irrespective of the long-term consequences for themselves, their citizens and the country at large.

In all this, the history, recent and distant, of the former Yugoslavia was a receptacle from which each could take the worst and best, in building the narrative that would legitimise the pursuit of power. The national politics that had been developing through the centrifugal evolution of the party-state (nationalism from above) had, by the late 1980s and early 1990s, touched fingers with the nationalism from below that had been preserved in the 'ice box', and that had remerged with the 'thaw' of collapsing communism. This double nationalist bind, and double intensification of nationalism under the strain of necessary adaptation to a new post-communist situation which required political openings and economic rationalisation, proved to be a challenge that those responsible for the future of the country could not meet peacefully. The dominance of the communist political sphere throughout the postwar period, its unaccountability, the impotence of society to react and take a grip on politics, the festering national grievances real and/or invented, the complexity of the construct of relations within Yugoslavia – all these things created a chemistry of breakdown that was, at the very least, highly likely to generate violence on a large scale.

Society and citizens – privacy without democracy

A deep sense of insecurity, or more precisely uncertainty, was introduced into the lives of the citizens of Yugoslavia by the recurrent changes of rules in the political, societal and economic spheres during the communist period. The four successive constitutions within a span of less than thirty years, the constant changes of legislation, procedures and rules created a situation of what has been termed legal nihilism or legal anomie. There was no legal security for medium-long-term planning of individual or minor private group endeavours. Communist instrumental politics dominated. The political sphere of power had an overwhelming influence on all aspects of life. It monopolised all other social and economic activities, and manipulated them for its own goals.

The initial postwar enthusiasm and mobilisation for rebuilding the country, and the ensuing economic boom and prosperity of the 1960s and 1970s, produced a rapid change in the social structure, with the decline of the agrarian population and the growth of the urban population, and of a middle class. The middle strata of society experienced accelerated social promotion, accompanied by feelings of greater material security and hopes that they were catching up with living standards in the Western societies that they were now able to visit regularly, due to the freedom of movement and open borders' policy of the ruling elite. The fact remains that the scope for private entrepreneurship was sharply limited. With the bulk of private property and economic activity located within the agrarian sector, dependence on the 'public sector' was the norm for the emergent social groups. And the 'public sector' was under the control of the League of Communists, whether at the highest levels of the party or down the hierarchical ladder at the level of local communities.

The time came, inevitably, when the new middle classes/strata had to face up to the limits of the communist system, both in terms of the scope for private initiative and investment, and of alternative political possiblities. In practice, these latter were strictly limited to the inner Communist Party sphere. Any political initiative external to the party came under immediate suspicion and was invariably suppressed. The middle classes were therefore faced with a blockage to their social development at the political level and, in due course, also with the beginnings of the economic crisis. They were thus forced to reduce their aspirations to the maintenance of their existing standard of living and the securing for their progeny of an adequate position in the existing social division of labour. In the absence of any possibility of doing so within legitimately autonomous spheres of society (which simply did not exist) or within professional organizations, they tended increasingly to establish informal relationships and groups outside the legal framework of the dominant system. The debt crisis of the early-mid-1980s, and the consequent decline in economic growth and the erosion of living standards, deepened the sense of uncertainty. As the struggle for everyday survival increasingly squeezed out other goals, resignation and lack of outlook came to dominate more and more in the consciousness of the people, breeding in turn anomie and apathy (Mrkšić, 1987).

It is useful to reflect on the pattern of evolution of attitudes that resulted from all this. The dominance of a dictatorial political elite and the rise of living standards throughout the postwar period led to a situation in which people increasingly defined their orientations in terms of personal and concrete societal needs (Zukin, 1975: 108). The fact that issues of a higher political, social and economic order were out-of-bounds for the Yugoslav citizen meant that no political learning process, such as might be conducive to the promotion of feelings of responsibility for the public good, was unfolding. On the contrary: individuals were being demotivated and driven to expend their 'civic' energies either through the tightly defined mechanisms of Communist Party life or through private consumption and personal image enhancement ('keeping up with the Ivanovićs').

The noxious effect of these negative political and social dynamics – fundamentally anti-modern in terms of what the republican tradition in political theory traces back to the renaissance ideas of the *vita activa*, *vivere civile* and *vivere libero* – bore its bitter fruit in the failure of Yugoslav society in the early 1990s (if indeed it still existed at that time) to counterbalance the activities of the regional political leaderships in their machinations in relation to the future of Yugoslavia.

A clear statement of this profound self-centredness of individuals, of this wholesome modernity at the level of the private sphere without spillovers into the public/political sphere, is provided by the following 'confession' (in the Rousseauesque sense) of a typical representative of the higher strata of the Yugoslav urban middle classes who, from within the walls of their relatively high material wellbeing, did not see the catastrophe of a violent breakdown of the country approaching, and hence took no counter-measures. (This particular person is a woman from Sarajevo, owner, with her husband, of an optician's shop, speaking from the thick of the war at the beginning of 1994.)

> Before, under the communist regime, we were not in the habit of protesting. It is also true that we were living something of a *dolce vita*. We reckoned, before the war, that we were earning more than the average French optician. In a sense we had it too good – everything was earned without effort or obligation. We spent weekends in Rome and Paris, we kept up with the fashions, and were always going out to restaurants. We went skiing at night on the illuminated slopes around Sarajevo; we spent our days at the terraces of cafés. Nobody was interested in politics. Had people like us and our friends engaged ourselves, we may have been able to avoid the worst. (Dominique le Guilledoux, 'Ici Sarajevo, là bas Zagreb', *Le Monde*, 6 January 1994: 3; my translation)

This sense of impotence *vis-à-vis* crucial issues, bred by the communist monopoly of power, had thus created a sense of political impotence and futility that effectively barred any *engagement* beyond the private sphere.

Of constitutions and electoral laws

One of the key false steps on the slippery, downward slope was the attempt, following the announcement of free elections in 1990, to create institutional arrangements conducive to the continuity of the existing power structure at the level of the republics – since the deadlock over the possible reform of the 1974 constitution had ruled out any possibility of political reform at the federal level.

The two key republics, Serbia and Croatia, i.e. effectively their respective communist leaderships, embarked on a constitution-building operation that was calculated to secure their victory in the first free elections. Both opted for electoral laws which basically followed the French model, rather than the proportional representation model. The two-round majority voting system (first-past-the-post) was supposed to secure the maximum number of parliamentary seats for a given number of votes (Vejvoda, 1991).

The communists of Croatia, under Raćan, and those of Serbia under Slobodan Milošević, were seeking to legitimate themselves through free elections, so that they could continue to reign within the new political multiparty setting. In the event, the elections in the two republics generated very similar numerical results – but with very different political outcomes. In April 1990 in Croatia the predictions and calculations of the communists (League of Communists of Croatia – Party of Democratic Change) were confounded, and it was the opposition Croatian Democratic Union (HDZ) of Franjo Tudjman that won 67.5 per cent of the seats in the lower house with 41.5 per cent of the vote, while in Serbia (in December 1990) the communists (now renamed the Socialist Party of Serbia) won 77.6 per cent of the seats with 46 per cent of the vote. Both ruling parties thus commanded overwhelming majorities in the new parliaments. Tudjman and his party proceeded to produce a new constitution for Croatia which effectively created a presidential system. In Serbia, Milošević and his party had pushed a new constitution through the old communist assembly, before the first multiparty elections. This constitution also gave great power to the president.

By the beginning of 1991, then, the political scene in the former Yugoslavia was dominated by one, salient fact. With no federal multiparty elections having been held, the two most important republics had, in their newly elected parliaments, ruling parties with absolute, unrivalled majorities, within the framework of presidential systems. This quite simply meant that two individuals, two leader-presidents, were in a position, virtually independently of parliamentary or any other kind of control, to decide the fate of the country.

Conclusion

The softness of the Yugoslav brand of totalitarianism in the end made no structural difference to the kind of power structure it induced. It allowed certain freedoms which were of great importance to the everyday life of private individuals and to the development of a feeling of individual dignity in a material sense – but *not* in a political or deeper societal sense. The social stratification that emerged from post-Second World War development was that of an urbanised society. But that urbanised society lacked the political institutions of a modern society through which interests and their conflicts could be mediated in a peaceful manner. The social actors whose pivotal rule in modern society is to moderate social and political strife and marginalise political and social extremes were simply unable to break out of the state of fragmentation and political impotence in which they found themselves trapped. The mechanics of republican statehood *à la yougoslave* divided the political, social and economic space of the country in such a way as to render coalitions across republic borders virtually impossible at a crucial time of crisis. The courageous attempts of liberal, democratically minded individuals and groups, aware of the dangers lying ahead, were of no avail. The population at large was reduced to rhetorical incantations of 'Why are they doing this to us?'. The 'they' were the political leaderships and *nomenklature*, the 'us' the population that had benefited from the material development of Yugoslavia since 1945, and were now ready to accept a *status quo* that had, in fact, become insupportable. Large segments, though not all, of the 'us' would be swept up by the winds of ethnic homogenisation, politically masterminded for power-preserving purposes, on the basis of the manipulation of genuine national grievances.

References

Allcock, J. B. *et al.* (eds) (1992) *Yugoslavia in Transition: Choices and Constraints* (New York: Berg).

Arendt, Hannah (1954) The difficulties of understanding, *Partisan Review*, vol. XX, no. 4, reprinted in Arendt, H. (1994) *Essays in Understanding 1930–1954* (New York and London: Harcourt Brace).

Bibo, I. (1991) The distress of East European small states. In I. Bibo, *Democracy, Revolution, Self-Determination* (Highland Lakes: Atlantic Research and Publications).

Biserko, S. (ed) (1993) *Yugoslavia: Collapse, War, Crimes* (Belgrade: Centre for Anti-War Action and Belgrade Circle).

Bowman, G. (1994) Xenophobia, fantasy and the nation: the logic of ethnic violence in former Yugoslavia, *Balkan Forum*, vol. 2, no. 2, June, pp. 135–62.

Brubaker, R. (1995) National minorities, nationalizing states, and external national homelands in the new Europe, *Daedalus*, vol. 124, Spring, pp. 107–32.

Burg, S. (1983) *Conflict and Cohesion in Socialist Yugoslavia. Political Decision-Making Since 1966* (Princeton, New Jersey: Princeton University Press).

Buvać, D. (1990) *Slom Hiperinflacije ili Jugoslavije* (Ljubljana-Zagreb: Cankarjeva založba).

Castoriadis, C. (1988) The Yugoslavian bureaucracy. In C. Castoriadis, *Political and Social Writings*, vol. 1, 1946–1955 (Minneapolis: University of Minnesota Press).

Cohen, L. (1993) *Broken Bonds: the Disintegration of Yugoslavia* (Boulder: Westview).

Crick, Bernard (1962) *In Defence of Politics* (London: Weidenfeld & Nicolson); 4th edn (1992) (Harmondsworth: Penguin Books).

Crnobrnja, M. (1994) *The Yugoslav Drama* (London, New York: I.B. Tauris).

Denitch, B.N. (1994) *Ethnic Nationalism: the Tragic Death of Yugoslavia* (Minneapolis: University of Minnesota Press).

Djilas, A. (1991) *The Contested Country. Yugoslav Unity and Communist Revolution, 1919–1953* (Cambridge, Mass: Harvard University Press).

Djukić, S. (1994) *Izmedju Slave i Anateme – Politička Biografija Slobodana Miloševića*, (Belgrade: Filip Višnjić).

Dragnich, A.N. (1992) *Serbs and Croats: the Struggle in Yugoslavia* (New York: Harcourt Brace).

Foucault, M. (1984) *Microfisica del Potere* (Torino: Einaudi).

Gellner, E. (1991) Nationalism and politics in Eastern Europe. In *New Left Review*, no. 189, Sept.–Oct., pp. 127–34.

Glenny, M. (1993) *The Fall of Yugoslavia* (Harmondsworth: Penguin).

Goati, V. (1989) *Politička Anatomija Jugoslovenskog Društva* (Zagreb: Naprijed).

Golubović, Z. (1991) Yugoslav society and 'socialism': the present-day crisis of the Yugoslav system and the possibilities for evolution. In F. Feher and A. Arato (eds) *Crisis and Reform in Eastern Europe* (New Brunswick: Transaction Publishers).

Gow, J. (1992) *Legitimacy and the Military: the Yugoslav Crisis* (London: Pinter).

Hayden, R. (1992) Constitutional nationalism in the formerly Yugoslav republics, *Slavic Review*, vol. 51, pp. 654–73.

Indjić, T. (1994) Jugoslovenska sociologija izmedju apologije i jeresi, *Književne Novine*, vol. 46, no. 879, 1 February, pp. 1 and 3.

Janjić, D. (ed.) (1994) *Religion and War* (Belgrade: European Movement in Serbia).

Jovović, D. (1991) *Jugoslavija i Medjunarodni Monetarni Fond* (Belgrade: Ekonomika).

Kaldor, M. (1993) The wars in Yugoslavia, *New Left Review*, no. 197, pp. 96–112.

Kovačević, Dj. (1991) Jugoslavija: Osvajanje ili Gubitak Istorije. In R. Nakarada, L. Basta Posavec and S. Samardžić (eds) *Raspad Jugoslavije – Produžetak ili Kraj Agonije* (Belgrade: Institut za Evropske Studije).

Kovačević, S. and Dajić, P. (1994) *Chronology of the Yugoslav Crisis 1942–1993* (Belgrade: Institut za Evropske Studije)

Lefort, C. (1986) *The Political Forms of Modern Society. Bureaucracy, Democracy, Totalitarianism* (Cambridge: Polity Press).

Linz, J. and Stepan, A. (1992) Political identities and electoral sequences: Spain, the Soviet Union, and Yugoslavia, *Daedalus*, vol. 121, no. 2, Spring, pp. 123–39.

Macesich, B. (ed.) (1992) *Yugoslavia in the Age of Democracy: Essays on Economic and Political Reform* (Westport: Praeger).

Magaš, B. (1993) *The Destruction of Yugoslavia: Tracking the Breakup 1980–1992* (London: Verso).

Meister, A. (1972) *Où Va l'Autogestion Yougoslave?* (Paris: Anthropos).

Milanović, B. (1990) *Ekonomska Nejednakost u Jugoslaviji* (Belgrade: Ekonomika).

Mrkšić, D. (1987) *Srednji Slojevi u Jugoslaviji* (Belgrade: IIC SSO Srbije).

Offe, O. (1993) *Ethnic Politics in East European Transitions* (Bremen: Zentrum fur europaische Rechtspolitik).

Palau, J. and Kumar, R. (1993) *Ex-Yugoslavia: from War to Peace* (Valencia: HCA & Generalitat Valenciana).

Paqueteau, P. (1995) Sous la glace, l'histoire. Les rapports du nationalisme et du communisme en Europe de l'Est, *Le Débat*, no. 84, mars–avril, pp. 105–20.

Pavlowitch, S. (1971) *Yugoslavia* (London: Ernest Benn).

Pavlowitch, S. (1988) *The Improbable Survivor: Yugoslavia and its Problems 1918–1988*, (London: Hurst).

Pejić, N. (1992) Media and responsibility in the war, *Peuples Mediterranéens – Yougoslavie, Logiques de l'Exclusion*, no. 61, Oct.–Dec., pp. 35–46.

Perović, L. (1991) *Zatvaranje Kruga – Ishod Političkog Rascepa u SKJ 1971–72* (Sarajevo: Svjetlost).

Perović, L. (1995) Beg od modernizacije – obnova prošlosti postaje program za budućnost, *Republika*, vol. 7, no. 112, 16–31 March.

Popov, N. (1990) *Jugoslavija pod Naponom Promena* (Beograd: Izdanje autora).

Popov, N. (1994) Le populisme serbe (parts 1 and 2), *Les Temps Modernes*, vol. 49, no. 573, April, pp. 22–63 and no. 574, May, pp. 22–84.

Prpa-Jovanović, B. (1995) The making of Yugoslavia. In D. Gojković and J. Ridgeway (eds) *Yugoslavia's Ethnic Nightmare – The Inside Story of Europe's Unfolding Ordeal* (New York: Lawrence Hill Books).

Puhovski, Z. (1989) Mogućnost pluralističke konstitucije Jugoslavije, *Theoria*, vol. 32, no. 1, pp. 79–85.

Puhovski, Z. (1990) *Socijalistička Konstrukcija Zbilje* (Zagreb: RS SOH, Školska Knjiga).

Ramet, S. P. (1992) *Balkan Babel: Politics, Culture and Religion in Yugoslavia* (Boulder: Westview Press).

Schapiro, I. (1990) Three fallacies concerning majorities, minorities, and democratic politics in majorities and minorities. In J.W. Chapman and A. Wertheimer (eds) *Majorities and Minorities, Nomos XXXII* (New York and London: New York University Press), pp. 79–125.

Schierup, C.-U. (1994) 'Eurobalkanism – ethnic cleansing and the post cold war order', in D. Janjić (ed.) *Religion and War* (Belgrade: European Movement in Serbia), pp. 125–45.

Seligman, A. (1994) Some thoughts on trust, collective identity, and the transition from state socialism. In C. Rootes and H. Davis, *Social Change and Political Transformation* (London: UCL Press).

Seroka, J. and Pavlović, V. (eds) (1992) *Tragedy of Yugoslavia: Failure of Democratic Transformation* (Armonk: M.E. Sharpe).

Shoup, P. (1968) *Communism and the Yugoslav National Question* (New York and London: Columbia University Press).

Shoup, P. (1992) The role of domestic and international actors in the Bosnian-Herzegovian drama. In J. Palau and R. Kumar (1993) *Ex-Yugoslavia: from War to Peace* (Valencia: HCA & Generalitat Valenciana).

Tepavac, M. (1994) *Demokratija ili Despotija* (Zrenjanin: Gradjanska čitaonica).

Tepavac, M. (1995) 'Tito's Yugoslavia', in D. Gojković and J. Ridgeway (eds) *Yugoslavia's Ethnic Nightmare – The Inside Story of Europe's Unfolding Ordeal* (New York: Lawrence Hill Books).

Thompson, M. (1992) *A Paper House: the Ending of Yugoslavia* (London: Hutchinson).

Thompson, M. (1994) *Forging War: The Media in Serbia, Croatia and Bosnia-Hercegovina* (London: Article 19).

Tilly, C. (1975) *The Formation of National States in Western Europe* (Princeton, New Jersey: Princeton University Press).

Udovički, J. and Ridgeway, J. (eds) (1995) *Yugoslavia's Ethnic Nightmare – The Inside Story of Europe's Unfolding Ordeal* (New York: Lawrence Hill Books).

Vaćić, A. M. (1989) *Jugoslavija i Evropa – Uporedna Analiza Privrednog Razvoja Jugoslavije 1971–1987* (Belgrade: Ekonomika).

Vejvoda, I. (1991) Electing for war, *Yugofax – A Critical Briefing on the Conflict in Yugoslavia*, no. 5, 12 October, p. 7.

Vejvoda, I. (1994) Yugoslavia and the empty space of power, *Praxis International*, vol. 13, no. 4, January (Special issue on *The Rise and Fall of Yugoslavia*).

Vujačić, V. and Zaslavsky, V. (1991) The causes of disintegration in the USSR and Yugoslavia, *Telos*, no. 88, Summer, pp. 120–40.

Woodward, S. (1995a) *Balkan Tragedy – Chaos and Dissolution After the Cold War* (Washington DC: The Brookings Institution).

Woodward, S. (1995b) *Socialist Unemployment – The Political Economy of Yugoslavia 1945–1990* (Princeton, New Jersey: Princeton University Press).

Zukin, S. (1975) *Beyond Marx and Tito – Theory and Practice in Yugoslav Socialism* (New York: Cambridge University Press).

Zurcher, A. J. (1933) *The Experiment with Democracy in Central Europe – A Comparative Survey of the Operation of Democratic Government in Post-War Germany and in the Russian and Austro-Hungarian Succession States* (New York: Oxford University Press).

Chapter 3

The Disintegration of Yugoslavia: Causes and Consequences of Dynamic Inefficiency in Semi-command Economies

VESNA BOJIČIĆ

Introduction

The break-up of Yugoslavia came at a time of radical change across the whole of the socialist part of Europe, a time which also witnessed the dissolution of two other federations: the Soviet Union and Czechoslovakia. Most analyses of the causes of disintegration in these countries emphasise internal factors, in particular political factors which found expression in the shift from a one-party to a multiparty system and the revival of nationalism in historical context, with the role of economic factors relegated to the background. What is largely missing in these analyses is any account of the specific interaction between the internal problems of the countries in question and the process of change in its wider environment. This certainly played a very important role in exacerbating the weaknesses of the given systems, and their eventual collapse.

As far as Yugoslavia in particular is concerned, there is a tendency for its break-up to be ascribed to the specific problems of the unique experiment with the self-managed socialist market economy. The fact is, however, that Yugoslavia, with all its institutional peculiarities, suffered from exactly the same systemic weaknesses as all the other command-type economies, including the semi-command economies: low economic efficiency, a lack of technological dynamism and an inability to adapt. These weaknesses became increasingly obvious against the background of the wider processes of change, characterised by increasing interdependence and globalisation, which intensified in the 1980s and 1990s.

In this chapter we focus on the particular way in which the complex interaction between economic and political factors limited the development potential of semi-command economies, making them extremely vulnerable to any process of change. Thus in Yugoslavia, in our view, although specifically political elements played a pivotal role in the saga of dissolution, a process of economic disintegration conditioned by underlying political factors that had evolved over decades played the decisive part.

In seeking to the identify the main factors behind Yugoslavia's economic disintegration and political fragmentation, we proceed as follows. In the first part of the chapter, the economic system, the efficiency of that system, and the development strategy the system was called on to implement are examined, with particular emphasis on the period after 1965, i.e. the period of evolution and implementation of the socialist market economy concept. Investment, technological development and structural change provide the focus of the second part. These are the crucial elements in any explanation of the key problems of distorted economic structure, and the implications of that distorted structure in terms of the lack of dynamic efficiency and capacity for sustainable growth. Some specific aspects of regional development policy – a critical component which can provide a degree of structural cohesion in a heterogeneous country such as was Yugoslavia – are discussed in the third part. The main theme running through this chapter is the peculiar interconnectedness of economics and politics in Yugoslavia's postwar development. And in part four, before concluding, we summarise the pattern of ascendency of politics over economics in the specifically Yugoslav context.

Development strategy, economic system and economic efficiency in postwar Yugoslavia: factors of disintegration

Rapid growth was a distinguishing feature of Yugoslavia's postwar development, with an average annual growth rate of national income of 5.3 per cent in the 1953–89 period. For one part of this period – 1953–60 – an average growth rate of 8.9 per cent was recorded, while in some parts of the country, notably in the autonomous province of Vojvodina, the average annual growth rate was as high as 12.1 per cent, 1953–60. All this placed Yugoslavia among the fastest growing economies in the world at the time (Boltho, 1982; *SGJ*, 1991: 412).

The immediate postwar period was characterised by a highly centralised Soviet style of development, with strong emphasis on industrialisation in pursuit of the fast overall growth of the economy. The aim was to rebuild the industry destroyed during the war, but mainly and most importantly radically to transform the largely agricultural profile of Yugoslavia's prewar economy into a modern industrial one. While central planning as such was abandoned within a few years of its being set up, the Soviet-style development strategy would continue to underlie economic policy-making in Yugoslavia for many years to come.

The strategy of development was country-based, with centralised institutions and policy-making designed to ensure the effective mobilisation of resources under the central planning mechanism. It implied a unified, Yugoslavia-wide market, with unrestricted circulation of people, goods and capital. The cost of building up a comprehensive, vertically integrated industrial structure, against the background of a generally underdeveloped economy, yet with significant regional variations in terms of existing preconditions and needs, was never likely to be met fully from domestic sources. The solution discovered in the years immediately after the split with the Soviet Union in 1948 – to take full advantage of Yugoslavia's relatively easy access to international capital markets, compared to other socialist countries – turned out to be of critical importance for the subsequent economic decline and dissolution of Yugoslavia. The drive for fast overall growth, and the heavy industry bias promoted in the pre-reform period, also set the stage for the disintegrative processes that emerged in the course of economic and political reforms, as each republic tried to set up its own comprehensive industrial base. Particularly in the later stages, as the resources to accommodate such a development orientation became increasingly scarce, this tended to result in a mad scramble for resources on the part of the individual republics.

Apart from the short period of highly centralised planning, and excluding the three final years of Yugoslavia's existence, it is possible to identify four distinct periods in terms of efficiency performance, three of which can be identified with major systemic changes. (See Table 3.1; for a detailed account of the systemic changes see Lydall, 1989 and Dyker, 1990.) These are:

- 1953–64: the period of self-management, supported by only limited market-oriented reform;
- 1965–73: the period of full-scale market socialism;
- 1974–79: the 'contractual economy' period, during which collective control was reasserted; and
- 1980–89: the period of economic crisis, not associated with any key changes in the system.

With all the high overall growth rates, several characteristically negative features of Yugoslavia's development pattern were already in evidence in the pre-1965 period: falling rates of growth of GDP, and of industrial and agricultural production; increasing rates of unemployment; rising inflation and sluggish growth of labour productivity. For most of the period rates of growth of exports and imports were also trending downwards, thus completing the picture of low and declining economic efficiency in the Yugoslav economy. Poor economic performance as expressed through these key macroeconomic indicators was one of the major reasons lying behind repeated attempts to reform the system.

That said, a very rough systemisation in terms of more and less successful periods is justifiable, with 1965 as the dividing point. The official introduction of self-management in 1951, and the reinstatement of the role of the market in the

Table 3.1 Main performance indicators of the Yugoslav economy (average annual growth rates, %, except*)

	1953–64	1965–73	1974–89	1974–79	1980–89
GNP	8.6	5.3	2.8	6.3	0.7
Industrial output	12.7	6.9	4.3	7.6	2.4
Agricultural output	7.2	1.8	0.7	2.4	0.5
Employment	6.3	2.0	2.8	4.5	2.0
Labour productivity	2.3	3.2	0.0	1.7	−1.3
Unemployment rate*	6.6	8.0	14.2	13.0	15.1
Personal consumption	7.3	5.1	2.0	5.8	0.1
Gross fixed investment	11.4	3.4	−0.3	8.9	−5.1
Retail prices	4.0	14.1	68.5	18.2	108.7

* The unemployment rate is calculated in the Yugoslav statistics as a percentage of the non-agricultural population.

Source: Žižmond, 1991: 161.

years that followed, still allowed for a significant degree of administrative regulation in the economy, particularly in terms of income distribution and investment. The Federal Investment Fund, abolished only in 1963, acted as an effective vehicle for directing the course of development. On this basis, the overall economic performance of Yugoslavia in the period up to the 1965 reform can to a large extent be explained in terms of a relatively efficient strategy of centralisation of capital allocation in the context of the early phases of building socialism, notwithstanding significant supplementary growth impulses that resulted from radical changes in the foreign trade, monetary and banking system in 1961, as 'market socialism' evolved. Overall macroeconomic performance was additionally boosted by a generous inflow of foreign aid, which for the 1951–59 period totalled $1bn, with a further $274mn of military aid and $219mn in long-term credits and grants from other Western governments (Plestina, 1992: 69).

The impressive growth performance of the Yugoslav economy in this period was of the 'high cost' variety, based on investing an average of some 35.3 per cent of GDP over the 1953–60 period (*SGJ*, 1991). Providing inputs to meet plan targets often involved deep erosion of the country's natural resource base, while the emphasis on material growth went in parallel with deterioration in the social infrastructure. The costs of rapid industrialisation also manifested themselves through disinvestment in some sectors, sluggish development in agriculture, and massive impoverishment of the agricultural population.

The roots of Yugoslavia's distorted industrial structure, which was both the source and the outcome of the conflicting interests of individual republics throughout Yugoslavia's postwar development, and one of the major obstacles to dynamic development, can be traced back to the early 1950s. The concept of forced industrialisation prescribed that the bulk of investment should go into capital-intensive, basic industries. In the event, these industries not only failed to produce adequate results in terms of increasing production, productivity and employment, as the ultimate goals of any development strategy, but proved to be unviable in terms of the limited size of the Yugoslav market. For that reason they generated an enormous wastage of resources.

Under the policy of decentralisation, with each republic trying to create its own integrated industrial base, the problem of limited market size was further exacerbated, evolving, as it did, into the problem of 'duplicating' industrial capacities on a regional basis – again preempting economies of scale and functional integration. Distortions in relative price structures that favoured final products over raw materials formed another structural obstacle to the success of the development strategy. They discouraged the development of extractive industries and directly induced increasing import dependence in relation to inputs. Against the specific regional industrial pattern, they contributed enormously to the strengthening of the tendency to fragmentation.

Yugoslavia's respectable growth performance up to the mid-1960s was the result of extensive growth, based on increased, rather than improved, utilisation of inputs. In the context of the typical growth fetishism of socialist-type development, efficiency was largely neglected and no institutional framework to foster it was put in place. Hence the basic rationale behind the 'market reform' of 1965 was precisely to switch to more intensive forms of development, through the strengthening of the market mechanism as a complement to planning.

Reform was also implemented in the political sphere, with the system being decentralised further. Although the new socioeconomic system that emerged out of this reform was formally conceptualised as a market socialist, self-managed economy, the practical outcome of the reform of the economic and political system in 1965 was 'republican etatism'. This was in a way a logical stage in the process of the fragmentation of the economic and political system that had been going on virtually from the start of socialist development. Political determination was not enough to counter the autarkic tendencies that the economic system and development strategy bred.

One of the most important shortcomings of the 1965 reform in terms of disintegrative forces in the economic system and the development strategy of Yugoslavia was its failure to establish the market principle in the sphere of fixed capital formation. Although the reform provided a framework for markets in goods, services and labour, it was only really in goods and services that a functioning market was established. The labour market remained grossly imperfect and distorted, as evidenced by the vast disparities in incomes across firms. The capital market simply never came into existence, as autarkical republican regimes restricted the movement of the capital to within the territory from which it originated. Attempts to reform the banking system on a territorial principle provided institutional backing for the generally inward-looking attitude of the republican political oligarchies which had, through the process of extensive decentralisation (see Chapter 2), become the principal players in matters of investment decision-making.

With all the emphasis on factor productivity growth proposed by the 1965 reform, the institutional framework and economic policy orientation ensured that the extensive use of capital, facilitated by negative real interest rates, continued. Consequently, increases in the volume of capital rather than in its productivity came through as the decisive element underpinning growth performance at that time. Labour, still relatively abundant, continued to be overpriced, which simply ruled allocative efficiency out of the question.

In terms of efficiency performance, the eight-year period following the 1965 reform was one of decline in all major aggregate performance indicators compared to the previous eleven-year period, except for a one percentage point increase in the rate of growth/labour productivity. The average annual rate of inflation of 14.1 per cent over the 1965–73 period was 3.5 times the inflation rate for the 1953–64 period; the unemployment rate went up to 8.0 per cent from 6.4 per cent (Žižmond, 1991: 161), while the total foreign debt in 1973 reached $4.4bn (Dyker, 1990: 120). There was also a further worsening of the gap between the more and less developed republics. By 1970 the gap between Slovenia and Kosovo in terms of per capita GDP had increased to1:6 (it had been 1:3.8 in 1952). Finally, growing interenterprise debt reflected the failure of development strategy, and of systemic reforms that attempted to provide an efficient mechanism of macroeconomic regulation and control. All these problems continued to intensify right up to the dissolution of Yugoslavia in the early 1990s, making it ever more difficult for such a heterogeneous country to preserve the degree of tolerance and the sense of solidarity which would have been a minimal condition for its survival.

Overall, the 1965 reform failed in its aims, partly because of its incompleteness and inconsistency, and partly on account of the obstacles erected by the political elites at various levels. The motives behind the systemic changes introduced in 1973, centred round the 'associated labour' concept, were both economic and political. Deteriorating economic performance called for reform, while the strengthening of the industrial managerial elite, together with the increasing role of the banks, called – at least in the eyes of the leadership – for a reassertion of the leading role of the party.

The promulgation of 'integral self-management', as enshrined in the 1974 constitution, represented a reversal to a *non-market economic system*. It effectively rejected the market mechanism, macroeconomic steering and indicative planning, and substituted a system of self-management agreements, social compacts and overall social planning, in which localised political and planning authorities came to exercise a key role (Bartlett, 1991). The process of the decentralisation of the political system, under pressure from the republics, produced deeper and deeper cleavages along regional lines, effectively turning Yugoslavia into a political confederation, which was implicitly recognised in the 1974 constitution (see Chapter 2). This crucial inconsistency between a non-market economic system and a highly decentralised political system, against the background of Yugoslavia's specific regional-cum-ethnic issues and deteriorating economy, certainly contributed enormously to the acute crisis Yugoslavia entered in the early 1980s, and to its 'national bankruptcy'[1] in the 1990s.

Most macroeconomic indicators improved after the 1973 reform, except for labour productivity and inflation. But this reflected a return to extensive development, which had indeed started as early as the late 1960s, and was based on a further increase in investment ratio. Expansion in investment was financed through increased borrowing on international markets, so that over the 1971–79 period an average of 38.3 per cent of Yugoslavia'a gross fixed investment was financed through foreign borrowing. Yugoslavia's total foreign debt in 1980 reached $17bn,[2] signalling the impending exhaustion of the economy. And this was the final and definitive demonstration that Yugoslavia's postwar development policies had produced weak and fragmented economic structures, incapable of providing for stable and sustained development.

Because of the peculiarities of Yugoslavia's economic and political system, and in particular of the interaction of the two, the abundance of foreign capital had, over the longer run, a number of significant counter-productive effects. It helped divert attention from the key problems of the system and its functioning, such as the issue of structural adjustment and the growth in regional disparities. It also provided a material basis for the proliferation of particularistic interests pursued by the political elites of individual republics and provinces engaged in competition for resources, conveniently justified in terms of their own republic's (nation's) interests.[3] The

---

[1] The term comes from Žarković-Bookman, 1994.

[2] Yugoslavia's GDP in 1980 expressed in dollars at $1 = 17 dinars was around $23bn.

[3] Note that in Yugoslavia the administrative boundaries of the republics largely corresponded to the ethnic distribution of the population, with the notable exception of the republic of Bosnia-Hercegovina. See Chapter 2.

result was a gradual shaping up of six 'national' economies within the system, which effectively excluded integrative and reintegrative forces.

The corollary to this process was extreme distortion in the pattern of Yugoslavia's integration into the international division of labour.[4] Each republic insisted on forging its own links with the outside world, the consequence of which was a profound peripheralisation of a country as a whole. Systemic changes promoted through the application of the associated labour concept in the period 1973–79, in combination with the institutions of workers' self-management, significantly contributed to the internal dynamics of disintegration. They created almost insurmountable obstacles to the mobility of labour, capital and technology, thus blocking both technological progress and competition, and seriously undermining the organisational efficiency of self-managed enterprises. Basic economic infrastructure, such as the rail system, postal and telecommunication services, etc., also fell victim to disintegration, thus undermining the very material and physical preconditions for a viable unified market – to the extent that it had ever been really operational.

By giving local governments and political bodies full powers without responsibility, these changes also exacerbated the major structural imbalances that already existed at the level of firms and banks, industrial and service sectors, and at the macrolevel itself. The ascendancy of politics over economics translated itself in practice into preference for economic autarky, particularly at the level of republican governments, which stopped at nothing to protect what they perceived as their own interest. This often extended to measures to cut out competition from other republics, and to an effective closing-off of the republican economies, not only from unwanted competition from other parts of Yugoslavia, but also from abroad. *In terms of overall development, Yugoslavia effectively ceased to exist.* It is against this background that the severest crisis of the postwar development of Yugoslavia set in at the beginning of the 1980s, with differentiating effects on different industries and different parts of the country.

The 1980s was the decade of the culmination of the crisis, when Yugoslavia's internal economic and sociopolitical problems and changes in the global environment came into baleful confluence. In the 1980–90 period, the average rate of growth of national income was 0.5 per cent: the worst performance in Europe. Labour productivity started to fall sharply. Investment declined by between 6 per cent and 7 per cent annually, while the annual inflation rate averaged 108.7 per cent 1980–89,[5] and on a rising curve, leading to hyperinflation by 1989. All this was happening against the background of the country's rising international debt, and as the conditions in international financial markets significantly changed compared to the years of affluence of the 1970s.

The crisis of the 1980s is usually referred to as a 'debt' crisis, as servicing the huge foreign debt of around \$22bn by 1982 set the scene for a series of hectic, stop-go efforts to arrest negative tendencies within the economy. However, under the dictate of IMF stabilisation programmes,[6] and in the context of the specific

---

[4] Some specific features of this pattern are described in Schierup, 1992.
[5] Source: *Ekonomska Politika*, no. 2033, 1991: 15–16; Žižmond, 1991: 161.
[6] Prasnikar and Svejnar point out how little impact key variables in these programmes had on the efficiency of Yugoslav firms. See Prasnikar, Svejnar and Klinedinst, 1992.

characteristics and problems of the Yugoslav economy at the time, the situation only worsened. Supply-side bottlenecks originating in the economic system itself represented a major cause of the crisis. What systemic changes were implemented had little impact on these bottlenecks, as they did not challenge the basic incentive structure of the system. Thus, at its very outset, the IMF-style austerity programme stood little chance of success. Its immediate effect was a sharp drop in demand and imports, which further lowered the levels of output and aggravated the economic and political crisis. The impact was particularly severe in the less-developed parts of the country. To the extent that this stabilisation programme adopted in 1983 achieved anything, it achieved it through purely administrative measures.

The 1983 stabilisation·programme was confronted with more or less the same problems as had the previous reforms. Disagreements over the aims and provisions of the reform itself conspired with the extremely slow and complicated decision-making process to block its implementation. What was different this time around was that these problems came into the open, which had significant implications for the overall social and political atmosphere. Mutual recriminations among republics over alleged exploitation, and growing ethnic and cultural intolerance within populations faced with severe economic hardship beyond anything experienced thus far, came increasingly to dominate political and social agendas.

As the economic crisis deepened, the confrontation among the republics not only over the key aspects of economic policy, but also over the future profile of the economic system and indeed the future of the country as such, sharpened. The inability of the federal government to affect the course of events and bring republics into compliance with federal rules and regulations was painfully exposed. The need for a genuine, far-reaching reform to remove structural and functional blockages to economic flows was clear for all to see. But decades of systemic reform aimed at decentralisation had seen a process of withdrawal of the state from many aspects of economic life, and with it a profound weakening of the state at all levels. Consequently, the state was in no position to perform the important tasks envisaged by the radical reform proposed in 1989 which would, finally, have produced the revolutionary changes in property rights without which reform is a non-starter. In this last stage of Yugoslavia's existence, it became obvious that the long process of economic disintegration and fragmentation of the federal administrative structure had left in place very little in the way of any functioning mechanism that could keep the country together.

Investment, technological development and structural change

The basic parameters of investment policy in Yugoslavia were set by the development strategy of forced industrialisation. As stated earlier, the investment effort in Yugoslavia as measured by the gross investment/GDP ratio was by any standards exceptionally high for most of the period, and particularly in the second half of the 1970s.[7] Except for the 1980s, rates of growth of investment constantly outpaced overall growth rates.

---

[7] Uvalić (1992), p. 69, quotes Yugoslav official statistics to the effect that the share of gross investment in GMP (Gross Material Product) was on average 40.6 per cent in the 1970s. Even when account is taken of the differences between the GDP and GMP concepts (the latter does not include 'non-productive' services such as health, education, public administration, etc.) the reported investment ratios remain extraordinarily high.

The bulk of investment went into the expansion of industry, with basic industry being a priority. Although favoured by investment policy, priority sectors recorded below-average growth rates, so that they were a drag on the growth of industry as a whole. The emphasis was on projects in highly capital-intensive basic and energy sectors, which ate up enormous volumes of resources and took a long time to complete. At the same time their final products suffered price discrimination, so that they were unable to take their fate into their own hands through self-financed investment. Thus both patterns of investment in basic industry and systemic measures *vis-à-vis* basic industry conspired to hold back the development of the sector, with all the inevitable structural problems that that entailed.

At the same time, the manufacturing industries which were supposed to absorb the inputs of basic industry turned to imports and grew fast, increasing their share in total industrial value added. The growth of this segment of industry was largely based on the availability of foreign credits and shaped by the preferences of individual republics. Manufacturing also benefited extensively from preferential treatment in the system of income distribution and foreign trade regulation. Thus a situation was created in which this segment developed more or less independently of the rest of industry, with little impact on the dynamics of the sector as a whole.

The whole issue of priorities in the development strategy of Yugoslavia worked as a significant impediment to its sustained development. It is clear that policies that favoured rapid growth, exports and employment and, at the same time, in trying to achieve those goals, relied on production priorities within the primary sector, could not succeed. The process of defining development priorities was vitiated by a badly conceptualised development strategy, and economic policy measures and instruments based on a non-market economic system. In the final stage, all selectiveness in priorities was lost, so that consequently almost all sectors were declared priority, causing not only disorientation in development strategy, but also a large-scale wastage of resources.

Inefficiency was thus the central characteristic of the investment pattern in Yugoslavia. If we look at the incremental capital/output ratio, we can identify a continuous deterioration: from 3.60 in 1966–72, to 4.29 in 1976–80, up to an incredible 24.43 in the 1981–85 period (Papić, 1989: 202). Thus, in spite of the enormous investment effort forced on the economy through rapid industrialisation, the actual impact of investment on development was rather disappointing, and investment worked as a strong regenerator of structural and technological imbalances in the Yugoslav economy.

There were some other features of the investment pattern in Yugoslavia which complete the explanation of why this was so. The share of construction work in gross fixed investment in 1965–85 was around 54 per cent (*SGJ*, 1987: 69). A comparatively low proportion of new investment went into capital equipment, and this was one of the reasons why the technological gap between Yugoslavia and the advanced countries was constantly deepening. The intrinsically extensive character of investment policy in Yugoslavia was also manifested in a strong emphasis on investing in new capacities as opposed to the reconstruction and modernisation of existing ones.[8] Consequently, the process of the continuous upgrading of production

---

[8] The share of investment in new capacities within total investment in the socialised sector was almost 50 per cent (SGJ, 1991: 500).

capacities was largely absent, which directly undermined the competitiveness of the industrial sector.

A number of characteristics of the Yugoslav economic system that persisted throughout the postwar period – price distortions, the short-term profit orientation of firms, inappropriate arrangements in the foreign trade sphere, limited domestic savings and distorted market structure – conspired to sideline the issue of technology and technical change in the context of development strategy and policy. By suppressing any form of genuine competition, the economic system excluded the possibility of effective incentives for technological awareness at the level of the enterprise, or of well-defined and systematic policy at the level of government that would motivate investment in technological search. The development strategy of forced growth promoted competitiveness based on cheap material and labour inputs,[9] while the issue of technology was resolved either through imports or, where this was too expensive, by directing resources into low-technology, labour-intensive projects.

Nothing resembling a strategy of technological development existed in Yugoslavia until the late 1980s. Technology policy was limited to technology transfer, which was conducted in a fragmentory and highly inefficient fashion. Firms developed their links with foreign partners and suppliers of technology on an individual basis, with the result that a variety of systems and different technological generations were often to be found in the same technical and technological area.[10] Not infrequently, technology was licensed from abroad, even though it could have been obtained locally. A multiplicity of standards resulted, which worked directly against closer cooperation among the firms of a particular locality (Schierup, 1992: 93), and to a significant extent prevented the development of more complex technologies such as would require complementary indigenous technological effort.

Over a number of years Yugoslavia was paying more for technology transferred from abroad than she was investing in its development at home. In just four years, 1979–83, Yugoslavia spent some $1.27bn on imports of equipment, these being mostly technically advanced systems,[11] in contrast to the heavy imports of basic technologies characteristic of the 1950s.

The import of patents and licences held up well as the Yugoslav economy moved into crisis. Over the period 1973–86 some 1050 patents and licences were bought, mostly from Western Europe.[12] This confirms that Yugoslav firms generally did have access to modern technology, although mainly in the form of buy/lease arrangements. The problems of the preparation and implementation of technology transfer arrangements, which required substantial knowledge and experience on the part of local firms with respect to the selection and eventual mastering and adaption of the technology, were numerous. As a result, many arrangements for the transfer

---

[9] This is illustrated by the composition of Yugoslavia's industrial exports. In 1970–86 exports of raw-material-intensive industries made up 38.3 per cent of total exports to the OECD, while the share of exports of labour-intensive industries was on average 23.4 per cent (OECD, 1988: 63).

[10] Notably in the electronics industry.

[11] *Ekonomska Politika*, 30 May 1985.

[12] *Ekonomska Politika*, 23 January 1988.

of technology were made on unfavourable terms for the recipients of the technology, and the deficiencies generally associated with the arrangements for the transfer of technology to developing countries were much in evidence.

All this contributed to the profound weakness of Yugoslavia's science and technology base, which was, in turn, among the causes of the disarray on technology issues. The extremely fragmented research and development base suffered from both insufficiency and inefficiency. The amount of R&D spending decreased steadily throughout the 1980s, oscillating around 1 per cent of GDP (*SGJ*, 1989). R&D units within enterprises made up less than 15 per cent of the total number in the country, compared to 75 per cent in some developed countries. The majority of R&D institutions were small in size, dealing mainly with small-scale research projects, and suffering from lack of funding, personnel and equipment. Thus problems of inadequate capacity and capability on the supply side of the technology factor greatly contributed to the slow rates of technological advance and adoption within the economy.

The reasons for the disappointing impact of technological development on Yugoslavia's economic performance are primarily to be sought, not so much in an inadequate or obsolete technical base, as was the case with most of the former socialist countries, but rather in wider organisational and managerial shortcomings at the level of the firm, lack of expert technical knowledge, weak links between industry and the R&D sector, and a lack of coordination at the federal level between the different components of science-technology policy and industrial development. Significant resources that could have been invested in building up domestic technological capabilities were frittered away on payments for foreign technology. The motivation and capability of local enterprises to acquire, develop, improve and re-transfer technologies were thus systematically undermined, as was, consequently, the flexibility and adaptability which is the key to efficiency at the enterprise level. Technical inefficiency, as distinct from allocative inefficiency, was in consequence an important cause of low and declining productivity in Yugoslavia. On a more general, macroeconomic level, by neglecting the significance of technology (and of education and skills) for dynamic and efficient economic development, and by not providing at least some unifying elements with respect to technological development, Yugoslavia missed a critical opportunity to create some degree of structural cohesion – a key condition of sustainability – within the economy.

The peculiar pattern of investment and the eccentric treatment of technological change, both determined by the nature of the economic system and the development strategy, resulted in a distorted pattern of structural change as the Yugoslav economy developed. These elements taken together explain the creation of a rigid economic structure incapable of transforming itself, despite a series of reform attempts through the post-1965 period, which was in itself a major structural blockage to the dynamic development of the Yugoslav economy (Killick, 1995).

At the level of the economy as a whole, trends in output and employment reveal a process of prolonged industrialisation, which however never entered its mature stage whereby industry should become a nodal point and a structuring force for the development of the other two sectors within the global structure. The share in total value added of the secondary sector, of which industry is the core, remained in

Yugoslavia at a higher level than typical for that level of development, and this was also the case for the primary sector. After 1970, the share of the tertiary sector in total value added actually fell, contrary to the experience of other countries at a comparable level of development.[13] On the other hand, from 1965 there was, in fact, an acceleration in the rate of the shift in employment from the primary to the secondary sector, which supports the argument that this was still an early stage in Yugoslavia's industrialisation, despite the speed and intensity with which it progressed.

The intensity of structural change was directly related to the dynamics of growth, so that the loss of growth momentum in the late 1970s halted what structural change there was. The result was a global structure in which the primary sector was oversized, the industrial sector was not fully integrated into the global structure and failed to exercise its potential propulsive impact on the rest of that structure, and finally the underdeveloped tertiary sector was unable to play its proper role in the economy.

As far as any change in the branch composition of industry is concerned, emphasis on the overall dynamics of the sector as a whole resulted in a profound disregard for its internal structure. Problems of structural adaptation within the sector were seen in terms of balancing basic and manufacturing industries, this reflecting, among other factors, the prevalent attitudes towards technological progress and the failure to grasp the complex relationship between technological progress and economic growth and development. The importance of the adoption and adaptation of modern technologies, and of structural adjustment in manufacturing as the leading sector, was never properly appreciated in development plans and strategy. The fact is that so-called development plans lacked any clearly defined overall strategy of industrial development on which the sustainable growth of the economy could be based. There was also a link here with Yugoslavia's trade strategy, which was to a considerable extent tied up with the countries of the former Soviet bloc, and as such suffered from a fundamental lack of adequate incentives for the dynamic development of industry. At the same time, two other important sectors enjoying clear-cut comparative advantage – agriculture and tourism – were not, until very late in the period under review, at the focal point of development strategy. This indirectly affected industrial development too.

The pattern of structural change in Yugoslavia was predominantly shaped by excessive domestic demand and a long-term commitment to import substitution, whereas two other potentially equally important factors of structural change – exports and input-output relations within industry – had much less effect. The manufacturing sector itself, the central focus of industrial growth in Yugoslavia, was broken up into suboptimal capacities and was heavily dependent on imported inputs. It was, consequently, very sensitive to the balance-of-payments situation, a critical factor in Yugoslavia's development throughout. The core of manufacturing was made up of industries of medium and low technological intensity (as defined in OECD, 1988), which were particularly affected by the wave of changes related to

---

[13] For an exposition of the typical patterns of structural change see Chenery, Robinson and Surquin, 1986.

the spread of information technologies in the 1980s. Their output was generally unsophisticated in terms of quality, technical standards and service content. Consequently they were not up to the task of adapting to the new technologies and increasing exports, as required by the economic policies of the 1980s.

To sum up, the process of forced industrialisation was pursued without adequate coordination, in spite of the formal role of planning in Yugoslavia's economic system, and this resulted in a weak and stagnant manufacturing sector. Thorough restructuring and revitalisation of the manufacturing industry became the highest priority precisely at the time of Yugoslavia's severest crisis, when none of the necessary conditions of that restructuring and revitalisation, from finance to political consent, were at hand.

Regional development

The problems relating to the manufacturing sector are but a part of a general picture of an economic structure which was inherently fragmented and lacked the flexibility to adapt to internal pressures and external shocks. Yugoslavia's regional development policy was an important element in the emergence of that structure. In fact, all the issues that we have touched on so far have a specifically regional dimension in one way or another. Only when taken together in that regional dimension, do they offer a full explanation for the massing of centrifugal, disintegrative forces and the break-up of Yugoslavia.[14]

Regional development policy in Yugoslavia involved a complex interplay of economic, political, social, cultural and historical factors, which made the officially declared goal of the reduction of the enormous inherited economic disparities and social inequalities among the Yugoslav nations very difficult to achieve. The problems of uneven development were present not only between 'North' and 'South', but also between individual republics and autonomous provinces and within them, which made a coherent regional development policy extremely difficult to conceive and implement. Although the achievements of regional policy can by no means be reduced to pure numbers (an argument frequently and forcefully put forward by party officials under the old regime), the overview of basic indicators of development for all Yugoslav republics presented in Table 3.2 gives an approximate idea of what was accomplished.

Several points with implications for the assessment of the effects of regional policy emerge from the above figures. Demographic statistics show that population growth was faster in the less-developed republics, i.e. Bosnia-Hercegovina, Macedonia and Montenegro (all three were classified in this category for most of Yugoslavia's postwar development) and the autonomous province of Kosovo than in the three developed republics and the autonomous province of Vojvodina. Although Table 3.2 contains data for two (variable) benchmark years only, it is clear that the rate of growth of the less-developed republics constantly lagged behind the

---

[14]   Plestina (1992) presents a comprehensive study of regional development as a critical factor in the disintegration of Yugoslavia.

Table 3.2 Basic indicators of Regional Development in Yugoslavia

	Year	SFRY	BH	Mon.	Croa.	Mac.	Slov.	Ser.*	Kos.
Population	1953	100	16.7	2.5	23.2	7.7	8.8	41.1	4.8
	1990	100	19.0	2.7	19.7	8.9	8.2	34.5	8.3
GMP	1953	100	14.4	1.8	26.7	5.2	14.3	37.6	2.2
	1989	100	12.9	2.0	25.0	5.8	16.5	38.0	2.1
GMP	1953	100	83	77	122	68	175	86	43
per capita	1989	100	65	71	124	65	200	88	40
Average growth of GMP (%)									
1956–90		4.9	4.6	5.0	4.6	5.2	5.1	5.1	5.1
(per capita)		3.9	3.2	3.7	4.0	3.7	4.1	4.3	2.3
Fixed assets	1955	100	107	49	100	68	124	93	85
per worker	1989	100	93	134	110	75	138	87	89

* Serbia as a whole.

Source: Plestina, 1992: 180; *SGJ*, 1991: 410–12.

country's averages, so that in terms of GMP per capita they registered a deterioration of their position over the four decades, implying a widening of the gap in the levels of development (social indicators provide supporting evidence). Except for Bosnia-Hercegovina, however, the less-developed republics significantly increased their share in Yugoslavia's fixed assets per worker. Why was this so?

The typical Yugoslav investment pattern, marked by high rates of investment, *repeated itself in the less developed republics in an even more pronounced form*, with investment ratios rising constantly and, in some less-developed republics, and in Kosovo in particular, being maintained above the Yugoslav average. Exactly the opposite relationship held with respect to investment efficiency as expressed through the incremental capital/output ratio, which meant that in order for the less-developed parts of the country to achieve the same economic performance as more developed republics, the investment input *had* to be significantly higher. And if the data on population growth is included, a picture of a vicious circle of poverty emerges, with per capita income in the poorer areas growing only slowly, from a low base.

A recent study of the efficacy of regional policy in Yugoslavia (Babić, 1992) argues that all this was primarily the consequence of variations in the efficiency of utilisation of the factors of production between developed and less developed regions, and plays down the importance of differences in economic structure – and therefore of the differentiating effect of economic policy as such. Consideration of the inherited characteristics of the two groups of regions, such as the more advanced industrial base and infrastructure, higher levels of skills and qualifications of the work force, etc. in the more developed parts, undoubtedly speaks in favour of such an argument. The fact remains that the developed regions had more manufacturing industry, with the less-developed regions remaining predominantly

Table 3.3 Gross Fixed Investment,* Incremental Capital-output Ratio and GMP† 1953–89, by Region

Period	Yugoslavia	Bosnia-Hercegovina	Montenegro	Croatia	Macedonia	Slovenia	Serbia	Kosovo
Gross fixed investment*								
1953–60	19.3	22.2	52.7	16.7	26.0	16.9	18.9	18.4
1961–70	20.4	20.8	36.5	18.8	32.9	16.4	20.9	39.4
1971–80	22.7	28.3	39.6	21.0	26.6	21.4	21.5	42.0
1981–89	16.3	18.8	21.9	15.7	13.0	14.9	16.4	25.3
1953–89	19.5	22.6	32.6	18.2	22.1	17.5	19.2	32.9
ICOR								
1953–60	2.2	3.0	8.9	1.9	3.2	1.9	2.0	2.3
1961–70	3.2	3.9	4.4	3.0	4.2	2.4	3.4	5.6
1971–80	4.0	5.1	6.4	3.9	4.6	3.5	3.7	7.6
1981–89	32.3	15.3	1408.5	297.3	13.9	126.7	26.6	23.8
1953–89	3.7	4.7	6.3	3.6	3.9	3.2	3.5	3.0
GMP†								
1953–60	8.9	7.4	5.9	9.0	8.1	9.1	9.7	7.9
1961–70	6.3	5.4	8.4	6.3	7.9	6.9	6.1	7.0
1971–80	5.7	5.5	6.1	5.4	5.8	6.1	5.9	5.5
1981–89	0.5	1.2	0.0	0.1	0.9	0.1	0.6	1.1
1953–89	5.3	4.8	5.2	5.1	5.6	5.5	5.4	5.3

* Ratio to GMP
† Average annual rates of growth.

Source: Vojnić, 1994: 282.

basic-industry-oriented. This was one of the key reasons behind the conflicts of interest between these groups of regions. Arguments of a 'centre-periphery' type were not uncommon in the debates over regional policy.

It is precisely in the particularist interests of the individual republics that we find one of the biggest and most durable obstacles to the implementation of systemic reforms. While the more developed parts favoured decentralisation and a market economy, the less-developed argued rather for centralisation and income redistribution. This basic disagreement over the content and pace of the reforms, which obviously had different implications for the more and the less developed regions, worked in time as a powerful disintegrative force.[15]

It can plausibly be argued that overall dynamic development of the economy was a common interest of both more and less developed regions. But with the devolution of power that accompanied the reforms of the system, and with the availability of foreign loans, growth in the less-developed republics became decoupled from growth in the country as a whole, which directly undermined the efficacy of regional policies. Regional development policy was meant, at least officially, to have a country-wide focus, providing for the more balanced growth of different regions within a Yugoslav context. In practice, however, very few of its priorities was achieved. Rather regional policy was simply based on a mechanism of redistribution, which was, although from different perspectives, continually challenged *by developed and less developed republics alike.*

Decentralisation of the economic and political system had very important repercussions for regional policy. It placed the prerogatives of economic and political authority in the hands of republican and local bureaucracies whose main concern was to obtain sufficient resources to finance their own favourite development projects, aimed at as high a degree of self-sufficiency as possible. In the case of the less developed regions, this frequently meant going for prestige projects, offering very little productive return for their regional economies, or directing resources into programmes which could not be supported by the skills and qualifications of the local workforce, or by the local infrastructure, or both.

The inefficiency of the investment pattern in less developed regions was constantly raised as an issue by the more developed republics, which felt exploited – particularly in view of the fact that within the more developed republics there also existed less developed parts that needed assistance. The issue of contributions to the Fund for Development of the Less Developed Republics and Autonomous Provinces came to a head with the sharp economic decline from the late 1970s, and was one of the strongest arguments put forward in favour of the secession by Slovenia and Croatia, the most developed republics in Yugoslavia.

The problems associated with development strategy and regional development policy, with their origins in the character of the economic system as such, resulted in contrasting degrees of integration into the Yugoslavia-wide market on the part of the two regional 'blocks'. Interregional trade indicators have become political tools

---

[15] Vojnić (1994: 281) argues that the less developed regions, while recognising the potential benefits from increased efficiency associated with greater reliance on the market mechanism, in practice tended to press for the preservation of a more centralised system.

in the arguments over the causes of the collapse of Yugoslavia, and over the costs and benefits for the individual republics, now independent states, of that trade. They are therefore always likely to be disputed by someone. But it can be said with some confidence that the less-developed republics were generally more open to interregional trade than the more developed republics.[16] Awareness of this fact was an important element in the perceptions of the latter group as to its likely prospects after secession.

The lack of a coherent regional policy was partly responsible for the systematic undermining of the overall productivity performance of the Yugoslav economy. Instead of looking at the needs and problems of the less-developed regions, regional policy *de jure* focused on the political centre's notion of what was good for the development of the country as a whole, and *de facto* represented little more than a pay-off to keep the political bosses in the poorer regions minimally happy. All this reflected the dominant political influence of the developed republics at that centre. To conclude, regional development policy failed to fulfil its goals, or indeed provide any force of cohesion, in a country of pronounced regional diversity.

The supremacy of politics over economics

The predominant role of the political elite in economic matters was never eliminated in Yugoslavia (nor indeed in any of the other semi-command economies), in spite of all the reforms of the system. It could be further argued that the modifications to the economic system that were implemented – by a political elite whose primary concern was to strengthen its own position – actually created, within the specific framework of Yugoslavia's national, ethnic and regional diversities, major structural obstacles to the country's dynamic long-term development.

The key to the successful management of Yugoslavia's economy would have been the operationalisation of a unified market, with unified monetary and fiscal policies. This would have imposed competitive pressures on domestic producers and induced a more efficient allocation of resources. However, the concept of a unified market, with a free flow of correctly priced resources, was not acceptable to the political elite, as it would have implied the dissolution of its power base, namely social ownership. Thus even the introduction of self-management could be explained in terms of the political elite looking for a way of appearing to provide more economic liberalism while preserving its powers, by trading off Yugoslav-level federalism against republican etatism.

The disastrous implications of the predominance of politics in economic matters were perhaps most obvious with respect to regional policy. The decentralisation of power through the concept of self-management, combined with federalism, was seen as a pragmatic way to accommodate the different economic interests of the regions and the legacy of prewar Yugoslavia – which was never openly acknowledged by the regime as a cause of possible serious discontent. While political

---

[16] Steinherr and Ottolenghi (1993: 235) discuss this issue and present statistics to back up the claim.

stability was, at least formally, guaranteed through a constitution that implied the statehood of all major Yugoslav nations, the more concrete preconditions of economic equality was less easy to guarantee and achieve. In an atmosphere of general shortage of resources to underpin investment ambitions mediated through political elites at different levels, the political bureaucracy often resorted to populist-nationalist slogans which, against the background of growing regional discrepancies in levels of economic development between republics, created a breeding ground for the rise of ethno-nationalism. This was particularly the case in the 1980s, by which time the League of Communists had already become caught up in serious internal strife and had in practice abandoned its principle of democratic centralism. Thus, with the political system in disarray and the economy in deep crisis, a major impetus was given to the rise of the economic and political separatism which eventually led to the collapse of Yugoslavia.

Concluding remarks

Yugoslavia was the first of the former socialist, command-type economies to embark on the path of economic reform. The reforms set in train were generally aimed at the decentralisation and liberalisation of the socioeconomic system and at greater reliance on the market mechanisms of resource allocation. The aim was to remove, or at least to ease, the barriers to dynamic growth. In spite of the substantial institutional changes that were implemented, the economic system of Yugoslavia was not liberated from the typical and fundamental features of the socialist economic system. Thus its failures can be attributed primarily to the shortcomings of the planned administrative system in general. But they were nevertheless significantly exacerbated by the socialist self-management system introduced in Yugoslavia in the early 1950s.

The objectives of the reforms in Yugoslavia were never fully accomplished. The reforms were partial in their character, and never tackled the basic problem of the Yugoslav socioeconomic system: namely, social ownership over the means of production and, implicitly, the ascendency of politics in relation to fundamental economic issues. For most of the postwar period, development policy in Yugoslavia was predominantly concerned with fostering dynamic growth at the level of the economy as a whole. The need to create and preserve a certain degree of structural cohesion such as would have provided for the structural adaptability of the system as such, and accordingly created conditions for stable long-term development, was simply overlooked. As a result, two crucial effective nodes of development policy – technology policy and regional policy – were simply missing.

The entire systemic set-up of the Yugoslav economy tended, even after reform, to suppress and even eliminate any potential for the technology-related structural adjustment of the economy. The bulk of investment was channelled into activities in which Yugoslavia *de facto* had comparative disadvantage, causing wastage of resources through low efficiency and lack of competitiveness. Elimination of the regional economic disparities in Yugoslavia was never accomplished, which was another important source of economic and political instability. Apart from the general issue of insufficient economic resources, the combination of administrative system and political climate created a fertile ground for economic regionalism and further aggravated the problem of economic inefficiency and the structural inflexibility of the system.

When limits to the chosen development path were reached, internally and in terms of radical economic and political changes in a wider environment, the system confronted major structural blockages to further growth. It became obvious, as was the case with the other semi-command economies, that the basic preconditions for switching to a different mode of development in terms of human and capital resources, organisational and managerial practices, research and communications infrastructure and institutions, simply did not exist. This was a direct consequence of the decades of 'non-negotiable' forced growth strategy, and a socioeconomic system shaped by a peculiar, and ultimately disastrous, relationship between economics and politics.

References

Babić, S. (1992) Regionalna X-efikasnost 'otkrivena' metodom indeksnih brojeva, *Ekonomska Misao*, Beograd, vol. 25, no. 1, pp. 13–30.

Bartlett, W. (1991) Economic Change in Yugoslavia: from Crisis to Reform. In O. Sjoberg and M. Wyzan (eds) *Economic Change in the Balkan States* (London: Pinter).

Boltho, A. (ed.) (1982) *The European Economy: Growth and Crisis* (Oxford: Oxford University Press).

Chenery, H., Robinson, S. and Surquin, M. (1986) *Industrialisation and Growth: a Comparative Study* (Oxford: Oxford University Press).

Dyker, D. (1990) *Yugoslavia. Socialism, Development and Debt* (London: Routledge).

Ekonomska Politika, weekly, Belgrade, various issues.

Jovanović-Gavrilović, B. (1989) *Kvalitet Privrednog Rasta* (Beograd: Savremena administracija).

Killick, T. (ed.) (1995) *The Flexible Economy – Causes and Consequences of the Adaptability of National Economies* (London: Routledge).

Lydall, H. (1989) *Yugoslavia in Crisis* (Oxford: Oxford University Press).

Milanović, B. (1987) Patterns of regional growth in Yugoslavia 1952–83, *Journal of Development Studies,* vol. 25, pp. 1–19.

Milanović, B. (1989) *Liberalization and Enterpreneurship – Dynamics of Reform in Socialism and Capitalism* (London: M.E. Sharpe).

OECD (1988) *Science, Technology and Innovation Policies: Yugoslavia* (Paris: OECD).

Papić, Z. (1989) Reforma Razvojne Orijentacije. In *Privreda u Reformi* (Belgrade: Ekonomike), pp. 198–213.

Plestina, D. (1992) *Regional Development in Communist Yugoslavia: Success, Failure and Consequences* (Boulder: Westview Press).

Prasnikar, J., Svejnar, J. and Klinedinst, M. (1992) Structural adjustment policies and productive efficiency of socialist enterprises, *European Economic Review*, vol. 36, no. 1, pp. 179–201.

Schierup, C.-U. (1992) Quasi-proletarians and a patriarchal bureaucracy: aspects of Yugoslavia's re-peripheralisation, *Soviet Studies*, vol. 44, no. 1, pp. 77–99.

Schierup, C.-U. (1993) Prelude to inferno – economic disintegration and political fragmentation of Yugoslavia, *Balkan Forum*, no. 8, pp. 89–120.

Sjoberg O. and Wyzan, M. (eds) (1991) *Economic Change in the Balkan States* (London: Pinter).

Statistički Godišnjak Jugoslavije (*SGJ*, Statistical Yearbook of Yugoslavia), various years.

Steinherr, A. and Ottolenghi, D. (1993) Yugoslavia: was it a winner's curse? *Economics of Transition*, vol. 11, no. 2, pp. 209–43.

Uvalić, M. (1992) *Investment and Property Rights in Yugoslavia – The Long Transition to a Market Economy* (Cambridge: Cambridge University Press).

Vojnić, D. (1994) Ekonomske dimenzije dezintegracije, *Ekonomski Pregled*, vol. 45, no. 3–4, pp. 261–89.

Žarković-Bookman, M. (1994) *Economic Decline and Nationalism in the Balkans* (London: Macmillan).

Žižmond, E. (1991) *Specificnosti Inflacije u Jugoslaviji* (Zagreb: Naprijed).

Chapter 4

The Degeneration of the Yugoslav Communist Party as a Managing Elite – a Familiar East European Story?

DAVID A. DYKER

Introduction

To say that there are significant, even critical elements of continuity between the old communist regimes and elites of Eastern Europe, and the new regimes and elites which have taken control of the region since 1989, is merely to state the obvious. Even in the 'clean-break' countries like Poland and Czechoslovakia/the Czech Republic, the fact that the handover of power was wholly peaceful, that there was no revolution as such, and that the human and financial assets of the old *nomenklatura* remained largely intact, made it inevitable that those who had wielded power and influence under the old order would resurface under the new. Nor would it be appropriate to issue any blanket condemnation of such a trend. To the extent, for example, that the '*nomenklatura* capitalists' of Poland have money, expertise and contacts, they may be able to play an important role in the transformation of the Polish economy. Again, no one could accuse the neo-communist governments presently in power in Poland and Hungary of betraying the cause of transition towards a fully fledged capitalist system. *What is absolutely clear is that we cannot hope to understand the 'new' politics and economics of the region if we do not understand the old.*

In broad-brush terms the former Yugoslavia fits in to this pattern as well as any other sub-region of Eastern Europe. The level of continuity at the presidential level is somewhat higher than average for the transition countries. Kučan in Slovenia, Tudjman in Croatia, Milošević in Serbia and Gligorov in Macedonia are all former members of the top elite of the Communist Party/League of Communists of Yugoslavia. Their patterns of 'personal transition' vary between the two extremes of Franjo Tudjman, once a communist, then a nationalist dissident, finally a nationalist president – and Slobodan Milošević, the classic '*nomenklatura* nationalist' (see Dyker, 1995), whose transmogrification from communist *apparatchik* into nationalist *caudillo* was almost imperceptible. In the spectrum which runs from legitimate business to outright gangsterism in the former Yugoslavia, the old elites are similarly prominent.

But surely, the reader may interpose, the Yugoslav communist system was fundamentally different from that of the rest of the communist-controlled part of the world? Dictatorial certainly, but with a commitment to decentralised and market-based procedures unique, even among reforming communist systems, and which excluded, by definition, the kind of active, mobilisatory role which central planning gave the *apparatchik*, and which formed the basis of the latter's unique *insider* attributes, attributes only too easily transferable from old to new systems? Surely the specifically nationalist element in Yugoslav politics was equally unique, and surely it is this that represents the key element of continuity between old and new systems?

All these points are absolutely valid. In accommodating them, however, I will argue three critical points:

1   While the role of the *apparatchik* in the former Yugoslavia was certainly circumscribed, it was not negligible. In particular, the continued predominance of politicised decision-making in the area of investment decision-making meant that the top political elite still played a key role in relation to medium-to-long-term strategic economic decision-taking, even if they were largely exempt from the kind of day-to-day firefighting which the tyranny of short-term output targets imposed elsewhere in the region.

2   While the *apparatchik* was the lynch-pin of the *nomenklatura,* the ranks of the latter went well beyond the confines of the professional party secretariat, to embrace the managing elites of all the key sectors of the economy and of public life. The maintenance, to the very end, of the one-party system meant that in this respect Yugoslavia was much less different from the other countries – and indeed tended to become less different in its period of decline. Thus in reasserting party control after the crisis of Croatian nationalism in the early 1970s (see below and Chapter 11), the central party leadership reaffirmed the central importance of 'cadres policy' – based on the principle that everyone under consideration for a key job in any walk of life should be positively vetted by the party secretariat – which was the essence of the *nomenklatura* system as practised throughout the former communist world (Dyker, 1990: 89).

3   The nationalist element in Yugoslav politics, under old and new regimes, is an extreme manifestation of a *general* attribute of communist and post-communist systems, rather than something uniquely Yugoslav. '*Nomenklatura* nationalism' – certainly exemplified by a number of the Yugoslav successor states – has come through as the dominant political strain in most of the post-Soviet states and also in Romania. Going back to the old systems, it is clear that while it was only in some communist states (again the best example after Yugoslavia is the Soviet Union) that nationalism appeared as a major spring of behaviour within the *nomenklatura*, the *territorial principle of organisation* was common to *all* the communist parties in power. Party apparatuses revolved around provincial and city party committees and their full-time secretaries, and central committees were dominated by the latter. As 'General Secretaries' Brezhnev and Gorbachev in the Soviet Union were in a sense nothing more than the grandest of those full-time secretaries. It is perhaps not surprising, therefore, that *apparatchiki* tended instinctively to think of territorial solutions to almost any problem with which they came

face to face – with explosive results, as we shall see below, in cases where adminstrative territory coincided with ethnic identity.

Still, Yugoslavia *was* different. And the purpose of this chapter is to demonstrate the differentness as well as the sameness. We begin by charting briefly the development of the apparatus and the *nomenklatura* in the Soviet Union, and then trying to pick out the main elements in the pattern of decline that set in there. We then essentially repeat the same process, but in greater detail, for the former Yugoslavia, before returning to the task of generalisation and, finally, trying to draw some conclusions.

The Soviet Communist Party – model of control, model of decline?

The development of the Soviet Communist Party apparatus is inextricably intertwined with the development of Stalinism. It was Stalin who, as General Secretary, first started to build up the secretariat and the nationwide network of city and provincial party secretaries in the 1920s. It was, in turn, these fledgling *apparatchiki* who, increasingly dominant within the Central Committee of the Soviet Communist Party, gave Stalin the monolithic support to defeat his political enemies (and erstwhile allies) in the late 1920s. It was they also who implemented (brutally and inefficiently enough) the collectivisation campaign of the early 1930s, which massively increased their sphere of power by extending the control of the party to the predominantly agrarian regions which had retained a measure of effective self-government under the New Economic Policy of the 1920s. And the successes of the early five-year plans in building up the Soviet Union's heavy industrial strength were critically dependent on the emergence of the urban *apparatchik* as the key mobiliser, expediter and trouble-shooter of Stalinist central planning. It is, indeed, no exaggeration to say that without the *apparatchik* in that role, central planning would have collapsed under the weight of its own top-heaviness and inflexibility (Dyker, 1992: 67).

The 1930s also witnessed the flowering of the *nomenklatura* system in the Soviet Union. With the rapid pace of industrialisation, the demand for highly trained and/or managerial manpower grew rapidly. The political presuppositions of Stalinism rendered it essential to develop a system of political control over these burgeoning elites, and the job of managing the twin lists of key jobs, and individuals considered fit to hold them, fell to the cadres department of the Central Committee. Thus while industrialisation demanded that the *apparatchiki* share power with the *tekhniki* ('technocrats'), the ultimate political control of the former over the latter, through the *nomenklatura* system, was never in doubt.

But that could not prevent the emergence of serious tensions between *apparatchiki* and *tekhniki*, tensions which finally came out into the open after the death of Stalin. Those tensions flowed ultimately from the fact that the party and industrial elites were organised on diametrically opposing principles: the party on the territorial principle, the industrial elite on the industrial/sectoral principle. It is clear that the party could not have been organised on any other basis, at least as long as political control was a paramount consideration. The logic of central planning, with its hierarchy of plan targets and obsession with industrial/sector priorities, had seemed in the period of high Stalinism to point just as clearly in the direction of the departmental principle. But as Nikita Khrushchev, Stalin's successor as party chief, began the process of political de-Stalinisation, he decided to test that latter principle. Soviet economic performance was already beginning to falter in the mid-1950s, and Khrushchev was inclined – with some justification – to pin the blame on the 'narrow departmentalism' of the industrial ministries. As it happened, Khrushchev did have political opponents within the industrial/administrative hierarchy. By abolishing the industrial ministries and replacing them with regional economic councils (*sovnarkhozy*) he was able to kill two birds with one stone – strengthening his grip on the reins of power and pursuing his chosen strategy for a new Soviet economic take-off. Since the *sovnarkhozy* were in most cases coextensive with the existing political units within the country, he at the same time reinforced the power and prestige of the regional party secretaries – his own staunchest supporters.

Politically adroit, Khrushchev showed himself in all this to be economically inept. The *sovnarkhozy* turned out to be disastrous failures. Because the administrative reform was not accompanied by any marketisation of the economy, they behaved in exactly the same narrowly bureaucratic way as the ministries had before them. But because they were so small (there were more than 100 of them), and because their boundaries in many cases made no economic sense, they lacked the minimal organisational/economic logic that, say, a ministry of ferrous metallurgy has. Not surprisingly, Soviet economic performance continued to deteriorate during the *sovnarkhoz* period (1957–65) and this was one of the main reasons why Khrushchev was voted out of office by the Central Committee in 1964 (Nove, 1969, Chapter 12).

But the *sovnarkhoz* experiment had opened up a Pandora's Box which could not be closed again. In increasing the power and privileges of local apparatuses, it increased the scope for the abuse of office through corruption, nepotism, etc., and accelerated the process of degeneration of the Communist Party apparatus into a bastard-feudal ruling class. At the same time, it gave some legitimacy to local nationalism, for the first time in Soviet history. Particularly in the predominantly non-Russian areas, like the Caucasus and Central Asia, it witnessed just the beginning of the emergence of a new consensus between elites and masses, based not on class loyalties, but rather on national consciousness – the consensus that would form the basis, twenty years later, of the crucial alliance between mass nationalism and *nomenklatura* nationalism.

Under Brezhnev the process of political degeneration of the apparatus continued steadily, with nepotism (even within the family of Brezhnev himself) and bribe-taking now becoming increasingly the rule. But in reinstating the ministerial system of industrial administration and at the same time introducing the limited marketisation of the economy that had been missing from the *sovnarkhoz* reform, Brezhnev did manage to re-establish a kind of stability in the Soviet economy – only a kind of stability, because with growth rates continuing to fall, and productivity stagnant by the early 1970s, slow-down was already easing into the stagnation that presaged the economic collapse of the late 1980s. What was also evident from the early 1970s was a renewed assertion of the political primacy of the Communist Party apparatus, a trend that was sufficient to kill the limited economic reforms which Brezhnev (or rather his prime minister, Kosygin) had introduced in 1965 and ensure that there would be no rational response to the onset of stagnation.

That was the situation that Mikhail Gorbachev inherited on succeeding to the General Secretaryship of the Communist Party of the Soviet Union in 1985. In making one last attempt to reform the Soviet economy, Gorbachev mauled the ministerial structure with reorganisations, amalgamations and sackings. But it was in his attempts to move towards a genuine introduction of the market principle that Gorbachev set in motion a train of events that would finish with the break-up of the Soviet Union. For in trying to go much further than any previous Soviet leader towards the re-establishment of the autonomy of economic life, Gorbachev, a man of impeccable apparatus background, chose a pattern that could surely only have been born in the mind of a man wholly conditioned by the peculiar pattern of territorialism characteristic of the Soviet Communist Party.

The pattern chosen was 'republican *khozraschet*' (the term *khozraschet* here denoting not just 'economic accountability', but also self-financing and hard budget constraints). Apparently oblivious of the fact that business corporations in the West are hardly ever organised on a territorial basis, Gorbachev essentially went back to Khrushchev's formula of the 1950s, setting up existing political sub-divisions of the country as economic units. The difference was that this time a degree of real marketisation was involved. That ensured that this time the specific economic perversities of the *sovnarkhoz* system were avoided. But with the underlying nationalist consensus stronger than ever, it left the whole Soviet system deeply vulnerable to a build-up of centrifugal forces. By the late 1980s, the ministerial system had irretrievably broken down. In the Baltic republics, which were used as laboratories for the republican *khozraschet* system, the notion of 'Estonia/Latvia/Lithuania plc' slipped over almost imperceptibly into the notion of national independence. In achieving national independence in 1990, the Baltic countries effectively removed the cornerstone from a Soviet edifice that would finally come tumbling down at the end of the following year. By early 1992 the Soviet Union had been replaced by fifteen independent republics, most of them ruled by high-ranking members of the old Soviet Communist Party apparatus.

What themes and elements from this Soviet story can we generalise to serve as a foundation for our analysis of the Yugoslav material?

- Communist party structures, and the people who man them, tend to think instinctively in territorial terms. Because *any* system of economic administration, whether planned or market, tends to work more in terms of *lines of communication*, tensions and clashes between the territorial principle and the line principle are inevitable in countries ruled by such structures.
- The underlying dynamic of the degeneration and ultimate fragmentation of communist systems lies in the progressive deterioration in economic performance, and the inability of the apparatus, *qua* Communist Party apparatus, to respond to these economic-performance problems rationally.
- As the party apparatus degenerates and becomes corrupt – thus adding effectively to its privileges – it becomes increasingly entrenched in its opposition to economic reform, until a critical point is reached at which it

perceives a 'class' interest in switching to a nationalist platform, necessarily incorporating some genuine commitment to market reform.
- If a genuine radical succeeds to the leadership of such a system late in the day, he is likely to precipitate, rather than avert, the collapse of that system.

The Yugoslav communist system – evolution and degeneration

During the period of 'hard-boiled dictatorship', 1945–50, Tito modelled his communist dictatorship very much on the Stalinist Soviet system which he and the other leaders of the Yugoslav Communist Party so admired (Hoffman and Neal, 1962). The watchword was *bratsvo i jedinstvo* (brotherhood and unity). That meant that while the new socialist Yugoslavia was constructed as a microcosm of the Soviet Union and a living embodiment of Stalin's own nationalities policy, with constituent republics and within one of them 'autonomous regions', all based on ethnic criteria, the party ruled over the whole structure with a rod of iron. The details of the structure introduced did, however, reflect a genuine desire to lay the ghosts of the prewar and wartime periods. Though Serbs dominated postwar Yugoslav politics as they had dominated prewar, Serbia was 'cut down to size'. Macedonia was established as a separate republic in what had been 'south Serbia', and its own Slav language, more similar to Bulgarian than to Serbo-Croat, was elevated to the status of an official language. Montenegro was hived off as a separate 'union republic'. The Albanian-majority area of Kosovo was given nominally autonomous status – as was Vojvodina in the north of Serbia, even though here the ethnic group concerned, the Hungarians, were only a substantial minority. Croatia was established as a republic within generous borders, and the Serb-minority areas of Krajina – which were to figure so prominently in the dramatic events of the early 1990s – were *not* given any special status. The one area of Tito's Yugoslavia that defied a Soviet/Stalinist solution was Bosnia and Hercegovina. Here there was a mixed population – of Serbs, Croats, and Serbo-Croat-speaking Muslims – with no group having the numerical strength to claim the prerogative of titular nationality, and the Muslims not even being recognised as an ethnic group, but rather as a population 'in the process of declaring themselves Serb or Croat'.

Following the split with Stalin and the Soviet Union in 1948, and after an extended period of 'agonising reappraisal' in the early 1950s, the Yugoslav communist leadership started to move towards a radically different interpretation of socialism. Years before anyone else in Eastern Europe, they started to re-establish the market as the nexus of economic activity. To ensure that the market would be a socialist one, or at least have socialist trappings, *workers' councils* were established in each enterprise. And as they moved towards a more market-based economic system, the Yugoslav communist leadership felt constrained to move towards a more genuinely federal system. This represented much more than just a mechanical application of Soviet principles of territorial organisation: the fact is that the Soviet Union would not actually begin to grapple with these issues for another decade or so. Rather Tito seems to have realised that if, in the context of a less overtly repressive dictatorship, and with the memory of wartime ethnic sectarian atrocities still fresh, he was to keep control over the national dimension of Yugoslav political life, he would have to compromise with nationalism. The form that compromise took was typically communist, but with a uniquely Titoist twist. In moving towards a kind of market economy, the leadership chose to devolve a substantial degree of power over key economic variables – in particular investment finance – to regional governments. But in the initial phase of the building of Yugoslav self-management, this power was invested largely in the local-level *communes* rather than in the republics themselves, so that devolution should not take too explicit an ethnic-regional form. At the purely political level a quite un-Soviet tendency towards the federalisation of *the Communist Party itself* (now renamed the League of Communists) began.

The critical phase of development of the Yugoslav communist system came in the 1960s, as successive reforms sought increasingly to extend market principles into the sphere of investment, with a view to raising the quality of decision-making in this key area while the economy shaped up to the need for transition from extensive to intensive development (see Dyker, 1990, Chapter 4). The strategy was to shift control out of the political sphere and vest it in a banking system operating on commercial principles. In practice, the strategy backfired badly. Because most of the big banks, which had previously been little more than government departments, had their head offices in Belgrade, the federal capital but also the capital of Serbia, they tended to be seen in the other republics as Serbian banks, operating in Serbian interests. Now that they were free to pursue profit-oriented policies, those interests were increasingly perceived, especially in Croatia, in terms of the economic exploitation of the non-Serbian periphery.

This constituted one of the main elements in the build-up of nationalist sentiment in Croatia from 1967 onwards, transforming a primarily politico-cultural movement (*Declaration on the Croatian Literary Language*, 1967) into a concrete set of demands for increased regional political and economy autonomy. The initial reaction of the authorities in Belgrade was accommodating, and constitutional amendments passed in June 1971 turned Yugoslavia into something very close to a confederation. But the crisis continued, and in late 1971 President Tito, himself a Croat, decided that he had had enough. In early 1972 a wholesale purge of 'fascist-totalitarian tendencies' in the Croatian League of Communists was launched. In the succeeding months the leaderships of most of the other republical/provincial leagues were also purged.

But Tito was as clear in the early 1970s as he had been in the 1950s that it would be no use simply repressing nationalism. Now, as then, nationalism would have to be allowed a degree of articulation, so that it could be mediated and assimilated into the official political culture (Dyker, 1977). Tito's policy line in the years after the purges of 1972 consisted of two main policy elements:

- The economic system was revamped with a view to taking some of the ethnic divisiveness out of the area of investment finance and investment decision-taking. A comprehensive system of *planning agreements* was introduced: vertical ones, linking enterprises and governments were called 'social compacts' (*društveni dogovor*) and horizontal ones – 'self-management agreements' (*samoupravni sporazum*) – linking enterprise to enterprise. The planning agreement idea, it should be noted, was popular among left-of-centre parties in Western Europe at the time (NB it was *not* a Soviet idea!) as a way of socialising the investment decision-taking process. The Yugoslav leadership's reasoning was that planning agreements would help to build consensus in this most sensitive area, in such a way as to ensure that no party to any investment project could ever plausibly claim that they were being exploited.

- On the political side, Tito did not reverse the trend towards constitutional confederalism. The new constitution of 1974 preserved the changes introduced by the constitutional amendments of 1971. It gave each republican/provincial government a virtual veto over federal government decisions and effectively created a system where republics and provinces delegated powers to the federal government, rather than the other way around (see Chapter 2). In so doing, it appeared, at the strictly constitutional level, to be going far further than simply accommodating regional/nationalist sentiment. But there was more to Tito's strategy than constitutional reform. If the republics and provinces were to be given their head in government committees, who would look after the national interest? The Titoist/Leninist answer was: the party. The early-mid-1970s witnessed a reassertion of the 'leading role' of the party, buttressed by the reintroduction of a formalised system of 'positive' vetting by League of Communists committees of candidates for all key jobs, i.e. of the classic Soviet *nomenklatura* system.

Cleverly constructed though it was, Tito's compromise in the event was a colossal failure, a failure that was in turn a key factor in the pattern of degeneration, fragmentation and ultimately dissolution that set in from the mid-1970s. The essence of that failure lay in the *peculiarly Yugoslav* dimension that was added to the archetypally Soviet principle of cadres policy. For when Tito decided to go back to a Leninist *nomenklatura* policy, he conceded the right to do the positive vetting to party committees working within *regional* structures – so that the line of authority on cadres policy led up to the level of republican/provincial governments and not beyond. In the context of the specific pattern of political regionalism in Yugoslavia, this was a fatal error. It ensured that the planning agreement idea – by no means devoid of good antecedents or indeed of good sense – would be easily twisted and distorted in the interests of the regional elites. Instead of building national consensus, those elites concentrated on building autarkic little empires, finding willing allies among local business leaders ever eager to cut out any actual or potential competition from other regions. In so doing they tapped rich sources of traditional political culture through the medium of *veze i poznanstva*: the web of contacts and influence which had often offered the only basis for political survival in the old 'colonial' days under the Habsburgs and Ottomans. The specificity of this reversion to traditional political modes in Yugoslavia in the 1970s is that it took a thoroughly corrupt form. Significantly, the incidence of corruption was growing at around this time in virtually every other communist country, including the Soviet Union. But the specific forms of corruption which came to the fore in Yugoslavia (see discussion of the classic Agrokomerc scandal in Dyker, 1990: 146) represented what was, perhaps, a unique blend of degenerate communism and traditional local 'pork-barrel' (see Tullock, 1976) politics. A distinguished Yugoslav journalist could sum up the situation in the late 1970s thus:

> It is much more profitable to hike up prices, make on imports, and collar the domestic market with the help of the state. In a certain sense it is even easier than in that biblical, pre-reform period, for now everyone has his own local state, partial towards him, with full powers, but not with full responsibility. (Gavrović, 1979)

The principle of power without responsibility had far-reaching and baleful results at the level of the government of Yugoslavia. By creating a *liberum veto* situation at the level of the federal government, the blighted compromises of the 1970s produced a policy environment reminiscent of Poland in the eighteenth century (significantly, just before Poland disappeared from the map of Europe for a couple of centuries) or the pre-Luxembourg Compromise Council of Ministers of the EC. As a result, all sorts of vital government functions were simply turned on their heads. Thus while a 'normal' state seeks to minimise, or at least keep under control, the deficit on balance of payments, the regional leaderships of 1970s Yugoslavia vied with other to see who could 'get away with' running the biggest deficit, while the federal government and the National Bank stood helplessly by.

With the private multinational banks, replete with petrodollars, ready to lend to anybody that seemed to pass a minimal political stability test, and therefore presenting the ideal partners for corrupt politicians, it was easy enough to finance the huge deficits that Yugoslavia was running up by the late 1970s. But as global macroeconomic conditions started to change sharply from 1979 and interest rates shot up, the burden of debt service escalated dramatically. It came as no surprise, then, that in 1982 Yugoslavia found itself no longer able to meet its debt-service obligations. The IMF duly arranged a rescue package, but the economic shock of the debt-service crisis – particularly in terms of living standards – was something from which Yugoslavia never recovered (see Chapter 3).

There is much here that seems, at least at first sight, to be peculiarly Yugoslav. It was the perverse political compromises of Tito's declining years, against the background of Yugoslavia's unique national/regional problems, that allowed the balance of payments to run out of control as corrupt local politicians borrowed and borrowed internationally, knowing that they would not ultimately have to bear responsibility for repayment.

Yet exactly the same sort of thing was happening elsewhere in Eastern Europe at the same time. In Poland, the economic collapse of 1979 can be traced directly to the international borrowing and spending spree embarked on by a ruling elite whose descent into corruption was evidently that much more dramatic than elsewhere in Eastern Europe. In Hungary the level of corruption may have been lower, but the results in terms of debt-service problems were, by the early 1980s, just the same. Yet both these countries exhibit a high degree of ethnic homogeneity, and both have been governed on a unitary basis throughout the postwar period. Indeed, of the variables now under consideration, the *only* common one between Poland, Hungary and Yugoslavia in the 1970s and 1980s is a communist elite in degeneration.

Of course the two interpretations are not mutually exclusive. The peculiarly

Yugoslav dimension of the Yugoslav story concerns its *mechanics* rather than its *essence*. That dimension left Yugoslavia that much more vulnerable that much earlier to the process of conversion of public property into the private property of the *nomenklatura* – a process which did not get fully under way elsewhere in Eastern Europe until the beginning of 'wild' privatisation in the late 1980s, and in the Soviet Union not until the early 1990s, with the state about to break up and the flow of illegal capital export rising to critical levels (*Russian Economic Trends*, 1995: 4). It probably meant – though the hypothesis is speculative and impossible to verify – that Yugoslavia, a quasi-market economy with a good record in some areas of manufacturing export, sank much deeper into international debt, and therefore into domestic economic stagnation, than was unavoidably necessary, even with a communist regime-in-degeneracy. It certainly meant that the whole process was accompanied, in the Yugoslav case, by much higher levels of macroeconomic imbalance and much higher levels of inflation than elsewhere, as regional fragmentation affected the National Bank itself. This made it increasingly difficult for the Bank to implement any kind of national monetary policy, and left regional governments with what amounted to a 'license to print money' as '[regional banks] ... became *sui generis* finance ministries of para-state political structures' (Gavrović, 1979). But the *underlying* pattern was remarkably similar to that observable elsewhere in the region.

The Yugoslav nomenklatura *and the break-up of Yugoslavia*

In the light of all this it is hardly surprising that Yugoslavia's reaction to the debt-service crisis of 1982 was essentially a temporising one. The federal government was, in fact, quick to bring the balance of payments into surplus, and the current account remained consistently in the black from 1983 until the dissolution of Yugoslavia. But this was not achieved through the medium of exporting performance – total exports hardly grew at all through the 1980s – but rather through cuts in imports in function of the exchange rate policy – and of the fact that from 1982 economic growth simply ceased in Yugoslavia. More critical from the viewpoint of political stability was the sharp fall in living standards, as the net inflow of goods and services produced by the trade deficits of the 1970s was cut off. In 1988 average real net income was just 70 per cent of what it had been in 1978 (*Statistički Godišnjak Jugoslavije 1990* (1990): 150). But while these economic trends did much to discredit the communist regime, the interregional political deadlock continued to paralyse federal economic policy-making as before. One of the best illustrations of this comes from the field of energy policy. In a situation of extreme energy shortage, and with energy utilisation per unit of industrial production continuing to deteriorate, the republics and provinces were in 1988, five years after the breaking of the crisis, still unable to reach agreement on:

- a timescale for the exploitation of energy resources;
- the allocation of amortisation funds for new investment;
- the basis on which rental payments for the exploitation of non-renewable resources should be calculated;

- procedures for repayment of loans; and
- the question of ownership of the brown-coal deposits of Kosovo (did they belong to Kosovo, or to Serbia, or to Yugoslavia?) (Dyker, 1990: 141).

It is difficult to imagine what they had managed to agree on!

But amidst all this, and despite the rapidly falling stock of the League of Communists, especially in the north-west republics, the 1980s witnessed some remarkable reversions to classic Bolshevik behaviour patterns among League of Communist activists. There were attempts to launch politicised export and quality campaigns, and to use political pressure to stop firms putting up prices and top management (including the top party management!) putting up their own salaries. Significantly, most of these initiatives originated from the regional or local political level. And in the late 1980s there was a renewed tendency for local League of Communists bosses to interfere directly in the management of 'their' enterprises, even to the extent of 'sacking' directors. None of this had any real impact in economic terms. But it did demonstrate how, right to the end, the Yugoslav Party elite was prepared, if only occasionally, to take quite extreme measures to pull the rest of the *nomenklatura* into line. And it is all uncannily reminiscent of the odd little Chernenko interlude in the Soviet Union, when, for a couple of years (1983–84) before Gorbachev was finally handed the leadership, 'the leading role of the party' was once again being pushed as the key to the solution of the problems of economic deterioration. It seems that in Yugoslavia-in-degeneration, as in the Soviet Union-in-degeneration, the prenationalist *apparatchik* could think of nothing better to do, in times of deep crisis, than to throw his weight around.

As the 1980s progressed, the rate of inflation escalated dramatically in Yugoslavia, reaching nearly 2500 per cent on an annualised basis at the end of 1989. Behind the inflationary trend lay a striking tendency, through the decade, for the money supply to be increasingly hijacked by sectional interests. By 1984, so-called 'selective', i.e. ear-marked, credits from the National Bank were accounting for some 97 per cent of annual emissions of primary money (Bjelica, 1985: 150). The great bulk of selective credits were supposed to go to agriculture and exports. In practice, they were largely diverted to other purposes:

> The key factor reducing the effectiveness of monetary and credit policy, in the sense of controlling the money supply and credit policy, was the rigidity, the extreme inelasticity, of the system of approval of selective rediscounted credits to banks from primary emission. This rigidity flows from established practice, customary rights, social conventions, compromises, pressures, and not from the basic legal prescriptions ... Selective credits are now ... the main factor influencing the lending capacities of the commercial banks. (Golijanin, 1985: 25)

Many of those pressures emanated from the regional dimension, and the bulk of those compromises were mediated through the regional dimension. Regionally based commercial banks provided regional elites with credit as and when local political priorities demanded it. In ultimately accommodating those credits through increases in selective emissions, the National Bank of Yugoslavia fed inflation and also connived at the erection of a whole complex of unsound financial structures which only served to obfuscate further the real and critical issues of economic structure facing Yugoslavia.

But in 1990 Yugoslavia went through a brief but extraordinary period of stabilisation. Just for a moment, it seemed as if the country – and its economy – might be saved. The new prime minister, Ante Marković, a man of technocratic background though also a trusted member of the *nomenklatura*, introduced a policy package based on the Sachs Plan for Poland. A new dinar was introduced, tied strictly to the German mark. A commitment to fiscal and monetary rectitude was proclaimed – backed up by the knowledge that with an effectively fixed exchange rate it becomes virtually impossible to accommodate *any* degree of inflation. Foreign trade and foreign investment regulations were to be liberalised and a privatisation programme set in motion.

The package was initially extraordinarily successful in terms of macroeconomic stabilisation. By June 1990 the rate of inflation had fallen (from the December 1989 rate of nearly 2500 per cent annualised) to −0.6 per cent on a monthly basis. But while the National Bank of Yugoslavia did much to reassert its authority over the commercial banks, the latter, still very much in the political grip of republican governments, continued to extend financial support to insolvent enterprises. As a result, the end of 1990 witnessed a major crisis of insolvency in the commercial banking sector (Grličkov, 1991b). In November 1990 Serbian leader and archetypal *nomenklatura* nationalist Slobodan Milošević prevailed on the Serbian national bank, nominally a subsidiary of the National Bank of Yugoslavia, to discount Din 18bn of commercial bank loans, thus implicitly creating new, 'high-powered' money to the tune of some 10 per cent of the Yugoslav stock of money at that time. This enabled the Serbian government to pay salaries and pensions to millions of state employees, retired people, etc. for the first time for months, and just a few days before the Serbian elections, which Milošević, in the event, won by a landslide. All this was in clear contravention of the new banking regulations introduced by Marković in early 1990 with a view to reasserting the control of the National Bank of Yugoslavia over the money supply. But the 'Great Bank Robbery' effectively destroyed Marković's programme, followed, as it was, by similar *demarches* in Montenegro, Slovenia and Croatia (Grličkov, 1991a). It showed with brutal clarity how even this most sensible and well-organised federal prime minister, *nomenklatura* member though he was, was completely powerless once the regional political bosses had moved against him.

But why did they turn against him? Surely Marković's programme, in promising (and indeed delivering, if only for a short period) stable prices and a strong balance of payments, was bound to restore, at least to a degree, the credibility of the communist system in Yugoslavia, and thus indirectly to strengthen the power base of regional communist leaders? Had the mortal blow against Marković been struck by the now openly separatist governments of Croatia and Slovenia, there would have been no puzzle. But it was Milošević, after making the skin-deep change from communist to socialist, who delivered the *coup de grâce*. Why?

There seem to be two main reasons. First, Marković's draconian monetary regime threatened to deprive local political bosses of their cherished *license to print money*. Under the old system of automatic selective credits, finance could almost always be found for local pork-barrel projects – and this was one of the principal underlying reasons for the strength of the inflationary tendency in the system. The Great Bank Robbery represented, quite simply, a reassertion on the part of Milošević of this key prerogative. Second, by this time the great majority of regional leaders, including those who still called themselves communists, had, it seems, become convinced that communist ideology could no longer provide political legitimacy on a long-term basis. If the communist element in national communism was going to be dropped, then Ante Marković and his programme were simply an encumbrance, a nuisance, the more so the more successful they were. In this context the differences between Milošević, *apparatchik* to the end, Kučan and Gligorov, *apparatchiki* turned separatists, and Tudjman, renegade communist turned nationalist separatist, are revealed as essentially minor.

How familiar is the story?

The detailed circumstances of the break-up of Yugoslavia and its bloody aftermath, as rehearsed in the other chapters in Part I, are clearly unique. Yet there is an underlying pattern, which derives from the general characteristics of *nomenklatura* regimes, and which corresponds quite closely to the pattern as it unfolded in other parts of Eastern Europe, especially in the Soviet Union. The sense of 'rats deserting a sinking ship' is even more clearly delineated in the Soviet case than in the Yugoslav. In Ukraine, Kazakhstan, Uzbekistan and Turkmenistan local political bosses who were already hitching their wagons to the nationalist star (they felt increasingly threatened in their party positions by Gorbachev's *perestroika*), abandoned communism as one man when the unsuccessful coup against Gorbachev in August 1991 deprived the traditional Soviet ideology of its last vestiges of credibility. The 'license to print money' issue could not possibly have arisen in countries in which central planning still ruled, where there was no active money and where, indeed, key *nomenklatura* members, particularly top *apparatchiki* and ministerial-industrial leaders, retained the right of direct, physical disposal over large blocks of assets. But it is striking that in the immediate aftermath of the break-up of the Soviet Union, during the brief interlude of the 'rouble zone', the governments of the newly independent republics other than Russia (we also exclude here the Baltic states), most of them representing virtually intact survivals of the old Soviet/republican governments, centred their economic policies largely on the manipulation of the framework of the rouble zone in such a way as to implement large-scale transfers of real resources from Russia (Dyker, 1994). Equally striking is the way that, with the demise of the rouble zone and the establishment of separate national currencies in all the post-Soviet republics, the majority of those new currencies quickly descended into hyperinflation, as *nomenklatura* nationalist governments used the printing press to finance huge budget deficits.

The story is clearly quite different in the other multinational post-communist state to split up into its constituent ethnic parts since the revolution of 1989–90 – Czechoslovakia. But that is not surprising, and indeed tends to reinforce rather than refute our hypothesis. For the Czech regime of Vaclav Havel and Vaclav Klaus is a classic 'clean-break' regime, with no links whatsoever with the old *nomenklatura*. The Meciar regime in Slovakia has a less clear-cut profile. Meciar is a former communist, but was never a member of the *nomenklatura*. Both Klaus and Meciar are, in their different ways, nationalists. But they are not *nomenklatura* nationalists.

How much difference does it make?

The reader who is prepared to accept the argument that there is a particular pattern of degeneration of elite communist into *nomenklatura* nationalist, of which the former Yugoslavia represents one of the best but by no means the only example, will certainly follow up with the question: So what? Given that all East European leaders at the present time are in some sense nationalists, does it matter where they come from, whether they are 'clean-break' nationalists or *nomenklatura* nationalists? An answer to the question has already been hinted at at the end of the last section. If we are to seek to reply to it more systematically, we must be prepared to formulate a general, predictive theory of *nomenklatura* nationalist behaviour. We can do this in terms of three main elements:

- just as the *nomenklatura* member under the old system was almost *defined* in terms of his 'license to print money', so the *nomenklatura* nationalists of the post-communist period are by their nature inclined to use the printing press to finance their public and private spending plans. So a *nomenklatura* nationalist regime is by definition one that is weak on fiscal and monetary discipline – which means high rates of inflation. In the specifically post-Yugoslav context, 'the political and social nature of the independence movements, and the relationship of the pro-independence forces to communist elites, is central to the fate of the soft-money coalition' (Kraft, 1995: 470);
- just as the *nomenklatura* member under the old system tended to territorialise every issue, so the *nomenklatura* nationalist in power has an obsessive tendency to involvement in territorial disputes, large and small;
- just as *nomenklatura* members under the old system tended to adopt a kind of feudal-proprietorial attitude towards all the assets within *their* territory, so *nomenklatura* nationalists can be expected to go slow on privatisation, or at least on 'real' privatisation such as would alienate all property rights over the given blocks of assets.

The most striking thing about the post-Yugoslav pattern is that on macroeconomic balance the theory simply does not work. All the successor states have remarkably (in the cases of Serbia/Montenegro and Macedonia quite improbably) good records on monetary and fiscal discipline and inflation (Kraft, 1995). That elements of fiscal 'sleight of hand' have been present, especially in Serbia/Montenegro, is indubitable. Whether macroeconomic stability can be maintained into the medium term remains an open question. The fact remains that the *nomenklatura* nationalists of the former Yugoslavia have simply not followed their post-Soviet compatriots in exploiting the prerogative of the printing press.

Equally striking is that fact that the other two predictions turn out to be extremely accurate. In the case of Serbia/Montenegro, the obsession with territorial issues has been grotesquely evident. But even 'sensible little Slovenia' has not been able to avoid getting involved in a dispute over borders and territorial waters with neighbouring Croatia, a dispute that has sometimes reached the proportions of a virtual trade war. Again, the pace of privatisation has been extremely slow in all the successor states. And what privatisation there has been has been predominantly insider, i.e. *nomenklatura* privatisation. In Croatia, for instance, the state sector still accounts for some 80 per cent of economic activity. The bulk of the rest is now in the ownership of former managers, i.e. former *nomenklatura* members (Kraft, 1995: 483–4). In Serbia/Montenegro, at mid-1995, 65.5 per cent of business-sector (*privreda*) capital stock was still in social ownership, with 26.8 per cent in various forms of mixed ownership. Just 5.8 per cent was in private ownership (Grličkov, 1995: 14). By the time of writing the situation in Serbia had changed little, though there had been significant progress in Montenegro (see Chapter 10).

Why such a stark contrast between the former Yugoslavia and the former Soviet Union, on the one key indicator, that of macroeconomic stability – all the more sharply delineated against the background of a high degree of similarity in relation to the territorialisation of political issues and feet-dragging on privatisation? Two alternative arguments can be advanced. The first, the 'minority report', looks at the case of Poland, a classic 'clean-break' post-communist regime (the subsequent return to power of a reformed communist party does not alter that), with an excellent record on macro-stabilisation and a clean sheet on territorial disputes. The pace of privatisation in Poland has been extremely slow and what privatisation there has been has been predominantly of the *nomenklatura* variety. The Polish economy has nevertheless continued to perform well – perhaps better than any other transition country. This, the argument runs, demonstrates two things:

1   A significant element of *nomenklatura* privatisation is probably inevitable in
    any transition process.
2   A sensible transition government like the Polish understands that it is
    restructuring that matters, not privatisation *per se* (cf. the Russian
    experience). By refusing to force the pace on privatisation, it allows the
    economy to restructure 'organically', by responding to new technological and
    market opportunities as they arise.

There are, certainly, remarkable similarities between the Polish and Slovenian cases. In both countries renewed economic growth has been firmly based on the growth in productivity, which suggests that genuine restructuring *is* going on, despite the slow pace of privatisation. Place the blame for the territorial dispute firmly and exclusively on the shoulders of Croatia, and Slovenia emerges as a model transition economy, tough on macro-stabilisation and wisely cautious on privatisation, with no real symptoms of *nomenklatura* nationalist mind-set, despite the fact that both president and prime minister come from classic *nomenklatura* nationalist backgrounds. On this reading of the evidence, the whole *nomenklatura* nationalist theory falls apart.

The alternative argument is a more subtle one. It is based on the proposition that the great freedom extended to *nomenklatura* capitalism in the Yugoslav successor states, and the particularly close links between *nomenklatura* nationalist governments and the *nomenklatura* capitalists in these instances, are precisely among the key reasons why it has been possible to maintain such a high degree of macroeconomic discipline:

> Perhaps the preoccupation of the managerial elite in Slovenia with 'spontaneous privatisation' has limited their opposition to the end of soft money. While obtaining subsidies from the government remains important, it may be that Slovene managers have decided that making money in 'normal' market-oriented ways is the thing of the future. Or, less happily, they may be finding that the enrichment possible via spontaneous privatisation outweighs the importance of subsidies ... [In Croatia] many managers have become owners by taking out questionable loans from insurance companies, sometimes with the unsecured shares in the enterprise to be bought as collateral. Apparently, the HDZ tolerated this in the interest of the most rapid transition to capitalism possible, and also perhaps as a convenient way to bring in privatisation revenue ... On the other hand, the stabilisation experience of 1994 suggests that the highest echelons of the government can force the managers into line when they want to. (Kraft, 1995: 477–8, 484)

This interpretation saves the theory – for that reason alone I am inclined to favour it – and shows how the differences between post-Yugoslav and post-Soviet *nomenklatura* nationalist behaviour can be explained in terms of a more sophisticated, long-term view on the part of the former group *of their own self-interest*. Given the long history in the former Yugoslavia of quasi-market institutions and greater openness to the West, this is entirely plausible. But the macroeconomic 'truce' will only hold indefinitely if the *nomenklatura* capitalists of the successor states use their insider privileges to give real impetus to the root-and-branch restructuring which is the only long-term hope for any transition economy. In the case of Slovenia, the chances of this happening are fairly good. In those of Croatia, Serbia/Montenegro and Macedonia the forecast is much less certain. Either way, it is surely the *nomenklatura* nationalists and *nomenklatura* capitalists who hold the key.

References

Bjelica, V. (1985) Rigidnost selektivne politike i politike visokih kamatnih stopa. In *Aktuelna Politika i Politika Kamatnih Stopa* (Belgrade: Srpska akademija nauka i umjetnosti).

Dyker, David A. (1977) Yugoslavia: Unity out of Diversity? In A. Brown and J. Gray (eds) *Political Culture and Political Change in Communist States* (London: Macmillan).

Dyker, David A. (1990) *Yugoslavia. Socialism, Development and Debt* (London: Routledge).

Dyker, David A. (1992) *Restructuring the Soviet Economy* (London: Routledge).

Dyker, David A. (1994) *Establishing Conditions Conducive to the Expansion of Trade among Countries in Transition*, STEEP Discussion Paper no. 12, March (Sussex: Science Policy Research Unit, University of Sussex).

Dyker, David A. (1995) *Nomenklatura* nationalism: the key to the new East European politics?, *Australian Journal of Politics and History*, vol. 41, no. 1, pp. 55–69.

Gavrović, M. (1979) Jedanaesta teza o reformi, *Privredn Vjesnik*, 28 May, p. 5.

Golijanin, M. (1985) Za uravnotežniji odnos restriktivnih i stimulativnih elemenata u monetarno-kreditnoj politici. In *Aktuelna Monetarna Politika i Politika Kamatnih Stopa*, (Belgrade: Srpska nkademija nauka i umjetnosti).

Grličkov, V. (1991a) Upadi u platni sistem, *Ekonomska Politika*, 14 January, p. 11.

Grličkov, V. (1991b) Sudar koncepcija, *Ekonomska Politika*, 13 May, pp. 10 and 12.

Grličkov, V. (1995) Preživljanvanje, *Ekonomska Politika*, 29 May, pp. 14–16.

Hoffman, George W. and Neal, Fred W. (1962) *Yugoslavia and the New Communism* (New York: Twentieth Century Fund).

Kraft, Evan (1995) Stabilising inflation in Slovenia, Croatia and Macedonia: how independence has affected macroeconomic policy outcomes, *Europe-Asia Studies*, vol. 47, no. 3, pp. 469–92.

Nove, A. (1969) *An Economic History of the USSR* (London: Allen Lane, Penguin Books).

Russian Economic Trends (1995) Centre for Economic Reform, Government of the Russian Federation, April.

Statistički Godišnjak Jugoslavije 1990 (1990) (Belgrade: Savezni Zavod za Statistiku).

Tullock, G. (1976) *The Vote Motive*, Hobart Paperback no. 9 (London: Institute of Economic Affairs).

Chapter 5

The Collapse of Yugoslavia – Between Chance and Necessity

SLAVO RADOŠEVIĆ

Welcome to Europe 2000. Sarajevo is your future.
(Haris Pašović, theatre director, to a group of foreign visitors
at Sarajevo airport, as reported by Mary Kaldor)

Introduction

The basic idea of this chapter can be expressed in the form of two questions. Is there anything historically new in the Yugoslav collapse? Was the Yugoslav collapse inevitable and predetermined, or the entirely unexpected outcome of a specific constellation of factors?

We can distinguish between different approaches to the explanation of the Yugoslav *débâcle* in terms of whether they are *monocausal* or *complex*. Monocausal explanations are those that emphasise one particular factor exclusively – sociocultural or economic factors, for instance. The most common monocausal explanation is the one which sees the Yugoslav conflict as a problem of historically embedded hatred. Schierup (1993a) calls it the 'pressure cooker' approach: the social explosion is to be explained in terms of totalitarian regimes suppressing historical, culturally grounded conflicts which erupt when the 'lid' is lifted as a result of 'democratisation'. Thus the current conflict is portrayed as the expression of innate and age-old ethnocultural identities. The economic explanation argues, in equally monocausal terms, that the disintegration was inevitable, either because Yugoslavia never really managed to integrate economically, or simply because regional differences and redistributional requirements were so huge (Steiner and Ottolenghi, 1993).

Both these groups of explanations are essentially ex-post rationalisations. Much rarer are the attempts to unravel the nature of collapse by taking into account the interaction of several qualitatively different factors. These more complex explanations do not feature built-in inevitability of conflict. For example Golubović (1993) offers a complex interaction of social, political and cultural factors as an explanation for the collapse of Yugoslavia. Schierup (1993a, 1993b) sees the failure to break the vicious circle of underdevelopment and political authoritarianism – endogenously determined but constantly reproducing in new forms in reaction to changes in the world economy – as being central.

Here I argue that monocausalist explanations are fundamentally wrong. The Yugoslav disintegration will be analysed in this chapter in terms of the interplay of technicoeconomic, political and anthropological factors. A starting premise is that politics and economics are deeply intertwined and powerfully interactive. There is a crucial political dimension to economic processes which sharply limits the explanatory power of either political or economic analysis taken by themselves in cases like this. The inability of political agents to formulate a new social consensus in the years of the decay of the old system, and the protracted political battle that resulted, created a pervasive crisis of morals, values and identity in the society. A universal ontological insecurity was created and maintained by political manipulation. That sense of insecurity affected collective memories deeply, transforming latent tensions into acute ones, in that myths entered as a part of reality. But if we want to understand why nationalism was an answer to the identity crisis, we must look at the cultural heritage of patriarchal societies in which collectivism and tribal ties play an important role. At the same time, it is clear that identities are not autonomous and given, and that they can only be understood in political context. Following Schierup (1993a, 1993b) I discuss ethnic nationalism in terms of identity, but also in political-economic terms.

An equally important distinction is that between *disintegration* and *collapse*. What is so terrifying about the Yugoslav conflict is not so much the political disintegration of a country as the collapse of primary social ties and the destruction of the primary social fabric. A collapse involving the displacement of four million people is of such a degree of intensity that a qualitatively new dimension of social transformation enters the equation, so that economics and politics, even in combination, cannot provide a sufficient explanation. The distinction between disintegration and collapse is critically important, because the future prospects of a former Yugoslav region would have been quite different had the country disintegrated in a peaceful way.

These distinctions allow me to develop two corollaries. First, a collapse has its own dynamics and goes through several qualitatively different phases. As Oklobdžija (1993: 92) argues, the conflict did not begin as an ethnic conflict, and the *creation* of enemies was a prerequisite for war. Indeed, the conflict started at the top of the social structure, 'very far from the level occupied by the average citizen of any of the nationalities' (Oklobdžija, 1993; see also Zimmerman, 1995). Once it had gathered momentum, it turned into a civil war, which totally devastated local communities. This in turn brought mafia-type groups to power at the level of both state and military apparatuses and strongly influenced the subsequent dynamics of the conflict.

Second, the Yugoslav crisis is the result of an interplay of long-term and short-term processes. As Vesna Bojičić demonstrates in Chapter 3, the structural causes of the crisis flow from a protracted period of failure to adjust to external changes. On the other hand, the social and psychological preconditions of conflict were created in a very short period of just a few years, sometimes even just a few months. How the mental picture of 'others' could change so radically in only a few months, and how it could lead to such a downward spiral of conflict, remains to be analysed by social psychologists and anthropologists. Here I merely hint at some possible explanations.

So what is historically new in the Yugoslav conflict? I argue that it is an unfortunate constellation of economic, political and anthropological factors, the mutual interaction between which brought about what was, even for the 'directors of the war scenario', an unexpected outcome. While anthropological phenomena (culture, collective memories and identities) do provide important elements towards an understanding of the collapse, they operate, as Schierup (1993b: 90) puts it, against the background of structural parameters that demand profound scrutiny as categories of political economy. In addition to that, the Yugoslav conflict is contingent on global economic and technological changes. The ability to compress time and space through electronic media, for example, played an important role in the dynamics of collapse.

What follows is intended to be not a final answer, but rather an outline of my own understanding of the Yugoslav collapse. Allcock (1993) argues that our knowledge of the human world is fundamentally compromised by our attachment to the subject of our research. I hope that my personal attachment will in this case serve, if not as a guarantee of detachment, at least as a safeguard against the oversimplified pictures and new myths that are daily built around the Yugoslav human and political tragedy.

Technico-economic factors of the disintegration of Yugoslavia, and the structural sclerosis of the 1980s

As of the late 1980s, Yugoslavia seemed to enjoy definite advantages in relation to the process of transition towards post-socialism. As a socialist country, but with a developed goods market and a degree of openness to the world economy, the Yugoslav economy appeared to be one that could be relatively easily transformed into a full-blooded market economy. The pricing of goods was predominantly free – not continuously and not for all goods, but there was never any doubt about the primacy of the market principle in price formation. On the other hand, factor prices (wages and salaries, interest rates, exchange rates) were formed in a different way. Generally, factor prices were determined by regulations or even by laws. As a rule, wages were variable and employment fixed. Workers could be hired, but it was virtually impossible to fire them. Only state and parastate institutions could authorise the establishment of new firms. The closure of firms was almost unheard of.

The only market that did not exist in any form was the capital market. The interest rate was regulated by parliamentary (effectively government) acts. Banks functioned to an extent as firms but also as a part of the state administration, so that they were constrained by the decisions of local and federal authorities. There was no foreign currency market as such and regulations on foreign currency were subject to administrative decision.

The efficiency problems in the functioning of Yugoslav firms were not directly linked to labour management as such, but rather to its Marxist ancestry, which showed up in the social ownership of the means of production and in the treatment of capital rents. As Stiglitz (1993) demonstrates, the argument against social ownership cannot be grounded on the dimension of managerial inefficiency, but must rather be pursued on the grounds of government (in)ability, in the given context, to pursue a tight competition policy and to desist from subsidisation. This latter dimension, coupled with the absence of capital markets, represents a critical systemic feature which inhibited the entrepreneurial potential of the Yugoslav economy.

The main problem was not the principal – agent conundrum, as generations of Western scholars on self-management tried to argue – but rather state-enterprise relationships.

The entire system of management of the capital stock and establishment of new firms contained many elements of the command economy. Indeed, the Yugoslav system could be classified as a semi-command economy (Kračun, 1991; see also Chapter 3 by Vesna Bojičić in this volume). Enterprises were endowed with socially owned capital that workers were supposed to manage. This endowment provided the pretext for continual interference on the part of the authorities in enterprise decision-making, in order to prevent 'misbehaviour' by workers-managers. Because the economy was a highly regulated one, politicians tended in any case to become deeply involved in all the important problems of the enterprise. The most powerful instruments in the hands of politicians were the rationing of credit and foreign exchange, various subsidies and tax exemptions, and selective price and wage regulation.

These were the main systemic characteristics of the 'Yugoslav model', most of the elements of which the majority of republic leaderships wanted, by the late 1980s, to get rid of. However, the Yugoslav crisis cannot be reduced to a crisis of a specific socialist system. It is also a developmental crisis, independent of the political system, and similar to the crises of other middle-income economies, mostly in Latin America, that have followed the import-substitution strategy. Even in some of its economic characteristics, especially in terms of export structure, the Yugoslav economy was more similar to developing than to centrally planned economies (Glissman, 1989).

The Yugoslav crisis coincided with the wave of structural change in the world economy at the beginning of the 1980s. The new framework to which Yugoslavia had to adjust could be described in terms of a few catch-phrases like post-Fordism, globalisation, liberalisation, privatisation. This is not the place to try to evaluate how well-grounded these concepts are, and whether they really reflect the shifts that occurred in the world economy at the beginning of the 1980s. What is incontrovertible is that a country has to adapt to the changing technicoeconomic requirements emanating from the world economy. I will sketch this problem as it affected Yugoslavia, from the macroeconomic as well as from the microeconomic perspective.

Economic diversification became, during the 1970s, the dominant impulse in most of newly industrialising economies (NICs) among which Yugoslavia was numbered in economic terms. However, if we apply a standard index of structural change, we discover that Yugoslavia, even in the period 1965–80, was below average for developing countries (an index of 12.01 as compared to. 13.83)[1] (OECD, 1991). The Yugoslavian rate of structural change was half the Spanish (24.73),

---

[1] The standard index of structural change is calculated on the basis of the degree of correlation between the pattern of shares of aggregate value added by sector in two benchmark years. If the correlation is high, the corresponding index is low, signifying that there has been little structural change. Where the correlation is low, the index of structural change is high.

much less than the Korean (31.37) and Brazilian (30.03), and less even than India's (20.8) and Mexico's (14.83). In terms of GDP and manufacturing value-added, however, performance was satisfactory up to the 1980s. That means that growth was not achieved through diversification and structural change, but rather through heavy investment in the same industries. The low rate of mobility of capital, caused by the institutions of social ownership, contributed greatly to this structural stalemate.

The post-Second World War industrialisation of Yugoslavia was based on domestic raw materials, cheap labour and holding down agricultural prices as a way of extracting surplus. On that basis a programme of *extensive industrialisation* was implemented, centred on the creation of new capacities and the achievement of quantitative goals. This relatively successful programme eventually generated significant cost inefficiencies. Economic criteria were not preeminent in investment decision-taking, and industries were developed with the main goal of increasing employment or substituting for imports. A significant capital-goods sector was created on the basis of this pattern of extensive development. Initially, the policy of import substitution combined with the extensive growth model allowed the domestic market to dominate the development of the majority of industrial sectors. But in the 1980s domestic aggregate demand began to slacken, especially in the machinery sector, as both consumption and investment fell in the face of extreme pressure to force exports in order to reduce a balance-of-payments disequilibria.

The problem of rigidities constraining the ability to adjust to changing requirements can be more easily discerned at the micro-level. First, as a result of historical factors as well as of an industrialisation policy based on big systems, the Yugoslav economy was dominated by big- and medium-sized firms. Medium-sized and large firms (more than 100 employees) accounted for 94.1 per cent of the overall employment in manufacturing, 91.7 per cent of capital stock, 93.8 per cent of manufacturing GDP and 71.7 per cent of firms in 1987. The share of small firms in employment was only 10–30 per cent of what is common in Western countries. In the socialised sector there was practically no entry or exit of firms and the growth of firms was achieved mainly through diversification. Existing firms were hardly ever downsized, though there was substantial hidden unemployment in many of them.

Yugoslav firms were, then, mainly fairly big, often with strong, quasi-monopolistic positions on regional markets. The lack of competitive pressure created medium-sized and large conglomerates, vertically integrated, which tended to keep the bulk of auxiliary production under their own control. As a result, there was a lack of demand for the kinds of products in which small firms have a comparative advantage. A high degree of vertical integration in parts and components production seriously impaired firms' flexibility and adaptability, thus reducing the opportunities for entrepreneurship. Consumers paid for this rigidity through the high prices of a protected domestic market.

The changed conditions of the 1980s brought into sharp relief the drawbacks of such a pattern for the competitiveness of the Yugoslav economy. The uncompetitive market structure blocked the development of efficient markets and suppressed entrepreneurship. The passage of constitutional and legal amendments in 1989, which, after ten years of ideological struggle, finally allowed the free formation and closing of enterprises of all ownership types, had an immediate impact, but came much too late.

The second rigidity lay in the position of labour as a fixed cost. The law permitted only full-time employment. Only 1 per cent of employment in Yugoslavia was part-time, and this reflected largely involuntary part-time employment (pregnancy, invalidity). Voluntary part-time contracts were not introduced until 1990. Since labour was a fixed cost, the rationalisation of the work force could not be a central objective. In the period of extensive development, when increases in production were in fact the central goal, this rigidity was not felt as a serious constraint.

Wage demands were a recurrent feature of the Yugoslav economy, as they are of the market economies, albeit for different reasons. Pressure on wages was exerted through the mechanisms of self-management (Dyker, 1990, Chapter 4). It was not until 1990 that the first genuine collective agreements aimed at controlling levels of wage demands were introduced.[2]

The development of the economy was largely financed by internal savings and the import of foreign capital through financial and commodity credits. But there was no domestic financial market to which people could direct their savings, and they tended to purchase durable consumer goods rather than save. So the investment requirements of extensive growth had to be met, to a greater extent than would have been necessary in a 'normal' economy, from abroad. With limited refinancing, with no equity financing and with foreign medium-term loans from public institutions and private banks the prevailing form of external financing, liquidity problems were inevitable.

Third, the pattern of internal organisation of the firm developed largely in response to ideological pressures. Up to the 1970s, the organisational structure of large firms was similar to that familiar in market economies at that time: decisions about production were centralised in special divisions. This was appropriate to the general technicoeconomic requirements of the Fordist regime. However, at the beginning of the 1970s there was a strong ideological drive for decentralisation – but without any coordination. This contributed directly to economic deterioration. It was an heroic – but foolish – attempt to decentralise decision-making in the absence of clearly defined property rights over capital, or of fully developed markets for capital and labour (Simonetti, 1989), and might best be described as fragmentation without market liberalisation. Far from providing the greater flexibility the new global conditions required, it led to even stronger political surveillance of the economy, and in practice made the system more rigid through the all-embracing system of 'planning contracts' (see fn. 2) it introduced. It was not until the 1980s that these constraints were removed – and even then it was not supported by the transformation of institutions and legal rules on the macro-level. Finally, a struggle against the

---

[2] These collective agreements were signed by trade unions and government. In political and economic terms they were quite different from the 'social compacts' and 'self-management agreements', introduced by the 1974 constitution, which had a much narrower compass. Social compacts were essentially vertical planning agreements, linking government to business chambers and the chambers to production organisations, while self-management agreements were horizontal, interenterprise contractual linkages (Dyker, 1990: 86).

decaying Yugoslav version of Fordism was launched at the end of the 1980s, under conditions of weak and hesitant impetus towards structural change – and again much too late.

In the 1980s economic policy was based on devaluation and interest rate and monetary policies as prime policy tools – this reflecting an overly macroeconomic view of competitiveness. It was in practice at best a short-term salve, leading ultimately to a vicious circle of devaluation–inflation–further devaluation. To understand the dynamics of the Yugoslav collapse it is extremely important to bear in mind that the 1980s were also years of stalemate in the structure of the economy: a stalemate mainly caused by the political stalemate. Yugoslavia entered the 1980s with a system of 'total' self-management, which was in practice a highly politicised economic hierarchy in which not only republics but also provinces and municipalities had a say in negotiations on key economic issues. Tito's death in 1980 and the subsequent weakening in the legitimacy of the Communist Party opened up a window of opportunity for change. This chance was missed, however, and the 1980s turned out to be years of protracted crisis caused by the inability of the political elites to formulate responses to the crying need for change.

Standard economic indicators show a clear-cut economic deterioration throughout the 1980s, which significantly inhibited the scope for achieving a social consensus. After an average annual rate of growth of 5.5 per cent in 1971–80, Yugoslavia experienced virtual stagnation in GDP levels in the 1980s (0.5 per cent growth p.a. 1981–88). The aggregate volume of investment activity in 1987 was 47 per cent of its 1979 level. The investment/GDP ratio fell over the same period from 27.3 per cent to 18.8 per cent. After continuous increases throughout the 1950s and 1960s, real wages decreased by an average of 2.2 per cent annually 1978–89, i.e. 24 per cent cumulatively. Consumption decreased from 64 per cent of GDP (1972) to 60.5 per cent (1982) and 58.8 per cent (1987). Public consumption was more resistant to change. The share of social infrastructure expenditures in GDP grew from 42 per cent in 1971 to 52.5 per cent in 1986, adding to inflationary pressure. These latter trends changed remarkably little when GDP growth performance deteriorated sharply in the first half of the 1980s.

The extent of structural sclerosis of the Yugoslav economy, especially during the 1980s, is confirmed by a whole range of indicators. It is visible in the stagnant share of the service sector (Ratković, 1990), in the relative decline of the information sector[3] (Radošević, 1991), in the deterioration of technology flows (Medenica, 1991), and in the strikingly low rate of new business formation during the 1980s (entrepreneurial repression) (Radošević, 1991). At the same time over-employment in the social sector was extremely high: as much as 15–20 per cent (Simonetti, 1989).

The protracted economic crisis had a noticeable effect on human capital formation. From an average level of 5 per cent of GDP in the 1970s, expenditure on education decreased in the 1980s to about 3.5 per cent of GDP. The efficiency of the educational system deteriorated, with around 25–35 per cent of high school pupils

---

[3] The information sector includes all activities relating to the production, processing and distribution of information, and to the information infrastructure. See OECD, 1986.

leaving school without qualifications. Deterioration in the human capital stock was one of the factors in the increasing impoverishment of the population. Over the period 1978–89 the absolute number of people living in poverty grew from 3.4m (17.2 per cent of the population) to 5.4m (23.6 per cent of the population) (Pošarac, 1991). (It is important to note that half of the population living in poverty lived in the countryside. This was a prime reason for the absence of social unrest, as owner-ship of land permitted the rural population to be self-sufficient in food.)

In short, Yugoslavia suffered a comprehensive economic crisis during the 1980s which slowly but surely shifted the balance of political power and cut off the possi-bility of a new social consensus. The solution to accumulated economic problems required political preconditions which were never present at any point during the 1980s.

Regional differences and development trends

Yugoslavia never managed to develop a common development pattern and become a truly integrated economic area. The problem first appeared with the dissolution of the Austro-Hungarian Empire (1918). The creation of the Kingdom of the Slovenes, Croats and Serbs meant merging several very heterogeneous economic areas (Pertot, 1971). While this diversity might have been turned to advantage, it was never exploited during the seventy years of Yugoslavia's existence. In that context the question posed by Steiner and Ottolenghi (1993) as to whether Yugoslavia was ever 'an organic, tightly interwoven economic construction' seems very relevant. Indeed, analysis of trade structure (see Table 5.1) shows a relatively low level of trade integration among regions.

In the postwar period the roots of this fragmentation can be traced back to the institutional concept of 'working people' who are vouchsafed constitutional rights over the value-added created within the region – in order to prevent the 'exploita-tion' of one region by another. As Simonetti (1989: 22) argues, the main task of politicians in an economic system like that is to stop any federal policy that might have a negative economic impact on any dimension on their territory. With such a framework it is impossible to have a consistent economic policy.

Table 5.1 Structure of Trade by Region (per cent of GDP, 1987)

	Intraregional trade	Interregional trade	Foreign trade
Slovenia	59.7	18.3	22.0
Croatia	66.9	17.6	15.5
Serbia	61.0	19.8	19.2
Vojvodina	59.4	24.0	16.6
Montenegro	52.4	31.5	16.1
Bosnia and Hercegovina	50.9	30.6	18.5
Macedonia	58.5	21.8	19.7
Kosovo	57.3	30.9	11.8

Source: Based on Steiner and Ottolenghi, 1993.

The issue of economic exploitation of one region by another was a favourite theme of politicians. In fact, it is difficult or almost impossible to show a systematic bias in redistribution running along specifically regional lines – not surprisingly, perhaps, in an economy where redistribution was so far-reaching and pervasive. (For discussion on this see Dubravčić, 1993, and Bojičić, in Chapter 3 of this volume). Sočan (1989: 16) argues that the process of subsidising or penalising firms, sectors or regions and populations operated in two main directions; first, subsidisation through artificial cost reductions (non-payment of foreign loans, interest rates and even bills, or negative real interest rates, etc.) and 'under the table' income appropriation (official/National Bank of Yugoslavia or grey credit/money creation, subsidisation of losses, administered and monopolistic prices on the domestic market, undervaluation of the dinar in relation to the currencies of countries with which Yugoslavia had clearing agreements, etc.); second, penalising through artificially high costs (ever-growing taxes and social security, etc. contributions, levels of wages not merited by levels of productivity, administered or monopolistic prices of inputs, high customs duties, import taxes and quantitative restrictions, failure to observe reasonable delivery times on the part of suppliers, inadequate performance and quality of inputs, extremely high positive real interest rates for those firms (about half) which were actually paying interest, etc.) and through administrative and monopolistic diversion of income (negative real interest rates on savings, inflationary devaluation of money, overvaluation of the dinar in relation to the hard currency area, obligatory reserves at the National Bank of Yugoslavia, etc.). The economy was unable to sustain such enormous administrative and monopolistic redistributions, in particular as the subsidies involved were practically 'giveaways', without any kind of developmental conditionality.

In conclusion, the system was full of elements of redistribution which inhibited economic development in general, and thus regional development in particular. Virtually constant relationships in the structure of regional GDP confirms a kind of 'regional repression'. This provided a basis for competing political claims in which problems relating to the non-market character of the economic system and regional problems were intentionally mixed up and exploited for diverse political purposes.

The process of economic disintegration and the late modernisers

By the end of the 1980s, after ten years of intensive political battles, it was finally accepted ideologically that marketisation was inevitable. The economic modernisers, by which I mean here the professional groups in society (managers, private owners, highly skilled groups) which shared the views of the last federal prime minister, Ante Marković, came to full legitimacy in the period when the party elite had already lost its credibility (see Chapter 4) and the new political elite had not yet come to power. Although these mainly technocratic groups had little time to articulate themselves politically, a window of opportunity did open and there was hope that the country could be modernised and transformed peacefully. The agenda of the economic modernisers consisted of the following main points:

1   Transformation of the state legislature in accordance with the principles of a *rechtstaat*. This was largely achieved by the 1989 reforms, which were

drafted by a group of competent administrators and academics supported by a few forward-thinking politicians and ministers.

2   Adjustment to a new growth strategy, through organisational change and managerial improvements at enterprise level. All this was based on a clear understanding that legal changes by themselves are insufficient for the actual transition to a market economy.

The scale of economic adjustment required was enormous and the task simply impossible without political backing. A policy aimed at bringing wages into line with productivity and efficiency, making firms pay the actual costs of capital and introducing proper depreciation procedures for housing, communal and other infrastructure, would always be politically highly sensitive, as the cases of the other economies in transition confirm. In addition, the financial implications of restructuring were colossal. For example, the cost of restructuring the steel sector alone were estimated by British steel consultants at $10bn. Clearly, undertakings on that scale can succeed only if they are backed by firm political will.

The reality was that political conflicts – especially about modes of privatisation and especially between the federal and republic levels – critically retarded the process of modernisation during the 1989–90 period. The Federal Law on Privatisation provided for several methods of privatisation, but stressed the sales of internal shares to the workers at a discount price, and with the workers being given ten years to pay. Parallel laws in Croatia and Serbia stressed the nationalisation of a considerable portion of the stock of socially owned assets. The Federal Law specified that about 1500 public enterprises should be privatised through the sale of internal shares to workers. In the event, only twenty enterprises were totally sold to workers or other citizens in 1991. The federal plan would have led to insider privatisation on a large scale, which would have created a critical mass of alliances for market reform. The option of nationalising socially owned assets was preferred by the republics, because it would naturally legitimise and increase the power of the new states.

The economic modernisers attempted to reorganise the social structure and reform the economy while keeping the political system (temporarily) unchanged. Although at the time that might have seemed the only feasible option, from today's perspective such an approach looks politically naïve. The project of modernisation of Yugoslavia as one state came too late, at a time when political power had already shifted to the republics, with the loss at the federal level of the prerogative to impose price control, and the loss of federal control over collection of taxes and customs and over the budget. In this drama *démarches* like the Serbian 'Great Bank Robbery' (see Chapter 4) were but the final act. If we wish to understand fully the origins of the drama, we have to go back to an earlier period.

The socialist political elite and the victory of national liberalism

Effective policy-making for post-socialist transformation requires a political process that allows disciplined, tough decisions and also long-term time horizons. Powerful corporate interests must often be challenged to ensure adequate domestic competition. A politically secure government, continuity in the civil service, and the ability to cut monopolies down to size and resist lobbying are almost necessary conditions for such a transformation (Porter, 1990). It seems obvious, from today's perspective, that the kind of political system that allows continuity and offers some resistance to the pressure of interest groups simply did not exist in Yugoslavia.

The political system created by the 1974 constitution introduced self-management as a total system covering not only enterprise-local community but also enterprise-parastate-body relationships. The character of this system was more collusive than competitive. It required universal contractual bargaining across the economy and polity, and was characterised by *decentralisation without liberalisation*. An excessively multilayered government apparatus was formed, based on parastate institutions. These institutions were implanted throughout the economy and infrastructure, which allowed them to build their own interests, channels and instruments and to act almost as equal partners of the state bodies. The range of disparate economic interests could not be successfully mediated in an economic system that required or allowed such a degree of political interference.

From a political perspective, Yugoslavia, like many other middle-income economies, lacked an institutional structure and policy regime which would systematically encourage and reward the exertion of economic effort, while penalising firms which failed to make the effort or misdirected their efforts towards unproductive (i.e. non-productivity enhancing) activities. In an economy heavily dependent on quantitative import restrictions and various forms of administrative redistribution, any attempt at a reduction of factor-price distortions, which constantly reappeared as an objective, automatically generated pressure to secure the vested interests of different lobbies through the intensification of the administrative redistribution of costs and incomes. Generally speaking, the extent of the redistribution of costs and incomes forced on the federal government by business, regional and political lobbies (including the army) increased after 1985.

In political terms the decade of the 1980s could be reinterpreted as a confrontation between a neo-liberal attempt at reform and an old type of developmental model. Since there were no political preconditions for any new kind of developmentalism or third way, the old lobbies could survive only through redistribution. In such a situation, neo-liberalism was less a temporary need than the only possibility. The 1980s had seen the global emergence of 'deregulationism' as a theory of the state and this helped legitimise similar strands of thinking in Yugoslavia at that time.

However, neo-liberalism requires that the state should be competent and resistant to the pressures of group interests. As Hodgson (1993) points out, a neo-liberal or other alternative model of development can only be defined in terms of structural forms fashioned outside the sphere of commodity exchange and supported by political and social norms and agreements. Thus regulationism does not mean less demand on state administration. It *does* entail reducing the power of lobbies and the implementation of market-friendly methods of intervention. But it may lead to a stronger state than under the old developmentalism. If a government wishes to push through a liberalisation programme regardless of widespread opposition, the state may have to become more coercive and, paradoxically, more *dirigiste*. As Fortin *et al.* (1988) put it, given the potentially conflictual and redistributive implications of economic liberalisation, in the short and medium term at least, a stronger and more authoritarian state may be seen as necessary to enforce those implications. In the Yugoslav case, cumulative and deep-seated social and interrepublic conflicts simply did not allow the federal government to behave in such a way.

The weakness of the federal administration contributed significantly to the disintegration of the federal state. Excessively bureaucratic, excessively politicised and to a great extent simply incompetent, the administration was incapable of implementing transparent and developmentally justified policies, incapable of maintaining the stability of the system by taking the role of automatic pilot in times of tough political conflict. The flood of acts and laws, described by some analysts as 'normative optimism', which continued unabated until the 1989 reform, merely served to show up the low administrative capability of the state. Legislative proliferation led to a situation where enterprises had to devote a huge amount of time to understanding the legal environment. As the laws were often inconsistent, overlapping and poorly drafted, they had frequently to be revised and amended. Bad administration meant that government(s) and enterprises considered themselves to be enemies. In such a situation both sides tried to cover all contingencies to protect themselves from misbehaviour on the other side. The result was a vicious circle of normativism.

Why was it the republic political elites fell heir to supreme political power as the old system collapsed? The important role of individual politicians, above all of Milošević, apart, are there other structural characteristics of the political system of the former Yugoslavia which contributed to this pattern?

First, Yugoslav society was not sharply polarised in terms of (the whole of) society versus (the whole of) the state as in other east European societies. The structure of the oligarchic elite was concealed under the façade of self-government (Golubović, 1993). As a result there were no opposition social movements of significant size, unlike in other eastern European countries. The state simply could not have been taken over by new political forces, as it itself was so diffused, in terms of federation and republics, and in terms of individuals delegated from the republics to the federal government and administration. Once the old ruling social coalition of working class and political elite (Županov, 1983) had fallen apart, a vacuum appeared which it was only too easy for populists like Milošević to fill.

Second, grass-roots political articulation could not compensate for the weakness of the state itself in terms of pushing the neo-liberal project. The pressure for privatisation does not come from the workers. As Kornai (1990) puts it 'there are no strikes or street demonstrations in favour of increasing economic efficiency at the expense of state protection. As a result, there does not exist a grass-roots movements for the decentralisation of the state-owned sector.'

Third, in a society where the property rights of people, enterprises and regions remained undefined, and the identification of social groups weak, political actions were ineluctably only weakly linked to economic interests (Goati, 1991). As a result, voting in multiparty elections tended not to be for defined interests of social groups as such – because interests could not be properly defined in that system. Where there are no differential individual, social and economic interests, politics is inevitably mainly about collectivist interests (previously class, now nation).

In the old Yugoslavia, the only interests that could be articulated at federal level were economic interests relating to redistribution. This in turn bred *national liberalism*, whose main claim is that the key problems of the nation stem from an oppressive federal association. The realisation of the national liberal objective is interpreted in terms of all political and social interests being subsumed under the interests of the nation, or at least suppressed until the new state is consolidated. As Salecl (1993: 83) puts it, 'an essential feature of the ideological efficiency of the nationalist parties was their ability to subordinate all real (economic) problems to the problem of national identity; in so doing they succeeded in convincing the voters that solution to the national question would solve all other questions as well'.

Collective memories, identity and ontological insecurity in the dynamics of collapse

As we noted earlier, the intensity of collapse in the Yugoslav region does not follow from the scale of the economic and political troubles in which they found themselves at the end of the 1980s. On the contrary, a rational observer could have found plenty of evidence to show that a human tragedy on such a scale was unthinkable. In order better to understand the collapse, we have to try to get to the bottom of factors which were so powerful as to be able to destroy elements of the primary social fabric like neighbourhood and local communities. The question is especially intriguing if we take into account that 'historically rooted hatred' was not the outcome of the everyday experience of millions of inhabitants of Yugoslavia before 1991. In a matter of months, however, the dynamic of conflict created a situation in which different ethnic identities became sharply polarised, and everything that had been shared was forgotten. This could not have happened if it had not been for systematic daily attacks on people's perceptions of 'others'. In Bosnia especially, where ethnic cultures were not geographically segregated, new identities could be generated only by systematically imposed 'forgetting', or by systematic terror.

Obviously identity is not something fixed, given and unchangeable. So we have to look at the factors that create knowledge about ourselves, which create 'reality'. As Giddens (1994) argues, reality is no longer just direct human experience, but has become extended to what the press and electronic media present. Thus information is no longer merely descriptive of reality, but becomes a constituent part of it. In a world in which information is constitutive to reality we get, manufactured uncertainty, as Giddens calls it, which affects our daily lives fundamentally. Information about events regularly enters and reconstructs the environment. Who is a 'good guy' and who a 'bad guy' is no longer something we can determine on the basis of our direct experience: it is now determined on the basis of the total information environment by which we are surrounded. In a world of manufactured uncertainty, ontological insecurity can become acute if mechanisms of political manipulation target the very core of accepted beliefs and conventions. This fragility is especially marked in societies which are, in cultural terms, still patriarchal. It may well be because people find it impossible to live in a world of manufactured uncertainty that they are easily pushed towards national fundamentalism – which reduces subjective uncertainty. For anyone with everyday experience of Yugoslavia on the eve of the war, this analysis seems entirely plausible. Within a matter of months, people had radically changed their attitudes and identities. For most of them a shift towards collectivism and tradition was the only solution. This massive opportunism was reinforced by the gradual but systematic creation of a picture of 'others' as 'devils' and 'us' as victims. Finally, the rediscovery of tradition was reinforced by a reinterpretation of the party's systematic denial of 'national identities' in their strong form. In reality, all the nations of the former Yugoslavia had suffered equally in this respect. In the reinterpretation, 'our national identity was suppressed more than any other in the former system'.

As Giddens argues, fundamentalism allows us to avoid the problems of manufactured uncertainty by externalising uncertainty. The historical novelty of the Yugoslav situation lies in the fact that there was so much uncertainty to externalise. When uncertainty regarding the future becomes as pervasive as it did in the former Yugoslavia, fundamentalism spreads from the margins into the mainstream of society. It is reinforced by the systematic preclusion of political dialogue and the demonisation of 'others'. With dialogue rejected and cultural autoerotism and self-sufficiency in the ascendency, newly rediscovered old 'imagined communities' started to acquired a social function – as effectively the only collectivity in a country that was still formally multinational. They gradually started to fulfil the need 'for belonging and security, and to allow one to move within known forms without having to make constant efforts of analysis and interpretation' (Oklobdžija, 1993: 96).

However, a 'new reality' cannot be formed *ex nihilo*. It must touch, as Županov (1993) argues a 'repertoire', or collective memory. These are shared myths and beliefs which do not form part of our direct experience, but which mediate signals and impute values and importance to different signals that we pick up from the environment. If the message is compatible with our 'repertoire', it will be accepted as a reality. This 'repertoire' in the Yugoslav case was obviously conducive to the messages of fear and mistrust which local political elites were disseminating so wildly through the press and TV.

On the other hand, as Županov rightly argues, we should be aware that collective memory is a latent category, which is activated only when someone systematically seeks to activate it. A powerful propaganda and political machine, supported by paramilitary groups which are working to provoke conflicts, is a *sine qua non* for such a course of events. How passive xenophobia was transformed into active xenophobia in a very short period in the Yugoslav case remains to be analysed more systematically than is possible here. Pervasive insecurity, most often unconscious, seems to be the most important explanatory factor. Another factor is the loss of 'analytical power' on the part of the population. The banishment from the public scene of the political groups that can pinpoint the inconsistencies in the image of 'others' being purveyed by the new dominant political elements further limits this 'analytical power'. Paradoxically, the provision of more information, even when it is different, does not solve the problem, because it only increases people's sense of uncertainty and thus reinforces their attachment to the fundamentalist world view.

In the world of the 'fundamentalist syndrome', i.e. where values or identities are temporarily absolutised and are not subsumed into any political dialogue, 'rational actors' get things systematically wrong. For example, the 'tactical rationalism' of the international community in the Yugoslav conflict did nothing to help bring the conflict to an end. On the contrary, *the international community lacked precisely that intensity of irrationality, beliefs and commitments which would have been necessary to force the parties to the conflict to accept some kind of rules of the game.* Another example is the Marković programme, which had only rationalist elements and lacked the necessary element of political irrationalism. It did not target the critical parts of the collective memory and therefore failed to get its message across. By focusing on economic reforms and postponing political action, Marković found out too late that economic change is dependent on the way the problem is symbolised through ideology. As Salecl (1993: 83) puts it, what matters in a political battle are not hard facts, like unemployment and poverty, but how those hard facts are perceived and symbolically mediated and structured.

Fortunately, the manufacture of uncertainty on the scale it was manufactured in the course of the Yugoslav conflict cannot be kept going indefinitely – no more can the 'fundamentalist world view' be reproduced permanently. As long as the political and war machinery is able to keep up tension and produce horrors 'to order', the bulk of the population will be trapped in the dominant (manipulated) perception of what reality is. However, as armed conflict becomes a permanent state, and as the political propaganda begins to be too repetitive, the population starts to get back its 'memory', i.e. its ability to compare the new with the old situation.

The return of memory opens up the possibility of the re-examination of identity and a more realistic assessment of knowledge about ourselves. Even when in political or military terms a situation may not seem to be changing much, things may be very different from the anthropological perspective. A return of memory brings an understanding of one's own past, and alternative interpretations of one's own identity and perceptions of the current situation. Although people's new identities remain different from the old ones, there is a new readiness to accept some of the incompatibilities between national identities as facts. This softening of the 'fundamentalist' stance is a sign of preparedness to accept an alternative political perspective – something unthinkable in the acute phase of ontological insecurity.

The reacquisition of the ability to face facts was particularly striking in the case of the Serbs of the Croatian Krajina. In the wake of the Croatian military offensive in August 1995 they fled in fear from their own land on an unimaginable scale, on the basis of a realistic assessment of the new military balance. Had there been more political will for a peaceful settlement on the part of the Croatian authorities, they would, no doubt, have been equally prepared to accept a compromise political solution. The key point here is that the prospects for a settlement of the conflict were in no way compromised by the 'fundamentalist syndrome'. In this case people reacquired 'analytical power' rather rapidly. In a situation where perceptions of 'others' are now much more realistic, there is a real possibility that military activity may eventually lead to political activity conducive to a final resolution of the conflict.

The limits of irrationality and the re-emergence of economics?

The basic objective of the Yugoslav war, which was to solve the problem of national identity through national states, was not achieved – even with the mid-1995 'simplification' of the maps of Croatia and Bosnia and Hercegovina. This creates an insuperable problem for all those political forces which have the creation of a mononational state as their main objective.

Since the national question on the territory of the formerYugoslavia cannot be solved in terms of states, or through the wizardry of cartographers, the key problem is how new states can become democratic and able to tolerate 'others'. This would sooner or later lead to the reformulation of national political programmes, an issue that is especially important regarding Serbia and its future political role in this region. As Janjić (1993: 105) rightly points out, the key mistake of Serbian nationalism was that it posed the Serbian national question in state, rather than in democratic terms. Cviić makes exactly the same point in relation to Croatia (see Chapter 11). If the Serbian national programme gives up its 'small imperial dream' and makes a move towards a more democratic solution, that will surely significantly speed up the transformation of the other protagonists in the conflict as well.

Newly created identities and political structures must sooner or later come to terms with economic realities. The paradox of all the great national projects in the region is that, even if they were all realised (which is geographically impossible), they would not overcome the main economic weakness of the old Yugoslavia: the low level of economic interdependence. It is difficult to believe that Greater Serbia, Greater Croatia or Muslimia would be 'organic, tightly interwoven economic structures', capable of ensuring a much higher level of intrastate economic interdependence than was the case in the past with Yugoslavia. Thus whatever political and border arrangements are made, economic reality will force political changes, as well as modifying basic attitudes towards the 'others'. With the return of 'remembering', and a shift from mass paranoia towards a more complex perception of reality, the new states will, irrespective of how they have come out of the territorial 'game', be compelled to step back from the economically and politically irrational behaviour of the early 1990s.

Unfortunately, the new political elites are not up to the task of 'late late modernisation'. With the exception of Milošević, they came to power after the first republic-level multiparty elections, coming not from strata with established economic power, but rather from a purely political environment (S. Bolčić, as quoted in Goati, 1991). They do not constitute a class seeking to legitimise its economic power in a political way. On the other hand, their political power has enabled them to take over economic control of the society. Control over what was previously 'social capital' is the cornerstone of their power and is used to consolidate that power rather than to transform the economies in question. To make matters worse, the war has radically thinned out the social groups which would be expected to be the main standard-bearers of modernisation. The 'ruralisation of the cities', the reintroduction of political criteria for many professional functions: all this is further reducing the size of those groups. Finally, the populist semi-rural-semi-urban cultural background which emerges from the war as victor is quite inappropriate for the modernisation process. Modernisation requires openness and understanding of 'others', appreciation of local specificities in relative and not in absolute terms – in a word, all the things that are incompatible with strong national programmes.

Paradoxically, the political groups that created the new states might turn into the biggest constraint as far as international integration is concerned. In their current shape (with the exception of Slovenia) the successor states are in no position to integrate themselves through a wide network of market and democratic institutions. The prospects for international reintegration will depend critically on how long it takes to construct a new political elite. For that reason, despite the inhospitability of the present sociopolitical 'landscape', it is almost (but not quite!) inevitable that, sooner or later, the late late modernisers will have their day.

The new states will slowly realise that zero-sum nationalism based on the notion that others are always to blame for 'our' losses, is counterproductive and must eventually exhaust itself in the production of ever new objects of blame. They will progress just as fast as they retreat from hard nationalist positions. By the same token, the very process of integration will lead to the transformation of national identities. Obviously this will be a highly politicised process. What is absolutely clear is that statist nationalism in its narrowest interpretation of total sovereignity in all matters affecting the citizens of the given country is no longer feasible, given the likely pattern of economic interdependence with the other countries. Even while the war was still going on, there were plenty of examples of infrastructural interdependence of warring parties, operating as useful pressures for a return to a more rational assessment of the situation. But the economic prospects of the successor states, and the political prospects of the late late modernisers, will be primarily determined by the internal national and social consensus – or lack of it. A nationalism which accepts 'others' as part of 'us' is the only viable one economically.

References

Allcock, John (1993) Involvement and detachment: Yugoslavia as an object of scholarship, *Journal of Area Studies*, no. 3, pp. 144–60.

Bazler-Madžar, Marta (1991) Politika regionalnog razvoja – savremene tendencije, *Politika Razvoja*, no. 4, April 1991.

Buvač, Drago (1994) Krepke sankcije, *Feral Tribune*, 19 September 1994.

Dubravčić, Dinko (1993) Economic causes and political context of the dissolution of a multinational federal state, *Communist Economies & Economic Transformation*, vol. 5, no. 3, pp. 259–72.

Dyker, David A. (1990) *Yugoslavia. Socialism, Development and Debt* (London: Routledge).

Fortin, J., Moore, M., Roberts, R. and White, D.G. (1988) *The Politics of Economic Liberalisation in the Third World* (Sussex: Research Proposal, Institute of Development Studies, University of Sussex) mimeo.

Giddens, Anthony (1994) 'First global society', lecture delivered at the University of Sussex.

Glissman, Hans (1989) *EC 1992: Strategic and Policy Issues for the 1990s – with Special Reference to Developing Countries and Yugoslavia*, paper presented to a workshop of the Institute of Economic Research in Ljubljana, Kiel Institute of World Economics.

Goati, Vladimir (1991) Spoticanje 'pećinskog antikomunizma', *Borba*, 13–14 April 1991.

Golubović, Zagorka (1993) Nationalism and democracy: the Yugoslav case, *Journal of Area Studies*, no. 3, pp. 65–77.

Hodgson, Geoffrey (1993) *The Economics of Institutions* (London: Edward Elgar).

Jahoda, Maria (1992) *World within World, Nationalism: a Danger to the Management of Global Problems*, EC report to the FAST Programme, Theme C, FOP 322.

Janjić, Dušan (1993) Socialism, federalism and nationalism in (the former) Yugoslavia: lessons to be learned, *Journal of Area Studies*, no. 3, pp. 102–19.

Kornai, Janos (1990) *The Affinity Between Ownership and Co-ordination Mechanisms: The Common Experience of Reforms in Socialist Countries*, paper prepared for the Round Table Conference on 'Market Forces in Planned Economies' organised by the International Economic Association jointly with the USSR Academy of Sciences in Moscow, 28–30 March 1989.

Kračun, Davor (1991) *Yugoslav Semi-Command Economy and its Conversion into a Market Economy*, working papers EDP, Institute for Economic Diagnosis and Prognosis, Maribor, vol. 21.

Medenica, Djuro (1991) Tehnološka razmena Jugoslavije, JU-TET seminar (Brioni: Federal Secretariat for Development).

OECD (1986) *Trends in the Information Economy,* Information, Computer and Communication Policy Series, no. 11, Paris.

OECD (1991) *Background Report Concluding the Technology/Economy Program*, Paris.

Oklobdžija, Mira (1993) The creation of active xenophobia in what was Yugoslavia, *Journal of Area Studies*, no. 3, pp. 191–201.

Pertot, Vladimir (1971) *Ekonomika Vanjske Trgovine Jugoslavije* (Zagreb: Informator).

Porter, Michael (1990) *The Competitive Advantage of Nations* (New York: Free Press).

Pošarac, Branka (1991) *Analiza Siromaštva u Jugoslaviji* (Belgrade: Ekonomski Institut).

Radošević, Slavo (1991) *Uvod u Tehnološku Politiku Jugoslavije* (Zagreb: Ekonomski Institut).

Ratković, Marija (1990) *Medjuzavisnosti Tehnoloških i Strukturnih Promena i Zaposlenosti u Jugoslaviji, Deo 1, Razvoj Ljudskih Resursa u Jugoslaviji* (Belgrade: Institut Ekonomskih Nauka).

Salecl, Renata (1993) Nationalism, anti-semitism, and anti-feminism in eastern Europe, *Journal of Area Studies*, no. 3, pp. 78–90.

Schierup, Carl-Ulrik (1992) Quasi-proletarians and a patriarchal bureaucracy: aspects of Yugoslavia's re-peripheralisation, *Soviet Studies*, vol. 44, no. 1, pp. 79–99.

Schierup, Carl-Ulrik (1993a) *Eurobalkanism: Ethnic Cleansing and the Post-Cold War Order*, paper for international conference on the Yugoslav War and Security in the Balkans and in Europe, Bologna, 10–11 December 1993.

Schierup, Carl-Ulrik (1993b) Economic disintegration and the political fragmentation of Yugoslavia, *Balkan Forum*, no. 2, March, pp. 89–120.

Simonetti, Marko (1989) *Comparative Analysis of Yugoslav and Western Enterprises (Theory, Institutional Framework and Prospects for Improved Compatibility)* (Ljubljana: Institute for Economic Research).

Sočan, Lojze (1989) *Adaptation of the Yugoslav Economic System and Policies in Order to Improve Economic Compatibility with the EC* (Ljubljana: Institute for Economic Research).

Steiner, Alfred and Ottolenghi, Daniel (1993) Yugoslavia: was it a winner's curse?, *Economics of Transition*, vol. 1, no. 2, June, pp. 209–44.

Stiglitz, E. Joseph (1993) Some Theoretical Aspects of Privatisation: Applications to Eastern Europe. In M. Baladassarri, L. Paganeto and E. Phelps (eds) *Privatisation Processes in Eastern Europe: Theoretical Foundations and Empirical Results* (New York: St. Martin's Press).

Zimmerman, Warren (1995) The last ambassador: a memoir of the collapse of Yugoslavia, *Foreign Affairs*, March/April, pp. 2–20.

Županov, Josip (1983) Znanje, društveni sistem i 'klasni interes', *Naše Teme*, no. 7–8, pp. 1048–54.

Županov, Josip (1993) Budjenje demona u dobrim susjedima, *Nedeljna Dalmacija*, 3 November.

Part Two

In the Eye of the Storm

Chapter 6

Bosnia and Hercegovina – State and Communitarianism

XAVIER BOUGAREL

The outbreak of war in Bosnia and Hercegovina[1] in April 1992 was immediately followed by the outbreak of polemics on the nature of the war, and indeed on the nature of Bosnian society itself. While some invoked 'five hundred years of toleration and democracy', others, following Ivo Andrić, painted a picture of 'a land of hatred and fear'. Crossroads of civilisations, Bosnia is certainly a land of encounters, of coexistence and, occasionally, of symbiosis. On the periphery of more than one empire, it is also a land where, with extraordinary regularity, other peoples' wars have nourished and have been nourished by the internal conflicts of Bosnian society. Thus the words 'tolerance', 'hate', 'coexistence' and 'fear' are all equally applicable. In essence, they are complementary or consecutive rather than contradictory.

But if there is one word that is not appropriate to Bosnia and its history, it is 'democracy'. In the first place, the regimes which have ruled successively in Bosnia, from the Ottoman Empire (1463–1878) to Yugoslav communism (1945–90), have been in no sense democratic. Only with the end of the Austro-Hungarian occupation (1878–1918) and the birth of the Yugoslav monarchy was some semblance of parliamentary life introduced. In the second place, the concept of democracy is presumed, in general terms, on that of citizenship. In fact, the principle which has given structure to the Bosnian political order has not been citizenship, but rather communitarian identity. All elections held in Bosnia since 1910 have been dominated by national parties.

That does not mean that communitarianism in Bosnia is immutable and incontestable, nor that the wave of democratic and civic aspirations that swept over Central and Eastern Europe in the 1980s passed by this republic of the former Yugoslavia. But it does mean that the present crisis cannot be understood unless we take account of this key dimension of Bosnian reality – obfuscated by some, distorted by others.

---

[1] Hereafter Bosnia.

State and communitarianism in Bosnia: from *millets* to nations

In the early centuries of the Ottoman period, the Islamisation of a large proportion of the Bosnian population, and the installation of substantial orthodox populations and smaller Jewish populations, gave Bosnia its contemporary confessional profile.[2] But in this period social status and confessional identity still did not coincide completely. Christians continued to occupy a significant place among the military and feudal elites, while Christian and Muslim *rayas* (subjects, labourers) to a great extent shared the same lot. Confessional identity was, moreover, very fluid in the early centuries of Ottoman rule. And there were a number of peasant revolts in this period which pitted Muslim peasants against their Muslim feudal lords.

From the middle of the eighteenth century, as the slow sclerosis of the Ottoman Empire set in, community divisions became more rigid (Sugar, 1973; Mantran, 1989). With the organisation of the Christian populations into *millets* (religious communities enjoying a large measure of internal autonomy), the churches came to play a key social and cultural role. But none of this stopped the deterioration in the economic status of the Christians. The latter trend was particularly marked in Bosnia, the frontier of the Ottoman Empire, with the local Muslim elites monopolising power to their personal advantage, and the Christian populations perceived as potential allies of the Austro-Hungarian Empire.

The result was a Bosnian society structured along communitarian lines. The millets not only decided on a range of juridicial questions (tax regimes and the division of jurisdictions by millets), but were also identified, within the towns, with particular areas and particular guilds. In the countryside, they were heavily identified with the cause of socioeconomic opposition. As late as 1910, more than thirty years after the end of the Ottoman presence in Bosnia, 91.1 per cent of the landed proprieters having *kmetovi*[3] (tenant farmers with feudal obligations) were Muslims, while 95.4 per cent of the *kmetovi* were Orthodox or Catholic.

As a result, the fluidity of confessional identity and relationships was increasingly replaced by a closed communitarianism. The informal institution of *komšiluk* (good neighbourliness) certainly continued to be the rule in everyday dealings between the communities; but it was based on a constant reaffirmation of community identities and codes, and not on their effacement. *Komšiluk* never developed into intimateness. In terms of the relationships it established between the public and private spheres, between communitarian identity and social bonds, it represented the inverse of citizenship, rather than its premise.

The relationship between the millets and political modernity, symbolised in the nineteenth century by the development of nationalism, is certainly more ambiguous (Jelavich and Jelavich, 1963; Karpat, 1963). The institutionalisation of the millets –

---

[2] In 1879, at the end of the Ottoman period, the population of Bosnia was 38.7 per cent Muslim, 42.9 per cent Orthodox (Serb) and 18.1 per cent Catholic (Croat). The corresponding figures for 1991 were 43.7 per cent (Muslims in terms of national identity), 31.4 per cent and 17.3 per cent. The Jewish population of Bosnia fell from 11,248 in 1931 to just 377 in 1953.

[3] Singular *kmet*.

which came rather late in the day – must be seen in the context of the efforts at modernisation and reform undertaken by the Ottoman state in the nineteenth century. So while the nationalist movements of Eastern Europe place the state in the centre of the political order, the communitarian mobilisations which took place in Bosnia in the same period sought to keep it at a distance. Both the insurrection of the Muslim feudal lords against the Ottoman reforms in 1831 and the anti-tax revolt of the Serb peasants of Hercegovina in 1875 were effectively revolts against the reinforcement of the role of the state. The first certainly represented no kind of nationalist movement; the second only turned into one after the intervention of the youthful neighbouring Serbian state and the internationalisation of this first Bosnian crisis.

Thus the creation, in the wake of the Austro-Hungarian occupation of 1878, of a modern state apparatus in Bosnia constituted a fundamental rupture. The slow transformation of the communitarian identities and relationships inherited from the Ottoman period must be understood in the context of this political modernisation, and of the beginnings of economic and cultural modernisation (Sugar, 1974; Donia, 1981; Čupić-Amrein, 1987).

Initially, the Austro-Hungarian Empire, anxious to counteract the influence of Serb and Croat nationalism, sought to promote a global Bosnian identity, taking control of the religious structures of Bosnia (nomination by the Emperor of Catholic and Orthodox bishops, and of the Muslim *Reis-ul-Ulema*), and even forbidding the use of the terms 'Serb' and 'Croat' in the titles of cultural associations. This arbitrary policy found some support among the emerging modernisers among the Muslim elites, but was met with hostility by the Orthodox elites (Serbs), the Catholic elites (Croats), and by the traditional Muslim elites.

With the new Christian commercial and administrative elites in Bosnia making Serbian and Croatian nationalism their own, nationalist sentiment developed rapidly within the Orthodox and Catholic communities of the territory. The Muslim community, for its part, mobilised around its religious and territorial elites, demanding cultural and religious autonomy – a kind of 'millet in reverse' for the Muslim population. From that time, the Austro-Hungarian Empire started to accept, and then even to favour, the consolidation of the communitarian structure of social and political life in Bosnia.

On the economic side, the Habsburgs gave privileges to the Catholic elites (local or from the rest of the Empire) within the administration, and preserved the land-owning privileges of the Muslim elites, in exchange for their loyalty. On the political side, the Dual Monarchy conceded cultural and religious autonomy to the Serb community in 1906 and to the Muslims in 1909. In the latter case, the agreement involved the establishment of an elected *Reis-ul-Ulema* (subject to confirmation by the *Sheikh-ul-Islam* in Istanbul), and of an autonomous administration for the *vakufi*,[4] and also for the maintenance of shariat courts for matters of personal status. One year later, a provincial constitution instituted a Bosnian parliament, elected on a restricted suffrage and made up of distinct 'colleges' (thirty-seven Orthodox

---

4 Singular *vakuf*. These were endowments for the support of Muslims and the advancement of the Muslim faith.

deputies, twenty-nine Muslim, twenty-three Catholic and one Jew). Thus the introduction of parliamentarianism in Bosnia *went hand-in-hand with the institutionalisation of communitarianism.*

During the Austro-Hungarian period economic, social, cultural, and even sporting life continued to be structured on a communitarian basis. It was the same in political life. The national parties – the MNO (*Muslimanska Narodna Organizacija –* Muslim National Organisation), the SNO (*Srpska Narodna Organizacija –* Serbian National Organisation), and the HND (*Hrvatsko Narodno Društvo –* Croatian National Society), all of which came into existence between 1905 and 1910, dominated the first parliamentary elections. And it is this period that sees the birth of a Bosnian style of political life characterised by coalitions of interest between the political elites of different communities (a Serb-Muslim coalition on the question of cultural and religious autonomy up to 1909, and a Croat-Muslim coalition on the agrarian reform issue from 1911), by the mediating and pendular role of the Muslim community within the context of growing Serb-Croat rivalry, a tendency for the communities to use appeals to the state as a tactical device, and the instrumentalisation of intercommunity conflicts by that same state.

The First World War, which had its origin in Sarajevo, overturned the geopolitical equilibrium of the Balkans and disturbed, for the first time, the stability of relations between the communities (violence against the Serbs in 1914 and against the Muslims in 1918). But while the integration of Bosnia into the Kingdom of the Serbs, Croats and Slovenes (renamed Yugoslavia in 1929) made radical changes to the economic and political balance between the communities (agrarian reform and seizure of control over the state apparatus by the Serbs), it did not raise any immediate question marks over the communitarianism inherited from the Austro-Hungarian period.

In the elections of 1920 for the Constituent Assembly, the voting pattern of the Bosnian population – and indeed of the Yugoslav population as a whole – continued to be communitarian. Out of sixty-three deputies elected in Bosnia, only the four communist deputies could be considered as definitely not belonging to a party explicitly or implicitly communitarian. While the Serb and Croat communities were each represented by a number of parties, reflecting the various currents within their respective nationalisms (Behschnitt, 1980; Banac, 1984), the Muslim community was represented by just one: the Organisation of Yugoslav Muslims (JMO – *Jugoslovenska Muslimanska Organizacija*). The deputies from the JMO, every one of whom had been in the MNO, continued the strategies worked out during the Austro-Hungarian period. In March 1921 they agreed to vote in favour of a centralist constitution, and indeed to join the government, in exchange for guarantees on the maintenance of Bosnia as a distinct territory and of the Law on Religious Autonomy of 1909, and on compensation for landowners who had lost their land in the land reform of 1919. In February 1922, however, they changed sides and jointed the opposition headed by the Croatian Peasant Party (HSS – *Hrvatska Seljačka Stranka*) (Purivatra, 1969a; Banac, 1984).

In the longer term, economic, cultural and above all political trends within the Kingdom of Yugoslavia conspired to produce a grave crisis of communitarianism in Bosnia. The Serb and Croat populations of Bosnia looked more and more to

Belgrade and Zagreb, while the conflict between Serbs and Croats deepened rapidly. At the same time, the decline of the traditional Muslim elites produced a profound crisis of identity within the Muslim community. Exposed to the advances and pressures of Serb and Croat nationalism, the Bosnian Muslims were increasingly inclined to take refuge in national indeterminacy and a tactical Yugoslavism.

As the Serb-Croat conflict intensified, the margin of political manoeuvre for the JMO narrowed. In 1929 Bosnia was divided into four *banovine*,[5] and the autonomy of the Islamic religious structures was suppressed. In 1935, however, the JMO agreed to rejoin the government, in exchange for the re-establishment of this autonomy. Three years later it joined an electoral coalition led by the Serbian Radical Party – the party in power. For the first time, however, in these elections of 1938, JMO candidates did not obtain a majority of Muslim votes. Communist and Pan-Islamist groups were already multiplying among educated young Muslims.

When, in August 1939, the Serb prime minister D. Cvetković and the leader of the Croat Peasant Party, V. Maček, agreed on a territorial partition of Bosnia, with part of it being integrated into the new, big *banovina* of Croatia, this crisis of identity and of the representation of the Muslim community came to a head. A movement for the autonomy of Bosnia was created by leaders of the JMO and Islamic religious organisations (Redžić, 1987), only to break up in April 1941, after the collapse of the first Yugoslavia and the annexation of Bosnia by independent Croatia. That signalled the beginning, in Bosnia, of a conflict of rare intensity, with resistance against the occupiers mixed in with the massacre of Serb populations by the Croat Ustashas, of Muslim populations by the Serb Chetniks, and of reprisals against the same.

This destruction of institutionalised communitarianism by territorially oriented and exclusive nationalisms was paralleled by an internal fragmentation within each community. Thus the Muslim community, in a deep crisis of identity and representation, saw its leaders dispersed and inclined to play a waiting game and its populations organised, for better or worse, in a multitude of self-defence militias. The Serb community, for its part, was exposed to a policy of calculated genocide and largely abandoned by a Chetnik movement inclined to descend into brigandage and collaboration.

Tito's Partisan Movement was able, gradually, to win the support of substantial sections of the Bosnian population. And this was not just because the Partisans could give them physical security, still less on account of an abstract Yugoslavism or anti-fascism. The political advances in Bosnia on the part of the Partisans were also to a substantial extent due to the willingness of the Partisan leadership to champion the rural populations' demands for agrarian reform, *and to reproduce a communitarian structure on this basis* (Denitch, 1976).

Between 1941 and 1945, proclamations by the Partisan movement in Bosnia were invariably addressed to 'Serbs, Muslims and Croats', even though most of the Partisan activists were initially Serb. At its first session of 25 November 1943, the Antifascist Council of National Liberation of Bosnia and Hercegovina (AVNOBiH – *Antifašističko Vjeće Narodnog Oslobodjenja Bosne i Hercegovine*) proclaimed

---

[5] Singular *banovina*.

Bosnia reconstituted as a distinct territory, in which 'full equality of all Serbs, Muslims and Croats would be guaranteed'. It was around this time that Muslims started to join the Partisan movement in large numbers. Special Muslim detachments were created, within which Muslim precepts – especially with respect to food – were respected (Purivatra, 1969b).

In the post-1945 period the the relationship of the Yugoslav communists to communitarianism was ambiguous, to say the least (Shoup, 1968). The Yugoslav Communist Party attacked the traditional religious and communitarian structures (the shariat courts and *Preporod* (Renaissance) – the Muslim cultural association – were dissolved in 1946, and the madrasas (Muslim seminaries) closed in 1947), less to liquidate the communitarian structure than to put it under exclusive communist control. Recognition of the Macedonian and Montenegrin nations in 1945, and then of the Muslim nation in 1968, provide good illustrations of this phenomenon. More important, in generating a very substantial turnover of economic and political elites, the Communist Party of Yugoslavia gave support to the survival of the constituent mechanisms of communitarianism (Cohen, 1989).

Throughout the whole of the Yugoslav territory, and in particular in Bosnia, communitarian relationships were articulated in terms of two key factors: control of the state apparatus and control of the land. These two factors were in turn closely tied in with the question of relations between town and country, with town tending to dominate country economically, and the elites of the dominant community always seeking to take control of the towns (Tomasevitch, 1955). Certainly from 1878, every war in Bosnia was accompanied by sharp changes in the pattern of power relationships between the communities (taking control of the state apparatus and redistributing land), and by the eviction of the old urban elites by the new elites coming in from the countryside. This is the origin of the abrupt and erratic changes in the ethnic composition of the Bosnian towns, and of Sarajevo in particular.[6]

In this respect, the accession to power of the Yugoslav Communist Party was marked by almost perfect continuity. Not only were the lands confiscated from German owners in Slavonia and Vojvodina redistributed to partisans from Bosnia and Montenegro, but the old economic and political elites were largely replaced by new. Certainly the Serb community continued, in this initial period, to be overrepresented in these new elites, in Bosnia as in Yugoslavia as a whole. But whereas the Serbian elites of the first Yugoslavia had been recruited largely from Serbia proper, and had quickly found themselves in conflict with the rural Serb populations of Bosnia and Croatia, those of socialist Yugoslavia came largely from the peripheral Serbian populations, who supplanted the old Serb elites, from Sarajevo to Belgrade.

The really distinctive feature of socialist Yugoslavia lay in an attempt at modernisation aimed at the eventual disappearance of national peculiarities. But the profound process of modernisation to which socialist Yugoslavia was committed, far from leading to a revolutionary fusion of the Yugoslav peoples, led in fact to a

---

[6] In 1885 the population of Sarajevo was 60.1 per cent Muslim, 16.9 per cent Orthodox (Serb) and 12.7 per cent Catholic (Croat). In 1910 the corresponding figures were 35.6 per cent, 16.3 per cent and 34.5 per cent, and in 1948 34.6 per cent, 36.0 per cent and 23.3. per cent.

reinforcement of national identities (cf. the crystallisation of Macedonian, Montenegrin and, above all, Muslim national identity), and ultimately to a resurgence of communitarian ways of doing things, and of nationalist ideologies.

The resurgence of communitarian politics and nationalist ideologies in socialist Yugoslavia

As noted by a number of observers, socialist Yugoslavia evolved progressively from a relatively centralised federal system to a confederal system under which power lay essentially with the constituent republics and autonomous provinces, and their corresponding Leagues of Communists (Rusinow, 1977; Burg, 1983; Ramet, 1985; Krulić, 1993; Vejvoda, Chapter 2 in this volume). The trend is particularly noticeable in the period between 1966 (fall of Aleksandar Ranković, chief of the secret police and champion of the centralized state) and 1974 (adoption of a new, decentralising constitution).

The 'Croatian Spring' of 1971, marked by a confrontation between the Croatian League of Communists on the one hand, and the other Leagues of Communists and the Yugoslav National Army on the other, showed how, at the same time, nationalities policy was becoming, for the rival republican political elites, a favoured locus of confrontation − and *relegitimisation vis-à-vis* their respective national communities (see Chapter 11).

There are many different explanations for this decentralisation of the Yugoslav institutional and political system − all of them essentially complementary (Ramet, 1984; Golubović, 1986; Pawlovitch, 1988; Sekelj, 1990). First, the rapid industrialisation and urbanisation of Yugoslavia after 1945 was marked by disequilibria − of two sorts. The first, between the developed regions of the north (basically Slovenia and Croatia) and the underdeveloped regions of the south, aggravated the conflicts between the republics and autonomous provinces. The second, between the urban communes benefiting from economic development and the marginalised rural communes, rekindled the eternal frustrations of the peasant world.

In addition, the new population groups born of modernisation (the new economic and scientific elites and the educated urban population), fired by new political and cultural aspirations, themselves began to contest the legitimacy of an ideology and a political elite inherited from the Partisan movement. The confrontation between the new economic and scientific elites and the old political and military elite *reactivated old rivalries between different national communities,* as, for example, again with the Croatian Spring and also with the crisis in the League of Communists of Yugoslavia (LCY) 1986–89.

In Bosnia, decentralisation and the resurgence of communitarianism took quite specific forms. The 1960s witnessed the political emergence of the Muslim community, at the expense of the hitherto dominant Serbs, with the Muslims recognised, successively, as a constituent nation of Bosnia and of Yugoslavia (Bougarel, 1992). And in the context of Bosnia's unique situation among the Yugoslav republics, in that it did not correspond to a specific national community, and in the absence of explicit communitarian institutions within the republic, communitarian rivalries tended to express themselves through fundamental, if largely concealed, conflicts within the League of Communists of Bosnia, or through national-cultural institutions external to Bosnia (The Serbian Academy of Sciences and the Croatian *Matica Hrvatska* organisation) and religious organisations – primarily the Islamic Community (*Islamska Zajednica*).

With the death of Marshal Tito in 1980, the uncontested arbitrator of the Yugoslav political system had gone. As the economic crisis deepened and the communist ideology increasingly lost its credibility, nationalism took an ever stronger hold, as witness the Albanian demonstrations in Kosovo in 1981. This increase in the strength of nationalist sentiment can be explained in terms of a 'nationalist transfer' of economic and political frustrations. Thus, for instance, the Albanian demonstrators in Kosovo demanded their own republic – as a solution to the problem of economic underdevelopment in the province. A few years later, Serb demonstrators were seeking to explain the Serb emigration from Kosovo – essentially economic in nature – in terms of hypothetical 'Albanian pressures'. This 'nationalist transfer', encouraged by the rival political elites, cannot be reduced to simple manipulation on their part. It sprang ultimately from the communitarian patterns of behaviour and conceptions of the populations themselves.

In addition, as Shkelzen Maliqi notes in connection with the crisis in Kosovo, this 'nationalist transfer' of political and economic frustrations represents a 'statist reduction of consciousness', by means of which (in that particular case) 'the Kosovo problem is reduced to a national problem ... while other more important aspects of Kosovo's contradictory reality are put to one side'. At the same time the national problem itself is reduced to 'the conquest of the state, permitting the enthronement of a national bureaucracy' (Maliqi, 1989; see also Chapter 8 by Maliqi in this volume). The rise of nationalisms in Yugoslavia cannot, therefore, be analysed without taking into account the ambigious attitudes to the state on the part of populations formed by the Ottoman Empire, the communist system and, more specifically, by a federal and self-managing Yugoslavia in which *the state was both everywhere and nowhere.*

As the Yugoslav crisis worsened, the phenomenon of 'nationalist transfer' gradually spread to all the communities and republics. The 1980s were marked everywhere by a re-evaluation of national and religious identities, and a *rapprochement* between all or part of the communist political elites and the religious and opposition elites. The 'Milošević phenomenon', which emerged in 1986, and the role of the Orthodox Church and the Academy of Sciences in the same, is the rule rather than the exception in this context.

There were, certainly, substantial differences between the republics. The Leagues of Communists of Serbia and Montenegro, under the leadership of Slobodan Milošević, embodied an aggressive and authoritarian nationalism. In Slovenia and Macedonia the Leagues represented a moderate, reformist nationalism, while those of Croatia and Bosnia remained more conservative – and were accordingly wiped out by the nationalist and anti-communist parties in the free elections of 1990. This is why the LCY broke up in the course of its XIV Congress in January 1990. Throughout Yugoslavia, the Titoist principle of 'divide and rule' had been replaced by the nationalist principle 'divide up and rule'.

At the end of the 1980s the League of Communists of Bosnia (LCB) remained, on account of its multiethnic composition, the strictest in its continued support for the Titoist dogma of 'unity and brotherhood' – but also the most enfeebled by communitarian clientism, rivalries and the settling of accounts. The Agrokomerc scandal, which broke in August 1987, revealed the degree of corruption and internal decomposition present in the LCB. Beginning as a financial scandal, the affair rapidly took on a political dimension and ended up with the fall of the leading Muslim among the communist leadership, Hamdija Pozderac, the patron of Fikret Abdić, the director of Agrokomerc and veritable 'baron' of the Cazinska Krajina region. Abdić himself was dismissed and jailed.

In the years that followed, scandals, political disagreements and national conflicts multiplied, feeding on each other, within the structure of the LCB. Its last Congress, in December 1989, designed to prepare for the XIV Congress of the LCY, witnessed confrontation between local organisations of differing national composition, but at the same time victory for the conservative faction, led by the Muslim president of the Central Committee, N. Duraković; this was accompanied by the adoption of watered-down, obsolete resolutions (reaffirmation of Titoist dogma, rejection of Serb and Slovene proposals for constitutional reform, rejection of the multiparty system). In May 1990 the LCB was involved in an attempt to reconvene the XIV Congress of the LCY, and only transformed itself into the Party of Democratic Change (SDP – *Stranka Demokratske Promene*) in September 1990.

The legalisation of multipartyism came late in Bosnia. It was initially accompanied by a ban on 'any association based on national or religious allegiance, except as permitted by the existing law on religious communities' ('Zakon …', 1990). Aimed at preserving Bosnia from the rise of nationalism, this provision probably had the opposite effect, to the extent that it reinforced the imported and confessionally-based nature of the nationalist mobilisation. Thus, for example, the first Serbian mass rallies in Bosnia in 1989 were in response to the crisis in Kosovo and the conflict between Serbia and Slovenia, and were a direct product of the 'anti-bureaucratic revolution' in Serbia proper. In the same way, the first Croatian mass rallies of spring 1990 were closely tied in with the launching of the electoral campaign of the Croatian Democratic Union (HDZ – *Hrvatska Demokratska Zajednica*) in Croatia. The Serbian Democratic Party (SDS – *Srpska Demokratska Stranka*) of Radovan Karadžić and the HDZ Bosnia of Stjepan Klujić, formed, respectively, on 12 July and 18 August 1990, were both modelled on their homonyms in Croatia (Goati, 1992a).[7]

Again, it was the Serbian Orthodox Church of Bosnia which, in 1989, organised a succession of demonstrations commemorating the Battle of Kosovo – sometimes with the participation of local communist organisations. More generally, the opening of new churches or mosques increasingly provided an occasion for nationalist demonstrations; Duraković, the chairman of the Central Committee, was moved to denounce a wave of what he called 'national-religious euphoria'. He went on:

---

[7] The Croatian SDS was the dominant (Serbian) political party in the Serb-minority regions of Croatia.

'What is going on is a massive politicisation and indoctrination on a religious basis, unprecedented in the postwar period. Passions are being rekindled, divisions, settling of accounts, distrust and suspicion stirred up.'[8]

The central role of religious organisations in the nationalist mobilisation was particularly blatant in the case of the Muslim community. It was within the structure of the *Islamic Community* that a current of Islamic thought and action had been reestablished in the 1970s, with Alija Izetbegović already the central figure. The collapse of the communist system in 1989 set off a wave of disputes within the Islamic Community generally called the 'Movement of the Imams'. Izetbegovic's grouping were able to take advantage of this to come on to centre stage within the Community and seize control of its official publication, *Preporod*.

A few months later, on 27 March 1990, representatives of this grouping, associated with the leaders of the Islamic Community in Zagreb, announced the creation of the Party of Democratic Action (SDA – *Stranka Demokratske Akcije*), as a 'political alliance of the citizens of Yugoslavia belonging to the historical-cultural sphere of Islam'.[9] Initially regarded as marginal, the SDA succeeded, within a few months, in pulling together all the main actors and currents of Muslim nationalism and organising, in its turn, impressive mass demonstrations.

The pattern of internal evolution of the SDA can be illustrated by the case of Cazinska Krajina, a rural area in which the population is 90 per cent Muslim. The SDA organisation in this area was created by a small group of educated Muslims and Islamic Community activists. But it was unable to attract mass support until it had secured the support of Fikret Abdić, now once again director of Agrokomerc, and of his 15,000 workers. Thus the SDA, a party initially constituted on a clear-cut ideological base, turned gradually into a 'catch-all' party, based on the client networks of local notables, religious and lay. This did not prevent the founding caucus from retaining its control – through the personnel commission directed by O. Behmen. In September 1990, A. Zulfikarpašić and M. Filipović, representatives of the secular Bosnian nationalist trend, denounced the 'fact that the party is ruled by eleven people – of conservative and generally religious orientation – and that it is run by a closed and privatised council, held together by family ties'.[10] Not long afterwards, these individuals were thrown out of the SDA during an extraordinary assembly of the party. They proceeded to create the Muslim Bosnian Organisation (MBO – *Muslimanska Bošnjačka*[11] *Organizacija*).

The nationalists were the main winners in the election of 18 November 1990. In the elections for the lower house, the SDA obtained 30.4 per cent of the votes, the SDS 25.2 per cent and the HDZ 15.5 per cent, leaving 28.9 per cent for the nonnationalist parties. The new collective presidency was composed of 100 per cent of

---

[8] *Oslobodjenje,* 24 July 1989.

[9] SDA, Programska deklaracija, *Muslimanski Glas,* vol. 1, no. 1, November 1990.

[10] *Oslobodjenje,* 20 September 1990.

[11] This adjective has a strong overtone of national identity, in contrast to the alternative *Bosanska(i),* which is purely territorial in connotation, and therefore politically essentially neutral. But the use of *Bošnjački* as a synonym for *Muslimanski* is a political innovation of the contemporary period, and has no historical justification.

members of the three nationalist parties. A study of the electoral results reveals that support for the nationalist parties was particularly strong in the economically under-developed areas, in ethnically homogeneous areas, among the rural and neo-urban population, and among the lower and less educated socioprofessional groups. Thus the voting pattern in Bosnia shares many of the characteristics of the voting pattern in Serbia and Croatia. The nationalist vote in Bosnia is also identified with strongly religious social groups, still structured on the communitarian model. The non-nationalist or 'civic' parties were supported rather by the urban intellectual elites and the working-class, social strata created by the economic development of the postwar period, integrated into economic and cultural modernity and identified, dur-ing the 1980s, with democratic and trade-union movements which transcended communitarian frontiers (Bougarel, 1992).

Reflecting thus the changing and unchanging aspects of the Yugoslav socialist system, this communitarian pattern of voting is also rooted in some of the political practicalities of that system. Over a period of forty years, in the absence of political pluralism, the only chance the inhabitants of Yugoslavia had to express a free and individual choice was … in the census. These were held regularly, so that every individual had a regular opportunity to declare his nationality – or to declare no nationality. This fed the rivalries and clientism of the competing political elites, in that the results of the censuses served as a base for the distribution of top posts, according to the principle of the 'national key' (proportional representation of the various national communities).

At the same time, from the 1960s onwards, limited choice was introduced at elec-tions to local and republican legislatures, even if 'the introduction of electoral choice … was a rather manipulated affair: not only was the option of competitive parties, or even competitive socialist parties, ruled out, but the occupational and especially the ethnic backgrounds of candidates were an object of scrutiny and con-trol' (Cohen and Warwick, 1983: 17). With the rare occasions of multiple candida-cies with candidates of different nationalities always ending up with a communitarian voting pattern, the LCY decided never to oppose two candidates unless they were of the same nationality. Thus the 'national key' was effectively enshrined in an *ex ante* division of the seats up for election. While this procedure avoided any underrepresentation of, or open confrontation between, the different communities, it did undoubtedly help to reinforce among Yugoslav electors the notion that they were only represented politically to the extent that they were repre-sented ethnically.

It is hardly surprising, then, that some commentators have described the results of the elections in Bosnia, in all their communitarian starkness, as 'national plebiscites'.[12] It remains for us to try to understand the mechanisms and political consequences of these national plebiscites.

---

[12] E. Habul, in *Oslobodjenje*, 25 November 1990.

The tripartite coalition and the communitarian dismantling of the state

The electoral victory of the nationalist parties was also in part a result of their peculiar political strategies and practices – and in particular their *de facto* electoral alliance. Opposed to the incumbent communists, the three nationalist parties were, in their anti-communism and their championing of the market economy, very close in terms of programmes. They represented, in part at least, political alternatives to the 'civic' parties that had emerged from the League of Communists and its mass organisations.

In more concrete terms, the electoral system adopted, in particular the method of designation of the collective presidency, forcing the nationalist parties into a *de facto* electoral pact. While the seven seats on the presidency were effectively shared out among the various national communities (two Muslims, two Serbs, two Croats and one representative of other nationalities), so that a Muslim, for example, could only stand for one of the two seats reserved for Muslims, each elector had the right to vote on every seat in the presidency, whatever his nationality. The communists had introduced this as a device for moderation in the spring of 1990, reckoning that Serb and Croat votes would prevent the election of a nationalist Muslim candidate, Croat and Muslim votes the election of a nationalist Serb candidate, etc.

Faced with this institutional blockage, the nationalist parties called on their supporters to vote for *all* the nationalist candidates. We should not be surprised, then, that Alija Izetbegović, on the occasion of the founding assembly of the SDS, declared that 'we have been waiting for you for some time – for this Bosnia needs you',[13] and averred, just before the elections, that 'it would be very good if we could establish an SDA-SDS-HDZ coalition in Bosnia, and thus a Muslim-Serb-Croat coalition'.[14] The leaders of the three nationalist parties spoke warmly of each other and exchanged courtesy visits, even as the meetings they organised produced clashes between the respective partisans, at Foča in particular, where interethnic tensions rose to such a pitch that a state of urgency was declared in September 1990. This situation, perceived at the time as tragicomic, is far from being as paradoxical as it appears. In order to mobilise in their favour their respective communities, the leaders of the nationalist parties needed to increase interethnic tension – and to show that they were the only people capable of containing it.

This double strategy was encapsulated in a whole series of *double binds,* outside the context of which it is impossible to understand the rise of nationalism and the outbreak of war in Bosnia. The first of these double binds lies in the difference between the political conception and the everyday conception of community relations. The communitarian alignment at the political level is counterbalanced by the practice of *komšiluk* at the everyday level. The practice of *komšiluk,* on the other hand, represents not so much abstract tolerance or social interaction, as a permanent guarantee of the pacific nature of relations between the communities, and thus of the security of each of them. If political developments place a question-mark over

---

[13] *Oslobodjenje,* 13 July 1990.
[14] *Oslododjenje,* 7 November 1990.

this pacific nature, each community will seek to ensure its security through communitarian mobilisation and isolation, tending in this way to reinforce the general feeling of insecurity and precipitate breakdown in the codes of *komšiluk*.

The pre-election appeal of the SDA is typical of this way of thinking. In it, Alija Izetbegović told Muslim electors:

> Free elections are coming, and with them the day that the Muslim nation has been waiting for for more than a hundred years. This is a historic moment, in which there can be no 'don't knows' or neutrals ... That is why I am asking you to help on that day, by voting for the SDA, for liberty, and for Muslims. The other Yugoslav nations are going to do it for themselves. Why should the Muslims of Yugoslavia be the exception?[15]

It is upon this deep logic of Bosnian society, reminiscent of the sociological theories of the 'prisoner's dilemma' and the 'self-fulfilling prophecy' (see Gosztonyi, 1993), that the nationalist parties based their efforts to mobilise their respective communities, politically and subsequently militarily. And it is this logic that explains how a Bosnian population, which had in mid-1990 pronounced itself 74 per cent in favour of a ban on nationally or confessionally based parties,[16] could, six months later, vote in the same proportion for precisely such parties.

On 18 November 1990, the *de facto* three-party electoral coalition transformed itself into a governmental coalition. The post of chairman of the presidency went to Alija Izetbegović (SDA), and those of prime minister and chairman of the parliament to J. Pelivan (HDZ) and M. Krajišnik (SDS). From government, through ministries down to the majority of communes, the entire Bosnian state apparatus was divided up on the same principle – a veritable caricature of the Titoist 'national key'.

This dividing-up of power and resources soon provoked multiple conflicts over the control of firms, banks, police stations and schools. That in turn produced a progressive paralysis of public institutions and services, a comprehensive dismantling of the state, and was accompanied by the growing criminalisation of economic and political life (nepotism, corruption, 'wild' privatisation, etc.). In June 1991 the minister of the interior, A.Delimustafić (SDA), declared that:

> The minister of the interior is blocked by the three parties in power, or rather by their leaders. Those leaders have insinuated into the ministry 'their' people, cosy but incompetent, who have payed for their 'enthronement' by giving financial support to these parties ... When we arrest one of them, Izetbegović, or Karadžić, or Kljujić calls us and says: 'Don't do that; he's a good Serb, Muslim or Croat, and he's given DM10,000 to the party.' With the Ministry of the Interior parcelled up like that, we will end up with a Lebanon-style police force.[17]

This 'Lebanonisation' of Bosnia finally escalated into a territorial carve-up. At the local level, power conflicts always ended with the break-up of the commune councils, the creation of self-proclaimed, monoethnic communes, or the transfer of particular villages or neighbourhoods to neighbouring communes. At the level of the

---

[15] *Muslimanski Glas*, vol. 1, no. 1.
[16] According to a public opinion poll published in *Danas*, 22 May 1990.
[17] *Oslobodjenje,* 9 June 1991.

republic, the SDS was quick to brandish the threat of a violent partition of Bosnia. D. Balaban, an SDS minister, declared in May 1991:

> If Bosnia becomes an independent and sovereign state, the Serb nation is not going to be a national minority within that state. If that happens, the associated [Serb] communes will break away and create their own autonomous province, with all the functions of a state ... Within 24 hours at least one military unit will be set up in each Serb commune. The Serbs will not allow themselves to be surprised as they were in 1941.[18]

The fact is that, from November 1990, the three nationalist parties were diverging in their conceptions of the future of Yugoslavia. Not surprisingly, the SDS supported the centralist federal proposal put forward by Serbia and Montenegro, and the HDZ the decentralising confederal proposal favoured by Croatia and Slovenia. The SDA, following the JMO line from before the war, concentrated on the preservation of Bosnia as a distinct territorial unit. In the negotiations between the republics, it hedged between the federal and confederal proposals, before finally getting in behind the proposal for an 'assymetrical federation' put forward by Izetbegovic himself and Kiro Gligorov, the Macedonian leader.

The break-up of Yugoslavia in June 1991 brought the issue of the future of Bosnia herself to the forefront. The SDS called for Bosnia to remain within a reduced Yugoslavia, or else be partitioned on an ethnic base. The SDA insisted on the sovereignty and territorial integrity of Bosnia. When, on 15 October 1991, after several months of paralysis, the Bosnian parliament adopted a 'declaration of sovereignty', proposed by the SDA, and supported by the HDZ and the civic parties, the SDS demanded 'the implementation of the right of self-determination – including secession ... and the organisation of plebiscites for the constituent nations of Bosnia – the Serbs, Croats and Muslims'.[19] The SDS leader, Radovan Karadžić, threatened that 'The road you have chosen is the same road that took Croatia into Hell, except that the war in Bosnia will take you into a worse Hell, and the Muslim nation may disappear altogether.'[20]

At the same time, the SDS started to implement its threat to partition Bosnia. Between September and November 1991, six Serbian Autonomous Regions (SAO – *Srpske Autonomne Oblasti*) were proclaimed on Bosnian territory. In these self-proclaimed SAOs, the SDS monopolised the top posts – economic, political and, above all, military (Ministry of the Interior and territorial defence), and started to pursue a policy of discrimination and terror against non-Serb populations. On 26 October 1991 a 'parliament of the Serb nation in Bosnia' was created, made up of SDS deputies and chaired by M. Krajišnik. The self-proclaimed parliament organised on 10 November 1991 a plebiscite of the Serbs of Bosnia, and then announced on 21 December 1991, on the morrow of the official request from Bosnia to the European Community for recognition, the forthcoming creation of a 'Serb Republic of Bosnia-Hercegovina', attached to Yugoslavia.

While the SDS took the logic of communitarian dismantlement of the state to its ultimate conclusion, the other nationalist parties appeared more hesitant. The HDZ

---

[18] *Borba,* 14 May 1991.
[19] *Oslobodjenje,* 15 October 1991.
[20] Ibidem.

declared in favour of the independence and territorial integrity of Bosnia, but in November 1991 created two Croat autonomous regions: Herceg-Bosna (Western Hercegovina and Central Bosnia) and Posavina (Northern Bosnia). This ambiguity on the part of the HDZ was brought into the open after the replacement of Kljujić by Mate Boban as HDZ Bosnia leader on 5 February 1992. The HDZ then demanded a reformulation of the wording of the referendum on self-determination called by the Badinter Commission of the European Community (see below), and scheduled for 29 February and 1 March 1992. The HDZ wanted the referendum question rephrased in terms of 'constituent and sovereign nations' organised 'in their national areas (cantons)',[21] an idea taken up later on by J. Cutilheiro, mediator of the European Community.

This amendment was finally abandoned by the HDZ, in the face of opposition from the Catholic Church and the SDA. The attitude of the HDZ shows, nevertheless, that the result of the referendum of 29 February – 1 March 1992 (63.7 per cent of registered voters and 98.9 per cent of votes cast were in favour of independence, with the SDS having boycotted the poll) was less the product of Bosnian citizenship/statehood triumphant than of a double communitarian mobilisation. The Serbian barricades which appeared on the evening of 1 March 1992 around Sarajevo gave notice that the SDS were moving on to a counter-mobilisation – not just political, but also military.

The SDA also behaved ambiguously, if in another way. Continually and insistently pronouncing in favour of 'a democratic, sovereign state of constitutionally equal citizens and nations in Bosnia,'[22] the SDA boasted of its commitment to a 'civic' Bosnia. But at the same time it supported the partition argument, as advanced outside Bosnia by its branch in Sandjak, a predominantly Muslim area of Serbia and Montenegro. The SDA had proclaimed a Muslim National Council of the Sandjak (*Muslimansko Nacionalno Vjeće Sandžaka*) on 11 May 1991, and then organised a referendum on self-determination on 25 October of the same year. In the face of an omnipresent, repressive apparatus, the SDA can certainly not be accused of discrimination or terror against non-Muslim populations. Rather it was content to homogenise its own population, proposing, for example, that 'a roll of shame, containing the names of all those who work consciously against the general interest of Muslims, should be published regularly in *Muslimanski Glas* [the official SDA publication]. We must isolate these people.'[23]

In Bosnia itself, the desire of the SDA to harness to its advantage the civic discourse did not stop it from participating fully in the communitarian dismantling of the state. While this dismantling reinforced the communitarian clientism and rivalries on which the nationalist parties were based, it also met with strong resistance within Bosnian society. More than the civic parties, courted as they were by the SDA, it was the media, the trade unions and the student and pacifist movement that opposed the progressive intrusion of the nationalist parties into economic, social and cultural life. But those nationalist parties remained unanimous and united in

---

[21] *Borba,* 10 February 1992.
[22] *Oslobodjenje,* 12 October 1991.
[23] *Oslobodjenje,* 16 December 1991.

condemning and snuffing out any sign of an emerging civil society, despite the conflicts which set them at odds with each other and which in April 1992 broke out into an open and bloody war.

The confrontation between the emerging civil society and the nationalist parties in coalition peaked on 5 and 6 April 1992, even as fighting in the suburbs of Sarajevo first started. On 5 April, in response to an appeal from the pacifist movements, the trade unions and the television station, between 60,000 and 100,000 demonstrators massed in front of the Bosnian parliament, booing the parties in power and demanding that new elections be held. Invading the first floor of the parliament, the demonstrators installed a 'committee of national safety'. Condemned in almost identical terms by the SDS and the SDA, isolated by Serbian and Muslim militiamen, who blocked the arrival of convoys of miners and steel-workers from Tuzla, Zenica and Kakanj, abandoned by the civic parties, the demonstration was dispersed on the afternoon of 6 April 1992 by SDS snipers deployed on the roof of the Holiday Inn. (SDA snipers may also have been involved. See Vuković, 1993.) On 9 April 1992 the 'committee of national safety' dissolved itself. That was the last play of the emerging Bosnian civil society in its efforts to remove communitarianism from the political sphere. Momentarily disoriented, the nationalist parties wreaked their vengeance by bringing war into everyday life.

The events of 5–6 April 1992 throw into relief the internal causes and dimensions of the war in Bosnia, a civil war in the true sense of the word, in the sense that it was a war against civilian populations, against civil society. In using the term civil war, we do not ignore the external causes and dimensions of the conflict, the dimension of a war of territorial conquest. But by concentrating on the internal dimension, we can better situate those external dimensions within the complexity, the communitarian logic, of the Bosnian crisis.

In 1990 Franjo Tudjman, president of Croatia, put forward a proposal for what amounted to a Serb-Croat partition of Bosnia, as a solution to the Serb-Croat conflict. This proposal was apparently discussed at a secret meeting between Tudjman and Milošević on 25 March 1991, and then put to Izetbegović at meetings on 12 and 19 June 1991. But that does not mean that Serbia and Croatia had stable and unambigious policies towards Bosnia. In June 1991, Serbia was supporting an ephemeral 'historic Serb-Muslim accord', concluded between the SDS and the MBO, and guaranteeing Bosnia's territorial integrity within a reduced Yugoslavia. On 21 May 1992 Croatia and Bosnia signed at Zagreb a political and military cooperation agreement; two weeks previously, at a secret meeting in Graz, Boban and Karadžić had been mapping out the foundations of a Serb-Croat territorial compromise on Bosnia.

On the military side, the JNA had, apparently, prepared a plan for the military occupation of Bosnia, under the name RAM, as early as 1991. But the JNA was divided between a Greater-Serbian element, which openly supported the SDS and its militias, and a Titoist element, which tended to think of Bosnia as a last refuge in case of confrontation with Milošević.[24] The meetings of Izetbegović with Yugoslav

---

[24] On the role of the JNA in the Yugoslav crisis see Gow, 1992, and Chapter 7 in this volume.

Defence Minister, Veljko Kadijević, in December 1991, and with the commander of the Sarajevo military district, M. Kukanjac, in January 1992, suggested that Izetbegović was himself inclined to seek a *rapprochement* with this latter element. For the rest, where the RAM plan envisaged the provocation of interethnic incidents and the occupation of strategic points by the JNA, it looked mainly to the SDS militias, recruited among the Serb population of Bosnia. The paramilitary formations of the other nationalist parties, such as the Patriotic League, created by the SDA in March 1991, were largely staffed by Croat and Muslim officers who had deserted the JNA.

From the dismantling of the state to the disintegration of the communities

On 7 April 1992, the new 'Serb Republic of Bosnia-Hercegovina' was proclaimed at Pale, a village outside Sarajevo. The SDS proceeded to recall its two representatives from the collective presidency, and appealed to Serbian ministers, civil servants and policemen to break with the Bosnian state, recognised the previous day by the European Community and the US. On 19 May 1992 the formal withdrawal from Bosnia of the JNA, required by the Security Council, was counterbalanced by the creation of an Army of the Serb Republic (VRS – *Vojska Republike Srpske*), which brought together units of the JNA, the territorial defence organisations of the SAOs and a multitude of local militias. Assisted by the militias of Z. Arnjatović (Arkan) and V. Šešelj from Serbia, the Serb army thus fashioned already controlled more than 60 per cent of the territory of Bosnia. It had within the range of its guns the lines of communication and cities of Bosnia – including Sarajevo.

On 8 April 1992 the collective presidency of Bosnia decreed the mobilisation of the republican territorial army and gave the countless militias which had sprung up all over the territory of Bosnia one week to integrate into it. The same day, a Croatian Defence Council (HVO – *Hrvatsko Vjeće Odbrane*) was set up, and on 3 July 1992 a 'Croatian Community of Herceg-Bosna', bringing together all the territories controlled by the HVO. On 5 July 1992 the collective presidency announced the creation of the Army of Bosnia and Hercegovina (ABH – *Armija Bosne i Hercegovine*) as the sole armed force of the young Bosnian state, after the HVO had rejected a proposal to regroup with the Bosnian territorial army under a single command.

What exactly did this Bosnian state represent? Its authority, rejected by the Serb Republic and recognised in a purely formal way by the Croat Herceg-Bosna, did not exercise control over more than 10–15 per cent of the territory of Bosnia. If that fact is largely explained by the military situation, the policy of the SDA was certainly a subsidiary factor. The SDA obstinately refused, in the course of the first, decisive weeks of the war, to create a government of national unity, or to transfer the government to Tuzla, a town controlled by the civic parties. Only on 31 May 1992 did the SDA finally accept the conditions set by the civic parties, in particular the resignation of Izetbegović from the presidency of the SDA and the formation of a new government.

The final entry of the civic parties into the collective presidency (M. Pejanović and N. Kecmanović, quickly replaced by L. Ljuić-Mijatović) and into a reshuffled Pelivan government, barely concealed the perpetuation of communitarian behaviour. At the institutional level, the HDZ accepted the dominance of Izetbegović's entourage within the presidency and the government. In exchange, the SDA tolerated the dominance of the HVO in Hercegovina and Central Bosnia. This division of power between the SDA and the HDZ would hold up the establishment of an effective state in Bosnia for many long months.

The renewed coalition between two of the nationalist parties revealed its fragility and absurdity as relations between the ABH and the HVO soured at the local level. In May 1992 the issue of control over arms factories and depots had already begun to lead to violent clashes. From September 1992 confrontations between the ABH and the HVO in Central Bosnia grew more frequent. In the territories under their control, the HVO began to follow a policy towards the Muslim population that was increasingly discriminatory and intimidatory. As late as November 1992, however, Izetbegović condemned the creation in Mostar of a Council of Muslims of Hercegovina (*Vjeće Muslimana Hercegovine*), opposed to the HDZ, and ratified the formation of a new Bosnian government under the leadership of M. Akmadžić (HDZ) and the (unconstitutional) replacement of S. Kljujić by M. Lazić (HDZ) in the collective presidency. The representatives of the HDZ, it must be said, subsequently accepted the constitutionally dubious reappointment of Izetbegović to the chairmanship of the collective presidency.

An extension of the communitarian dismantling of the state, the war also played the role of destroyer of Bosnian society itself, through the medium of ethnic cleansing (*Le Nouvel Observateur/Reporters sans Frontières*, 1992). The systematic practice of both the Serb Army and the HVO of Hercegovina, ethnic cleansing does not aim only to put the conquest of a given territory beyond doubt and guarantee ethnic homogeneity. The invariable initiators of ethnic cleansing were militias coming from outside. But these militias always sought the participation of local people – *in despite of the spirit of komšiluk, and indeed with the precise aim of destroying that spirit.* Thus good neighbourliness turned, in many cases, into intimate murder. Ethnic cleansing aimed to destroy everything that might be an obstacle and a counterweight to the rationale of extremist communitarianism and nationalism. That explains why cleansers sometimes imposed ethnic cleansing on their own group. The HVO, for instance, put pressure on Croats to leave Central Bosnia. It also explains why urban populations identified the preservation of multiethnicity with resistance to the totalitarianism of the ethnic and mafia militias.

Ethnic cleansing was accompanied by the systematic pillage and blackmail of civilian populations, thus creating a predatory economy such as is characteristic of Bosnia in wartime. The various military formations in effect obtained their essential resources from plunder. Some of the forms that this plunder took, such as looting and extortion, can be rationalised in terms of communitarian extremism. Others tended in exactly the opposite direction. In particular, the imposition of levies on humanitarian aid and supplies to besieged towns was based, to a greater or lesser extent, on cooperation between military formations theoretically opposed to each other. Either way, the militia economy impoverished civilian populations and weakened the internal cohesion of the communities.

The idea of an alliance for the defence of the territorial integrity of Bosnia between the SDA and the HDZ, between the ABH and the HVO, was always an illusion. The territorial compromise sketched out by Karadžić and Boban at Graz on 6 May 1992 was translated, in the months that followed, into a voluntary retreat on the part of the HVO from the towns of Bosanski Brod and Jajce, in return for the JNA giving back Prevlaka, on the Croatian-Montenegrin border, to the Croats. On 4 April 1993 the HVO gave notice to the ABH to quit the territories specified in the Vance–Owen plan as Croatian provinces. The conflict between the two 'allies' then burst into the open with the destruction of the HVO at Zenica and Travnik, and the encirclement of the ABH in the eastern part of Mostar. The Croat enclaves in Central Bosnia (Žepče, Vareš, Vitez and Kiseljak) could hardly have resisted without increasingly open support from the Serbian army.

This reversal of alliances was a function of both military and local economic considerations. While the HVO at Žepče cooperated openly with the Serbian army, at Tešanj and Posavina, a few dozen kilometres to the north, it was integrating into the ABH. The Serbian army, which hired out tanks and heavy artillery to the HVO at Vareš and Kiseljak, hired out the same to the besieged Bosnian army at Mostar. These increasingly localised and criminalised military configurations, the chopping-up of the territories under Bosnian and Croat control into a multitude of isolated enclaves, inevitably led to the progressive social and political disintegration of the communities themselves.

In order to understand this paradoxical phenomenon, we have to recall the internal conflicts that wrack each of the national communities in Bosnia. The most deep-seated of these are, without a doubt, of a regional nature. Within each nationalist party there exist veritable regional lobbies, with invariably divergent interests. There are multiple lobbies within the SDA – Sarajevo, Central Bosnia, Hercegovina, Cazinska Krajina and Sandjak. Within the SDS there is the Bosanska Krajina lobby, centred on Banja Luka and also involving a breakaway from the SDS – the SDS-*Otadžbinski Front* (Patriotic Front); an East-Hercegovinian lobby led by B. Vučurević; and the Eastern Bosnia lobby, tightly controlled by the centre at Pale, and by Karadžić himself. The HDZ was divided into two main lobbies: Central Bosnia, represented by Kljujić, and Western Hercegovina, led by Boban. As already noted, the latter was able to take overall control in February 1992.

These regional conflicts, momentarily masked by the war, were exacerbated by the breakdown of communications and the differences in the situation in the various regions that resulted from that. To this must be added, in the Muslim and Croat cases, the repercussions of the conflict between the ABH and the HVO on relations between the nationalist parties and the religious authorities. Both the *Islamska Zajednica* and the Catholic Church condemned the Croat-Muslim clashes, and held the leaders of the SDA and the HDZ responsible. While the SDA managed, in April 1993, to oust the *Reis-ul-Ulema*, J. Selimovski, and to regain control of the *Islamska Zajednica,* the Catholic Church and the Franciscan Order continued to be important focal points for the Croatian political forces opposed to Boban and Tudjman.

While the presentation of the Vance–Owen plan on 2 January 1993 was probably a factor exacerbating the latent Croat-Muslim conflict, its replacement by the 'Washington Programme' on 22 May 1993, in turn replaced by the Owen–Stoltenberg plan on 29 July 1993, was certainly the detonator of an explosion within the Muslim community. As the prospect of military intervention receded, and the idea of a partition of Bosnia into three units, proposed on 16 June 1993 at a meeting between Milošević and Tudjman, was taken up by the international community, a grave crisis broke within the collective presidency of Bosnia. At the heart of the crisis lay a clash between those who wanted to carry on with negotiations, and those who wanted to break them off, between those who stood by the territorial integrity of Bosnia, and those who gave their conditional support to the idea of partition.[25] At the same time, the central power was increasingly being challenged by the supporters of Abdić in Cazinska Krajina, and by some of the civic elements in Sarajevo and Tuzla. The Muslim population itself, exhausted by the mindless bombardment of the towns, the terror inflicted by some gangster elements within the ABH and the cutting-off of humanitarian aid, and demoralised by the defeat on Mount Igman in August 1993, was sinking into defeatism.[26]

Izetbegović was thus compelled to adopt a compromise position, based on a reconvening of the negotiations at Geneva and conditional acceptance of the Owen–Stoltenberg plan. He declared to the Bosnian parliament on 27 August 1993: 'Our task today is to save what we can of Bosnia. That is our task here and now – so that, perhaps, at some point in the future, the whole of Bosnia may be saved. There is, however, no reason to be defeatist. We have not been conquered and they are not conquerers.' He then went on to enumerate his conditions for acceptance of the Owen–Stoltenberg plan (outlets to the sea and the river Sava, the restitution of territories which had a Muslim majority in 1992, military guarantees from NATO and the present of American troops).[27]

The compromise position was adopted by the Bosnian parliament on 29 August 1993, and confirmed by it one month later. All this helped to stave off the inevitable confrontation between an SDA increasingly tempted by the idea of partition, and the civic parties, still attached to the idea of territorial integrity, though for that reason little inclined to deprive the Bosnian state of the modicum of reality and legitimacy it still had. But the compromise position also addressed the desire for immediate peace now dominant within the civilian population, and it was through this that Abdić tried to apply pressure.

In July 1993 Abdić had appealed publicly to Izetbegović to accept the Owen–Stoltenberg plan, on the grounds that 'the prosecution of this bloody war could result in the physical disappearance of our people'.[28] In September he accused Izetbegović of 'bellicosity', and called for a referendum on the Owen–Stoltenberg plan.[29] Failing to obtain the political support he expected in the rest of Bosnia,

---

[25] It should be noted that the lines of division were not identical on the two issues.

[26] The journalist E. Stitkovac, generally well informed, reports that there were pacifist demonstrations in Tuzla and Zenica in September 1993. See *Borba,* 1 November 1993.

[27] *Ljiljan,* no. 33, 1 September 1993.

[28] *Oslobodjenje* (European edition), no. 20, 30 July 1993.

[29] *Borba,* 6 September 1993.

Abdić proclaimed an 'autonomous province of Western Bosnia' on 27 September 1993. A few days later the first armed clashes between Abdić's supporters and members of the V Corps of the ABH still loyal to Izetbegović occurred. At this moment, the Muslim community was on the verge of implosion.

But it was not the only community to experience this kind of internal difficulty. The acceptance of the Owen–Stoltenberg plan by the parliaments of the Serb Republic and Herceg-Bosna also provoked strong reactions within the Serb and Croat communities, in particular in the territories that would have to be ceded. Local governments and populations appealed to national mythologies in attacking the policies of their nationalist leaders. While the authorities in Livno and Stolac accused Boban of wanting to install on 'sacred Croatian soil ... the [green] flag whose very colour burns our eyes',[30] the war widows of Kupres rejected the cession by the Serb Republic of 'territories ethnically Serb for centuries, strategically important and with an exceptional economic potential, and strewn with communal graves containing more than 10,000 Serbs whose throats were slit by Ustasha hands'.[31]

The most serious internal problems of the Serb Republic and Herceg-Bosna, however, were related to the militia economy and the impoverishment of the civilian population. On 10 September 1993 two brigades of the Serb army rose up and took control of Banja Luka. The leaders of these 'September 93' mutineers issued a communiqué, complaining bitterly that the Serb fighters 'have become beggars and foreigners in their own country; while we fight ... slick manipulators lead a comfortable and fashionable life at the rear – with the blessing of the ruling power, amassing their fortunes and implementing their dark political designs', and proceeded to arrest 'war profiteers.'[32]

The exact origins and circumstances of the mutiny at Banja Luka, which fizzled out after a week without having achieved any significant results, remain obscure. It certainly reflected an exacerbation of the hostility of the Krajina Serbs towards those of Eastern Bosnia, the urban Serbs of Banja Luka towards Pale, the 'capital' of the Serb Republic. It was accompanied by demonstrations of discontent in a number of other units of the Serb army, and among the civilian population, directed against the 'war profiteers' and the leaders of the SDS.

The fact that the 'September 93' mutiny and the proclamation of the 'autonomous province of Western Bosnia' happened almost simultaneously may be fortuitous. But it does underline the similarities in the process of disintegration under way within the various national communities of Bosnia. Izetbegović commented on Abdić's secession in Cazinska Krajina thus: 'The Muslims have finally reached the state of becoming a political nation, capable of creating its own state. I think that here we have an attempt to turn the clock back fifty years, to divide us up into tribes again, with one tribe in Krajina, one in Tuzla and, finally, one in Sarajevo.'[33] Faced with the risk of a total political and military collapse of the Muslim community, the

---

[30] *Borba,* 8 September 1993.
[31] *Borba,* 3 September 1993.
[32] *Borba,* 11 September 1993.
[33] *Oslobodjenje* (European edition), no. 30, 8 October 1993.

SDA was left with the task of re-establishing a state which it itself had helped to destroy.

Return of the state, return of the communities?

On 25 October 1993 the collective presidency of Bosnia dismissed Messrs Boras, Lazić and Abdić from its membership, and coopted in their place N. Duraković, chairman of the ex-communist SDP, I. Komšić, former vice-chairman of the SDP and then chairman of the Croat Peasant Party (HSS – *Hrvatska Seljačka Stranka*) of Bosnia from its creation in April 1993, and S. Kljujić. The same day it asked Haris Silajdžić (SDA), incumbent minister of foreign affairs, to form a new government.

The formation of the Silajdžić government signalled the replacement of the SDA-HDZ coalition by a coalition between the SDA and the civic parties, and a rejigging of the connections betweeen the central government and the regions through the nomination of four ministers responsible for regional coordination (Tuzla, Zenica, Mostar and Bihać). Among the priorities of the new government, Silajdžić mentioned, on taking power:

> the survival of the population, for hunger and cold threaten the population throughout the free territory … the reinforcement of the capacity of the country to defend itself, and in particular of the ABH … the revival of industry and the reactivation of commercial and financial circuits … [for] a time of war demands a war economy … protection of human rights and the reinforcement of legality and security of property … [for] every act of violence, injustice or illegality against individuals … gives rise to a feeling of general insecurity among the citizenry.[34]

The reassertion of the power of the state was symbolised by the elimination, on 26 October 1993, of two mafia commanders: M. Topalović-Caco and R. Delalić-Ćelo, who had been blackmailing and terrorising the civilian population in Sarajevo. The same day, S. Halilović, commander of the ABH until June 1993 and representing the important Sandjak lobby within it, was placed under house arrest. The reassertion of government power extended throughout the territory under Bosnian control. Several military commanders were replaced and a number of maverick units, like the 'Green Legion' and the 'Dagger Division' in Central Bosnia, were integrated into the ABH.

Not known for his sympathies with Marshal Tito, Izetbegović declared around the same time on Bosnian television:

> We must learn the lessons of everything that was good in the last war … When the Chetniks and Ustashas arrived, the population fled, because these were armies which killed civilians. When the Partisans arrived, they did not flee … The Partisans were brutal, and very tough on their enemies, but it is a fact that they did not kill women and children. And that is why they won. We must never forget that, and we must draw the lessons. We will win if we have the reputation of being an army which does not kill women and children. We must be what the Partisans were. We must be a *people's army.*

---

[34] *Oslobodjenje* (European edition), no. 34, 5 November 1993.

On the territory controlled by the ABH we must create an area in which the rule of law holds, in which civilisation is preserved, and in which democracy reigns and the simple rule that no one should be persecuted for his religious or national identity, his political convictions is observed. We must realise this model within the Bosnian state ... By the force of this political model, we could banish the shadows in which some parts of Bosnia live, and will live for some time to come ... and that will open the way to the reintegration of Bosnia.[35]

In reality, the re-establishment of the Bosnian state was accompanied by a reassertion of SDA control over everything. Perhaps here, too, Izetbegović found some inspiration from Marshal Tito. The SDA was, certainly, in a minority within the collective presidency. But the main function of that latter body was international legitimisation. The real executive was elsewhere – in the Silajdžić government, largely controlled by the SDA, and within which the ministries responsible for regional coordination were all the leaders of the SDA in the regions concerned.

This process of reining-in the regions – where ex-communists had retained a significant degree of power, in the economy and in the police – was also evident in the army. Not content to monopolise the top army posts in the political field and in relation to morale, the SDA managed, following the November 1993 reshuffles, to gain control of a majority of corps commands. On 25 and 26 March 1994 R. Delić, the commander of the ABH, attended the first session of the SDA leadership to be held in Sarajevo since April 1992. On this occasion B. Alispahić, minister of the interior, and F. Muslimović, chief of military security, were coopted on to the party leadership.

The session of the Bosnian parliament which, on 29 September 1993, reiterated its conditional support for the Owen–Stoltenberg plan was preceded by a session of a novel political institution – the Bosnian Assembly (*Bošnjački Sabor*). Composed of representatives of various organizations within the Muslim community (*Islamska Zajednica,* the Congress of Muslim Intellectuals, *Preporod,* etc.), the Bosnian Assembly is in fact largely controlled by the SDA. It decided at its inaugural session to abandon the name *Musliman* in favour of that of *Bošnjak*,[36] and to offer conditional approval of the Owen–Stoltenberg plan. The subsequent vote of the Bosnian parliament in great measure simply ratified that of the *Sabor.*

The existence and role of the *Bošnjački Sabor* shows that the re-establishment of the Bosnian state was not marked by any break with communitarianism, but rather by a reorganisation of the communities by the state. In the months that followed, an Assembly of Croats of Bosnia and Hercegovina (*Sabor Hrvata Bosne i Hercegovine*), presided over by I. Komšić, and a Serbian Civic Council (*Srpsko Gradjansko Vjeće),* presided over by M. Pejanović, were held in Sarajevo. These two structures, by their nature communitarian, for all their claims about a 'civic' Bosnia, purport to represent the Croat and Serb populations of the territories under Bosnian control. Created from above, and with the support of the Bosnian state, these institutions give that state a basis for contesting the representativeness of the self-proclaimed parliaments of Herceg-Bosna and the Serb Republic.

---

[35] *Oslobodjenje,* 26 November 1993.
[36] See footnote 11.

The Croat-Muslim Federation: one state or two?

This rally on the part of the Muslim community was soon translated into a reversal of fortunes in the Croat-Muslim clashes. The fall of Vareš, in November 1993, reduced Croatian territory in Central Bosnia to a few isolated and exhausted enclaves. The intervention of the Croatian army certainly saved Herceg-Bosna from total military defeat. But it precipitated an internal political crisis within the Croatian community. In Croatia itself, the opposition parties accused the Croatian defence minister, Gojko Šušak, the principal representative of the Hercegovinian lobby in Zagreb, of having sacrificed the Croat populations of Central Bosnia on the altar of Herceg-Bosnia. The only organisations/individuals concerning themselves with the protection of civilian populations in Central Bosnia by this time were the Catholic Church and the Croat representatives in the collective presidency.

Meanwhile Croatia was, in its turn, being threatened with economic sanctions by the UN. At this point, events began to move very fast. On 8 February 1994 Mate Boban was replaced as head of Herceg-Bosna by Krešimir Zubak. On 10 February 1994, after a murderous bombardment of Sarajevo, NATO threatened the Serbian army with aerial strikes if they did not pull their heavy artillery back from Sarajevo. The Serbs conformed to the ultimatum before its expiry on 21 February 1994. Finally, in Washington on 1 March 1994, Haris Silajdžić and Mate Granić, the Croatian minister of foreign affairs, signed accords putting an end to the Croat-Muslim conflict and establishing a Croat-Muslim Federation, itself confederated to Croatia.

It was thus the internal political crisis within the Muslim and Croat communities themselves that paved the way for the creation of the Croat-Muslim Federation. But while its creation represented the first indication of the possibility of a reconstitution of Bosnia, the Croat-Muslim Federation has shown itself to be in practice a limited exercise. It amounts to no more than the setting-up of an institutional mechanism, ever more complex, but at the same time inefficient, and the establishment of military cooperation between two armies that remain distinct. The superimposition of one political entity on another (Republic of Bosnia-Hercegovina, Croat-Muslim Federation, Republic of Herceg-Bosna), the monopolisation or paralysis of institutions at the local level, shows that the Croat-Muslim Confederation is not the final word in the process of constitution of national entities on Bosnian territory.

The HVO had by now been effectively absorbed by the Croatian army, and Herceg-Bosna integrated into Croatian economic and monetary space. In the territories under Bosnian control, non-Muslim staff were progressively replaced in the administration and the army, and the representatives of the civic parties again marginalised in the collective presidency. On 3 August 1995 the SDA pushed a major constitutional amendment through the Bosnian parliament: the chairman of the presidency, hitherto chosen by his peers on the basis of the principle of rotation, would now be elected by Parliament and the post effectively reserved for a Muslim.

In the mixed cantons and the villages affected by ethnic cleansing, the SDA and the HDZ have competed for the control of local institutions and, through those, of the territories themselves. At the global level, they have recognised each other's right to rule over the respective populations and are united in snuffing out any 'civic' aspirations. Thus this new coalition between nationalist parties threatens the last refuges of 'civic' Bosnia – and ultimately also the Croat-Muslim Federation itself, as is evident from the attacks by the SDA and the HDZ on prime minister Silajdžić, its principal architect. The process of the destruction of Bosnian society has continued just the same. The pace of the return of victims of ethnic cleansing has remained slow, while the exodus of Serb and Croat populations from territories under Bosnian control is accelerating.

The Serb Republic in crisis

Parallel with all this, the internal political crisis of the Serb community, brought into sharp relief by the Banja Luka mutiny of September 1993, has grown ever deeper. While the Bosnian state has managed, more or less, to reorganise its economy, the economies of the Serb Republic and of Serbia and Montenegro have been strangled from the outslide by the economic sanctions decreed by the UN in May 1992, and undermined from the inside by a criminalisation of the economy beyond measure. This is reflected in the fragmentation of the apparatus of state, to the advantage of informal and gangster networks, the material and moral exhaustion of the army, and an inexorable demographic decline, due in equal measure to the systematic expulsion of non-Serb populations and to individual strategies of escapism among the Serb population itself.

Serbia, eager to obtain a lifting of sanctions, as a condition of economic recovery and therefore also of the long-term maintenance of her military superiority, pressed the leaders of the Serb Republic to accept the new peace plan proposed in July 1994 by the 'Contact Group'. When, one month later, the Serb Republic rejected the plan, Serbia imposed her own economic embargo on her erstwhile client. While the embargo was not systematically enforced, it marked a rupture betweeen Serbia and the Serb Republic and shattered the political cohesion of the latter. The handful of members of the Serb Republic 'parliament' belonging to civic parties at this point formed an independent parliamentary group led by Milorad Dodik, the member for Banja Luka,[37] while a number of other parties opposed to the SDS were reconstituted or reactivated.

In spring 1995 the first Serb military reverses in Croatia (Western Slavonia) and in Bosnia (Mount Vlasić and the Livno plateau) exacerbated the internal conflicts in the Serb community. Within the structure of the Serb Republic, the political and regional dissensions already present were further complicated by a clash between the political apparatus, dominated by the local notables grouped around Radovan Karadžić, and the military hierarchy under the command of General Ratko Mladić. In April 1995 Mladić told the 'parliament' of the Serb Republic that they must choose, while there was still time, between the proclamation of a 'state of war', with a view to facing up to the military confrontations of the future, and acceptance

---

[37] In November 1990 Dodik had been elected on the list of the League of Reform Forces (*Savez Reformskih Snaga*), led in Bosnia by Nenad Kecmanović, Serbian candidate for the collective presidency, and Selim Beslagić, Muslim mayor of Tuzla.

of a territorial compromise. Sunk in their dreams of power and their financial scams, the Serb members took no notice of the warning.

Like the period February–March 1994, that between May and September 1995 was thus marked by a brutal acceleration of the course of events. In May, 300 members of UNPROFOR were taken hostage, in retaliation against the NATO aerial strikes that followed the bombing of the Tuzla market place. Then in July the destruction of the Muslim enclaves of Srebrenica and Žepa seemed to indicate continued superiority, and indeed invincibility, on the part of the Serb army. But it was these actions that led to the adoption of a plan for massive aerial strikes by the 'Contact Group' (London conference, 21 July 1995), and to the reinforcement of military cooperation between the Croatian army, the Bosnian army and the HVO, under the Split Agreement of 22 July 1995.

When, at the end of July 1995, the armies of the Serb Republic and the Serb Republic of Krajina, supported by the forces of Fikret Abdić, tried to take the Muslim enclave of Bihać, a Croatian offensive swept away the Serb Republic of Krajina and the 'Autonomous Province of Western Bosnia' in the space of a few days, lifting the three-year siege on Bihać. One month latter, on 28 August 1995, another terrible bombardment of Sarajevo provoked massive aerial strikes against Serb military infrastructures. The Bosnian and Croatian armies took advantage of this to break through the front line, which had remained practically unchanged since the autumn of 1992, and take, in the space of a few weeks, 15–20 per cent of the territory of Bosnia. On 5 October 1995 a ceasefire was negotiated on the basis of this new front line.

The extraordinary rapidity of the reversal of the military situation precipitated an internal political crisis within the Serb Republic. In August 1995 the conflict between the political apparatus and the military hierarchy came out into the open, with Mladić being dismissed by Karadžić, and Mladić refusing to go, fortified by the support of his officer corps. In October, with Banja Luka seething with refugees, the 'Patriotic Front', consisting of a number of opposition parties and supported by the army, demanded the resignation of Karadžić. Karadžić then withdrew to the Sarajevo region, where he managed to regain control of the army, but with Banja Luka and the region around it slipping away from him, and eastern Hercegovina proclaiming its autonomy. It was now the turn of the Serb Republic to be threatened with implosion.

Turnabouts and continuities

The military turnabout of summer 1995 went hand-in-hand with a diplomatic turnabout. In July, an American mediator, Richard Holbrooke, replaced the EU and UN mediators and put forward a new peace plan. In September, the Geneva and New York accords provided the basis of an institutional and territorial compromise in Bosnia. Three weeks of difficult negotiations at Dayton (USA), 1–21 November 1995, produced a number of agreements on the various conflicts born of the Yugoslav crisis, most importantly on the Bosnian conflict. The Dayton agreements, which should, in principle, put an end to that conflict, were signed in Paris on 14 December 1995.

It remains for us to try to understand the exact nature of these turnarounds. Over the period 1992–95 the various military offensives affected the conflict less by their results on the ground than by the crises and political regroupings they provoked. In the same way, while the territorial collapse of the two Serb Republics was certainly a reflection of military exhaustion, it was undoubtedly amplified, even precipitated, by the Serb armies themselves.[38] The evolution of the political configurations of the conflict, between and within communities, remains more important than the balance of military power itself.

The offensives of the summer of 1995 set in train political realignments which were no less pregnant with significance for the future for having passed largely unnoticed. The disappearance of the Serb Republic of Krajina removed the principal obstacle to a rapprochement between Serbia and Croatia – while the issue of control over the territories recaptured by the Croat and Bosnian armies turned into a new source of tension within the Croat-Muslim Federation. The fragmentation of the Serb Republic seemed likely to increase the chances of it being taken under direct control by Serbia – which would be perfectly consistent with the whole pattern of the Bosnian conflict.

In the same way, at the international level, the American mediator Holbrooke's plan in practice went back to the basic dispositions of the plan put forward by the 'Contact Group', to wit a territorial partition between the Croat-Muslim Federation (51 per cent) and the Serb Republic (49 per cent), and the establishment of confederal links between those two units and Croatia, on the one hand, and Serbia on the other. It must be said that in creating a common institutional framework for the Croat-Muslim Federation and the Serb Republic, the Holbrooke plan simply adds another layer to the pyramid of concurrent sovereignties which is Bosnia. In other words, the Dayton agreements are likely to be difficult to implement and may, if the experience of the Croat-Muslim Federation is anything to go by, simply result in the creation of homogeneous and separate ministates.

Finally, the movements of the Serb population, provoked by the offensive of the Croat and Bosnian armies, the scorched earth policy and the installation of other displaced populations in the territories recovered, also reflect this logic of the dismantling of society which has animated and dominated the Bosnian conflict since the beginning. The Dayton agreements envisage, certainly, the disappearance of the term 'Herceg-Bosna' and the gradual reunification of the Croatian and Muslim parts of Mostar. But though they establish the Serb Republic as a recognised political unit, they also predicate the immediate return of the Serb quarters of Sarajevo to the Bosnian authorities, which carries with it a grave risk of a massive exodus of Serbs from that city. While the Dayton agreements represent an important stage in the Bosnian conflict, they do not guarantee a durable cessation of hostilities. They are more likely to lead to a definitive dismantling of Bosnian society than to its progressive reintegration.

---

[38] We may note that in September 1995 the Serb forces managed to hold on to strategically important points which were difficult to defend, like Doboj and Brčko, even while they were retreating elsewhere; and that the result of the changes in the front line was a reduction in the proportion of Bosnian territory held by the Serb Republic to around 50 per cent. We may speculate, therefore, that the territories lost were of limited interest to the Serbs in the perspective of the likely pattern of the territorial partition of Bosnia.

References

Andrić, Ivo (1987) Letter from 1920. In *Titanic et Autres Contes Juifs* (Paris: Belfond).

Banac, Ivo (1984) *The National Question in Yugoslavia: Origins, History, Politics* (Ithaca, NY: Cornell University Press).

Behschnitt, Wolfgang (1980) *Nationalismus bei Serben und Kroaten 1830–1914* (Munich: Oldenburg).

Bougarel, Xavier (1992) Bosnie-Herzégovine: anatomie d'une poudrière, *Hérodote*, no. 67.

Burg, Steven (1983) *Conflict and Cohesion in Socialist Yugoslavia* (Princeton: Princeton University Press).

Cohen, Leonard (1989) *The Socialist Pyramid. Elites and Power in Yugoslavia* (New York and London: Mosaic).

Cohen, Leonard and Warwick, Paul (1983) *Political Cohesion in a Fragile Mosaic. The Yugoslav Experience* (Boulder: Westview).

Čupić-Amrein, Maria (1987) *Die Opposition gegen die Österreichische-Hungarische Herrschaft in Bosnien-Herzegowina* (Bern: Peter Lang).

Denitch, Bohdan (1976) *The Legitimation of a Revolution. The Yugoslav Case* (New Haven CT: Yale University Press).

Dizdarević, Svebor (1993) Les présupposés inacceptables du plan Vance–Owen, *Le Monde Diplomatique*, February.

Donia, Robert (1981) *Islam under the Double Eagle* (Boulder: Columbia University Press).

Goati, Vladimir (1992a) Les effets de la démocratie majoritaire, *Peuples Méditerranées*, no. 61, October.

Goati, Vladimir (1992b) Politički život Bosne i Hercegovine 1989–1992. In S. Bogosavljević (ed.) *Bosna i Hercegovina Izmedju Rata i Mira* (Belgrade: IDN).

Golubović, Zagorka (1986) *La Crise de la Société Yougoslave* (Paris: Index).

Gosztonyi, Kristof (1993) Nationalitätenkonflikte in ehemals sozialistischen Ländern. Ein spieltheoretisches Model, *Ost-Europa*, no. 93, July.

Gow, James (1992) *Legitimacy and the Military. The Yugoslav Crisis* (London: Pinter).

Jelavich, Barbara and Jelavich, Charles (1963) *The Balkans in Transition* (Berkeley, Los Angeles: University of California Press).

Karpat, Kemal (1963) *An Inquiry into the Social Foundations of Nationalism in the Balkans* (Princeton: Princeton University Press).

Krulić, Joseph (1993) *Histoire de la Yougoslavie* (Brussels: Complexe).

Le Nouvel Observateur/Reporters sans Frontières (1992) *Le Livre de l'Ex-Yougoslavie. Purification Ethnique et Crimes de Guerre* (Paris: Arléa).

Maliqi, Shkelzen (1989) Kosovo kao katalizator jugoslovenske krize. In S. Gaber (ed.) *Kosovo-Srbija-Jugoslavija* (Ljubljana: ZSMS).

Mantran, Robert (ed.) (1989) *Histoire de l'Empire Ottoman* (Paris: Fayard).

Pawlovitch, Stefan (1988) *Yugoslavia: the Improbable Survivor* (London: Hurst).

Purivatra, Atif (1969a) *JMO u Političkom Životu Kraljevine Srba, Hrvata i Slovenaca* (Sarajevo: Svjetlost).

Purivatra, Atif (1969b) *Nacionalni i Politički Razvitak Muslimana* (Sarajevo: Svjetlost).

Ramet, Pedro (1984) *Nationalism and Federalism in Yugoslavia* (Bloomington: Indiana University Press).

Ramet, Pedro (ed.) (1985) *Yugoslavia in the 80s* (Boulder: Westview).

Redžić, Enver (1987) *Muslimansko Automastvo i 13. SS Divizija* (Sarajevo: Svjetlost).

Rusinow, Denny (1977) *The Yugoslav Experiment* (London: Hurst).

Sekelj, Laszlo (1990) *Struktura Raspadanja Jugoslavije* (Belgrade: Rad).

Shoup, Paul (1968) *Communism and the Yugoslav National Question* (New York and London: Columbia University Press).

Sugar, Peter (1973) *The Industrialisation of Bosnia-Hercegovina 1878–1918* (Washington DC: University of Washington Press).

Sugar, Peter (1974) *Southeastern Europe under Ottoman Rule 1354–1804* (Washington DC: University of Washington Press).

Tomasevitch, Jozo (1955) *Peasants, Politics and Economic Change in Yugoslavia* (Stanford and Oxford: Stanford University Press).

Vuković, Željko (1993) *Ubijanje Sarajeva* (Belgrade: Kron).

'Zakon o udruživanju gradjana', in TANJUG (1990) *Stranke u Jugoslaviji* (Beograd).

Chapter 7

The Yugoslav Army and the Post-Yugoslav Armies

MILOŠ VASIĆ

Introduction

The Yugoslav People's Army (JNA – *Jugoslovenska narodna armija*) died of natural causes in the spring of 1992, when the war in Bosnia began. After being cheated and humiliated in Slovenia, during the ten-day *drôle de guerre* (June–July 1991), after losing its moral credibility, reputation and popular support in the Croatian campaign (July–December 1991), the JNA was already mortally wounded when it had to leave Bosnia and Hercegovina on 19 May 1992. By that time its nature, name, insignia and most of its personnel had already changed beyond recognition: it was no longer Yugoslav, it was definitely not the People's and in truth it hardly merited the name army. The simple fact that Slobodan Milošević's police force currently outnumbers the Yugoslav Army should suffice to illustrate the point.

The JNA was hoodwinked, used, misused and abused by Slobodan Milošević: systematically weakened and misled – and then discarded. One might argue that the Yugoslav People's Army did not die a natural death, it was murdered. In fact, this was not the case. An army is a synergetic organism dependent on a powerful *esprit de corps* to give it the instinct for survival. The very fact that the Yugoslav People's Army was unable to detect and foil Milošević's plans points to the nub of the issue: the JNA, being the military arm of the Communist Party, inevitably shared the fate of communism: collapse and death from natural causes. Slobodan Milošević and his cynical and faithless *nomenklatura* managed to switch from one totalitarian ideology – communism – to another (and indeed the only one left) – chauvinism. The political choice faced by the Yugoslav People's Army around 1990 was a particularly painful one: liberal democracy or totalitarianism. By its very definition, the conceptual and political grounds on which it stood, its training, doctrine, personnel policy and underlying system of values, the JNA was unable to take the side of liberal democracy. Even worse, it was unable to save its own state, the Socialist Federal Republic of Yugoslavia. Confronted with the dilemma, whether to save Yugoslavia and let communism perish or to destroy the country trying to save communism, the JNA chose the latter. The result is well known. Both Yugoslavia and communism perished and the JNA perished with them. What remains is the populist-totalitarian chaos of present-day Serbia and Montenegro, a state which does not need an army, because it relies on its police and the police-controlled paramilitaries it has created. It comes down to a question of trust: the former JNA officers are suspect by definition; they are bitter, still impregnated by the Yugoslav idea, maybe – and very probably – resentful. The police force and its paramilitaries are strongly tied to the regime in terms of their salaries, privileges and the exigencies of sheer survival: the army might survive the fall of Milošević; few of the police top brass and none of the paramilitaries would.

Naturally enough, the latter-day 'Yugoslav' Army, VJ (*Vojska Jugoslavije*, the official name since April 1992), suffers even more than did the JNA the indignities of being a highly politicised armed force, utterly subjected to the ruling party and confined to the ancillary role of defensive force (foreign aggression being a highly remote possibility). The main and politically crucial role of 'civil war army' is allotted to the police force and its paramilitaries; the pattern here points clearly to the prevalent hierarchy of values: the need to preserve personal power inside Serbia comes first; the fate of Serbs in Croatia and Bosnia, the outcome of the wars going on there and the idea of Greater Serbia comes second.

Another illustration of Milošević's strategy is provided by the constant, concerted – and successful – efforts to keep the Army (both JNA and VJ) off balance, confused and insecure. Since 1987, when he took power in Serbia, Milošević has flattered the army, leading it on to the thin ice, encouraging it by raising false hopes of a restoration of communism, and manoeuvring it into no-win conflicts; treating it as a political partner and ally and then pulling the carpet from under its feet; letting it embark on highly questionable ventures and leaving it on its own when it desperately needed political support. And all of that worked perfectly, because Slobodan Milošević knew – and knows – the intimate inner workings of the system which created and conditioned the Yugoslav professional soldier. All those soldiers, including the best educated and the shrewdest ones, had one essential flaw: they were products and parts of a system that was itself fatally flawed.

The Yugoslav armed forces had sufficient practical means and legal grounds in 1990–91 to prevent war and the disintegration of Yugoslavia; besides, it was their constitutional duty. Forty-five years of admiration and flattery had spoiled the victorious, Second World War-hardened Partisan Army of Marshal Tito, but its moral credibility among the population of Yugoslavia remained almost intact. In addition, the JNA was rated fairly high on the list of European armies and courted by both NATO and the Warsaw Pact in terms of arms sales and the sharing of new technologies. So the Yugoslav military class had both the knife and the cake in their hands, as the Serb saying goes – and they lost both. Why? Why the critical lack of political wisdom, *esprit de corps* and civil courage?

Communism and Bonapartism

The answer is to be found in the very inherent characteristics, the underlying nature, of communist armies. Totalitarian as they are, communist societies stick very closely to their military doctrine as formulated by their classics: Lenin, Mao Zedong, Tito, General Giap, etc. The doctrine is simple and clear enough: the People has two arms: political – the Party – and military – the People's Army. The party, being the avant-garde, the spearhead and the 'collective intellectual' of the working class, is the ultimate expression of the political will of the given people/nation – and of the International Proletariat. Communism recognises no distinction whatsoever between politics and war, party and army; they are just two sides of the same coin of power, as indeed non-Marxist classics like von Clausewitz have argued. The hierarchy of values in a given communist society being set thus, the party must be the centre of gravity and the ultimate decision-making instance: the remaining power structures – commercial/industrial, police and secret service, diplomatic, military – are but ancillary executive services. They only implement the party's general line as formulated, spread and interpreted by the Politburo and its executive bureaucracies. Any attempt in a communist society to use control over particular groups of assets to build an independent power-base disturbs the established balance of power and is promptly branded in terms of a standard set of excommunication labels: if it is culture and arts, it is 'bourgeois decadence'; if it is the economy, it is 'pro-capitalist deviation' or (in Yugoslavia) 'anarcho-liberalism'; if it is the secret services and police, it is the 'Stalinist deviation'; and if it is the army, it is 'Bonapartism'.

In the communist book of sins, the term 'Bonapartism', used to describe the personal political ambitions of a military leader (especially a successful one) who wants all power for himself and thinks that being a successful military leader is enough to get it, is always considered one of the worst. The record shows, however, that a contender with his political power base exclusively within the military establishment never becomes leader of a communist country. Since Lenin's time – and he was the first to warn about Bonapartism – inhibitions about political ambitions have been systematically instilled into the communist military class. The conditioning has never failed: the slightest sign of political ambitions inevitably led to purges and premature retirements – if not worse (cf. Lin Biao in China). The word 'Bonapartism' has never been used in Serbia/Montenegro since the war began, but it is present all the time: some dangers, especially the greatest ones, do not have to be named. In pragmatic political terms, the JNA was the second most redoubtable enemy of Milošević's ambitions, after the reformed communists of Slovenia, Croatia, Macedonia and Bosnia and Hercegovina. In summarily disbanding the League of Communists of Yugoslavia in 1990, supported by the organisation of the LCY in the JNA, Milošević did, in fact, remove the key institutional obstacle to Bonapartism. Perhaps that was why he then turned against the army.

The history: from heroism to paralysis

On 21 December 1941 (Stalin's birthday, incidentally)[1] the First Proletarian Brigade of the National Liberation Army of Yugoslavia lined up for review in Rudo (Eastern Bosnia, now within the territory of Karadžić's self-proclaimed state). For six months already, ragged and scarcely armed guerrilla groups had been fighting the

---

[1] Later, that day became JNA day, having been moved to 22 December in 1948, the year that Tito broke with Stalin.

German Wehrmacht bravely and against all the odds all over what used to be Yugoslavia. It seems that Josip Broz Tito did not take the Stalin-Hitler pact of 1939 seriously, and his illegal Communist Party of Yugoslavia (some 12,000 members) began preparations for war as soon as the Wehrmacht invaded the Kingdom of Yugoslavia in April 1941. The Royal Yugoslav Army had simply fallen apart in the face of the German invasion, and had offered no serious resistance. On 4 July 1941 the decision was made by the Central Committee of the CPY to start a guerrilla war against Germany and its quisling states in Yugoslavia. The stakes were high: to fight against Nazism, the ultimate evil, was a moral choice on a planetary scale. Tito's Partisan movement decided to risk an all-out war against a superior enemy; the decision was based on a long-term strategic assumption that such a monstrous concept as Nazism simply could not win, and on a recognition that Nazi racism could mean only one thing for the South Slavs. In a way, the present position of the Bosnian Muslims is analogous: they are facing an ethnic-exclusivist force, driven by an ideology of hatred and ready to exterminate them just because they are Bosnian Muslims; the choice is clear – to fight back or be exterminated.

There was competition, too, in 1941: General Draža Mihajlović, the commander of the scattered remains of the Yugoslav Army, organised a royalist Chetnik movement, supported by the exiled king and his government. But General Mihajlović went for a different approach: he tried to conserve his strength by negotiating with the Germans, and he fought Tito's Partisans in the meantime, hoping to be able to snatch political power for the king once the war ended with victory for the allied forces. He terrorised the civilian population, especially the non-Serb population in Bosnia, but the anti-Nazi Serbs in Serbia too. By 1944, his force was hopelessly compromised and generally perceived as quisling. The end of the Second World War brought his defeat and death at the hands of the communists. Serb nationalism, however, always clung to the myth of Draža Mihajlović as national hero, and the Chetnik theme would surface again in the 1990s in relation to the fate of the Yugoslav People's Army.

Tito's strategy and tactics followed very closely the conceptual apparatus of what was later named the 'People's War' by classics like Mao Zedong and General Giap. His guerrillas 'swam through the people like fish in the sea', helping, supporting and defending the civilian population regardless of their nationality; the only criterion being anti-Nazism. Mass reprisals by the German authorities (100 hostages shot per one dead German soldier) only worsened the situation, just like in France: the civilian population was faced with a choice – to join the fight against Nazism or suffer the non-selective wrath of the terrible Waffen SS troops. The final victory in 1945 was indisputable: Tito and his 400,000-strong army had won the war in the Balkans and were welcomed as liberators. It was Tito's achievement, owing nothing to Stalin, who had little love for Tito. Through his unquestionable shrewdness and political skills, Josip Broz Tito managed to cheat Stalin three times (1937, when he survived the purges; 1941, when he launched his guerrilla war and cut all communications with Moscow; and 1945 when he proclaimed his own regime in Yugoslavia in spite of Stalin's agreements with Western Allies); Tito promised free elections and multiparty democracy to Winston Churchill in 1944 – and cheated him too.

In 1945 the Yugoslav People's Army was a redoubtable force – but it lacked trained officers. In the three years that followed VE Day, thousands of JNA officers and young soldiers were sent to Soviet military schools. The JNA was organised very much on Red Army lines, and was increasingly armed by Soviet weaponry. The total amount of Soviet military aid to Yugoslavia 1944–48 is still unknown; Bolotin (1986: 309) says that by 1 May 1945 the USSR had given to the Yugoslav People's Liberation Army 125,446 rifles, 38,210 sub-machine guns and 14,296 machine guns, to which can be added hundreds of tanks and aeroplanes and thousands of artillery pieces and mortars. It is interesting to note that many of those weapons (T-34 tanks, Mosin-Nagant rifles, M-41 Shpagin sub-machine guns and all manner of machine guns) were taken out of the depots and distributed to Serb rebels in Croatia and Bosnia in 1991 and 1992 ...

After the break between Tito and Stalin in June 1948, the defensive strategy and doctrine of the JNA shifted: the main threat was now coming from the East and the Warsaw Pact countries. The West took some time to decide to help Tito. In 1951, Tito's wartime Chief of Staff and new minister of foreign affairs, Kosa Popović, went to Washington and signed a *US Military Aid to Yugoslavia Agreement*. Between 1951 and 1956, some $20bn worth of arms and military equipment was delivered to Yugoslavia, including 34,000 Thompson M-1A1 sub-machine guns (most of those were used in the war in Croatia in 1991, in addition to other arms from the same source, especially artillery pieces). After the Yugoslav–Soviet reconciliation in 1957, the JNA tried – and managed – to maintain a certain balance in its arms' procurements and military technology transfers, while developing its own domestic production. Tito's in-between position, as the most important non-aligned leader, provided lots of political latitude: both parties in the Cold War courted him and he managed to build a respectable military force out of the JNA.

In doctrinal and strategic terms, the JNA was conceived, trained, deployed and educated as a purely defensive army. Facing two possibly hostile and by far superior military-political entities – NATO and the Warsaw Pact – the JNA was prepared to offer strong initial resistance, to buy time for further mobilisation, and then revert to guerrilla-style warfare based on hidden assets kept in a constant state of readiness. That meant primarily organised withdrawal to the mountains, where stocks of arms, fuel, food and military equipment would be waiting for the troops. Being a defensive army, the JNA relied on locally available logistical support for deployment in the case of war: the theory posited that the mobilisation of resources and logistical support should be organised locally, around main garrisons and deployment centres (military district HQs). That pattern of organisation was to prove fatal later on, in the civil war.

It goes without saying that such a defensive concept was based on the assumption of unquestionable political consensus among the population. That consensus was to be preserved by political means: the communist regime, police control, controlled media, etc. For forty-five years those prerequisites were present and the JNA was happy to live in its drab-olive ivory tower, courted, flattered and privileged, carefully isolated from the society it was supposed to defend. Officers and army personnel had their own apartment blocks, their privileged shops, their medical care, their courts of law; the army bank offered them privileged credits, their wives were employed without problems. And the Communist Party (League of Communists of

Yugoslavia) had a special grip on the army – of course. The JNA had its own Communist Party organisation (OSK JNA) and more than 80 per cent of professionals (officers and men) were party members. No one could be promoted without the explicit approval of his party organisation (and the approval of the Security Directorate of the JNA, which looked after discipline, loyalty and counter-intelligence). The grip of the party organisation inside the JNA was total and undisputed; it followed a vertical chain of subordination and was reinforced horizontally. Communist Party bodies in the different republics of the former Yugoslav Federation had no access to or influence over local military Communist Party organs. The only point at which influence could be brought to bear was the SKJ (League of Communists of Yugoslavia) Presidency, where the head of the JNA Communist Party organisation had a chair, together with the communist leaders of the six republics and two autonomous regions. In political and organisational terms, that made the JNA the only federation-wide centralised state agency under the semi-confederal 1974 constitution.

Set as it was in its bureaucratic ways, smug in its ideological correctness and unreflecting in its petty selfishness, the JNA hardly noticed the events of 1989 and 1990. It is true that its political directorate was making its usual worried noises about 'imperialist attempts to sabotage Socialism'. But no one *dared* to analyse what seemed to be a Europe-wide process of the decay of communism. Worse than that, no one dared to question the unchallenged belief that communism is here to stay forever.

Enter Milošević: the collapse of communism

The JNA top brass could not, howevever, help noticing the tidal wave of Serb nationalism unleashed by Slobodan Milošević in 1987. In spite of a certain uneasiness, JNA generals did not really object. Why not? Because Milošević used Kosovo as his launching pad; he followed the 1981 ideological misinterpretation of the Kosovo crisis, misnaming a demographic and social problem and presenting it as a 'counter-revolution'. Now the JNA was very worried about Kosovo, because in the course of the 1981 riots it had had, for the first time, to roll tanks and fly jets in to intimidate Yugoslav citizens; the generals had been confused by the Kosovo crisis; no serious attempt at analysis was made. When Milošević promised to pacify Kosovo, and captured the presidency of the League of Communists of Serbia on that platform (and after much plotting behind the scenes), the army was relieved to have found a man who spoke straight communist lingo, and who was going to sort out Kosovo.

There was another angle to it: by 1987 the voices of liberal dissent in Slovenia were growing stronger; the JNA was their favourite target, because of its ideological stiffness, and what young Slovenian journalists and intellectuals perceived as its obsolescence. Close to the West and its subcultures, younger Slovenes were mostly pacifists; they raised the issue of conscientious objection, which drove the JNA mad. In 1988 there was the scandal of the Ljubljana Four: a secret JNA contingency plan was published by *Mladina*, a Slovenian youth magazine (still one of the best weeklies in the Balkans). Four people were arrested by military counter-intelligence (one of them, Janez Janša, would be the first minister of defence in the independent Slovenia). Their trial by the military court in Ljubljana provoked a long and vociferous campaign of protests; the most basic values of Yugoslav communist society were openly questioned. It was too much for the army, and even more so for Milošević: he smelled a reformist rat and made an alliance with the army against the Slovenes. In the eyes of the bulk of the JNA officers' corps (predominantly Serbs and Montenegrins and all communists), Milošević was a saviour; he managed to identify Serbdom with communism for them. The deadly stereotype was established: Serbs are communists; *ergo* they are pro-Yugoslav.

In 1990 Slobodan Milošević practically disbanded the League of Communists of Yugoslavia, refusing to respect the procedures of the XIV Congress of the League, held in January of that year: reformist factions among Slovene, Croat, Bosnian and Macedonian communists had become too strong and were threatening to take it over. Federal prime minister Ante Marković had already launched his programme of economic and political reforms, threatening established communist control over the economy, administration and media; *political power itself* was in danger.

The role of the Yugoslav People's Army in the break-up of Yugoslavia was defined by two factors: its ideological and political inertia and its privileged status. By the end of 1990 the stage was set for the break-up: non-communist parties had won elections in Slovenia, Croatia, Bosnia and Hercegovina, and Macedonia. That could mean only one thing: that the Federation was dead, unless there were federal elections (see Chapter 2). General Veljko Kadijević, the minister of defence in Ante Marković's cabinet, gave some indications that the army might support the prime minister's reforms. In an interview in December 1990, Kadijević actually said so. In the same interview he officially discarded the doctrine of People's Defence, the holy scripture of the JNA for the previous twenty years. Introduced after the Warsaw Pact invasion of Czechoslovakia in 1968, that doctrine emphasised the time-honoured principles of People's War and the arming of the people. Its embodiment was the Territorial Defence network. By 1989, the JNA was seeking to take control of Territorial Defence stocks of arms, sensing dangers that were, as subsequent events proved, only too real.

The arming of Croatia

The electoral victory of Franjo Tudjman and his nationalist HDZ party in Croatia (May 1990) deeply upset the Serbs of Croatia, still traumatised by the genocidal killings in the Second World War, committed by the Croat quisling Ustasha regime (some 500,000–700,000 dead in mass-extermination camps, etc.).[2] Those fears were systematically amplified by Serb nationalist propaganda, under Milošević's direction. Milošević's secret services began infiltrating their agents into the Serb communities of Croatia as early as June 1990; those agents laid the foundations for future military formations and took control of local Serb political organizations. (JNA

---

[2] But see footnote 3 to Chapter 11.

counter-intelligence sources still claim that they were not aware of that infiltration.) The arms soon followed.

It must be emphasised that the Croat government and the new ruling party (HDZ) aggravated the situation beyond measure by their heavy-handed, haughty and tactless approach to the Serbs of Croatia. The HDZ's aggressive, triumphalist and menacing nationalism played right into Milošević's hands: moderate Serb politicians in Croatia were marginalised and replaced by extremists; more arms found their way into Serb regions of Croatia, and secessionism became the dominant slogan. The Croatian police grew in numbers and the strength of the police reserve was increased. They needed arms and equipment. The JNA-controlled military industry of Yugoslavia refused to supply the Croat police and Croatia went to the international black market. The US and USSR turned them down, but Hungary, Romania and some other countries and individuals agreed to sell. A large-scale covert operation began. Yugoslav military intelligence got wind of it quite soon and mounted a counter-operation.

By the end of 1990 the JNA had a pretty good idea of what was going on. The Security Directorate had material evidence of illegal arms' imports into Croatia and (on a much smaller scale) into Slovenia: video tapes, audio tapes, documents, witnesses, specimens. The story could no longer be contained; independent press workers noticed Singapore-manufactured SAR 80 assault rifles in the hands of the Slovene Territorials and started asking questions. By that time Croatia had already imported at least 40,000 Hungarian-manufactured AK 47 assault rifles, plus a number of Armbrust anti-tank weapons and other arms. The General Staff asked for a meeting of the collective Federal Presidency in its capacity of Supreme Command of the Armed Forces, and hinted about the evidence they had. On 9 January 1991 the Presidency issued an ambiguously formulated order: all paramilitary formations were to turn in their illegal weapons to the JNA. The very wording of the order made it unimplementable and self-contradictory: Croatia was arming its own perfectly legal police and police reserves and welcomed the order, arguing that it was binding on Serb paramilitaries on Croat territory. The JNA and Serbia had the Croatian police in mind, but were unable to reach a consensus within the Presidency and impose their interpretation. A half-hearted compromise was found and the Presidency order turned out to be a damp squib.

The army then decided to prepare a surprise for Dr Tudjman. In the early morning of 25 January 1991, special teams of the military police quietly arrested five men involved in the distribution of weapons in Northern Slavonia. In the early afternoon of the same day, Tudjman was shown a sixty-minute video tape which was to be broadcast that very same evening on Yugoslav TV. Although heavily edited, the film gave a rather fair picture of what was happening with the illegal arming of Croatia: it featured General Martin Špegelj, Croatian minister of defence, in a country house, giving instructions to a couple of JNA officers on how to kill their fellow officers when the time came. There were pictures of convoys of arms, incriminating documents, witnesses, the lot. The film – shown in prime time, just after the main TV news – was a shock, but it did not change much. After an initial, embarrassed silence, Croatia explained that it had to buy its arms from outside, because its own Territorial Defence arms had been taken away. And there the matter rested for the time being.

Saving communism and Milošević

Maybe the most fundamental document for an understanding of the role of the JNA in the critical year 1991 is an analysis of the Political Directorate of the MoD, distributed to JNA Communist Party members on 25 January 1991 and leaked to the press on 31 January. This restricted document was entitled *Information about the Current Situation in the World and in Our Country and the Urgent Tasks of the JNA*. Its message, tone and wording are definitely old-style communist – reminiscent of 1955. The text starts with the judgment that the USSR would survive the reform tendency which 'leads to perdition', and goes on: 'Socialism is not defeated and on its knees in Yugoslavia either. Yugoslavia ... has stood up to the first wave of anti-communist hysteria. There are still real prospects for the survival of a federal and socialist Yugoslavia.' The Gulf War is described as an attempt by the US and the West to secure 'cheap energy'. The 'screenwriters from the West' (conventional conspiracy theory concept) are blamed for all the key events in Eastern Europe, the USSR and Yugoslavia. 'Their basic strategy – destruction of the communist idea and the socialist option – has achieved some successes, but not its ultimate objective. Destruction of communism had not occurred in countries which had had genuine revolutions.' The document forecast two directions of attack against socialist Yugoslavia: attempts to depose communist regimes still in power at republic level; and attempts to break up Yugoslavia and then blame the communists for it. CIA and state department evaluations of the Yugoslav crisis are mentioned and the following conclusion is drawn:

> The essence of these messages is completely clear – to destroy socialism in Yugoslavia, even at the price of her break-up ... The support some Western circles evince for democracy is transparent demagogy, because democracy for them is only what suits their objectives and interests. For them, democracy in our context means in the first place – anti-socialism.

This document outlines three main tasks for the JNA: to help to reform the Yugoslav economy; to secure the federation (all confederal and other more flexible forms of state organisation are ruled out); and to make the newly formed SKPJ party (League of Communists – Movement for Yugoslavia) 'the main political force on Yugoslav territory and the linchpin for all left-oriented parties'. The latter task was singled out as being 'the most important'. However, impassioned appeals to join the SKPJ (nicknamed 'the generals' party' in December 1990 when it was founded) were met with very little enthusiasm by officers of the JNA, and the 'urgent tasks of the military' were soon swept under the carpet. But a clear warning had been given, though it was not heeded. The army top brass still had hopes that communism might be saved and they were looking for something to 'happen' in the USSR.

In the event, something happened in Belgrade. At the end of February 1991 the

Serbian opposition called a mass demonstration for 9 March against Milošević's control of radio and television. Milošević's secret service responded on 2 March by staging an incident in Pakrač, in Western Slavonia, between policemen in the local police station. Serb officers disarmed their Croat fellow officers and expelled them. A Croatian police special unit intervened and took control of the town, which had a mixed population. The JNA then intervened to take on what would be its main task in the succeeding months: preventing ethnic conflicts. The Pakrač diversion did not work (no casualties, in spite of Milošević's media claims of 'forty dead') and the 9th of March duly produced a demonstration. Milošević's police attacked some 40,000 demonstrators in the centre of Belgrade, creating a critical mass of anger; street violence lasted until the late afternoon and the police were effectively defeated and dispersed. Around 18.30 pm JNA tanks and armoured personnel carriers rolled into the capital and took up key positions. There were, it must be stressed, no incidents between the population and the soldiers.

For the first time since 1944 tanks were on the streets of Belgrade – and it was no parade.

A history of failed coups

That day, the JNA generals threw their lot in with Slobodan Milošević – reluctantly, as was discovered later, but definitively. Now, four years after the event, the whole affair is much clearer. The 9th of March 1991 was an attempted *coup d'état*; and not the first one. The first time a coup was seriously considered was at the end of 1990, as a way to deal with the arming of Croatia. Detailed contingency plans were drafted within the General Staff, but there was no political vision, no clear-cut political purpose, to back it up. It is easy to seize power in a classic *coup d'état*; but what to do with it, once seized? There was no Marshall Jaruzelski among them, nor a General Eanes of Portugal. The basic idea was to depose all the local rulers in the Yugoslav republics; but that meant Milošević too, and that broke their hearts – and was also dangerous, for his charisma was so strong … They had had signals from the West that a coup which would sweep away nationalist leaders and bring to power some liberal democratic political force supported by all ethnic groups (like Ante Marković) would have been at least tolerated, if not openly supported. But those signals had been weak, ambiguous – and deniable. And anyway such a coup would have destroyed communism and brought Yugoslavia into the Western world … On the other hand, a communist counter-revolution, a Thermidor which would have swept away all those non-communist parties and leaders and restored the Dictatorship of Proletariat and People's Democracy on the Chinese model was an even more dangerous venture. Finally socialism in the USSR was not exactly 'on its knees', but it was not on its feet either – and the USSR was so far away.

So in January 1991 the generals decided to wait and see. Then the 9th of March came. Now we know that 'wrong' police tactics were deliberately used on that day in order to provoke more violence. The President of the eight-member presidency of Yugoslavia, Dr Borisav Jović, Milošević's faithful clerk, started ringing up other Presidency members all over Yugoslavia and asking their urgent permission to use the JNA in Belgrade – because the situation was out of control and the constitutional order in danger. But he was phoning them about noon, and control was not 'lost' until 16.30 pm, when the police started using firearms. He had barely obtained the permissions before the army started moving into Belgrade. What was not known at the time was that the Chief of Staff, General Blagoje Adžić, and Milošević's Minister of the Interior, Radmilo Bogdanović, had been in contact throughout the day. The JNA wasn't fooled by Milošević's scam: its Security Directorate was following the events closely, and giving its assessments to the General Staff. According to some reports, General Kadijević felt strongly that the JNA had lost face by acting in support of an incompetent police force. The very next day armour was withdrawn from the streets of Belgrade, to the great relief of the embarrassed soldiers. On the evening of 10 March – after a violent clash with the police and lots of CS gas – students and young people invaded the city centre and held a ten-day sit-in. No further police action was taken and, indeed, Milošević was forced to take some conciliatory steps.

A meeting of the Yugoslav Presidency was held on 12 March 1991 in the underground operations room of the Ministry of Defence. General Kadijević proposed the declaration of a state of emergency. The details of the proposal remain unknown, but it can be safely assumed that far-reaching measures were considered: suspension of certain civil rights, parliamentary life and political activity for a certain period of time, direct control over the media and the economy, possibly federal elections in due course, the internment of certain individuals, etc. March 12 was the most frightening day Belgrade could remember since the early 1950s: sensible people didn't sleep at home, political parties hid their membership lists and sensitive files, and the air could have been cut with a knife. The outcome of the Presidency meeting was that Milošević's men voted against the coup. The explanation is simple: it was too dangerous for them; their operations among the Serbs of Croatia and Bosnia were already known; the meaning of their chauvinistic warmongering propaganda was clear enough; they were for war and they did not want the JNA to stop them.

General Kadijević paid a quiet visit to Moscow on 13 March and there met Marshal Yazov, the Soviet Minister of Defence. It is not known what they spoke about; some informed guesses have it that a shipment of arms (some 30,000 tons in seven ships due to arrive on 1 July) was negotiated. Other informed people suggest that what Yazov actually told Kadijević was: hold on with your coup until we have done our coup here. Either way, it is clear that a communist-inspired coup would not have worked without strong Russian political support. Kadijević came back the next day and kept his own counsel.

Milošević responded by creating an artificial crisis in the Presidency. He ordered Jović to resign. On 16 March Milošević gave his famous speech to the mayors of Serbia, in which he explained that Serbia was in danger; that there was a plot to restore the Austro-Hungarian Empire; that Greater Germany wants the Balkans, that the West hates us, that Croats and Slovenes are German puppets and 'if we don't know how to work, we know how to fight'. That piece of outrageous demagogy sank deep into the psyches of his SPS *nomenklatura* and became the order of the day. The war in Croatia was on its way and the JNA did nothing to prevent it. The most probable explanation for this inaction is that the JNA leadership saw an opportunity to repeat the operations at the close of the Second World War, with the HDZ regime of Tudjman playing the role of the quisling Croat state. That was the anti-Fascist option: overthrow the HDZ and keep Croatia inside Yugoslavia – under military occupation and with a puppet government. The anti-Fascist political option was to be the first delusion of the JNA and was to last until 19 August 1991, when the defeat of Marshal Yazov's coup in Moscow destroyed all hopes of a successful communist Thermidor in Yugoslavia.

Milošević wasted no time: special operations in Croatia were intensified and the Knin-controlled police units of Mile Martić, the self-styled Minister of the Interior of the Krajina, took control of the Plitvice police station on 26 March. The Croatian police hit back on 1 April and retook the station; there were two dead, one Serb and one Croat. Army units interposed themselves, as they were to do repeatedly over the next five months in Croatia. This was called 'preventing ethnic conflicts' – but the barrels of JNA weapons just happened to be pointing at the Croat side. Even so, the Serbs of Croatia were not altogether happy, and the JNA units in the field were branded 'traitors' by them – they had been expected to attack the Croats and do nothing to restrain the Serbs. Serb paramilitaries went on with their attacks on the Croatian police and against Croats who had previously lived in these neighbourhoods. Civilians fled and the Croatian police were helpless against the army. The order of the Presidency to disarm the paramilitaries was not applied to Martić's police: they were treated as a legal body by the army. Under such rules of the game, the JNA troops were slowly becoming the border guards of the future, self-proclaimed, Serb Krajina state within Croatia.

A Slovenian interlude

On 25 June 1991 Slovenia declared its independence. On 25–26 June the JNA took up 134 out of 137 designated key positions in Slovenia, as Stage One of General Kadijević's plan for keeping Yugoslavia together, and awaited further orders. The Minister of Defence then asked the Supreme Command to order the Fifth Army to proceed with Stage Two of his plan, which provided for the total military occupation of Slovenia if serious armed resistance were met. At that point, however, Jović, who had been reinstated as chairman of the Presidency, said that there was no use trying to keep Slovenia inside Yugoslavia by force – let them go was Milošević's message. Kadijević's plan went off at half-cock and the Fifth Army units in Slovenia was caught with their pants down. The Slovene forces did not waste their time: they surrounded the barracks and military installations of the JNA in Slovenia and eventually starved them into surrender. The army was humiliated and shocked. There were dramatic scenes at the headquarters of the Ljubljana Corps; there was talk of retaliating against vital civilian targets, but it was too late. Slovenia was gone – with Milošević's blessing.

The JNA was instrumentalised and deliberately forced into the Slovenian impasse for two reasons: Slovenia had to be thrown out of Yugoslavia, being a reformed-communist rotten apple and a *drôle de guerre* was the most elegant way for both parties to make the secession irreversible. Some sources claim that Slobodan Milošević and the President of Slovenia, Milan Kučan, actually came to an agreement about the secession. The second reason was that the last thing Milošević wanted was a strong army to provide political competition in 'the future state' (as General Kadijević calls it in his memoirs).

A war of expansion: Croatia

In the evening of 1 July 1991, an armoured-mechanised division of the JNA First Army left Belgrade, heading west, cheered by crowds. Instead of advancing straight into Croatia – as everyone expected – and consolidating a tenable frontline from the Sava river, across Western Slavonia, to the Hungarian border, the division was deployed on the border between Serbia and Croatia. At the same time, the Podgorica and Užice Corps increased their pressure on the Hercegovina front. The two most incomprehensible and most infamous operations of the Balkans Wars were about to begin: Dubrovnik and Vukovar. Both operations were marked by ominous signs for the JNA: a very low response to partial mobilisations in Serbia and Montenegro; frequent mutinies of reservists, even in frontline positions; unprecedented lack of discipline; looting and war crimes, killings of civilians and destruction of cities and other civilian targets; and very low combat morale. It seemed likely that it would not end well. And it did not.

Up until 19 August 1991 the war in Croatia trailed on rather slowly. Short of manpower, the General Staff issued in mid-July a secret order granting volunteers full status as members of the armed forces, a decision which would cost the army dear later on: those volunteers were only too often members of extreme right-wing chauvinist parties, common criminals or Serbian secret service-controlled paramilitaries. They behaved in a wholly unsoldierly way, wearing all sorts of Serb chauvinist insignia, beards and knives, were often drunk (like many of the regular soldiers, too), looted, and killed or harassed civilians. Officers rarely dared discipline them, given the overwhelmingly Serb-nationalist political atmosphere in Serbia and the 'patriotic' jingoism and wild chauvinist propaganda of the state-controlled media. The image of the JNA had been badly tarnished in Slovenia and everybody talked 'treason'. Milošević's regime tolerated anti-communist excesses as long as they were directed against the JNA; officers were confused, and in any case often incompetent and afraid; regular non-commissioned soldiers did not care to resist the behaviour of 'volunteers' (why should they?). The combat morale of the JNA suffered accordingly.

When Marshall Yazov went for a coup in Moscow on 19 August 1991 Milošević's regime showed signs of premature joy – to be bitterly disappointed two days later. But Milošević had a back-up plan ready: to go for a Greater Serbia rather than a communist Yugoslavia. That is the only possible explanation for what actually happened in Croatia. The Serbs took territories where they were in the majority (and a little bit more), and expelled almost all Croats; the JNA took Eastern Slavonia, Baranja and Western Srem (what became UNPA East), destroying Vukovar in the process, because the infantry refused to charge and fight in close combat. On the Dubrovnik front, the war was mostly looting and indiscriminate shelling. The JNA failed to take Dubrovnik, in spite of Milošević's propaganda promise that it would become 'the capital of a great Serb state of Hercegovina and Montenegro'. The only rational explanation for the Dubrovnik operation is to be found, again, in General Kadijević's memoirs: it was part of a larger operation designed to take Split and the Dalmatian coast and 'reach the borders of the future state'.

The war in Croatia dragged on until the fall of Vukovar on 19 November 1991. It is now clear that the damage suffered by the JNA was much greater than the territorial gains made in UNPA East, the main theatre of its operations. Many barracks and garrisons were captured by the 'enemy'; large amounts of of weapons and equipment were lost. The Varaždin Corps case is typical. General Vlado Trifunović held the barracks and headquarters at Varaždin (located on the Croatian–Slovenian border) for months, against superior Croat forces, with just 400 soldiers. Belgrade promised help but none came, and Trifunović finally negotiated surrender and safe conduct for himself and all his men, after damaging and destroying as much equipment as he could (there were some 200 armoured vehicles and lots of other weaponry). His troops also did much damage to the city during the battles, and he was later sentenced as a war criminal in Croatia. When he finally returned to Serbia with his men, he was arrested and tried three times (acquitted twice, sentenced to seven years the third time). A scapegoat was needed and found; 'we needed you dead', he was told later; his appeal is still pending.

The war in Croatia brought with it a new phenomenon: attempted palace coups within the Ministry of Defence. The first one was on 24 August 1991, when a group of Air Force officers tried to replace their Commander-in-Chief, General Zvonko Jurjević, on the pretext that he was a Croat. General Kadijević intervened personally and defused the crisis. In the second one, on 28 September 1991, officers of the First Guards Mechanized Division took control of the Ministry buildings in Belgrade and tried to replace Kadijević with the Chief of Staff, General Blagoje Adžić. Adžić was outraged and would have nothing to do with the idea. General Kadijević showed remarkable courage; the crisis went on until the next morning, when the officers agreed to withdraw to their barracks. No action was taken against either group of officers, though they had committed grave breaches of discipline. This illustrates graphically the confusion, frustration and paralysis within the JNA.

The JNA came out of its Croatian campaign even worse than it had come out of Slovenia. Its reservists were demoralised and angry, feeling that they fought in vain for territories they did not feel to be theirs. The JNA was blamed for everything by everybody: for fighting such an infamous war in the first place, for not fighting it fiercely enough. Milošević kept repeating that 'Serbia is not at war', but rather Yugoslavia and the JNA. The generals kept repeating that they were 'an army without a state behind it'. The war in Croatia ended in a pathetic anti-climax. In Croatia – as in Slovenia – the JNA found itself in a false position because it was a defensive army, not a civil war army. Its doctrine was predicated on the support of the population, which had been lost before the fighting even started. There was no declaration of war and no general mobilisation. It goes without saying that there was no national consensus about the war either. What happened in Croatia was that an ethnic war was fought on cheap political ('anti-Fascism') and legalist ('secession') excuses. Paradoxically enough, it is impossible to say whether the JNA won or lost the war in Croatia, because the war objectives were never declared. It was claimed by some that the objective was the protection of Serbs in Croatia – but in the event almost half the Croatian Serbs remained under Croatian authority. The real – and never declared – objective was to create an ethnically pure Greater Serbia. On that criterion it is clear that the war in Croatia was lost. A viable Serbian state on the historical territory of Croatia was never built; the war was in vain.

A time of purges

There have been four great purges in the JNA, and its successor after 1992, the VJ. Those purges have left the army crippled and emasculated. They were made possible by Milošević's political infiltration of the officer corps: he corrupted the greedy, he flattered the ambitious, his secret service penetrated the army and intimidated the dissenters. The JNA's *esprit de corps*, the survival instinct of every organisation, was paralysed – if it ever really existed.

The first purge was in 1991, when almost all Slovene and Croat officers and men were forced to leave, regardless of their loyalty. Some left quickly and on their own initiative; some reluctantly once they had understood that non-Serbs were no longer welcome; some were simply fired. That purge left a considerable void in the ranks of the army: as many as 52 per cent of the Air Force flying personnel were non-Serbs, for instance. Other specialisms suffered too.

The second purge hit the army in early 1992: the victims this time were officers of strong Yugoslav persuasion, but whose loyalty to Milošević was questionable, or who did not share to a sufficient degree the currently fashionable commitment to Serb nationalism. General Kadijević resigned in January 1992, after an obscure incident in which a EU Monitoring Mission helicopter was shot down by the Yugoslav Air Force. General Blagoje Adžić was nominated as caretaker Minister of Defence. The first sign that a serious purge was imminent was the demotion of General Simeon Tumanov (an ethnic Macedonian), the deputy head of the Security Directorate of the MoD. That directorate was the first to be hit comprehensively once the purge was seriously under way, and by April it had been practically beheaded and taken over by Milošević's secret service and its proxies. There is a general belief that the war in Bosnia might not have started if the Security Directorate had been left alone.

One day in early May 1992 Milošević retired thirty-eight senior generals, and General Blagoje Adžić resigned in protest. Many Bosnian Muslim officers had already quit in early 1992, feeling uneasy and threatened by the growing Serb nationalism within the army and sensing the approach of war in Bosnia. General Života Panić became Chief of Staff. Thereafter Ministers of Defence were civilians.

This third purge practically cleansed the army of Bosnian Muslims and other non-Serbs. When the JNA split into the VJ and the BSA (Bosnian Serb army) on 19 May 1992, thousands of officers and men born in Bosnia and Hercegovina were ordered to join the Bosnian Serb Army. A similar thing happened in October 1993, when all remaining ethnic Serb military personnel born outside Serbia and Montenegro were ordered to join the BSA or Krajina Army immediately, or be fired with no pension rights.

The fourth purge was on strictly political grounds. After Milošević split with Radovan Karadžić, the Bosnian Serb leader, over the Vance–Owen peace plan (May 1993), he began quietly removing officers sympathetic to Karadžić and Vojislav Šešelj, an extreme right-wing chauvinist Serbian politician. Thus the pendulum of loyalty had reached another extreme point: now it was the turn of the Serb nationalists in the army to be purged. General Života Panić was retired and there was a reshuffle of the General Staff and the MoD. General Momčilo Perišić became the new Chief of Staff.

What kind of officers remained in the Yugoslav Army after so many purges? Bona fide communists and Yugoslav patriots were fired first; then non-Serbs, regardless of their political beliefs and loyalty; then those who were not for Greater Serbia; and finally those who *were* for Greater Serbia. Individual members of each purged group managed to survive, but the general impact of the purges was overwhelming: Milošević has succeeded in taking total control of the Yugoslav Army. The key to survival is clearly delineated: it is obedience to Milošević, regardless of his political manoeuvres, rather than allegiance to country, people, constitution or ideology.

The loss of Bosnia

Strategically, Bosnia is the key to the Balkans. Since 1918 Yugoslav military doctrines have been based on that fact. The experience of the Second World War illustrates the importance of Bosnia: it was where Tito's Partisans fled to; it was where they attacked from. Naturally enough, Yugoslav defence doctrine after 1945 stressed the importance of Bosnia in all sorts of ways. Fortified airports, underground command and communications posts and depots were built, and large quantities of weapons systems, ammunition, explosives and equipment were based in Bosnia. Some 60 per cent of Yugoslav military-industrial capacities were located in Bosnia. The loss of Bosnia and Hercegovina reduced the Yugoslav Army to its strategic size and importance as of 1912, if we do not count Vojvodina.

No serious historical study of the Balkan Wars of the 1990s can be attempted without answering the key question: Why did Milošević decide to start the war in Bosnia? The theory that Radovan Karadžić started it does not hold water: without Milošević's full political, logistic, police and military support there could have been no war in Bosnia. By starting the war in Bosnia, Milošević condemned to death the Serb state in Croatia, the Republic of the Serb Krajina (RSK): the Serbs of Croatia were persuaded to go for armed rebellion by promises that some kind of Yugoslav state would be there to support them in Bosnia. As late as April 1992 they were told by the highest Yugoslav officials (members of the Presidency and General Panić, the Chief of Staff) that 'the Yugoslav People's Army will remain in Bosnia for at least five–eight years', guarding them. It was a straightforward lie: the plans for the withdrawal of the JNA from Bosnia had already been activated at that point and on 19 May 1992 the Serbs of Croatia were abandoned, when the JNA was wound up.

We can only speculate as to what really happened: maybe Milošević really believed that Radovan Karadžić and Ratko Mladić would win and create a viable Serb state in Bosnia, securing the creation of Greater Serbia, the Holy Grail of the chimeric and pathetic latter-day Serb nationalism? But that does not sound like Milošević. There is a school of thought which believes that Milošević himself was unaware of the destructive power of the Serb nationalism he had unleashed; that the Pandora's Box of ethnic war went out of control and that he himself was surprised by the fact that the war of ethnic extermination gained such a momentum as to make it a self-supporting, suicidal machine. This author is close to that school of thought. The problem is that the relevant documents are not available; witnesses are either scarce or reluctant or afraid; lack of evidence hinders any attempt at serious analysis. What is beyond any doubt is that, by withdrawing from Bosnia, the Yugoslav Army reduced itself to the status of a second-rate regional force.

The three Serb armies

'The Yugoslav Army not only survived without a state behind it; it even created another two armies – the Serb Army of Krajina and the Army of the Serb Republic in Bosnia.' Thus the official propaganda line of the Yugoslav Army.

What were the losses of the JNA in Slovenia, Croatia and Bosnia? According to official estimates, rather reluctantly given and methodologically unclear (was the Territorial Defence weaponry counted?), the JNA left in Slovenia some 100-plus tanks and self-propelled artillery pieces, the same number of cannon and mortars, and unspecified numbers of other arms, ammunition, fuel and equipment. Unofficial sources suggest that Slovenia sold most of this hardwear to Croatia at inflated prices and conclude that the original numbers must have been higher. The losses in Croatia were on a larger scale: according to the official estimates, at least 21,000 assault and other rifles and machine-guns, 6 aircraft (mostly Mig-21s), 170 main battle tanks, 142 other armoured vehicles, 500 rocket launchers (of all calibres), 600 artillery pieces, 2000 anti-tank rockets, 13,000 mortar bombs, 30,000 land mines and hand grenades and 10 million rounds of ammunition were left in Croatian hands. The Serb Army of Krajina got some 200, mostly obsolete, tanks, several hundred armoured personnel carriers, 20-odd aircraft (fixed and rotary wing), several hundred cannon and mortars and unspecified numbers of small arms, vehicles and the like.

The JNA left in Bosnia 24 fixed-wing aircraft, 20 helicopters, 531 tanks (mostly obsolete), 4 missile squadrons (Frog-7), 87 multiple rocket launchers (128 mm and 262 mm) with many spare loads, some 5000 heavy mortars (120 mm) and 'many more' smaller ones (mostly 82 mm), some 220,000 small arms and unspecified (but by all accounts large) numbers of ordnance of all calibres, explosives, communications gear, vehicles and other equipment.[3]

Where does that leave the 'three Serb Armies' in terms of real strength, quality and combat preparedness?

---

[3] Combat losses not taken into account. Figures are from official sources and cannot be cross-checked against independent sources.

The Serb Army of Krajina no longer exists. It fled UNPA West in May 1995 and UNPAs South and North in August 1995, after well-prepared and quickly executed attacks by the Croatian Army. The real reason for those humiliating defeats was psychological rather than military. The Krajina Serbs did not take long to realise that the war in Bosnia was going badly and that Belgrade would not and could not protect them. Their state, the RSK (*Republika srpske krajine*), had already lost more than half its original population to ethnic cleansing of Croats – and the quiet emigration of Serbs. The remaining Serbs were disappointed, ageing and hopeless. Most of the 38,000 soldiers in the army were aged forty or over. There was no industry or economy worth mentioning to support the state and the army: in beginning the war, the Serbs of Krajina cut themselves off from their natural economic environment – Croatia. The better trained units of their army even fought as mercenaries for the Western Bosnian secessionist warlord, Fikret Abdić. Command, control and communications were poor in the Krajina army; the propaganda myths of the 'invincibility' and 'inherent heroism of Krajina Serbs', as compared to 'the cowardice of the Croats' provided a convenient excuse for the failure to build any fortifications.

What remains is UNPA East, defended by an army corps reinforced by reluctant refugees from Krajina, forcibly mobilised from all over Serbia/Montenegro against the law and all international treaties, and hastily trained as cannon fodder to a possible Croatian attack, so that the VJ does not have to be involved. Whatever happens there, the story of the Krajina Serbs in Croatia seems to be over: they took Milošević at his word – 'all Serbs shall live in one state' – and came to Serbia, all 180,000 of them.

The Bosnian Serb Army is in a similar situation. The fall of Krajina increased the length of the BSA frontline to almost 2000 kilometers, and exposed its western flanks to the Croatian Army, and to the freshly armed, supplied and relieved Fifth Corps of the Bosnian Army, one of the hardest fighting forces in the Balkans. Most of the huge BSA reserves of ammunition had been wasted during three years of indiscriminate shelling of civilian targets. It is not known how many of their tanks, APCs and aircraft were still serviceable at that point; the BSA suffers from an acute lack of spare parts and many of its tanks were already obsolete in 1992. The nominal strength of the BSA at mid-1995 has been estimated at close to 80,000 soldiers, but in terms of efficient and mobile units it was closer to 30,000, with the average age increasing, because youth has tended to emigrate to Serbia-Montenegro and abroad. There were few professional, highly mobile and well-trained units in the Bosnian Serb Army at mid-1995 and they lacked trained officers. Meanwhile the Croatian and Bosnian armed forces had continued to grow in strength, equipment and combat readiness. The Bosnian Serb Army had been in a strategically defensive mode since early 1994. The Bosnian/Croatian military triumphs against the Bosnian Serb Army in the autumn of 1995 (see Chapter 6) accordingly bore all the marks of the inevitable.

The VJ and Milošević's police today

The VJ's nominal strength in a normal situation must be somewhere between 70,000 and 90,000 men. What is called 'the transformation process' in the army has been slowed down by lack of funds. Its main principle was professionalism and the category of contract soldier has been introduced. But the objective of 30 per cent professionalisation has not been reached. Provision of critical technical resources was badly affected by the EU and UN sanctions. Salaries are lower than is good for an army, and specialised manpower is slowly leaving. As noted earlier, the VJ plays a secondary role in Milošević's defensive strategic planning, while the role of civil war army is given primarily to the police force.

There are some 80,000 people employed by the Ministry of the Interior of Serbia, most of them well-paid, uniformed officers. The Ministry also controls several combat-trained special police brigades, with helicopters, armour, mortars and anti-aircraft cannon. Beyond that, the police can mobilise its own reservists. These are the best-trained part of the general mobilisation pool – men in their prime who did their national service in the military police, border guards, elite and airborne units.

Contrary to common belief, paramilitaries, in the strict sense, have not played a significant role in the Balkan Wars. Legally, they simply do not exist. Serbian law gives the status of member of the armed forces to 'any person who takes up arms in defence of the country'. The term 'paramilitary formation' is, however, commonly applied to groups of armed volunteers organised by particular political parties. There have been several such groups (the Chetniks, the White Eagles, Arkan's Tigers, the Yellow Ants – the last nickname is a tribute to looting skills), but they were all organised with the consent of Milošević's secret police and armed, commanded and controlled by its officers. Attempts to organise paramilitary units outside the framework of police control have been quickly and efficiently discouraged. The only unit of any importance among these groups is the Serb Volunteer Guard (Arkan's Tigers), consisting of a core of some 200 well-trained and superbly equipped men, plus some reservists trained by them.

The paramilitaries were used as a psychological weapon in ethnic cleansing: they would enter a village or a city after the regular army units and start killing civilians, raping and looting. They would make sure that the stories spread, so that the next time, in the next village, no one would wait for them to come. Such units consisted on average of 80 per cent common criminals and 20 per cent fanatical nationalists. The latter did not usually last long (fanaticism is bad for business).

Croatia: a new power in the Balkans

The Croatian Army was formed in early 1991 from police reserves (some 40,000 of them). Under the name of National Guard Corps (ZNG), it fought the JNA and the Serb rebels of Krajina in 1991, in a war in which Croatia lost one-third of its territory. After the Vance plan had temporarily endorsed the Serb gains, Croatia started investing lots of money and effort in the creation of a new army. Foreign advisers were employed, sizeable funds were earmarked, privileges were established. Many trained JNA officers joined the Croat Army. An extensive campaign of arms-smuggling was started. Brigade after brigade was used in border skirmishes with Krajina Serbs and inside Bosnia, serving in shifts in order to acquire combat experience.

The Croatian Army relies on its eight professional Guards brigades, highly mobile, well-trained and well-equipped, supported by mobilised Home Guard units. The Air Force has 20-odd Mig-21 jet fighters (obsolescent) and some 6–8 Mi-24 Hind helicopter gunships. Armour is a rather strong asset – 450 main battle tanks (mostly T-55s and T-65s), some 600 APCs and other armoured vehicles. Artillery over 40 mm calibre runs to some 1000 pieces. Croatia keeps some 85,000 soldiers permanently under arms and can mobilise in short order another 50,000 without serious problems for its economy. The HVO (Croatian Defence Council) forces in Bosnia are practically an arm of the Croatian Army and have operated under Zagreb HQ planning, command and control since 1992.

After good planning and preparation, the Croatian Army attacked in 1995. Western Slavonia (UNPA West) was taken in the thirty-two-hour long 'Operation Lightning', on 1 May; almost all the 15,000 Serbs in the region left. Three months later, on 4 August, 'Operation Storm' took the rest of Krajina (UNPAs South and North) in a ninety-six-hour campaign; almost all the Serbs (this time some 180,000) left. Croatia's only remaining irredentum is Eastern Slavonia (UNPA East); in purely military terms it would be easy to take, but the proximity of Serbia would make it politically dangerous.

The fall of Krajina marked the bankruptcy of the idea of Greater Serbia and the emergence of a new power in the Balkans. Croatia is in fact not much of a threat to Serbia: the demarcation lines between those two states are drawn, the populations are resettled and the ideal of an ethnically pure state is achieved by both parties. Croatia's new self-confidence and strength is much more of a problem for Bosnia and for the Serbs in Bosnia. Croat nationalism has never renounced its ambitions in Bosnia, any more than Serb nationalism has. In 1993 Serb (BSA) and Croat (HVO) forces allied themselves happily against the Bosnian Army. It took a year of diplomatic effort and the resultant Bosnian-Croat Confederation agreement, forced on the parties by Washington, to neutralise that misalliance. The Confederation agreement was aptly described by Croatian minister of defence, Gojko Šušak: 'It's like swallowing a live frog.' The present strength of the Croatian Army presents the BSA with real dangers. The victory of the two in alliance against the Bosnian Serb Army in autumn 1995 makes those dangers that much more immediate.

The Bosnian Army and the People's War

The Army of the Republic of Bosnia and Hercegovina (ABH) was formed in the summer of 1992, when the very survival of Bosnia was at stake. As in Croatia, the initial organisational framework was the Ministry of Interior and its police reservists. There was a secret paramilitary organisation, the Patriotic League of the People (PLN), close to the SDA ruling party and active from March 1991, but its importance has been exaggerated. When the war began in April 1992, the critical battles around Sarajevo were fought by well-trained Bosnian police special units, supported by volunteers (some of them well-known Sarajevo gangsters). By mid-April the Bosnian Presidency had proclaimed a state of war, and all armed formations were reorganised within the framework of Territorial Defence. By that time some 260 officers of the JNA had already joined the Bosnian forces. Police and Territorial Defence forces took the Tuzla region in May 1992 and it has been the main stronghold of the Bosnian state ever since. On 1 July 1992 the Army of Bosnia and Hercegovina was officially founded and preparations for a prolonged guerrilla war began.

It is a miracle that the Bosnian Army survived at all during the winter of 1992–93: the enemy was far superior in numbers, weapons, logistics and transportation. That it did survive can be attributed to two main factors. First, the Bosnian Serb Army committed the grave (but inevitable) error of involving itself in the ethnic cleansing of territories where Serbs were not even in a majority, instead of going for the 'gravity centre' (von Clausewitz) of the Bosnian state. Second, the Bosnians stuck by the time-honoured doctrine of People's War (see Chapter 6), with its three stages. They survived the winter of 1992–93 by fighting a typical stage-one guerrilla war and defending their cities. Small, poorly armed units fought mostly for arms, cutting lines of communication, harassing the BSA by quick attacks and even quicker retreats into the mountains.

The very fact that the Bosnian Army survived to see the spring of 1993 was the key to future developments. The ragged bunches of haggard men armed with every imaginable kind of weapon did not look like an army at all; but in reality they were a formidable fighting force. They spent most of 1993 fighting both Serbs and Croats (the latter were supposed to be their allies) and emerged stronger. The Bosnian government began smuggling in arms. This had to be done over Croatian territory and Croatia top-sliced at least 50 per cent of every shipment, even after the hostilities between Bosnians and Bosnian Croats ceased. By mid-1993 the Bosnian Army was at stage two of the People's War, now disposing of bigger, battalion- and brigade-sized units – highly mobile and battle-hardened.

Their main strategy was to stretch Serb forces thin over a long frontline, always to attack at several points simultaneously, and to take as many strategically important locations as possible, primarily hill-tops and mountains from which future attacks could be launched. The territory held by the Bosnians is surrounded by Serb forces on three sides; the Bosnian Army perceived the advantage of operating inside the perimeter, forcing the BSA to move around it.

A very important development for the Bosnian state and army came in October 1993, when the army and the police eliminated in a swift and decisive operation several paramilitary gangs operating in Sarajevo (see Chapter 6). Those were the same gangsters who had helped defend the Bosnian capital in April and May 1992, and had then formed private military units, establishing political connections with certain factions of the ruling party SDA. They terrorised the non-Muslim population initially and everybody else subsequently. They tried to take over whole areas of Sarajevo. The decision to eliminate them and restore the rule of law was politically sensitive and it took courage and strength on the part of prime minister Haris Silajdžić and General Rasim Delić, Commander-in-Chief of the army, to do it. The government and the army emerged from that operation stronger and more respected, in Bosnia and abroad.

At the time of writing the Bosnian Army had about 120,000 soldiers in seven corps. Of these, some 100,000 men still did not have arms of their own. Since the Washington agreement on the Bosnian-Croat Confederation, arms have come more easily and the strength of the Bosnian Army is growing. It still has only a score of tanks and few armoured vehicles, but the emphasis is on mortars and artillery for the time being. If left alone by Croatia, the Bosnian Army will continue to grow stronger, and only a new Serb-Croat anti-Bosnian coalition could destroy it. While that seems highly improbable, the possibility is unlikely ever to be wholly dismissed from the minds of the Bosnian leaders

Conclusion

War is an extension of politics and cannot be considered separately from it. It is politics that determines whether an army will be used, abused or misused – to a degree, even, whether it will win or lose a war. The Yugoslav People's Army perished together with the Yugoslav political idea. Faced with the choice – to seek to preserve Yugoslavia and let communism perish, or to seek to preserve communism and forsake the state – the JNA choose the latter – and perished together with Yugoslavia. Instead of communism the army got Serb chauvinism, an obsolete, autistic and suicidal ideology. To quote General Kadijević again, the JNA did 'create three Serb armies': one has been defeated and no longer exists; one has been largely defeated; and one has been relegated to the status of a second-rate regional force. The JNA could have saved Yugoslavia (and itself): it only had to move against emergent chauvinist regimes in Belgrade and Zagreb, to support the liberal-democratic political programme of the last federal prime minister, Ante Marković, to defend the existing constitution and help change it later in a stable democratic political context, to agree to a confederal model or a loose federation, and to keep ever in mind that *anything is better than war.*

References

Bolotin, D. N. (1986) *Sovetskoe Strelkovoe Oruzhie* (Moscow).

Information about the Current Situation in the World and in Our Country and the Urgent Tasks of the JNA (1991) (Yugoslavia: Political Directorate, Ministry of Defence of Yugoslavia).

Kadijević, Veljko (1993) *Moje Vidjenje Raspada* (My View of the Breakup) (Belgrade: Politika).

Chapter 8

The Albanian Movement in Kosova

SHKELZEN MALIQI

The social framework

There are some very clearly delineated social phenomena in the post-communist
countries which have been taken in some quarters to represent the beginnings of a
new democratic system, but which are in practice quite different from – even the
opposite of – what they appear, and which create some real problems for the sociol-
ogy of politics. Under the rubrics of 'pluralism' and 'democratisation' we discover,
for instance, that there are a lot of parties that, as a matter of fact, are not parties;
that there are oppositions that are not authentic oppositions; and states that are not
real states. Any attempt to explain events in terms of these categories does, therefore, run a very real risk of simply creating misunderstandings, as Western politicians and social scientists have discovered. In the Balkans, misunderstandings have
come through as errors with tragic consequences, especially where Western politicians
have sought to bring calm and pacification at times of crisis. In practice, they have
tended to bring exactly the opposite.

The situation with respect to the Albanian movement in Kosova is no exception.
Formally, the movement consists of a number of political parties grouped together
in an opposition bloc. But that tells us very little about the true nature of the movement. It is true that in Kosova there is an Albanian Political Alternative, consisting
of twenty parties, none of which are in power, so that they can be described as being
in opposition, not only to the ruling parties, but also to the state, and to Serbia as a
political category. But the pluralism of the Albanian political scene in Kosova is
largely a façade, which sheds but little light on the true nature of Albanian Kosova
politics.

In reality, there is no genuine political alternative or opposition in Kosova, any
more than there is a real government. The essence of the Kosova situation over the
past few years has been a situation of total national confrontation between Serbs
and Albanians, expressed in different forms, bearing different intensities. On the
one side there is a military-police regime which continues to proclaim the goal of
total Serbian domination in Kosova. On the other side there are the Albanians who
make up 90 per cent of the population of the territory, but who have the status of
second-class citizens, even outcasts. That effectively excludes the option of playing

the role of opposition in the Western sense. In practice, the Albanians are seeking to establish a parallel public life in the margins, with an assembly and a government-in-exile, and with parallel institutions within Kosova (an independent educational system, stretching from primary schools up to university level; the elements of an independent health system; the beginnings of a relatively independent economic system, with instruments of self-finance, social security and 'national' trade unions; an independent system of sports representation; a parallel cultural life and elements of an independent information system).

The changes that have taken place in recent years among the Albanian population of Kosova, against the background – and stimulus – of police occupation are enormous, radical and irreversible. The old system has already been destroyed and a new one has been established. The very geography of social, political, national economic, etc. relations has been transformed. All this represents a deep *social* change, and political changes are no more than the tip of the iceberg. But it is those political changes – and the Albanian movement that emerged and promoted them after the breakdown of the old system from December 1989 – that constitute my main theme.

It was Serbian journalism and propaganda that dubbed this movement the Albanian Alternative – initially with a pejorative connotation. As long as the old one-party system still ruled, Serbian national-communists were able to use the term 'alternative' as a way of discrediting the revival of conscious 'opposition' among the Albanians of Kosova – by identifying it with pluralism. In the new political conditions, the terminology is used less frequently. But it is still legitimate to ask the question: Alternative to what and opposition to whom? Some believe that there is a real democratic and pluralistic opposition of alternatives. Others argue that there is a total, even totalitarian 'Albanian Liberation Movement', which tolerates no alternatives and whose pluralised form is a sham. Some of those who take the 'total' view see the 'Liberation Movement' as an anti-war alternative, articulated through a platform of non-violent, Gandhian resistance.

Harbingers of the Albanian movement – the demonstrations of 1968 and 1981

The Albanian national movement in Kosova achieved the status of mass movement only at the end of the 1980s. Under the first Yugoslavia (1918–41), the so-called Kacak (outlaw) Albanian movement was crushed, and the Xhemijet Party (representing the interests of Albanians and Serbo-Croat-speaking Muslims) was prohibited. Not a single Albanian organisation survived this period of Serbian repression to form the basis of a movement. But the disposition of the Albanian population remained strongly anti-Serb, as became evident during the Second World War, when the Albanians tended to view the Italians and Germans as liberators from the oppression of the Serbs. This was the main reason why in Kosova, unlike in Albania proper, the resistance movement against Fascist occupation was relatively weak.

After the Second World War, with the establishment of communist Yugoslavia (1945–91), the Albanians of Kosova were granted a degree of autonomy. They were thus able to organise a substantial official national movement. But nationalist and opposition groups operating illegally were small, limited in scope, and dispersed. Up to the 1960s, they had a generally anti-communist orientation and were predominantly linked to emigré organisations like Balli Kombatar (National Front) and Legaliteti (the royalist supporters of King Zog). From the 1960s, other groups, inspired by Enverism,[1] the Albanian variant of Marxism-Leninism (or, more accurately, Stalinism), became dominant. The best-known and most influential Enverist organisations were the Revolutionary Movement for Albanian Unity, founded by Adem Demaci, and the People's Movement for the Republic of Kosova. Though these groups and parties were active for many years, and had connections with Albanian emigré groups in the West and in Turkey, they were not able to establish credible party organisations on the new multiparty scene in Kosova after 1990.

Although the Albanian movement was weak and diffuse in communist Yugoslavia, it did foster a powerful sense of anticipation, which occasionally exploded in the form of mass demonstrations. The most important of these were the demonstrations of 27 November 1968 and March and April 1981. In both cases demonstrations were triggered by critical debates about 'federalism' within Yugoslavia, when even the communist authorities themselves were forced to discuss more openly the status of Kosova in particular, and of Albanians in Yugoslavia in general. In 1968 Tito's regime had reached a turning point, in terms of the decentralisation and partial confederalisation of Yugoslavia, while Kosova Albanian communists had taken advantage of Tito's settlement of accounts with Aleksandar Ranković in 1966[2] to demand republican status for Kosova. In the event, Tito and his compatriots devised an intermediate form of autonomy for Kosova, which gave the region *de facto* republican status, including the right of veto over federal government decisions, while keeping it formally within Serbia and denying it the formal right of secession, which belonged in principle, though not in practice, to the fully fledged republics.

The demonstrations that broke out in Prishtina, the capital of Kosova, on 27 November 1968, were in a way a response to the conclusion of the discussion on republican status for Kosova. The organisers of the demonstrations believed that they were a factor in the 'qualitative changes in the constitution of the Socialist Federal Republic of 1974' (which moved Yugoslavia even closer to confederalisation), and that they might have achieved more at that time if they had not been betrayed by 'Kosovo's bureaucratic clique' (Novosela, 1993: 94–5).

Compared to those of 1968, the demonstrations of 1981 (after Tito's death in May 1980) were on a much larger scale and claimed more victims.[3] They were organised as a series of sharp shocks, beginning with a student demonstration on 11 March. Social issues were to the fore at that demonstration, but there were also demands for a revision in the constitutional status of Kosova. The unrest surfaced

---

[1] Enver Hoxha (1908–85) ruled Albania with a Stalinist rod of iron from 1945 until his death.

[2] Ranković had been federal police chief and second in command in the Communist Party *nomenklatura* until his removal. Tito accused Ranković of misusing the Yugoslav secret police, and giving support to Serbian nationalism and hegemonism. Ranković was particularly brutal in his policies towards Kosova.

[3] One dead in 1968. Nine dead (officially) in 1981.

again on 26 March, when another student demonstration demanded the release of compatriots arrested at the first demonstration. But on the streets they were shouting slogans about the Republic of Kosova and the unification of the Albanian territories. The demonstrations were crushed with brutal force, with the help of the special federal police task force. The repression in turn provoked mass revolt by workers and citizens on 1 and 2 April. At that point the Yugoslav army intervened and a state of emergency was declared. The state of emergency continues until the present day (Kosumi, 1993).

The demonstrations of 1981 were proclaimed by the Belgrade authorities to be counter-revolutionary, and a long series of trials of Albanian 'irredentist' groups – in civil and military courts – began. The police 'detected' and tried by summary process around 200 'hostile and counter-revolutionary groups', half of them in the Yugoslav Army (Poulton, 1994: 61–2). A number of army officers of Albanian nationality figured among the condemned 'irredentists'. The verdicts were harsh: eight to fifteen years' imprisonment. The police repression, not to mention the treatment of the whole issue in the Serbian press, was so unselective and chauvinistic – in relation to the *whole* Albanian population – that it produced a pattern of defensive homogenisation on the part of the Kosova Albanians, initially on a platform of return to the constitutional autonomy of 1974. There followed mass protest marches in November 1988, with 300,000 participants, and a hunger strike by the Trepča miners against the suspension of Kosova's autonomy in February 1989 (Maliqi, 1990: 253–64). Under strong popular pressure, a Declaration of Independence was issued on 2 July 1990 by the 115 Albanian delegates of the Kosova Assembly – though they had been elected in December 1989 under the supervision of the League of Communists and the Milošević regime.

The Albanian movement in the late 1980s had two main streams. One, largely illegal (the Enverists), was composed of Marxist-Leninist groups, though without any common leadership or even a basic, agreed platform. The other stream was semi-legal (the Titoists), composed of intellectual and cultural organisations and institutions, management bodies within industry, and later on (late 1988–early 1989) even within parts of the state administration, the Assembly, and the League of Communists. Efforts were made to organise this latter stream into an institutionalised national movement. But these were unsuccessful and it was left to Milošević's 'anti-bureaucratic revolution' to forge the two streams into a single front, after the arrest of Azem Vllasi, the Kosova communist leader, in 1989, had left the semi-legal movement leaderless.

The formation of a pluralised Albanian movement under the threat of war

The main reason for the failure of the Albanian movement to impose itself more powerfully as a continuous force was its failure to free itself from the ideology of communism. Both Enverists and Titoists were followers of an ideology which had already lost its prestige and credibility by the 1980s. Although the Enverists were considered to be great patriots, and good and ardent nationalists, by 1990 they were simply old communists. For most of the 'frontline troops' of the old movement – people like Adem Demaci who had suffered in prison for their convictions – this was a fatal handicap in a new Albanian movement that was firmly anti-communist.

In 1990–91, ten years after its beginning, the crisis moved into a new stage of intensity. The division between Serbs and Albanians became total and confrontation became a way of life. It was difficult to predict what was going to happen next and Kosova became a zone of high war risk. The entire structure of regional administration was dismantled. The local police and security forces were disarmed (March 1990), all levels of local and municipal administration were suspended, big industrial enterprises were placed under direct administration, the mass media were occupied and the Albanian-language section of Prishtina University closed down (1991–92).[4] In this sense the Kosova problem increasingly took on the dimensions of the Palestine problem.

As a state with a high degree of military capability, Israel used all coercive means to 'liberate' and 'redeem' Palestine, as a 'sacred land' which had been 'usurped' by the Palestinians. In the same way the dominant state machinery of the 'unitary' republic of Serbia decided to apply all coercive means to the task of bringing Kosova back into the national possession of the Serbs, on the grounds that Kosova had been, historically, 'sacred Serbian soil', which had been 'usurped' by the Albanians a couple of centuries ago. In this sense, extreme Serbian nationalism adopted the key ideas of militant Zionism – the Serbs as a persecuted and historically tragic people, the notion of the historical right to gather all Serbs within one state, the idea of crusade against (in this case) the Albanians as an alleged vanguard of Islamic fundamentalism, the right to recolonise 'sacred soil', the right to impose demographic control over the 'usurpers'.[5]

In 1990–91 it seemed that the Serbian regime was preparing for war, more specifically for a quick and effective campaign to change the ethnic structure of Kosova. Simultaneously, following on the unofficial ratification of the Declaration of Independence of 2 July 1990, the proclamation of the constitution of the Republic of Kosova in Kacanik on 7 September 1990 and the election of an unofficial multiparty parliament of Kosova on 24 May 1992, the Albanians, supported by the majority of Kosova Serbo-Croat-speaking Muslims and Turks, proceeded to build their own uncompromising platform, based on the principle of separation of Kosova from Serbia.

In principle, this could only mean one thing: that the Albanians had accepted the challenge of war. Both government and opposition within Serbia considered

---

[4] *Kosova Watch*, no. 2, Kosova Helsinki Committee, Prishtina, 1994.

[5] There are some big differences between the Palestinian and Kosova situations. If we think in terms of life-threatening encirclement, then the similarity is between Jews and Albanians, rather than Jews and Serbs. Just as Israel is confined to a narrow coastal strip, and surrounded by the much more numerous Arabs, so the Albanians are largely confined to a narrow coastal strip on the Adriatic, with just a few little land corridors into the Balkan hinterland, and are largely surrounded by a Slavdom that stretches to the Urals and beyond. Just as Arab extremists declare of the Jews 'We will drive them into the sea', so Serbian militants say that they will 'first force the Albanians to flee beyond the Procletian Mountains, and then drive them into the sea'.

Kosova to be an inalienable part of Serbia, as laid down in the Serbian constitution of September 1990. So there was no possible basis for negotiation. Rather there were two irreconcilible national platforms, one based on the principle of plebiscitory self-determination, the other on historical rights and a certain conception of the state. The fact that war has not yet broken out in Kosova can be attributed to two factors: the decision by Albanian leaders to follow a policy of non-violent resistance (Maliqi, 1994), and the fact that virtually all Serbian military capacities have been taken up in the conflicts in Croatia and Bosnia and Hercegovina. But the war has only been postponed – because nothing has been done to remove its root causes. In the meantime the ethnic conflict in Kosova has turned into a kind of intense war of nerves, in which the one side stops at nothing, carrying out the most brutal violations of human rights and civil liberties, completely ignoring the protests of the international organisations which for a while kept monitoring teams in Kosova, while the other side bottles up its humiliation, despair, fury, rage and hatred – but for how long before it explodes?

In that context, a key question arises. What will happen if the Albanian movement is exhausted, either by the current war of nerves, or indeed by a real war in the future? What will happen if it remains the only option for Kosova, despite all the efforts to develop a pluralistic dialogue, to untie the Kosova knot? Before trying to answer this question, let us examine the Albanian political 'scene', its makeup, and the forces that populate it. We begin with the 'pre-history'.

The roots of Albanian political organisation

The new Albanian movement in Kosova has developed and attained a mass character during a period of deepening interethnic distance and conflict in the former Yugoslavia. It is easy to interpret its gradual development as a response to the closing of national ranks on the part of the Serbian minority within Kosova over a period of years, and to the creation of the Movement of Kosova Serbs (1985–89), as an anti-constitutional organisation aimed at putting pressure on the Kosova, Serbian and federal organs to limit or, indeed, abolish Kosovan autonomy. As a matter of fact, the Movement of Kosova Serbs in Kosova was from the beginning under the control of the Belgrade headquarters of the organisation, the goal of which was a redisposition of forces with the federation – in effect a restoration of Serbian hegemony at the Yugoslav level. The role of the Kosova Serbs was to 'prove' the injustice which had been done to Serbia by the constitution of 1974, and to place it in the context of a more general anti-Serbian conspiracy, hatched by all the 'dark' powers of the world (the Vatican, the Comintern, Germany, Islamic fundamentalism, Albania, the freemasons, etc.) in alliance with domestic traitors like Tito and his cronies, Croatia, Slovenia and the 'Kosova-Albanian mafia'.

The Albanian movement, as mentioned above, grew out of the discontent of the Albanian masses. The old communist regime of Kosova, under the tutelage of its masters (federal and Serbian), did nothing to allay those discontents, and continued to favour Serbian interests. Indeed the state 'annexation' of Kosova (in 1989) had been preceded, in October 1988, by a party annexation, as the autonomy of the

Kosova League of Communists within the Serbian League was liquidated. It is a surpreme irony that this was the last voluntary act of the party-state, and that indeed it was the first stage in the destruction of the foundations of Titoist Yugoslavia. Meanwhile, the unrestrained development of party pluralism and democracy in Slovenia and Croatia provided a vivid contrast to the aggression of the party-state in Kosova (and also in China, with the Tian An Men Square massacre), and the veiled threats that the Yugoslav People's Army might emerge as the final arbiter of the political crises in the country, and the 'last line of defence of the heritage of the Revolution'. In practice, the militaristic line favoured the extreme Serbian visions of a Greater Serbia within a restructured federation.

It has to be said that the Albanians formed their political alternative more through a concurrence of lucky events than on the basis of any definite plan or organisation. Several generations and teams of Kosova politicians, including the Kosova communist leader, Azem Vllasi, had already been politically liquidated, while the intellectuals were exposed to continuous persecution and harassment, all aimed at delaying for as long as possible the formation of a new Albanian political elite in Kosova. And yet, it was obvious that it was impossible to stop that process. Tiny opposition groups were created by intellectuals, as they were everywhere in the real-socialist countries of Eastern Europe, primarily within the framework of their associations: the Association of Writers of Kosova, the Association of Philosophers and Sociologists of Kosova, etc.

The Association of Writers, which under the old regime had been obedient, without being slavish (a kind of benign opposition), was rent apart in 1988 by the mass resignation of the Serbian writers from within its ranks (27 out of a total membership of 150), with the avowed intention of destroying the Association. In the course of the futile negotiations between the two sides in April 1988 the Albanian writers for the first time openly presented a draft of the Albanian national programme. Overnight, they found themselves promoted to the status of a beacon for the mobilisation of national forces. Dr Ibrahim Rugova, president of the Association, became the main figure of resistance for Albanians in that period, and his interviews to the foreign and domestic press finally gave the masses their voice.

The Association of Philosophers and Sociologists of Kosova (APHSK) had created its own oppositional nucleus at a much earlier stage, built around some members of the editorial staff and some of the collaborators of the *Thema* magazine and in particular its editor, Dr Muhamedin Kullashi. The Association become politically more assertive when Isuf Berisha was elected its president in 1989. It managed to organise the first real oppositional gathering, in spite of bans and cancelled hall bookings. In the first period of the pluralisation of the Kosova political scene, the APHSK emerged as an equal partner of the other parties and political groups, as the main organiser of the petition 'For Democracy, against Violence' (signed by 400,000 citizens of Kosova), and as the initiator of numerous appeals, announcements, declarations and actions. Later on, as political parties became properly organised, the Association decided to withdraw from the political scene, though its individual members remained active through the various parties – and party leaderships – they had joined. (They joined mainly the Social-Democratic Party of Kosova, but were also to be found among the leaderships of other parties. For instance, the influential scholar Fehmi Agani is the leading ideologist and vice-president of the important Democratic League of Kosova.)

For all the importance of these developments, there could not have been such a powerful and sudden turn of events in the direction of democratisation in Kosova, had it not been for the *deus ex machina* of sweeping democratisation across Eastern Europe, from the Baltic to the Black Sea, that accompanied the spectacular collapse of the Soviet empire. This dispirited and disorganised the last military bulwarks of Yugoslav Bolshevism and at the same time overturned Serbian plans for the Bolshevik pacification of Kosova. Neither the intensification of the state of emergency in the spring of 1989, when several hundred Albanian intellectuals were detained in 'isolation' (several months' imprisonment without investigation or trial), nor the Stalinist show trials of Azem Vllasi, some of the leaders of the Trepča strike and some demonstrators, could stand in the way of the tidal wave of democracy that swept the region after the fall of the Berlin Wall.

The Kosova alternative appeared as a mimetic opposition. There is nothing original in the Serbian nationalistic option for Kosova. All of its elements are *déjà vu* in terms of the populist, chauvinistic, nationalistic and totalitarian movements of the past, and of the well-tried techniques of manipulation of mass hysteria for state purposes. (Milošević himself has been compared to Mussolini and Hitler.) In the same way, there is nothing original in the Albanian alternative for Kosova. Since the adversary had chosen totalitarian ideology and behaviour, the Albanians were happy in turn to rely on the East-European model of democratic counter-action, which had proved to be very efficient in the fight against totalitarianism. The Albanians of Kosova simply took over the model and adapted it to the specific conditions of Kosova (permanent state of emergency and effective police occupation). The Gandhian tactic of peaceful resistance, itself a riposte to Serbian 'annexation', proved to be at least a propaganda success, in terms of fostering sympathy and a sense of affinity with the world Albanian community and world democratic public opinion.

Political organisations and parties on the contemporary Kosova political scene

The preconditions for opposition activity were already present in the last days of the former Yugoslavia, with toleration for the founding of opposition parties already established in some regions. Between December 1989 and February 1990 Kosova was quite rapidly overtaken by pluralism, with the sudden, catastrophic disintegration of the League of Communists, the Socialist Alliance,[6] and indeed all the other institutions of the system, with Albanian members resigning *en masse*. But it goes without saying that the pluralism came with a national bent, just as the previous policy had created an unbridgeable national gap. Even the founders of the Prishtina branch of the Union for a Yugoslav Democratic Initiative (UYDI)[7] were confronted

---

[6] The League of Communist's mass organisation.

[7] Among the founders of the UYDI in January 1989 in Zagreb were, from Kosova, Dr Muhamed Kullashi and Shkelzen Maliqi.

by this gap when they sought for multinational membership of the organization. In the event, only two Serbs joined it, in addition to several hundred Albanians.[8] From the Prishtina branch of the UYDI sprang the Kosova Alternative (founded on 7 December 1989), which was wholly Albanian in its composition.

In Kosova, as nearly everywhere else in the former Yugoslavia, it was the UYDI that broke the political monopoly of the League of Communists in the former Yugoslavia. The Prishtina branch of the UYDI, holding to the vision of the association, of a Yugoslavia reconstructed as a federation with sovereignty shared between consitituent republics and individual citizens, pressed for an Albanian option for Kosova within that framework. It played a very important role in initiating the foundation of a number of smaller parties and movements (Social Democrats, Greens). Under the leadership of the energetic Veton Surroi, the Prishtina branch of the UYDI facilitated the legalisation of many of the routine operations of the Albanian movement, such as the launching of the petition 'For Democracy, against Violence', the planning of mass, Gandhian protest actions, and the attempted organisation of dialogues with the Serbian government and opposition.

In the middle of 1989, a Council for the Defence of Human Rights and Freedoms (CDHRF) was founded in Prishtina, with Academician Idriz Ajeti and the energetic but mercurial historian Zekeria Cana at its head. Over a short period of time, the Council did an enormous amount of work aimed at transforming the passive attitude to repression which had been typical, up to then, of the Kosova Albanian masses and media. It collected a large number of testimonies on violations of human rights and police terror, and also on the mistreatment and even murder of Albanians in the Yugoslav Army. In 1991 Adem Demaci was elected president of the Council (*Knocking on Europe's Conscience*, 1992).

The Democratic League of Kosova (DLK), founded on 23 December 1989, was designed as a national party of Albanians in Kosova, with a brief to operate throughout the territory of the former Yugoslavia. For that reason, Democratic Leagues were initially established in Slovenia and Croatia, and also in Montenegro and Bosnia and Hercegovina. But with the rapid dismemberment of Yugoslavia, this concept of Yugoslavia-wide organisation had to be abandoned. The Albanians of Macedonia, in consideration of their special circumstances and in consultation and agreement with the DLK, decided to organise an independent national party: the Albanian Party for Democratic Prosperity (APDP). Both the DLK and the APDP were formed on the national/ethnic model.

In a short time – five weeks to be exact – the DLK managed to gather several thousand members. (They actually claimed that almost 700,000 had joined the party, but that would mean that nearly all adult Kosova Albanians had become members!) The explosion of membership of the DLK can be interpreted as a demonstration of Albanian discontent with the old regime, and the whole trend of

---

[8] It is at first sight paradoxical that Albanians joined in such large numbers an organisation openly committed to the preservation of Yugoslavia, while Serbs shunned it. The point is that the UYDI was primarily a *democratic* organisation – though it was also a Yugoslav one. As its leader, Žarko Puhovski, once said, 'If I'm forced to choose between Yugoslavia at any price and democracy, I'll choose democracy.'

developments in the old Yugoslavia. It also reflected a substantial personal vote for Ibrahim Rugova.

From the outset, the DLK started to develop a powerful network of branches and sub-branches throughout Kosova, and among the Albanian diaspora in Europe and the USA. The goal of the DLK leadership was to establish a Pan-Albanian, broad front, in which all groups within the population would find a place – women, youth, children, etc. – very much on the model of the old Socialist Alliance. Indeed, to a considerable extent the DLK was able to fill the void left by the disintegration of the old League of Communists and Socialist Alliance, right down to the local level.

The main strategic issue for the DLK was, from the start, the status of Kosova. Initially, in the spring of 1990, the call – by mimicry – was for 'full' or 'real' autonomy for Kosova. Demands then escalated steadily, first to a claim for equal status for the Kosova Albanians with the other nations of the federation, then to a demand for a Republic of Kosova within a reformed federation; and finally, after the referendum of 30 September 1991 'on a sovereign and independent state of Kosova', for independence or, as it was diplomatically packaged by Dr Rugova, for the establishment of a temporary protectorate in Kosova under a UN mandate.

During the first six or seven months of its existence, the DLK developed into a power centre with real authority in Kosova. It took control of the Albanian part of the Kosova Assembly, and even of the government of Jusuf Zejnullahu. By the spring and summer of 1990, accordingly, a competition had developed between the DLK and the Belgrade regime for control of Kosova's autonomous institutions. The outcome of this competition was finally decided in June 1990, with the liquidation of Kosova's autonomy by act of the Serbian parliament.

Other parties and movements were founded in the spring of 1990, although by that time the DLK had practically already conquered most of the broader political space. This blossoming came partly as an articulation of the feeling that it was high time to show that Kosova Albanians had made the transition to a new system and were moving towards genuine pluralism. The main new parties that date from this period are listed in Table 8.1.

In addition, there are the Republican Party of Kosova (two factions), the National-Democratic Party of Kosova, the Liberal Party of Kosova and the National Front (Balli Kombatar). Strikingly, there is not a single survivor from the old political elite in the leaderships of the new organisations.

During the first phase, the platforms of the Albanian democratic parties chimed in very closely with the aspirations of the masses: the establishment of comprehensive and real autonomy for Kosova, general democratisation, the settlement of national and other conflicts by a multiparty parliament, the release of all political prisoners, etc. In the event, the release of a certain number of political prisoners apart, the Albanian democratic movement did not manage to achieve any of these goals. Rather it was confronted by increasingly severe repression, and increasingly open provocation to start a war. So the Albanian movement was obliged to take on an essentially fire-fighting role. Its great success was in managing to persuade the Kosova Albanian masses to keep their tempers, and not start the war that Belgrade wanted.

The biggest burden, in restraining the revolt of the Albanian masses, fell on the

Table 8.1 Major Political Parties and other Political Organisations Created in the Spring of 1990

Name of party	Name of leader
Social Democratic Party of Kosova	Muhamedin Kullashi (1990); Shkelzen Maliqi (1990–92); Luljeta Pula Beqiri (1992–present); splinter group under Besim Bokshi formed in January 1994
Agrarian Party of Kosova	Hivzi Islami
Youth Parliament of Kosova	Halil Matoshi (1990–91); Veton Surroi (1991–93); Bajram Kosumi (1993-present)
Green Movement of Kosova	Nait Vrenezi (1990–91); Ilir Hoxha (1991–present)
Independent Trade Unions of Kosova	Hajrullah Gorani
Albanian Christian-Democratic Party	Lazar Krasniqi (1990–93); Mark Krasniqi (1993-present)
Forum of Albanian Intellectuals	Rexhep Qosja
Party of National Unity	Halil Alidemaj

shoulders of the smaller groups and parties, especially on those of the Youth Parliament of Kosova (YKP), which had a well-organised network and managed to root out the influence of the militant Marxist-Leninist groups which had been the main instigators of demonstrations, calling even for armed insurrection against Belgrade. The Marxist-Leninists had been to a considerable extent dispersed and disorganised by the imprisonments of the 1980s. The critical factor, however, was the statement from the Marxist-Leninists' revered leader, Adem Demaci, during his last month of imprisonment, in early 1990,[9] supporting non-violent resistance and the democratic option. Overnight, Marxism-Leninism became a thing of the past.

Although it had the strongest network, the DLK showed some hesitation and uncertainty in relation to the initial mass actions organised by the YPK and other democratic groups. Because the DLK tended to see itself as the legitimate heir to the old authorities in Kosova, and as the party truly representative of the national interest, it tended to concentrate on fighting internal political rivals within Kosova, instead of on taking on the real adversary: the Serbian authorities. Because some of the other parties and groups were more energetic in their political actions, the DLK leadership began to fear a haemorrhaging of membership towards those groups. The smaller groups had proposed from the beginning the establishment of a common political platform based on the formula: *first democracy, then the status of Kosova.*

---

[9] Demaci had been in prison for twenty-nine years.

The argument was that placing the priority on the status of Kosova was essentially a war option, which could postpone democratisation in Kosova and even in Serbia and Yugoslavia, while the victory of democracy might provide a starting point for negotiations on the future status of Kosova. But the DLK refused all proposals for the establishment of a Coordinating Body and Democratic Forum because it considered itself the only true representative of the national interest of the Kosova Albanians, and viewed the democratic option as a kind of national betrayal – potentially, if not actually. Their argument was that political 'tea-parties' and their self-elected leaders were prepared to trade the cause of Kosova's independence for a dubious democracy. Their slogan was: *free elections yes, but in a free Kosova.*

The suspension of the autonomy of Kosova by Serbia

As a result, the Albanian Alternative in the end fell into the trap of delaying democratic elections and insisting on the priority of the status of the Kosova question, thus effectively depriving itself of political manoeuvring space. The Declaration of Independence on 2 June 1990 was an attempt at a 'pre-emptive strike' against a 'constitutional' suspension of Kosova's autonomy by Serbia. But Serbia simply responded with an unconstitutional 'annexation', attacking Kosova's autonomy on all fronts and imposing a complete political and military occupation (Kelmendi and Kelmendi, 1992; *Knocking on Europe's Conscience*, 1992: 23–5).

The imposition of military administration on Kosova effectively neutralised the strategy – if it can be called a strategy – of the Albanian Alternative. With the democratic option foreclosed and non-violent resistance running out of time, the *sui generis* pluralistic complexion of the Albanian Alternative became increasingly inappropriate. In this context, the 'united national liberation front' option, as a form of mobilisatory strategy, began to look a much better prospect for the next phase.

With the suspension of Kosova's political life, Serbia promulgated, on the pretext that there was an imminent danger of secession, a series of sectarian acts, closing down the Assembly, abolishing the government of Kosova and introducing a system of direct colonial rule in the region. The Serbian Assembly took over all the property in Kosova that had previously belonged to 'society' under the fictitious rubric of self-management. They dismissed all Albanians employed in regional and municipal administration, and a comprehensive programme of 'ethnic cleansing' was then implemented in the management bodies of all social sector firms and cultural institutions. And the main task of the all-Serb 'emergency management teams' that were installed was to continue the process of 'ethnic cleansing' of Albanians at the lower levels – that of ordinary clerks and workers. Emergency measures of this kind were even introduced in hospitals and nursery schools. Out of a total of around 170,000 Albanians previously employed in the public sector, 115,000 – i.e. three-quarters – were fired, according to data from the Independent Trade Unions of Kosova (Fehatu, 1992).

Viewed from the Albanian side, all these measures were, above all, simply unconstitutional and coercive. According to the constitution of 1974 Kosova had the status of a fully-fledged federal unit, with the Kosova Assembly having the right of veto *vis-à-vis* the Federal Assembly and the Presidency of the former Yugoslavia. There was no constitutional basis for the suspension of the Kosova Assembly and government, whether in terms of the federal, Serbian or Kosova constitutions. As a matter of fact, Yugoslavia was effectively destroyed on 5 July 1990 when the Kosova Assembly was dispersed, in that from that moment on the highest representative body in the country, the Federal Assembly, could no longer legally and validly function, since one of its constituent elements, with the right of veto, had been forcibly abolished. No decision about the Kosova Assembly – not even a decision to suspend it – could be made without that Assembly's agreement. The action of 5 July 1990 was, therefore, effectively a *coup d'état*, which started Yugoslavia's descent into chaos. At the same time it compromised the cause of democracy and legality in Serbia, in that Milošević, who was under pressure to call democratic elections, decided that it was too dangerous to hold elections with the existing constitution – because they would almost certainly produce a vote for independence on the part of the Kosova population. So he decided to change the Serbian constitution first. But this was illegal in terms of the existing constitution, because that constitution stipulated that the Assembly of Kosova could delay adoption of any new constitution for a period of six months.

The impact of the suspension of Kosova's autonomy on the process of democratisation

With the postponement of elections, and through what amounted to a military occupation of Kosova, Yugoslavia – and that meant effectively Serbia – created a 'black hole' that continues to swallow up any attempt to democratise the Yugoslav/Serbian state and society. In dispersing the Kosova Assembly and making democratic articulation by the Kosova Albanians impossible, Serbia was actually foreclosing on its own chances of democracy, by destroying any basis for an effective Serbian opposition. And the disease has spread, through the creation, by coercive and undemocratic means, of a new 'Yugoslavia', a Serbian Republic in Bosnia, and a Serbian Krajina (now defunct) within the territory of Croatia. The apartheid in Kosova and the war in Bosnia all reflect the militaristic essence of the Serbian regime, all stem from the 'original sin' of the coercive 'annexation' of Kosova. In conditions such as these, it is impossible to talk about either Kosova Albanian or Serbian opposition. There are parties that declare that they belong to the opposition but the situation in practice precludes effective opposition, whether in terms of programmes or actions.

The Kosova Albanians have been invited on three occasions – 1990, 1992 and 1993 – to participate in multiparty elections and thus to enter the Serbian parliament, where they could have used parliamentary means to further their aims. The diplomatic representatives of democratic countries have exerted considerable pressure on Albanian political organisations to take part in these elections. But the Kosova Albanian line is that they cannot do this until the previous constitutional situation in Kosova is restored: more precisely, that the state of siege and the system of apartheid are lifted. Participation by Albanian parties in the elections in Serbia would, it is argued, represent a legalisation of violence, and a recognition of an illegal constitution and a system that was established without the consent of the population of Kosova. In this way, they would be signing a capitulation and committing an act of self-destruction, since the ruling party of Serbia, and most of the so-called Serbian opposition, calls in published documents for ethnic change to the advantage of the Serbs in the population of Kosova. So to swear loyalty to the Serbian state would mean recognising the 'property' rights, the rights of free disposal, of Serbs over Kosova – and that could mean the expulsion of a million Albanians from Kosova. Although, from the pragmatic point of view, participation in the Serbian elections might offer some advantages – it could be developed as a logical extension of the non-violent resistance strategy which Kosova Albanians have used in the past – it is a practice ruled out because it would represent a recognition of the Serbian *fait accompli* in Kosova, a denial of the right of self-determination, and a suicidal act in the face of the Serbian policy of assimilation and colonisation in Kosova.

As far as Kosova is concerned there is, unfortunately, still no Serbian opposition. This is, indeed, one of the main reasons why the Serbian opposition is so weak and helpless. It is unable to articulate any alternative, oppositional national programme, since its own programme presupposes exactly the same principle of unity of the Serbian lands as Milošević's. The situation is similar in Croatia and, indeed, in some of the other new states of the Balkans and Eastern Europe. A true opposition cannot, by the same token, be established in aspirant or self-proclaimed states like the Republic of Kosova. Kosova Albanian political organisations are not real parties, but merely pluralised elements of a national liberation movement whose overriding goal is the establishment of an independent Kosova.

The unofficial elections of 1992

In May 1992 multiparty elections for the (Alternative) Kosova Assembly were held. They were organised in a semi-legal fashion, under conditions of severe police harassment, mainly in private houses. It is remarkable that as many as twenty-four political organisations participated in them. Besides Albanian political parties, the Party of Democratic Action of Kosova (Serbo-Croat-speaking Muslims) and the Turkish People's Party of Kosova took part. Elections for the Parliament, and also for the presidency of Kosova, were organised. Only one candidate stood for the presidency, Ibrahim Rugova, the president of DKL, and the leader of the Albanian movement. Dr Rugova gained 99.9 per cent of the votes in the election for the presidency. In the elections for Parliament, out of 100 single-constituency seats, ninety-six were won by the DLK, two by independents who were members of the DLK, one by the Party of Democratic Action and one by the Parliamentary Party of Kosova (the successor organisation to the Youth Parliament of Kosova). The election procedures also provided for forty-two seats to be distributed on the basis of proportional representation to all parties gaining more than 3 per cent of the vote. This gave the Parliamentary Party of Kosova twelve seats, the Albanian Christian-Democratic Party seven, the Social-Democratic Party of Kosova one, and the Party of Democratic Action three. Thirteen seats, reserved for Serbian and Montenegrin parties on the basis of the proportion of those nationalities in the total population, were left vacant.

The May 1992 Parliament of Kosova did not manage to constitute itself, because the Serbian police stopped it. So in a formal sense it is impossible to talk about either government or opposition in the Kosova Parliament. There is no clearly artic-ulated parliamentary opposition to DLK, which exercises comprehensive political control. More genuine opposition is offered by some non-paraliamentary groups like the Forum of Albanian Intellectuals and the Party of National Unity, which are committed to immediate unification with Albania. Even this, however, is a variant of the national programme, rather than real opposition.

A path to the future?

The self-understanding of the Albanians of Kosova is reflected in their implicit col-lective decision and pledge to be free, to have nothing more to do with Serbia or the Serbs, and to achieve independence for Kosova. That is why the Albanians pro-claimed the Kosova Republic, and held their referendum on independence and elec-tions for a multi-party parliament. The next part of the fairy tale should bring punishment to the villain and reward the righteous.

In reality, however, in Kosova and in other places where problems of this kind have surfaced, Europe has to conceal its criminal past, and even its present. It does not wish to raise the question of the revision of borders, and seeks to solve the prob-lem of Kosova exclusively within the framework of safeguards for human and national rights and guarantees of the autonomy of Kosova within Serbia. After all, if Kosova were allowed to exercise the right of self-determination and secession through a plebiscite, why should such a right not be granted to the Corsicans, Scots, Catalans, Flemish or any other people in Europe left without their own state, or enjoying limited autonomy at best?

The current situation in Kosova is unbearable, a state of neither war nor peace – but still more war than peace. The problem must certainly be resolved through dis-cussions and negotiations and as soon as possible, bearing in mind the possibility of an explosion and massacre, and even a new Balkan war. But the determination of Europe and other international actors that the Albanians must live under the juris-diction of Serbia could produce a desperate situation – like a court judgment order-ing a married couple who hate each other, and can no longer live together, to share a flat. And if one of them wanted to partition the flat, the judge would say cynically: you will have your little autonomous corner in that flat where you can cry your heart out.

There are also some who say: things ought to be viewed in terms of the establish-ment of democratic institutions in the region. Kosova will have a new order, a new system, a new basis for intercommunity relations. Serbs and Albanians can live in mutual tolerance. But the crux of the problem of Kosova is precisely the absence of any prospects of establishing democratic institutions under the present circum-stances of absolute mistrust and absolute unwillingness to live together. Serbia is not prepared to lift the state of emergency and repeal the harsh measures limiting civil rights without a preceding declaration of loyalty by the Albanians. The Albanians for their part are not prepared to discuss coexistence with the Serbs without the restoration of the parliament and government of Kosova with all the state preroga- tives these bodies had prior to their forcible dissolution, and with due respect shown to the decisions of these bodies taken in secret sessions following dissolution, and in exile. Serious Albanian-Serbian talks could be conducted in the first instance only on the subject of self-determination for Kosova, on how to give Kosova indepen- dence, and only secondarily on the economic, political and other ties Kosova might have with Serbia.

The question arises, finally, of a possible negotiated solution of the Kosova ques- tion. On the Serbian side, opposition democratic circles have argued in favour of trying to reach an 'historic agreement' between Serbs and Albanians. It will be remembered, however, that, prior to the beginning of the war in Bosnia, in the sum- mer of 1991, the Muslim Bosnian Organisation initiated negotiations on an historic agreement of that kind between the Serbs and the Bosnian Muslims (see Chapter 6). We all know what happened to those negotiations: they failed, because the great majority of Bosnian Muslims did not trust Milošević's Serbia, *inter alia* because of the way it had dealt with the Kosova problem. It would clearly, therefore, be a pre- condition of any attempt at a resolution of the Kosova question that all the measures imposed in Kosova by Milošević's regime be repealed and that democracy be estab- lished in the region.

Let us assume that this point could be agreed. The question of the *framework* of Kosovan democracy then emerges. Some would like this framework to be the Serbian parliament, others the parliament of Kosova. And the issue is a critical one, for it was, after all, the parliament of Serbia which dissolved the Kosova parlia- ment, for fear that free elections in Kosova would establish the legally elected majority rule of the Albanians in Kosova – as a first step towards secession. Any Albanian-Serbian historic agreement would first have to untie this seemingly inex- tricable knot.

Resolution of the Serbian question in the former Yugoslavia has been sought, by the Serbs themselves, largely through the ideas and practices of *ethnic delimitation*. Viewed against this background, the Albanian-Serbian conflict over Kosova would appear to be one of the easiest to resolve in the whole volatile region of the Balkans. For here, delimitation between Serbs and Albanians could be carried out far more easily than delimitation between Serbs, Croats and Muslims in Bosnia, or Serbs and Croats in Croatia. In Kosova, and in Southern Serbia proper, Albanians account for a compact, two-thirds plus majority in all local communities, except in a few municipalities on the borders between Kosova and Serbia, the Sandjak and Montenegro (Zubin Potok, Leposavic, Medvedja). In Kosova itself, the Albanian majority hosts a very small percentage of the total number of Serbs in the Balkans (about 1.5 per cent). At the same time, 38 per cent of all the Albanians in the Balkans are accounted for by the Albanians of Kosova (together with the Albanians in Macedonia, they represent almost half of the Albanian people). Thus Serbian pre- tensions to treat Kosova as an exclusively Serbian territory create an unsustainable anomaly: namely the imposition of a regime of occupation and colonial status on 38 per cent of all the Albanians in the Balkans by 1.5 per cent of all the Serbs in the

Balkans. By the same token, it is clear that the maximalist objectives of the Serbian state for Kosova are largely unfeasible: they would require colossal funds and would, moreover, doom Serbia to continuing international isolation.

For the Albanian side the option is to leave Serbia, and the main trump cards here are peace and democracy. The Abanians are ready to enter any negotiations, but only as independent subjects, i.e. as a people participating in decision-making rather than as a minority, which they quite simply are not. If democracy is based on a majority decision-making process and the right to the self-determination of peoples, then the establishment of a democratic system will bring a demand for decolonisation and the *exercise* of the right of self-determination of the population of Kosova. Thus for the Albanians, all roads lead somehow to secession. This is true at present, in conditions of oppression and existential insecurity. It will be equally true under the putative democratic regime of the future.

References

Fehatu, Adil (1992) Temporary measures: an act of destruction of economic enterprises and social institutions in Kosova, English summary *Masat e Parkohshme* (Prishtina: BSPK).

Kelmendi, B. and Kelmendi, N. (1992) Dismantling and Serbization of the judicial system in Kosova, *Kosova Watch*, vol. I, no. 2, August.

Knocking on Europe's Conscience – Kosova: Evidence and Documents (1992) (Prishtina: CDHRF).

Kosumi, Bajram (1993) Pse i organizuam demonstratat me 1981 (How we organised the demonstrations in 1981) *Koha* (Prishtina), no. 6, 3 March, pp. 31–8.

Maliqi, Shkelzen (1990) *Nyja e Kosoves: as Vllasi as Millosheviqi* (Knot of Kosova: neither Vllasi nor Milošević) (Ljubljana: Krt).

Maliqi, Shkelzen (1994) Non-violent resistance of Albanians. In *Conflict or Dialogue: Serbian–Albanian Relations and Integration of the Balkans* (Subotica: Open University – European Civic Centre for Conflict Resolution).

Novosela, Selatin (1993) *Kosovo '68* (Prishtina: Renesensa).

Poulton, Hugh (1994) *The Balkans: Minorities and States in Conflict* (London: The Group).

Chapter 9

The West and the International Organisations

SUSAN L. WOODWARD

Introduction

The international aspects of the Yugoslav crisis pose a particularly difficult subject for analysis. The primary reason is methodological: the crisis was so much a consequence of, and an adjustment to, an international transition, and that international transition was itself being worked out so much in response to the Yugoslav conflict, that the causal relation between internal and external factors became increasingly difficult to disentangle as the conflict evolved. Because the domestic crisis evolved into separate nationalist struggles to create independent states out of one country, including competing claims for sovereignty over the same territory, moreover, the traditional demarcation lines between domestic and international spheres – the sovereign frontiers and prerogatives of the state – did not hold. Was the war in Bosnia, for example, as Western powers debated among themselves, a civil war or a war of external aggression? And are these the only two possibilities?

A second source of difficulty is political and psychological: the case represented a monumental failure for international and regional organisations of collective security and their member states, which had thought their principles and mechanisms were ready for the post-Cold War era. American leadership failed to materialise until late in the day and the Europeans were unable to exploit the opportunity this vacuum presented. The failure to manage the crisis, prevent the ensuing violence, or protect fundamental international principles in its aftermath did not, however, stimulate serious retrospection. The pattern was rather to avoid analysis and seek excuses. The powers and the international organisations did so by declaring the Balkans *sui generis,* and its crisis an unfortunate casualty of timing, occurring too early in the overloaded sequence of the end of the Cold War.

Most damaging to serious analysis, however, is the third reason, whereby these psychological defences constructed a new reality out of what happened. The path of the conflict, from the dissolution of the country to the creation of national states and then the ethnic homogenisation (so-called 'cleansing') of each territory, came quickly to be viewed as inevitable—the *natural* outcome of a logic of partition and nationalism *inherent* in the Balkans. Alternatives, choices and competing proposals and trends were lost in the fog of some distant past. Apart from regret that violence was not prevented, few questioned the proposition that this was a domestic quarrel, centuries in the making, and that the Yugoslav peoples chose their fate.

In fact, the crisis and path of the conflict cannot be adequately explained without reference to international factors, such as the interdependence between the nature of the Yugoslav socialist regime and its international environment, the fundamental economic, political and strategic changes in that environment during the 1980s, and to the principles and methods of international intervention to help manage the crisis. In fact, the Yugoslav crisis is not *sui generis,* but only a particularly dramatic example of the widespread phenomenon of political disintegration – the collapse of the governmental institutions and social norms enabling peaceful resolution or moderation of conflict – that becomes a contest over sovereignty itself and crosses the (normally) hard border separating *international* and *internal* politics. And the path that the conflict took was driven in part by the decisions of outsiders, by their methods of intervention, towards the self-fulfilling prophecies that the inappropriate categories and outmoded paradigms of those outsiders generated.

The external consequences of conflicts like the Yugoslav, in terms of refugees, the spread of lawlessness, ever deeper fragmentation and the defiance of international conventions, necessarily impel international action. Yet thus far the intervening powers and institutions in the Yugoslav case have found no solutions, either to the immediate problems of war and further disintegration, or in terms of the longer-term requirements of normalisation and regional stability. At the same time, their efforts to contain and end the wars in Croatia and in Bosnia and Hercegovina have become the primary context, in a process of trial-and-error and learning-by-doing, for redefining the international order in the post-Cold War period in the West.

Interdependence and transition: origins of the crisis[1]

Most analyses of the collapse of Yugoslavia, particularly those influencing the policies of governments that intervened in the crisis, have tended to focus on the role of political leaders, and in particular on the death of Yugoslav president Josip Broz Tito in 1980 and the rise to power in Serbia after 1987 of Slobodan Milošević. In this story, a domestic power struggle in the waning days of communist rule becomes an expansionary project of one nation against the others, in part through politicians' calculated revival of memories about national antagonisms and threats to the survival of their nation in the past from other nations within their common state (largely involving Serbs and Croats, or Serbs and the rest), and in part through their policies to stifle the emergence of pluralist democratic trends (said to be bursting forth in the republics of Slovenia and Croatia) by strengthening the central state and the socialist order. In these analyses there is a strong element of intention and planning, in accordance with the conspiratorial thinking that flourishes in regions and times where uncertainty is particularly pronounced. Like the theories of regime

---

[1] The documentation and detailed argumentation for the story presented here will be found in the author's full-length monograph on the collapse of Yugoslavia and the related international intervention. See Woodward, 1995a.

transition in South America, Southern Europe, or Central and Eastern Europe, they focus exclusively on domestic political variables (see O'Donnell, Schmitter and Whitehead, 1986).

The path that led to the dissolution of Yugoslavia was, however, far more contingent. To the extent that there were plans, their purpose was to protect national security and resolve an economic crisis generated by foreign debt, and they were largely written by military and economic professionals on the periphery of power, not the politicians they advised. Such plans and programmatic reform proposals were composed in reaction to events and changes in the international strategic and economic environment, or in alliance with representatives of international organisations and foreign governments. The changes that occurred in domestic policy and institutions, on the other hand, were the result of piecemeal political responses by individual actors who interacted to create the appearance but not the reality of a plan.

The issues at stake were the locus of control over economic assets and governmental power, and the defence of citizens' economic rights and social status (see Chapters 2–5). Thus the domestic political contest came to be focused on competing visions of the state and constitutional reform. Political mobilisation of elite and popular support used the language of constitutional rights and identities, and thus a rhetoric of national rights (Slovene, Croatian, Serbian and so forth) and of political revolution – the communist regime and anti-communism, democracy and authoritarianism. Outsiders responded directly to this rhetoric, either as ideological sympathisers or as mediators in what became an international issue once the battle lines were defined in terms of a struggle for national independence and sovereignty. And while the proximate causes of dissolution originated with policies of foreign economic adjustment adopted more than a decade before the fall of the Berlin Wall in October 1989, by the middle of the 1980s the positions on domestic, economic and political reform could not be separated from the transition taking place elsewhere in Europe and in the international system. It is possible that this adjustment would not have been so cataclysmic, and might have remained within the bounds of the evolutionary predictions of the transition-to-democracy school, if the international system had remained the same. But it did not, and it soon became painfully clear that the collective identity and internal order of socialist Yugoslavia 1945–90 had been shaped by and was inextricably tied to the Cold War international order (Woodward, 1995b).

The secret of Yugoslav President Josip Broz Tito's rule (1944–80), usually associated with his personal charisma or with communist dictatorship, lay in fact in the international balancing act he created to protect Yugoslav independence and to maximise its prosperity within a bipolar world of hostile ideological, strategic and economic blocs. The very political and economic identity of Yugoslavia as co-founder of the non-aligned bloc, for example, emerged as a response to exclusion from full membership in either Eastern or Western blocs in the period 1947–49. Although Yugoslavia's third way brought it international prestige and foreign trade flexibility, its independence was in fact a strategic resource that depended on the conviction of the Western powers that national communism in the Balkans was a propaganda asset, and that Yugoslav neutrality could be a vital element of NATO's strategy of containment in the east. The Yugoslav armed forces, under this policy, would defend Western Europe and the North Atlantic alliance against a Soviet onslaught through south-eastern Europe. In exchange it would receive privileged access to international financial institutions, public loans and Western capital markets. The consequence was a domestic system in part organised around the needs of defence, with economic benefits and international status depending on the maintenance of this system of defence and on perceptions of the country's strategic significance. The dependence grew over time, because the country's rapid economic growth was fuelled by three decades of borrowed capital, funding the import of intermediate goods and advanced technology, and because its political stability was in large part due to the consumerism, the rising standards of living and the relative equality in the distribution of the benefits of growth that that permitted.

The consequences of this international balancing act benefited not only Yugoslavs. It suited the Western powers. It prevented a major confrontation between West and East after the Second World War, against the background of the competition between Britain and the Soviet Union over the Balkans as expressed in the infamous October 1944 'percentages deal' between Churchill and Stalin: Yugoslavia would be shared fifty/fifty. In assuming the British imperial role by stages after 1946, most explicitly through the Truman Doctrine announced in March 1947, the United States in effect maintained the commitment to this division by being the primary (but not always constant) defender of Yugoslav neutrality. In the same way, after the First World War, the new Yugoslavia created at the Versailles Peace Conference had provided a regional compromise within the context of the new principles of international order: between the principle of national self-determination used to legitimise the dismantling of the eastern empires and the principle of the balance of power, under which the creation of a multinational state in the Balkans – the Kingdom of the Slovenes, Croats and Serbs – would act as a buffer against the emergence of large, potentially hostile powers (Italy, Austria, Serbia) in the region.

Multinational composition and national independence (and the role this gave to the armed forces and a non-aligned foreign policy) apart, international conditions initiated and shaped domestic Yugoslav economic policy and political change in the postwar period. Throughout the period after the system began to stabilise in 1952, governmental policy alternated between two tendencies that were defined, on the one hand, by East-West relations and their consequences for Yugoslav national security; and, on the other hand, by the availability of, and requirements for, the foreign financing for imports and infrastructural projects, and by the shifts in terms of trade and market access for Yugoslav exports and the effect of those shifts on factor prices for domestic manufacturers and federal customs revenue. The two tendencies in the dynamic of public policy reflected the pattern of microeconomic adjustment necessary to take account of external economic and strategic conditions – in terms of differing emphases in production and in corresponding systems of economic incentives, patterns of employment and political organisation for implementation – and accompanying adjustments in regulations on money, labour and constitutional jurisdictions of governmental authorities. The source of trade financing (public or commercial borrowing) directly defined federal-republican relations. Security threats (nuclear or conventional warfare; from the East or West) defined what had to be produced domestically for national defence and determined whether the technologically advanced federal army or the guerrilla-based Territorial Defence Forces in the localities were given priority. The pattern of demand for exports (primary commodities or finished goods in light or heavy manufacturing; and whether transactions were based on bilateral contracts in the East, governmental trade agreements in the South, or spot markets or supplier credits in the West) defined the firms, regions and industrial relations that policy would favour.

The decade of the 1980s began with a return to the policy tendency of liberal, 'efficiency-oriented' economic reform that had dominated policy in the 1960s. That policy orientation aimed at stimulating manufacturing exports to Western markets in order to repay foreign debt, reduce the trade deficit and restore liquidity to the external account. By 1979, the Yugoslav foreign debt had reached crisis proportions, at about $20bn, in part as a result of rising Western protectionism, the decline in foreign demand for Yugoslav labour (cutting the contribution of workers' remittances to the covering of the trade deficit from one-half to one-fourth by 1979), and the deteriorating terms of trade for Yugoslav exports. Commercial banks had initially reacted to the Polish debt crisis by stopping all further lending to countries in the area, including Yugoslavia. By 1982 the IMF was taking a much tougher line on conditions for loans, in response to a global debt crisis which had, indeed, resulted from overlending by multinational banks and IMF policy toward newly industrialising countries during the 1970s. The core of this liberal reform for Yugoslavia – a long-term macroeconomic stabilisation programme aimed at cutting domestic demand, labour costs and inflation – was introduced in 1982, in conjunction with yet another conditionality programme of International Monetary Fund (IMF) credits.

In addition to general austerity, with rising prices for most utilities and basic goods, tight quotas on imported consumer goods and a wage and salary freeze, the cuts that were required in public expenditure also put severe pressure on employment which had expanded during the 1970s, with the official unemployment rate rising to 14 per cent. More than half the jobless were young graduates under the age of twenty-five, and the decline in foreign demand for labour was cutting off the primary outlet for the rural labour surplus and for children of private-sector parents. The restrictive policies of the 1980s, oriented towards debt repayment, threatened with unemployment the beneficiaries of socialism – industrial workers and the children of the urban middle class. The government's programme for absorbing surplus labour – to send the actual and potential unemployed back to families, villages, and private sector agriculture and trades – was less than realistic because of the rapid urbanisation and the extension of university education of the 1970s. Transfers of administrative and professional staff to industry or private employment, and cuts in federal subsidies and welfare transfers and development credits for poorer areas, exposed all localities, regions and social groups to declining standards of living and rising unemployment; at the same time, they exacerbated social differences and inequalities. The government's stabilisation programme actually divided the country into two economic sectors of differential investment policy requirements: a high-wage, technologically advanced, export-oriented North and a low-wage, labour-intensive South. By 1985, the federal government was experiencing a fiscal crisis, and the federal system translated this directly into fiscal crises for the republics and localities. A spiral of hyperinflation began and people who held foreign hard currency were favoured even in domestic transactions.

To implement marketising liberal reforms that were meant to create a long-term capacity to service foreign debt and reduce reliance on internal savings and domestic sacrifice for recovery, governmental reform was needed. According to IMF economists and domestic liberals, the problem was the extreme decentralisation and segmentation of the economy embodied in the 1974 constitution (see Chapter 2) and the subsequent decentralisation to republican control of foreign exchange, foreign borrowing and foreign debt obligations. Delays in decision-making, financial indiscipline and a deadlocked, immobilised governmental administration seemed to point to the absolute necessity of a constitutional reform that would strengthen federal administrative capacity, improve macroeconomic management and create an independent central bank and a system of 'functional integration' appropriate to a market economy. And the League of Communists did indeed set up a commission for political reform that reported in 1985 with the first of a series of proposals to amend the federal constitution (and thereby the republican constitutions).

International conditions changed radically again in 1985–86. Commercial banks resumed lending, the United States Embassy and State Department organised a massive debt-refinancing programme (involving more than 600 banks), the EC[2] countries agreed to the implementation of a programme of further economic integration by 1992, Gorbachev's reforms began in the Soviet Union, East-West economic talks, involving the EC and the Council on Mutual Economic Assistance (CMEA) resumed, and the CMEA started to move from bilateral clearing to hard currency settlements at world prices for transactions. The first to seize the opportunity of a new opening in the East was the Vatican, while Austria and Italy began to expand economic ties eastwards.

But East-West tension did not subside, nor the threat from the Warsaw Pact, and the threat from NATO continued to mount. So there was little scope for cutting the federal defence budget. Under geostrategic pressures, the reformers' national security policy based on conventional-war doctrine and the decentralised structure of the Territorial Defence Forces was upstaged by a new arms race in sophisticated, high-technology weaponry, while JNA concern for defence of the cities against attack by air and sea mounted, and the perception of military threat in the eastern Mediterranean grew. Foreign developments seemed to require opposing policy orientations – a liberal economic programme and a defence-oriented programme – at the same time. The defence minister redrew borders of military districts across republican lines to improve coordination and prevent regional military cabals, and the army stepped up the campaign to reintegrate the country's major infrastructural systems of transportation, energy and communications. At the same time, foreign investment began to flow into Slovenia and Croatia, and regional organisations in trade and tourism developed links with provinces in Italy and Austria. New

---

[2] I refer throughout to international organisations by the title in use at the time in question. The European Community was renamed the European Union after the signing of the Maastricht Treaty in 1992, and the Conference on Security and Cooperation in Europe became the Organisation for Cooperation and Security in Europe in 1994.

opportunities in Western markets, for access to foreign capital independent of the federal government and, it was hoped, of eventual integration into the EC, reshaped the perception of opportunity in Europe. The question that had energised a left-wing intellectual and then political rebellion in Slovenia and Croatia in the 1920s and 1930s – 'Who are we in Europe?' – was again being asked, but this time by the political right.

The changes in the pattern of federal-republican relations entailed in the reform programme appeared, moreover, to deprive the republics and provinces of the sovereignty over economic resources that they had gained between 1968 and 1978. For Slovenia, which led the campaign against all elements that sought to revive federal capacity and authority, the critical resource at issue was foreign exchange. The recentralisation of control over monetary policy and the reform of the banking system and foreign exchange regime would mean the loss of the *right* to retain hard currency earned from exports by firms in a given republic that lay at the heart of the 1968–78 system and, for Slovenia, of the resources it had targeted for its economic programme for technologically driven global competitiveness and rising standards of living within the republic. As a primary export earner, at a time when the Helsinki Accords and CSCE talks had radically reduced its security threat from Italy and Austria, and when foreign investment and commercial bank activity were reducing the advantages of (manufacturing-friendly) federal price regulations and access to public loans, the Slovene republic saw its independent options multiplying. Protesting federal incomes policies that set restrictions on wages, salaries and credit, rising federal taxes, and the proposals to strengthen federal administrative powers, Slovene politicians increasingly campaigned against all manifestations of federal power and expenditure: federal wage regulations, the federal fund for the development of poorer regions, the federal army, federal administration, federal legislation and the supreme court. They began to canvass a proposal for a system of asymmetric federalism, within which Slovenia could define its own internal political system and economic relations with the federal government. By 1985, they were proposing that Yugoslavia should actually be transformed into a confederation of sovereign republics. Sensing the real threat of these proposals, Stane Dolanc, a long-time Slovene party leader known for his pro-Yugoslav views and his stint as federal minister of the interior, warned in January 1985 that a 'free, united Slovenia, joined in a Central European catholic federation ... means the destruction of Yugoslavia'.[3]

The external environment also influenced the domestic political battle over the economic and constitutional reforms in the other republics. The combination of an economic policy aimed at promoting exports to Western markets and declining domestic investment in transport, construction and industries such as mining, timber and heavy industry, were leading to deindustrialisation in the poor interior of Croatia and Bosnia and Hercegovina, areas which also happened to be ethnically mixed. The near collapse of markets in the Middle East as a result of the Iran-Iraq war and in the eastern CMEA bloc was disastrous, particularly for the economies of

---

[3] Dolanc on responsibility, debts, nationalities, *Delo,* 26 January 1985, as reported in Foreign Broadcast Information Service, *East Europe,* 4 February 1985: 116–17.

Macedonia and Bosnia and Hercegovina. Legislation to privatise firms and end the system of workers' self-management and protected employment in order to encourage foreign investment brought the first mass layoffs due to bankruptcy in forty years, beginning in Montenegro. When the largest firms of the republics of Serbia (Smederevo, steel), Croatia (INA, oil), and Bosnia and Hercegovina (the Agrokomerc food-processing conglomerate) were threatened with bankruptcy, and as the banking system attempted to socialise the debt among its members, a banking crisis began to engulf most firms in all republics, followed by a political crisis for republican politicians. Hard-pressed republican parliaments instigated tax rebellions, refusing to pay their federal obligations. They increasingly opposed any loss of governmental rights *vis-à-vis* the economy in the name of marketisation and, by October 1987, were coming to reject the explicit political conditionality for IMF and World Bank loans that required radical economic reform, functional integration of the country and effective federal power.

By 1988, the country was experiencing a social upheaval of revolutionary proportions as a result of the economic hardships occasioned by the debt-repayment stabilisation programme and the resulting ceiling on upward social mobility, the stricter criteria for employment in the public sector and the rising level of internal economic migration. Growing resentments over competition for jobs, unemployment and declining status and income found expression in anger at people and regions considered 'less efficient', at the country's system of proportional representation to protect national equality, at women and minorities, and at the privileges of party members or holders of foreign currency bank accounts. Young people started to play with right-wing symbols and ideas and, particularly in Slovenia and Croatia, developed links with anti-communist movements in East European countries. Growing activism on the part of the churches also introduced an external influence, since the major religions of the country were international and internationally organised: Roman Catholicism, Eastern Orthodoxy and Islam.

Although these developments had their own logic in terms of the domestic reform of a socialist, multinational and neutral state aiming to participate fully in the international economy, they were less and less separable from similar reforms in the Eastern bloc and from the imminent political revolution. By April 1989, the progress of Soviet reforms and of NATO-Warsaw Pact arms and force-reduction talks had persuaded the United States that NATO no longer needed the Yugoslav policy of armed self-reliance. The special relationship had lost its purpose and Yugoslavia was reclassified according to its pre-1949, geopolitical category, as part of South-East Europe. Gorbachev informed all communist parties that Soviet military and diplomatic aid would no longer be forthcoming. In the same year, Hungary took the decisions that opened the Berlin Wall and ended the Cold War and the Warsaw Pact. Yugoslavia now had to compete on equal terms with Central and East European countries for foreign aid, investment and agreements on entering Europe. The Europeans and the United States began to differentiate their approach to the region according to historico-cultural criteria, declaring the Central European, Roman Catholic countries of Hungary, Czechoslovakia and Poland to be better prepared for transition to Europe than the Orthodox, Uniate and former Ottoman regions. In Croatia, the conservative communist party leadership, seeing the writing on the wall in Poland and Hungary, began to open up to intellectuals pressuring for democratisation. The new differentiation in Western attitudes gave new urgency to the demands of Slovenia and the Croatian parliament for membership in Europe, if necessary as states independent of a Yugoslavia that appeared to be falling further and further behind in the queue.

As early as 1989, outsiders were taking explicit sides in the domestic quarrels over constitutional reform between confederalists and federalists, and in the debate over human and political rights that raged throughout the country, particularly in Slovenia, Croatia and Kosovo. United States Ambassador Zimmermann campaigned throughout 1989 against the Serbian repression of Albanian rights in Kosovo. Austrian foreign minister Mock began to tour Europe to mobilise attention on the impending crisis in Yugoslavia, and to canvass support for the Slovene decision, announced in September 1989, to begin a process of 'dissociation' from the federation. The Vatican openly lobbied for independence for the two Roman Catholic republics, Slovenia and Croatia. The German press, under the leadership of *Frankfurter Allgemeine Zeitung* publisher, Jorg Reismuller, and writer, Viktor Maier, waged a campaign on the dangers of Serbian nationalism, as personified in Slobodan Milošević, Serbian party leader from 1987. The multiparty elections in Slovenia and Croatia in April 1990, however, opened a new phase in international involvement, as the newly elected presidents and parliaments chose to move toward independence. Austrian support became more open, Slovenia began a serious public relations campaign in Western capitals, Croatia sought advice in Bonn, Oslo and Stockholm about how to proceed, and Slovenia and Croatia both made secret arms' purchases in Hungary, Austria, Germany and Czechoslovakia, to build up independent, 'national' armies. By 13 March 1991 this had resulted in an extraordinary resolution, in terms of international law and precedent, by the European Parliament, declaring 'that the constituent republics and autonomous provinces of Yugoslavia must have the right freely to determine their own future in a peaceful and democratic manner and on the basis of recognised international and internal borders'.[4]

At least as consequential as the growing support for Slovene and Croatian independence, and for the Slovene and Croat interpretation of the political crisis – that this independence was necessitated by Serbian nationalism and the ambitions of Slobodan Milošević to become a new Tito and to deny their freedom – was the declining foreign support for the federal government. Any internal solution to the crisis would have depended on common institutions for dialogue and compromise among the republican leaders and on progress in a federal reform programme that by 1989 was aimed at complete transformation to a market economy and political democracy. The primary source of federal domestic power and leverage was precisely its international role, including as intermediary for foreign credits and trade. Furthermore, given the growing nationalism within the republics, and the general economic deterioration, the declining numbers of moderates and reformists needed all the external support they could get. In practice, however, Prime Minister Marković was having ever greater difficulty in attracting economic assistance for

---

[4] See Gow, 1991. The reference to internal borders seemed to imply that Helsinki principles should also apply to republic borders.

his programme: appeals to Washington during the autumn of 1989 fell on deaf ears; renewals of association agreements with the European Community and the European Free Trade Association were repeatedly stalled by the EC and EFTA negotiators. The EC agreed in May 1991 to lend $4.5m towards the servicing of the foreign debt that year, but on condition that the country intensify economic reform and remain united. The Council of Europe paid little attention to the Yugoslav application for membership made in November 1989 by Foreign Minister Lončar with a view to buttressing Westernisers in the parliament. East-West confidence-building initiatives to de-escalate tensions continued to be focused on the two Cold-War blocs and did not move to incorporate neutral states, like Yugoslavia, or their armed forces. And no one within the federal government or in foreign circles wanted to entertain breaches in the prevailing international etiquette on interference in the internal affairs of a sovereign state.

Despite growing recognition by intelligence agencies and foreign offices during the autumn of 1990 that a break-up was imminent, and that the break-up would be accompanied by horrendous violence, meetings of NATO and the CSCE in November 1990 both voted not to take preventive action. According to the conservative approach of the Bush Administration toward European security at the time, Yugoslavia was 'out of [NATO's] area' of concern. The United States and the Soviet Union together vetoed CSCE action, arguing that the Yugoslav conflicts were an internal matter. The same month, the first of a series of US congressional actions to withdraw economic aid or impose economic sanctions on Yugoslavia for human rights abuses in Kosovo was introduced by Senator Don Nickles. When the Federal Presidency's effort in January 1991 to de-escalate armed conflict in Croatia between the government and the *Krajina* Serbs was extended to include troop movements by the federal army to secure the border and implement decisions to disarm all paramilitary and militia groups, the United States warned the army that it would not accept the use of force to hold Yugoslavia together. In the spring of 1991 EC delegations finally responded to Prime Minister Marković's request for economic assistance, and to Austrian appeals for mediation of the escalating internal conflict. But their approach was to begin to talk directly to the presidents of Slovenia and Croatia, bypassing the federal government altogether or treating it as a coequal party to international mediation. These subtle denials of Yugoslav sovereignty, reinforcing the view of the Slovene government, were hardly noticed at the time, but they were already helping to shape the outcome of dissolution. Those who needed the protection of the federal government, or an all-Yugoslav political space where they could mobilise sufficient numbers in favour of economic and political reform and against republican politicians willing to risk war for national sovereignty and states' rights, lost any hope of foreign support.

International intervention

The accelerating impetus of Yugoslav disintegration cannot be explained solely by domestic political struggles and constitutional disputes, because the constitutional reforms were part of the stricter terms of conditionality from international lenders

and because domestic actors were making their choices in terms of foreign developments – the changing structure of economic and political opportunity in Europe and
the changing security environment. The mixed messages from outside powers,
moreover, reinforced conflicts at home.

Those same outsiders like to make a distinction between 'politics as usual',
through which countries adjust to their external environment and outsiders actively
try to influence domestic behaviour, on the one hand, and explicit acts of international diplomatic or military intervention, on the other. That divide was crossed, in
the Yugoslav case, on 25 June 1991, when Slovenia and Croatia went ahead with
their announced intention to declare independence. By chance, at the same moment,
European Community foreign ministers were meeting at Luxembourg, making it
easier for them to act without delay. The 'troika' of foreign ministers (the EC mechanism for common foreign and security policy, made up of the three Member States
holding the current, previous and upcoming presidencies of the Council of
Ministers) was sent rushing to the scene. The equivalent body of the CSCE – its
Committee of Senior Officials (CSO) – followed a few days later to offer its 'good
offices', putting into practice for the first time a crisis-management mechanism for
emergencies adopted under United States pressure only two weeks previously.

The motivating factors behind these European offers to mediate the domestic
Yugoslav crisis were no different from those that had been pressuring engagement
since the fall of 1990: intelligence predictions that, if the country fell apart, there
would be terrible violence, and national competition to define the institutions and
mechanisms for guaranteeing European security after the Cold War. In particular, a
serious dispute in January 1991 among Britain, France and Germany, and between
them and the United States, over the appropriate pattern of participation in the US-
organised, UN-mandated coalition action in the Persian Gulf, 'Desert Storm',
revealed how far the Europeans were from being able to formulate a common foreign and security policy, only months before the Maastricht Treaty on further
European integration, due to be signed in December, was to make it a critical component (Chapter V) of the Union. At the same time, European non-members of the
EC, such as Austria and Hungary, were seeking a far more active role in European
affairs than had been possible during the Cold War. Supported by a United States
that was looking to reduce its financial burden in relation to European security, and
to Germany to take the lead in incorporating Eastern Europe into Europe, they were
pushing CSCE involvement in the Yugoslav disputes to demonstrate its capacity for
crisis management and conflict resolution as the best safeguard of European security after the Cold War. The Helsinki process had just been enhanced by the Paris
Charter for a New Europe, adopted in November 1990. For both the Europeanists
within the EC, such as its President, Jacques Delors, and the pan-Europeanists of
the CSCE, the Yugoslav crisis in the spring of 1991 appeared almost welcome, as a
test of their collective capacity for security policy-making independent of the
United States.

The policy shift in June 1991 reflected the temporary success of these proactive
Europeanists in the EC and CSCE in redefining the Yugoslav crisis as an issue of
European security, and as one that seemed to fit the institutions for conflict resolu-
tion they had available. The shift was rapid, from the bankers' approach of the EC

up to late May (promising loans in exchange for economic reform and adding the condition that the republican politicians must solve their disagreements and Yugoslavia remain one country) and the human rights approach of the United States (threatening to withdraw assistance and trade if the human rights record in Kosovo did not improve and (January 1991) if the army became involved in the constitutional quarrel, or in disbanding paramilitaries and illegal armies in Slovenia and Croatia), to crisis mode and the role of mediator on questions of sovereignty and borders. By June, both European and American foreign ministers had accepted the Slovene and Croatian declarations of independence at face value and declared these actions a matter of European security. That meant they had to uphold the principles of European security adopted at Helsinki in 1975 in relation to the newly emerging successor-states: territorial integrity, self-determination, human rights and the unacceptability of border changes implemented by force.

None of these approaches were appropriate to the circumstances, and there was a general refusal to acknowledge that there could be no effective mediation if Western powers did not first overcome their own disagreements about what should result, and recognise that the principles they were applying were in conflict. Political conditionality in exchange for loans assumed that compliance on the part of prime minister Marković was only a matter of his political will. States that refused active intervention, such as the United States, were simultaneously making intrusive demands in terms of the domestic actions of Yugoslav parties, such as the army and the Serbian government. Instead of choosing between the principles of territorial integrity and national self-determination, the Europeans chose to adapt their norms to their preferences and apply both principles to the federal republics, as if they already were states and the bearers of national sovereignty, and as if international law did not oblige them to apply the principles of territorial integrity and self-determination to the Yugoslav state, its entire population and its external borders. By assuming that conflicts over foreign exchange, federal taxes, the defence budget and the legitimate jurisdiction of the federal government in respect of the economy were indeed matters of national rights of self-determination, they accepted that territorial sovereignty rather than domestic reform was the issue at stake. By limiting their role to neutral mediation, they were forced to define the dispute between Slovenia and the federal government as a border dispute between two equal parties. And by defining the conflict as an issue of borders and sovereignty, they foreclosed the option of a domestic solution, including the protection of human rights regardless of national identity, and legitimated the view that this was an international conflict. The dominant view of most major powers, including the United States, Britain, France and the USSR was, as late as 1991, that it would be better to preserve Yugoslavia. But because the country lacked strategic significance for the West after the end of the Cold War, the powers had little interest in making that happen, and the assumptions lying behind the European intervention effectively ratified the break-up.

It is generally accepted that the international community, and particularly the Europeans, did too little, too late, to prevent the violence that began to unfold, first in Croatia and later in Bosnia and Hercegovina. In fact, there was plenty of international action. But at each stage it was troubled by disagreements among the major powers and an absence of common strategy and sustained commitment to see the crisis through.

The first disagreement, over which institutions and states should act in relation to Yugoslavia, was resolved temporarily by the crisis mediation of the European Community and the CSCE in June. The Brioni declaration of 7 July 1991 was its product: it predicated a ceasefire between the Slovene militia and federal army, under which the Slovene government (and also Croatia) would accept a three-month moratorium on moves toward independence, and that the army should return to barracks. Under CSCE mandate, the EC also set up a first-ever monitoring mission (the ECMM), thereby intervening directly in the internal affairs of a sovereign state – to monitor the Slovene ceasefire and the rising tensions in Croatia.

It soon became apparent, however, that crisis mediation was insufficient to stop armed violence, as incidents multiplied between Serb and Croat paramilitaries in Croatia, between local Serb authorities and the Croatian national guard, and eventually between the Croatian government and the federal army aiming to prevent Croatia from winning independence and to protect the Serb minority in border areas in the context of their expressed wish to remain within Yugoslavia. A second disagreement then arose over how to stop the fighting: whether to interpose foreign troops between the parties and negotiate a peace, or to recognise Slovene and Croatian independence, thereby declaring the actions of the federal army and the Serb minority to be illegitimate acts of aggression.

The proposal to send interposition forces demonstrated that the first disagreement – over who should act – had been only temporarily solved. If the United States continued to insist that the one source of organised, collective military force in Europe – NATO – should not be involved, could it also permit the Europeans to field their own forces? The answer, set out in the Dobbins Démarche of spring 1991, was no: a force put together by West European Union (WEU) planners was unacceptable, and the French suggestion to pursue French and German proposals for a Eurocorps calculated to replace a retreating American military presence in post-Cold War Europe was even less acceptable. Moreover, domestic politics in Germany had by late summer pushed its Foreign Minister, Hans-Dietrich Genscher, towards the view that Croatia had a right to independence – and also that the Serbs were aggressors and that immediate recognition of Croatian independence would defeat the Serbs and stop the army. Unwilling to confront Germany directly within the EC and to jeopardise the more important issue of the Maastricht Treaty, but strongly opposed to what Germany now called *preventive recognition*, Britain and France turned to the United Nations as an alternative institutional forum (where the non-permanent members of the Security Council at the time, Hungary, Canada and Austria, were already trying to draw attention to the violence). There, the Soviet Union and the United States vetoed intervention, but the proposal of the Yugoslav federal government for an arms embargo on itself, so as to restrict the scope for the escalation of the armed conflict (and, some would argue, to stop the illegal flow of arms to the secessionists) *was* adopted.[5] Secretary-General Pérez de Cuéllar sent an envoy,

---

[5] UN Security Council Resolution 713, of 25 September 1991, taken under Chapter VII of the Charter.

former US Secretary of State, Cyrus Vance, to investigate whether conditions were suitable for deploying United Nations peacekeeping troops.

Undeterred by the unavailability of troops and the lack of internal consensus, the EC also continued its efforts to mediate, with a more serious endeavour: a peace conference for all of Yugoslavia opened at the Hague on 7 September 1991 under the chairmanship of Lord Peter Carrington. By 8 October, when the three-month moratorium on secession had expired, an arbitration committee of legal advisers set up by the EC in August to help mediate the economic disputes of succession in relation to Yugoslavia (the Badinter Commission, named after its chair, French jurist Robert Badinter) gave its legal opinion, following a request by the conference, that Yugoslavia 'was in the process of dissolution', and that the republican borders were, on the principle of *uti possidetis* (keep what you have) legitimate international borders. European civil servants sitting in Brussels drafted a convention for a 'comprehensive settlement' of the Yugoslav question which proposed to the leaders of the Yugoslav republics and federal state that the six republics be recognised as sovereign states, that they form a customs union among themselves, and that special status (territorial autonomy) be given to national minorities in Croatia (the *Krajina* Serbs) and in Serbia (Kosovar Albanians). Meanwhile Lord Carrington continued to work to obtain a ceasefire between Croatia and the federal army. After fourteen signed but ineffective ceasefires, Cyrus Vance managed to make one stick on 23 November 1991, and over the following two months the conditions were laid for the deployment of United Nations peacekeeping troops to monitor the Vance Plan in Croatia. The federal army would withdraw, as had already occurred in Slovenia, but the areas of contested sovereignty in the Croatian *Krajina* would be placed under the protection of UN troops – 'without prejudice to the final political settlement' – while the EC Hague conference proceeded.

The second disagreement among the foreign powers – on the issue of recognition – was settled in favour of Germany, as it gained ever more converts to its policy of fast-track recognition in the course of the autumn of 1991. Within three weeks of the Vance-negotiated ceasefire, on 16–17 December 1991, the European Community agreed to recognise Slovenia and Croatia and invited (in a bargained compromise) the other four republics to request recognition. Unable to veto under the common foreign and security policy mechanism of the Maastricht Treaty, adopted the previous week, Greece abandoned its isolated opposition to the break-up in favour of a provision that would hold up recognition of Macedonia for another four years.[6] The German policy did, in fact, represent a renunciation of the EC policy committing the twelve collectively to a 'comprehensive settlement'. As Lord Carrington protested before the December decision, this would end the Hague conference. It would also, as UN Secretary General Pérez de Cuéllar protested, deprive the efforts of Cyrus Vance of any leverage over Croatia (and it did eventually undermine the United Nations mission by altering the political terms under which it was deployed). And, as Cyrus Vance, US Secretary of State James Baker, and Bosnian

---

[6] The provision specified that any state requesting recognition should have no territorial claims against any neighbouring EC state, and should not use a name that implied any such claim.

president Alija Izetbegović protested, the decision would ensure that war broke out in Bosnia.

Although the EC finessed this second disagreement, by in fact opting for both recognition of Croatian sovereignty and the deployment of interposition troops in Croatia under United Nations authority, the problem had to be resolved for Bosnia and Hercegovina. With the Germans insisting that the right to self-determination be legitimised through a popular referendum, as had been done in the case of German reunification in 1990 (but *not* accepted in that of the *Krajina* Serbs in Croatia), and on the legal advice of the Badinter commission, the EC now required a referendum on independence among the Bosnian population, in pursuance of the Bosnian government's request for recognition. At the same time, although the Hague conference was by now a dead letter, EC negotiators redirected their diplomatic effort to the three national parties governing Bosnia in coalition, in the hope of finding a political settlement over the political future of Bosnia prior to granting recognition.

The EC had finessed the contradiction in its own principles by dismissing multinational Yugoslavia as an artificial creation and applying both self-determination and territorial integrity principles to the republics, specifically in the cases of Slovenia and Croatia. However, this would not do for multinational Bosnia and Hercegovina. The negotiators, now at Lisbon, entertained proposals from Bosnian Croats and Bosnian Serbs for ethnic cantonisation, so as to prevent a break-up of Bosnia into national units. But when one-third of the population of Bosnia, namely one of its three nations, the Bosnian Serbs, rejected independence in the referendum held 28 February–1 March 1992, and the United Nations envoys, Cyrus Vance and Marrack Goulding, declared that conditions were not ripe to send peacekeeping troops to Bosnia, the worst-case scenario began to appear increasingly probable. Then, in a direct parallel with European actions *vis-à-vis* Croatia, the United States insisted on extending the German policy of preventive recognition to Bosnia and Herzegovina on 6–7 April 1992, ending all efforts at negotiating a settlement as localised clashes and ethnic terror erupted into full-scale war.

The spread of the conflict to Bosnia and Hercegovina once again confronted the West with its unresolved disputes: Who should be involved, should they send troops and what political outcome could they agree to support? In contrast to the Central European patronage of Slovene and Croatian independence, European policy toward Bosnia shifted to *containment* – to prevent the war from spreading further to Kosovo and Macedonia, which might ignite a full-scale Balkan war and could engage Greece and Turkey, obliging NATO to act. But while the Bush Administration had largely stayed on the sidelines during 1991, the US commitment to Bosnian independence and its Muslim president was reinforced in 1992 by its geopolitical interests in the Middle East.

Sharing the German view that the war erupting in Bosnia was also a case of Serbian aggression (based on a plan of President Milošević to create a Greater Serbia with the aid of the federal army), the United States now redefined the conflict in terms of the contours of its policies toward Iraq and Libya. Serbia was a *rogue state,* defying international norms, and extensive economic sanctions should be applied until it ended its cross-border aggression against Bosnian sovereignty. Under pressure from its Middle Eastern allies, Turkey, Egypt and Saudi Arabia, and from domestic lobbies pressing for intervention in support of Bosnian Muslims, the Bush Administration also began to pressure its NATO allies, through the UN Security Council, to take action that would further limit the military capacity of the Serbs (imposition of a no-fly zone over Bosnia, a naval and riparian blockade to enforce the sanctions, and possibly bombing the Serbs and lifting the arms embargo on the Bosnian government). At the same time, the Bush Administration continued to hold to its strategic view that Yugoslavia was not an issue of vital American interest, and was outside of NATO's area of commitment, which meant that it would not commit American or NATO combat troops to stop the fighting.

While lobbies in the US mobilised in support of the Muslim victims of Serb aggression (in the siege of Sarajevo and with the widespread terror, expulsions and cultural destruction taking place in eastern Bosnia) on the basis of moral principles and international humanitarian law, Europeans faced a new wave of refugees fleeing the fighting. Despite opposition from United Nations officials, French pressure now succeeded in committing the UN to an humanitarian mission to aid refugees, displaced persons and innocent civilians, beginning with the city of Sarajevo; Britain began to float the idea of safe areas in Bosnia, on the model of the intervention on behalf of the Kurds in Iraq, as a way of reducing the flow of refugees. The remit of the United Nations Protection Forces (UNPROFOR), created to protect four areas populated by the Serb minority in Croatia (and the Croatian minority remaining in these areas), was extended to the protection of humanitarian convoys of the United Nations High Commissioner for Refugees. This soon turned into the largest, most complex and most expensive operation ever undertaken by United Nations peace-keeping troops. While the United Nations came increasingly under attack for sending peacekeeping troops (lightly armed, acting under rules of engagement defined by consent, impartiality and the use of force only in self-defence) into a war (see Rieff, 1995), the mission reflected the criteria adopted by the European powers and the United States from the beginning: that the norms of sovereignty govern (and limit) international intervention, that the sovereign units were the republics of former Yugoslavia, and that because the area no longer affected the vital, strategic interests of any of the major powers, or of Europe in general, they should not send troops into combat. UN intervention suited the major-power interests of the Security Council, in that it neutralised domestic critics by sending humanitarian assistance, while containing the fighting and refugee exodus within Bosnia and Hercegovina, so that it did not spread to areas that *were* of strategic concern.

In contrast to the emerging American position – that the war would only end with the defeat of the Serbs (although they would not commit troops to that end) – the Europeans tended to view the Bosnian war as a civil war which required a political, negotiated solution. Under the British presidency of the Council of Ministers in the summer of 1992, the EC accordingly revived the idea of a peace conference. Joining offices with the United Nations (which under Vance had been more successful in the case of Croatia, and which the Serbs saw as a vehicle for engaging the United States, in the mistaken belief that it would be less anti-Serb than the Europeans), the EC called a new conference in London in August 1992 and established a permanent peace conference at Geneva – the *International Conference on Former Yugoslavia* (ICFY) – to negotiate all aspects of the succession crisis. Its co-chairmen, Lord David Owen for the EC and Cyrus Vance for the UN, soon became consumed by the task of only one of its six commissions – trying to negotiate an end to the Bosnian war. Like the Hague conference and the follow-up negotiations at Lisbon in February–March 1992, the ICFY drew up a set of political principles on sovereignty, a constitution and a map allocating territorial jurisdiction among the three warring parties. In place of the three-canton proposals made at Lisbon, the Vance–Owen peace plan of January 1993 divided Bosnia into ten provinces and aimed, by establishing a weak central government, to preserve a multinational and multiethnic Bosnia. When the plan was rejected by the Bosnian Serbs, Owen and Vance's successor, Thorvald Stoltenberg, drew up a new peace plan in August 1993 (revised as the Invincible Plan in September). This partitioned Bosnia again into three areas, but retained the extensive international monitoring of human rights from the Vance–Owen plan. This in turn was rejected by the Bosnian Muslims. The ICFY negotiators fell back on trying to keep communications open among all the parties, meanwhile quietly proposing that there could be no solution to the Bosnian war without a return to the comprehensive approach, based on the recognition of Bosnia's link to the rest of the former Yugoslavia: that meant finding a more global solution to the Croatian and Bosnian problems, proposing small adjustments in republican borders to satisfy the strategic interests (such as access to the sea) of independent states, and negotiating with the leaders seen to determine events, in particular Presidents Milošević and Tudjman. At the same time, the United States became re-engaged in the issue, under pressure from the European Commission and France, and began a series of manoeuvres with the opposite tactic: breaking down each conflict into ever smaller pieces and dyadic relations, rather than treating the crisis as a set of interrelated conflicts. It thus insisted on separating the Croatian and Bosnian conflicts on the principle of their recognised sovereignty and then, in the Washington Agreement of March 1994, negotiated (together with Germany) a ceasefire for half of Bosnia between two of its three parties, the Bosnian Muslims and Bosnian Croats.

The failure of the ICFY negotiations in 1993 left the major powers contributing troops to the United Nations protection force (above all, the UK and France), increasingly impatient with the Bosnian war. It also revealed that the larger problem remained – conflicts among the major powers and the continuing inability of those powers to work in concert toward an agreed objective. In practice, it seemed, the powers often worked at cross purposes, sending mixed messages to the parties that encouraged each to hold on to its maximal goals. By the end of 1993, there were three competing approaches in play at the same time. The United Nations forces sought to improve conditions for peace on the ground through classic peacekeeping principles: negotiating ceasefires, if necessary one village at a time, and using the lull in hostilities to restore daily life and open up communications across battle lines – e.g. through family visits, trade and restored utilities – in such a way as to rebuild the confidence and trust necessary to a political settlement in the long run. The ICFY negotiators shuttled tirelessly among the political capitals of Belgrade, Zagreb, Sarajevo, Knin and Pale, and gathered the leaders of the warring parties and neighbouring states in Geneva to negotiate a peace plan, with endless hours spent poring over detailed maps. And the United States talked incessantly of creating a military balance through the arming and training of Croats and Bosnians, air strikes against Serbs, and a military alliance between Bosnian Croats and Bosnian Muslims directed against the Bosnian Serbs.

The conflict between the ICFY and US approaches led in time to the demise of the ICFY and a loss of credibility on the part of of UNPROFOR, largely because of the encouragement the US position gave to the Bosnian leadership, under President Izetbegović and General Rasim Delić, not to sign a ceasefire with the Bosnian Serbs, and to seek an improved bargaining position through military offensives rather than accepting peace plans it did not like. By April 1994, the conference was being replaced by a third diplomatic mechanism: a 'Contact Group' of the five major powers (the United States, Germany, Russia, Britain and France). The peace plan presented, in July 1994, simplified previous plans to little more than a map dividing the territory of Bosnia and Herzegovina, 51–49 per cent, between two entities, a Muslim-Croat federation and the Bosnian Serbs. But when the Bosnian Serbs demanded adjustments before they would sign, the long-standing division between the US and Germany, on the one hand, and Britain, France and Russia, on the other, came out into the open. And, once again, disagreements led to diplomatic impasse, episodic attention from Washington, and growing impatience with the costs of the humanitarian mission and with the increasing risks to soldiers' lives as the war intensified.

By mid-1995, French pressure on the United States once more to take the lead, and the silent but steady withdrawal of British, French and Canadian troops from UNPROFOR, forced the issue. The Clinton Administration persuaded its allies that NATO bombing of Bosnian Serbs would complete the strategic reversal taking place on the battlefield through the medium of well-trained, well-equipped and well-informed Croatian troops, who had invaded and taken control of three of the UN protected areas in Croatia (one in May, and two in August) and overrun much of western Bosnia, expelling the Serbs (see Chapter 11). Meanwhile the Clinton Administration had come around to the European view that the Bosnian war could only end through a negotiated solution. Between August and November 1995, American negotiators ran a marathon of shuttle diplomacy between Balkan capitals. They managed to set up a new peace conference (under the name of 'proximity talks') in Dayton, Ohio, to get signatures on a political settlement and enable a NATO-led, peace implementation force (I-For), under American command, to replace UNPROFOR.

Toward new frameworks?

What are the prospects that international intervention in the former Yugoslavia will, finally, create, or stumble upon, new frameworks to promote stability in the region? Is the international transition, encompassing the transformation of Europe, coming to a tardy fruition in the Balkans?

Most Western leaders, policy-makers and diplomats are quick to insist, when looking at 1990 and 1991, that they could not have acted much differently than they did in the early stages of the Yugoslav crisis because the end of the Cold War brought a huge overload of problems, some of them, like the Iraqi invasion of Kuwait, of much greater strategic significance to the Western world than Yugoslavia. At the same time, however, they continue to insist that the institutions of European security – the OSCE, NATO, the WEU, the EU, the Council of Europe – are well-prepared to manage crises that threaten the stability of Europe.

In reality, not only did those institutions fail in the case of Yugoslavia, but they also revealed little capacity for learning. The actions of Western governments over the period 1991–96 repeated over and over the same approach, the same thinking – and the same mistakes. Certainly, the confrontation with the Yugoslav crisis has forced fundamental changes in those institutions – but the changes have been of a fumbling, *ad hoc*, reactive nature, rather than reflecting any strategy or learning. Thus, for example, Germany overturned its post-Nazi constitutional prohibition on participating in foreign wars, first sending pilots to help enforce the no-fly zone over Bosnia, then a hospital to Croatia to assist UNPROFOR in Bosnia, then Tornado fighter-bombers to police the no-fly zone, and finally troops to participate in the NATO implementation force. Russia was granted major power status, following the dissolution of the Soviet Union, through diplomatic partnership in the ICFY, the 'Contact Group', and the Dayton peace implementation process, sent soldiers to the Balkans for the first time since 1944 – but in blue helmets – and even placed troops under NATO and American command in I-For. And France took major steps to rejoin NATO. NATO engaged in its first military action since its founding – firing weapons to bring down Bosnian Serb aircraft in September 1994, deploying its Rapid Reaction Corps (created in 1991) to assist UNPROFOR in summer 1995, engaging in a massive bombing campaign against the Bosnian Serbs in September, and finally deploying fully as a peace implementation force in December of that year. Eastern European countries hoping to join NATO used participation in the NATO-led I-For to prove their readiness, and the WEU organised its first military operation: namely, joint patrolling with NATO of the naval blockade on the federal republic of Yugoslavia. The United Nations appeared on the ground in Europe for the first time ever, lost practically all credibility in terms of future peacekeeping missions, and saw its office of the High Commissioner for Refugees completely transformed in the process. The Nuremberg precedent was revived for the first time since 1945 with the creation of an International Criminal Tribunal for Former Yugoslavia at the Hague, to investigate, indict, and prosecute the perpetrators of war crimes.

Yet none of these changes amounted to a reaffirmation of the institutions for European and global security. The common foreign and security policy of the EU had proved a failure; its most ambitious ventures into the security field – the Balladur stabilisation pacts in eastern Europe – were structured around bilateral roundtables, and its Member States seemed ready to accept, by 1995, that Europe could not act in its collective interest without American leadership. Balkan initiatives for regional cooperation in security, transportation and trade relations taken in 1989–90 were interrupted by the Yugoslav wars and were being replaced, by 1994–95, by, again, a series of bilateral agreements. The CSCE had developed its instruments for human-rights monitoring and peacekeeping in Macedonia and the Caucasus, but had not overcome the limits imposed by sovereignty in its attempts to monitor in Kosovo, or the limits of political commitment on the part of its Member

States to fund and train a staff to organise and monitor elections and human rights in Bosnia. NATO's credibility was being tested not by war, but by peacekeeping in Bosnia and Hercegovina, its very survival tied to the uncertain outcome of a peace-implementation process in which NATO commanders insisted on the narrowest mandate so as to avoid the fate of UNPROFOR. Far from NATO and the EU containing Germany, in accordance with their original remits, Germany was now acting unilaterally to secure its eastern and southern flanks with a ring of friendly, prosperous, stable states from Poland to the Czech Republic, Hungary, Croatia and Slovenia, and without regard for the destabilising potential of this new, if invisible, border in eastern and south-eastern Europe. As a result of the Yugoslav crisis, a new forum for resolving major issues of European security is replacing existing institutions – an informal gathering of five major powers based on the 'Contact Group' set up in March 1994 to negotiate a Bosnian peace – which seems to imply a return to balance-of-power and balance-of-interest principles.

All the major players in the Yugoslav drama gave priority to national over collective interests. It was not only Austria, the Vatican, Germany and the EC Europeanists who saw the Yugoslav crisis as an opportunity to take advantage of changing times. France saw a chance to enhance its declining resources and prestige in Europe with its power in the UN Security Council and as a potential military guarantor of Europe. Britain used the crisis to bolster its status as a major power, balancing its own position to keep centre stage. Russia used it to gain acceptance at major economic forums (such as the G-7) and for financial assistance to its reforms. Turkey has found a new foothold in the Balkans, with its support of the Bosnian Muslims and a role delegated to it by the United States in equipping and training the Bosnian army. And the United States, while acting for the most part as a conservative power and reluctant leader, managed to protect NATO's centrality to European security and America's position of dominance in Europe and the Middle East.

Despite the conviction that dominated public commentary during 1991 that 'this is no longer 1914' (when an assassination in Sarajevo could ignite a world war) – because the institutions of collective security and common market had ended the era of national competition among the major powers for spheres of interest and local clients in the Balkan playground – the Balkans retain the capacity to lure the major powers into its local conflicts and create conflict among them over national interests. And, just as in 1914 and 1947–49, this capacity is not a reflection of some cultural predisposition on the part of the Balkan peoples, but of the state of relations among the major powers.

The powers' policy of containment *vis-à-vis* Bosnia and Hercegovina does, however, demonstrate some change relative to 1914 and 1939. On the pretext of preventing a local war from spreading, Europe and the United States *were* able to contain their own conflicts within peaceful channels. But the *ad hoc*, strategy-less character of their actions left them as unprepared in 1996 as they were in 1990–91 to manage successfully the remaining conflicts within the former Yugoslavia. Although patient diplomacy by American envoys (Cyrus Vance, Herbert Okun, Matthew Nimitz and Richard Holbrooke) had established a *modus vivendi* between Macedonia and Greece by September 1994 that appeared to resolve the main challenges to Macedonian sovereignty and survival, major issues between the two states remain unresolved. In addition, the interdependence between the two Albanian communities in neighbouring Kosovo and Macedonia, together with the economic disaster and its social and political consequences inflicted on Macedonia by the economic sanctions against Serbia and Montenegro, could still destabilise the new state (see Chapter 13). The scenario of a classic Balkan war to partition Macedonia, with all its wider consequences, which the policy of containment aimed to prevent, has still not been definitively put to rest.

Moreover, the Europeans have not yet addressed the conflict between different Helsinki principles that had wreaked such havoc in Croatia and Bosnia and Hercegovina. They have, therefore, no solution to the issue of Kosovo that might prevent the competing claims of sovereignty over the province between Serbia (of which it is legally a part) and the Kosovar Albanians (who form the vast majority and have voted for independence – see Chapter 8) from being resolved through war. Who has a right to a state, and what procedures exist to guide the process of 'state-creation' peacefully? The Croatian 'solution', to encourage the mass exodus of Serbs (whose position and claims in Croatia were very similar to those of Kosovar Albanians in Serbia), and the *de facto* partition of Bosnia into three areas of ethnically pure population, are surely not acceptable models for the future. Yet Europe and the United States continue to support Croatia, economically, diplomatically and militarily, and to accept the priority of sovereignty norms, under which human and minority rights are internal affairs of states. While they have opposed the population transfers, both voluntary and violent, in Bosnia and Hercegovina, they have done little to prevent them, and they continue to insist that the recognised borders of the republic are inviolable.

The most dramatic illustration of the absence of new frameworks to promote stability in the region (and regions like it) comes in the form of the (likely) outcome of the massive international intervention (which contrasts starkly with the approach taken toward Croatia) to implement a peace agreement and reintegrate Bosnia and Hercegovina. In the first months of the Dayton process, the combined efforts of NATO, the EU, the OSCE, the US, the IMF and World Bank, the UNHCR and hundreds of non-governmental organisations, were no more sufficient to reverse partition and put Bosnia back together than they might have been to prevent Yugoslav dissolution and war. The Dayton agreement, signed at Paris on 14 December 1995 was certainly a victory for the realists, but it came wrapped in the idealism of the moralists supporting the Bosnian government. In order to get signatures from warring parties, it created a constitutional system *with all the flaws of the former Yugoslavia*: extensive regional autonomy legitimised by national rights, and a weak central government with no functions that could bind the loyalty of all its citizens. Its ambitious deadlines for a political process that would enable international military forces to leave within twelve months will yield electoral results after nine months that give democratic legitimation to the three nationalist parties and produce a parliament stalemated by block voting and countervailing vetoes. International supervision of human rights for five years has been juxtaposed with a denial of constituent nation status to the Serbs within the federation, and of Croats and Muslims within the Serb Republic, and few safeguards for the rights of minorities (political and economic as well as cultural and religious) in any of the three, one-party-dominated areas. The international operation continues to talk to representatives of the three official parties who had gone to war, and who still control the armies, not to those who had opposed the war, the nationalist propaganda, and ethnic partition. American officials continue to favour the federation of Bosnian Muslims and Croats that their agreement of March 1994 created, and to treat the Serb Republic as an aggressive threat, to be isolated economically and diplomatically, whereas the Europeans insist that there will be no Bosnia if external programmes do not treat the country as an integral unit. An American policy, mandated by Congressional legislation and manifest in promises made to the Bosnian leadership at Dayton, to equip and train a Bosnian army that would be able to defend its state when the international force leaves after twelve months, is in sharp conflict with the European policy for long-term regional stability based on an OSCE-defined arms control regime, the 'draw-down' of all forces in the region rather than the 'build-up' of some, and Vienna-based negotiations to prevent a new arms race. If the three constituent units of Bosnia and Hercegovina choose to go their own way – to dissolve, as did former Yugoslavia – the international community will be faced again with a *fait accompli* it cannot recognise. Finally, the programme of economic assistance from the IMF, the World Bank and the European Union – on which the survival of Bosnia and Hercegovina depends – repeats the same conditionality, the same policies to ensure that debt is repaid, and that give little attention to the fiscal consequences of inevitable defence interests, and the same proposals for economic and political reform to create a market economy that raised all the political-legal conflicts over economic assets antecedent to the disintegration of Yugoslavia in the 1980s.

The ceasefire in Bosnia and Hercegovina, and the hopes that there will be no more war, has only brought the region's peoples back to the beginning: the process, first adumbrated in the 1980s, of transition of all the parts of the former Yugoslavia to a market economy, democratic government, legal safeguards for individual rights regardless of group identity, and a new position in a European and global order no longer based on strategic bipolarity and nuclear threat, has barely begun. And the external conditions in terms of regional and European economic integration and a stable, reliable European security regime that are so essential to the process, and that were so palpably missing in the 1980s, remain, in the late 1990s, just as uncertain and ill-defined.

References

Gow, James (1991) Deconstructing Yugoslavia, *Survival,* vol. 33, no. 4, July–August.

O'Donnell, G., Schmitter, P. C. and Whitehead, L. (eds) (1986) *Transitions from Authoritarian Rule,* four vols (Baltimore: Johns Hopkins University Press).

Rieff, David (1995) *Slaughterhouse: Bosnia and the Failure of the West* (London: Random House).

Woodward, Susan L. (1995a) *Balkan Tragedy: Chaos and Dissolution after the Cold War* (Washington DC: The Brookings Institution).

Woodward, Susan L. (1995b) *Socialist Unemployment: the Political Economy of Yugoslavia, 1945–1990* (Princeton, NJ: Princeton University Press).

Part Three

The Successor States

Chapter 10

Neither War nor Peace: Serbia and Montenegro in the First Half of the 1990s

JOVAN TEOKAREVIĆ

Introduction

Contemporary Serbia and Montenegro do not present an easy case for social analysis. Whatever methodology or sources of information we use, it is still difficult to explain the multitude of striking peculiarities and paradoxes of Serbia and Montenegro and their new federation: the Federal Republic of Yugoslavia (FRY). Unlike all the other East-Central European states, Serbia and Montenegro have not experienced a real regime change. The regimes in Belgrade and Podgorica have, since 1987 and 1989 respectively, really shown remarkable stability, strengthened rather than weakened by the ideological and policy changes they have introduced. Serbia and Montenegro have also escaped war on their own territories, although they helped in every possible way the Serbs fighting in Croatia and Bosnia and Hercegovina. For their involvement in the war in Bosnia and Hercegovina, Serbia and Montenegro were punished in 1992 and 1993 by the most comprehensive sanctions that the United Nations Security Council has ever imposed on any country. These sanctions, combined with a completely inadequate government economic policy, had resulted by the end of 1993 in a devastating economic crisis, coupled with a hyperinflation which surpassed even the German one of the mid-1920s. Serbia and Montenegro remain the only republics of former Yugoslavia which have not been internationally recognised, although they share the longest tradition of sovereign statehood among the ex-Yugoslav nations.

It is with a view to clarifying some of these issues that we now discuss the most important features of Serbian and Montenegrin political and economic development in the aftermath of the dissolution of the former Yugoslavia.

From peace to war

During the first half of the 1990s, political life in Serbia and Montenegro was decisively influenced by two factors: first, the change of political elite in 1987 in Serbia, and in 1989 in Montenegro; and, second, the disintegration of the Socialist Federal

Republic of Yugoslavia (SFRY) and the wars that erupted in Slovenia, Croatia and Bosnia and Hercegovina.[1]

The significance of the first factor can hardly be overemphasised. The political changes in Serbia and Montenegro were deeply interrelated events, in the sense that the latter was almost completely a consequence of the former. What were they about? In Serbia, at the VIII session of the Central Committee of the League of Communists of Serbia (LCS), held in September 1987, a hardline faction, led by LCS President Slobodan Milošević, defeated the more liberal faction led by Serbia's President, Ivan Stambolić, and Belgrade Party chief Dragiša Pavlović.

Through subsequent purges at all levels of the party and state hierarchy, Milošević's victory was turned into a complete triumph. It was praised by the most influential media, controlled by people loyal to Milošević, but it also gained the clear-cut support of the majority of the Serbian population. The main reason for this was not the form in which the new policy was established – for it added nothing new to the list of well-known communist techniques of coup and purge. The novelty was the content, i.e. the ideology of the new power-holders – nationalism. Milošević clearly understood the potential strength of nationalism in Serbia at that moment and relied heavily on it, backed by influential intellectual and military circles.

As an orthodox communist *apparatchik*, Milošević had no national programme of his own. He therefore began to borrow ideas from the nationalistic opposition (a habit he retains until this day), which had been supporting Serbs from the autonomous province of Kosovo since the beginning of the 1980s. During the 1980s, protests by the Serbs from Kosovo brought to the fore a fundamental problem facing Serbia: due to the high degree of autonomy granted to Serbia's provinces, Vojvodina and Kosovo, by the 1974 Yugoslav constitution, the republic was not able to exercise some of its basic constitutional rights on its own territory (see Chapter 2). The two autonomous provinces were not only directly represented in all federal political bodies and empowered to veto decisions of the Serbian authorities, but also had independent constitutional and legislative power, as well as their own administration and judiciary.

Vojvodina and Kosovo had effectively become 'states within a (Serbian) state', and Belgrade was eager to regain sovereignty over the whole territory of the republic. The issue seemed that much more important in that other Yugoslav republics, plagued with growing nationalisms of their own, were at the same time insisting on ever greater independence. Thus in the second half of the 1980s Yugoslavia was evolving from an already decentralised state into an association of eight states (six republics and two autonomous provinces). The Albanians of Kosovo, backed by the elites of some of the other republics, were set on cutting all remaining ties with Serbia and establishing their own sovereign republic. There was continuous Serb emigration from the province throughout the 1980s, under the pressure of the Albanian majority, and this brought the issue into the very centre of the republic's public life. Serbia was afraid of becoming the main victim of these parallel disintegration processes, within Yugoslavia and on its own territory. Of all the

---

[1] See Kovačević and Dajić, 1994, 1995.

Yugoslav nations, it had the most to lose: not only two provinces which it formally possessed, but also Yugoslavia, as the first state in history which had joined all Serbs from Croatia and Bosnia and Hercegovina with Serbia itself.

Milošević's sudden rise to the position of undisputed leader of the newly-born all-Serbian national movement should be understood primarily from the perspective of this uneasiness and anxiety which grew up in Serbia. Divided by ever harder republican borders, and afraid for their future in the Kosovo, Croatian and Bosnian environments – which had been extremely hostile to them in the not-so-distant past, during the Second World War – the Serbs from outside Serbia unexpectedly found a champion in Belgrade. Like no leader before him, Milošević promised to take care of them, working up their national feelings and raising their expectations. Having been witness to numerous vain efforts on the part of former Serbian leaderships to address the 'Serbian question' through institutions, Milošević quickly realised that he had to go another way. He turned to non-institutional methods and began to organise support for his policies through huge public rallies. That is how his 'anti-bureaucratic revolution' began. During 1988 and 1989 it was formally led by organisations of Serbs from Kosovo – but most probably carefully planned and directed by the Serbian regime. Kosovar Serbs would go from town to town, 'spreading the truth about Kosovo', as they said, and gathering tens or hundreds of thousands of participants. Participation on that scale, and with that enthusiasm, cannot be explained by theories of a specifically authoritarian national character, or in terms of mere manipulation through the media. The Serbs were reacting to a real and serious problem of the fragmentation of the Serbian nation within Serbia and Yugoslavia, and to their political underrepresentation, and implicitly rejecting any notion that these might represent a reasonable price to pay for the survival of Yugoslavia.

The problem was perhaps not so specific in itself, but the form in which it was presented, and the solution that was soon offered, *were* specific – and this is where the Serbian national awakening differs significantly from other, similar cases. The form was a wide-ranging, radical and exciting populist movement, created at a time when it still seemed that nothing – not even Mikhail Gorbachev's reforms – would ever challenge the stability of the East European communist regimes. The movement brought a new type of political legitimacy into the sclerotic and apathetic structures of late communism – one in which the leader defies institutions and relies on direct mass support.[2] But Milošević was still an old-style, hardline communist leader, with equally old-style political ideas. There was no place within the movement's basket of ideas for concepts like human rights, civil society, multiparty democracy … Communist-type collectivism was its first and last creation – only this time 'modernised' with almost limitless abuse of the most influential media, especially TV.

The solutions to the 'Serbian question' offered by the masters of the 'anti-bureaucratic revolution' did not in principle differ much from those spelt out by other Yugoslav nationalisms, in at least two aspects: first, there was an obsession

---

[2] Slobodan Antonić (1995) Vlada Slobodana Miloševića: pokušaj tipološkog odredjenja (The government of Slobodan Milošević: an attempt at a typological definition) *Srpska Politička Misao*, no. 1, pp. 96–7.

with the territory the nation should rule over; and, second, force was considered a legitimate means to achieve national goals. But in the Serbian case the two aspects were expressed with peculiar directness and intensity. This reflected the type of political leadership and also the fact that the Serbs were the most numerous nation in Yugoslavia. These two factors conspired to create a ruthless aggressivity and lack of preparedness (lack of perceived need, too) to make compromises with those who were weaker – indeed, with minorities of any kind.

Two of the most significant immediate results of the 'anti-bureaucratic revolution' were changes of political leadership in Vojvodina, Montenegro and Kosovo and suspension of the autonomy of the provinces. After repeated mass rallies, the Vojvodina leadership resigned on 6 October 1988, and the Montenegrin on 11 January 1989. A section of the Albanian Kosovar leadership was arrested in early March 1989, charged with organising a miners' hunger strike and demonstrations (see Chapter 8 on Kosovo). At the same time the Federal Yugoslav Collective Presidency proclaimed a state of emergency in Kosovo. After the Assemblies of Vojvodina and Kosovo had approved amendments to the constitution of Serbia – under extreme pressure from Belgrade – the Serbian Assembly passed them too, on 28 March 1989. The amendments took away from the provinces the right of veto on constitutional changes in Serbia, and removed part of the legislative, executive and juridical powers of the province authorities. These changes were confirmed a year and a half later, on 28 September 1990, when the Serbian Assembly passed the new constitution of the Republic of Serbia.

In a series of resolute protests, the Albanians from Kosovo made their stand against the suspension of autonomy. But their protests were put down by force, by large numbers of police (at first federal, afterwards only Serbian) and by the Yugoslav People's Army, which was deployed in the province.

The leaderships of the other republics, and a good part of the populations of those republics, became extremely concerned over Milošević's new, united Serbia. The old 'Serbia in three parts' (Serbia proper, plus its two provinces, Vojvodina and Kosovo) suited them; a united Serbia, with its three votes (from now on always in agreement) in the Yugoslav Federal Presidency, and with similar levels of Serbian representation in the Federal Assembly and the leadership of the ruling (and only) party, the League of Communists of Yugoslavia (LCY), did not.

By and large, Serbs considered this new balance of power within Yugoslavia a proper reflection of the size of their nation. Serbs should no longer be punished for their greater numbers, but should instead be given an appropriate share of federal power. This was the rationale behind the numerous suggestions which were coming from Serbian political and intellectual circles for the introduction of a new type of Federal Parliament in Yugoslavia. On the model of the US system, one of its chambers would have representatives of all the Yugoslav republics (all republics would be equal), while the other chamber would be elected (proportionally) in constituencies of equal size in terms of population over the whole territory of Yugoslavia. As the most numerous nation, Serbs would thus have a plurality in the lower chamber.

This and many other similar Serbian initiatives were interpreted in other republics as more or less disguised efforts to impose Serbian domination within Yugoslavia. To a great extent, such accusations were justified, at least as far as the

Serbian *regime* was concerned. This came out especially clearly in the regime's efforts to gain ascendency within the League of Communists of Yugoslavia. In the face of this threat, the Slovene and Croatian communists walked out of the XIV LCY Congress in January 1990. The ruling Yugoslav party thus practically ceased to exist, fully one and a half years before the country itself disintegrated.

The disappearance of the LCY had little in common with the 'anti-communist revolutions' that had just taken place in all the East European countries except Albania. Actually, Yugoslavia, and especially Serbia, was too busy with its own political struggles and ethnic tensions to absorb such a profound change.[3] Official Serbia claimed that the other countries of the region were only following her pattern of radical reform, as personified in Slobodan Milošević's new policy. The young Montenegrin ruling team had a better claim to the title of forerunner of the East European revolutions, since it really did come to power in a revolutionary-like situation. But this is where the similarity ends.[4] The new Serbian and Montenegrin *nomenklature* never wanted communism to end, and have not allowed it to end completely to this day. Ideological reasons and political aims and methods apart, they retain their communist ethos because at the time of the demise of communism elsewhere they had just arrived, they were fresh and ambitious, eager to stay in power and increase it. As such they were the very opposite of the senile, tired communist leaderships of the rest of East Europe.

It would be wrong, however, to say that the East European revolutions had no impact at all on Serbia and Montenegro. At the end of 1989, leading Serbian and Montenegrin intellectuals began to form opposition parties, although that was still not legally permitted. The League of Communists of Serbia did say, at its XI Congress in December 1989, that it had no reason or wish to hinder the formation of political parties. In the event, opposition political parties were actually legalised in July 1990, when the Serbian Assembly passed the Law on Political Organisations. Even this modest progress was achieved only after many protests on the part of opposition organisations. But it was also a sign that the Serbian and Montenegrin leaderships had realised that they had to adjust somehow to the new rules of multi-party political life, now common to all former communist countries, and to other Yugoslav republics. In mid-July 1990 the ruling Serbian party formally merged with the Socialist League of the Working People (an old and irrelevant umbrella organisation) under a new name – the Socialist Party of Serbia.

The stage would be finally set for the first multiparty elections in Serbia only a little later, on 28 September 1990, when the old (one-party) Serbian Assembly passed the new Serbian constitution. Milošević wanted to be sure that, whatever the results of those elections might be, he would continue to rule. That is why he did two things. First, he organised a referendum on 1 and 2 June 1990, and managed to persuade 97 per cent of the participants that it would be better to pass the new constitution first and have elections afterwards – the opposite pattern to all other countries of the region. Milošević's landslide victory at the referendum was a sign that

---

[3] See *Inter-ethnic Conflict ...*, 1992.
[4] See Srdjan Darmanović (1992) Montenegro: destiny of a satellite state, *East European Reporter*, vol. 5, no. 2, March–April, p. 28.

the Serbian population also wanted him on the throne – regardless of how the seats in the Assembly would be divided afterwards. Simply put, Milošević represented, for more than a convincing majority of Serbian citizens, the only guarantee that Serbian national interests would be properly protected.

The second thing Milošević did, in 'adjusting' to multiparty democracy, was to adjust the constitution of Serbia to his own needs. Serbia ended up with a mixed presidential-parliamentary system, but with a very strong and independent president, and an Assembly that is very much subordinate, and which can be dissolved by the president.[5] The new-style President of Serbia (Milošević was already chairman of the presidency of Serbia under the old constitution) was granted 'the power of a Roman emperor'[6] and the constitution was used simply as a legal form to legalise and rationalise almost unlimited personal power. After this, there was no doubt whatsoever as to who would hold the key to power – regardless of the results of the elections.

We shall return later to the analysis of multiparty elections in Serbia, Montenegro and FR Yugoslavia during the first half of the 1990s. For the moment, let us continue to develop the theme of the relationship between Serbia and the Serbs and Yugoslavia. We left the SFRY scene in January 1990, when the Yugoslav Communist Party effectively ceased to exist. With the federal government under the control of the reform-minded and totally economically oriented Prime Minister, Ante Markobić, the only institution which Milošević had at his disposal for his 'march on Yugoslavia' was the Yugoslav People's Army. Educated in Titoist anti-nationalistic and pro-Yugoslav spirit, most JNA generals were at first suspicious of the intentions of the Serbian president. He would begin to seduce a good part of them, not only those of Serbian origin, only in late 1990 and early 1991 – after he had shown his invincibility even in free elections, and after he had consolidated his propagandistic image as the defender of Yugoslavia, *vis-à-vis* secessionist forces in other republics. Decisive influence within the army, and later on full informal command over it, were crucial for Milošević's and Serbia's destiny from that time on (see Chapter 7).

Without the help of the army, the idea of uniting all Serbs from the SFRY into one state – the central idea of Serbian nationalism – would never have got off the ground. (The JNA, it should be said, were secretly arming the Serbs from Croatia and Bosnia and Hercegovina even before the outbreak of the war in summer 1991.) This 'Greater Serbia' programme, now adopted by the new Serbian leadership, traces its origins back to the document of September 1986 entitled 'Memorandum of the Serbian Academy of Arts and Sciences', an unofficial and unfinished

---

[5] See Miodrag Jovičić (1992) Parlamentarni sistem nasuprot predsedničkom i skupstinškom sistemu (The parliamentary system as opposed to the presidential and assembly system) *Arhiv za Pravne i Društvene Nauke*, vol. LXXVIII, no. 1; Lidija Basta-Posavec Ustavna demokratija i (ne)demokratska konstitucija društva (Constitutional democracy and the (un)democratic constitution of society). In Nakarada, Basta-Posavec and Samardžić (eds) (1991).

[6] Čavoski, 1991: 150.

document that became a symbol of the demand on the part of Serbs to unite, i.e. to live in one state,[7] on the basis of the controversial right to national self-determination.

In arming the Serbs in Croatia and Bosnia and Hercegovina and inciting them to rebellion, Milošević's regime was not the sole cause of the disintegration of Yugoslavia and the wars that erupted over three republics. But he did play a decisive role in an already volatile situation, and in the context of already fully developed militant chauvinisms among other Yugoslav nations, and the unconcealed desire on the part of these nations to put an end to Yugoslavia. Even where given elements could be justified by law, Milošević's policy carried an overlay of violent arrogance that overwhelmed any rational elements in it. A very good example is the reaction to the secession of Slovenia and Croatia in mid-1991. Serbia began by 'facilitating' secession (see Chapter 7) – and then started wars against both of them. The war in Bosnia and Hercegovina was a product of the same type of behaviour, and it is hardly surprising that it was punished with UN sanctions and total international isolation.

From war to peace

Economic sanctions against the Federal Republic of Yugoslavia were imposed by the United Nations Security Council on 30 May 1992 (Resolution 757). Sanctions were introduced because the Serbian and Montenegrin authorities had not complied with the previous resolution, no. 752 (15 May 1992), which – among other things – requested them to cease interfering in the armed conflict in Bosnia and Hercegovina, to withdraw the Yugoslav Army from Bosnia-Hercegovina, and to put all weapons under effective international control. Although the demand was addressed to all parties involved in the conflict, explicitly mentioning 'elements of the Croatian Army' as well as 'units of the Yugoslav People's Army', it was only FR Yugoslavia which was actually punished. By 21 May 1992 it really had withdrawn all soldiers born in other parts of Yugoslavia from Bosnia and Hercegovina. But it left enormous stocks of weapons to the Bosnian Serbs and continued to supply them.

The UN sanctions amounted to the most comprehensive and severe measures of economic embargo and diplomatic, cultural, etc. isolation, which the international community had ever imposed on a country, whether under the aegis of the League of Nations or the United Nations. They included a ban on all exports from Serbia and Montenegro, as well as on all imports except for food and medicines. International flights to and from Serbia and Montenegro were also forbidden and the level of diplomatic missions was reduced. Severe limitations were imposed on financial transactions, as well as on all kinds of transport links; all scientific, technical, cultural and sports cooperation was discontinued.

---

[7] See several critical articles on the Memorandum in *Balkan War Report*, no. 31, February 1995, and an *apologia* for it in Vasilije Krestić and Kosta Mihajlović (1995) *Memorandum SANU – Odgovori na Kritike* (The Memorandum of the Serbian Academy of Arts and Sciences – Reply to Critics) (Beograd: SANU).

These already harsh sanctions were reinforced three times during the following twelve months. UN Security Council Resolution 787, passed on 16 November 1992, prohibited the transit of key categories of goods through the territory of FR Yugoslavia, and authorised UN members to effect a blockade of Montenegrin sea ports, as well as to inspect and check cargoes travelling along the River Danube. On 18 April 1993 Resolution 820 again strengthened sanctions, with the introduction of a tougher transport embargo (cargo transport through FRY was forbidden); all capital of Serbian and Montenegrin firms held abroad was frozen. Monitors were installed on Serbian borders, on the Danube, and on the Adriatic coast too.

These last-mentioned measures were taken after the Bosnian Serbs, alone among the Bosnian groups, refused to accept the so-called Vance–Owen peace plan for Bosnia and Hercegovina. Serbia and Montenegro, exhausted after almost a whole year under sanctions, accepted the plan. But they were additionally punished for the 'sins' of their Bosnian brethern. Abandoning one after another the radical ideas of the 'Greater Serbia' project, Serbia and Montenegro started, from that time, to be increasingly 'cooperative' with the international community. In July 1994 they accepted the new peace plan for Bosnia, formulated this time by the so-called 'Contact Group'.

During the summer of 1994, after long negotiations, international monitors were finally allowed to station themselves on the Serbian-Bosnian border. It did not take them long to report that Serbia was no longer sending aid to the Bosnian Serbs. This radical turnaround in Serbian policy was confirmed by the introduction of the so-called internal Serbian-Serbian sanctions, imposed by the Belgrade regime on the Bosnian Serbs on 4 August 1994. A reward for this came in the form of some symbolic lifting of the UN sanctions on 23 September 1994 (Resolution 943). Belgrade airport was reopened for international flights, the ferry from Bar (Montenegro) to Bari (Italy) began to operate again, and sanctions were also lifted in the spheres of cultural and sports exchange. Sanctions were not lifted permanently, but temporarily suspended, conditional on a positive report, adopted by the UN Security Council, every 100 days. In the summer of 1995, Belgrade and Podgorica accepted yet another peace plan: this time the US one, hoping that they could finally get rid of sanctions. Sanctions were finally completely lifted at the end of 1995 with the signing of the Dayton agreement.

The most general reaction of the population of Serbia and Montenegro to the sanctions was that it is not the regime, but the whole nation, that was being (unjustly) punished by the entire international community. One could often hear murmurings about 'international conspiracy' and 'genocide' against the Serbs, and this kind of attitude was strongly reinforced by the regime-controlled media. A well-known Serbian expert on international law wrote at the time that 'Yugoslavia has been transformed into a kind of concentration camp, taking the early colonial period as a model', and that in both Serbia and Montenegro, as in Iraq, sanctions were 'genocidal in relation to the entire people, without discrimination'.[8]

---

[8] Smilja Avramov (1993) Sanctions in the post-cold war era, *Review of International Affairs*, vol. XLIV, no. 1018–22, July–November, Belgrade, pp. 7 and 8.

As in other countries which have experienced embargo, isolation very soon became a perfect excuse for all the weaknesses of the domestic government, and for any policy that the government cared to advance. In despite of foreign expectations,[9] sanctions were in practice an ally of undemocratic political forces and especially of the ruling elite. That elite used the pretext of sanctions to suffocate democratic opposition in Serbia and Montenegro as much as possible, and to create an hysterical atmosphere which feared and rejected everything foreign.

In judging the economic effects of the embargo imposed on Serbia and Montenegro, we should always bear in mind that sanctions are the main, but not the only, reason for the economic crisis and the radical deterioration in living standards.[10] There are at least three additional reasons for these latter developments: the dissolution of the 'second Yugoslavia', the war, and the unreformed economy of the Federal Republic of Yugoslavia.

The first serious blow to the Serbian-Montenegrin economy was the loss of the former Yugoslav market, with its 22 million consumers. The second was the very high price of supporting the 'Serbian war outside Serbia', and the several hundred thousand refugees from Croatia and Bosnia (in total, this swallowed up 20 per cent of GDP in 1992, 12 per cent in 1993 and 6 per cent in 1994). From the beginning of the 1990s, the economic crisis steadily deepened from year to year, ending in a record hyperinflation which finally reached an almost incredible 313m per cent in January 1994 alone (2 per cent per hour, or 116,545,906,563,330 per cent annualised!).[11]

In the year when sanctions were introduced (1992) Serbian/Montenegrin social product[12] fell 26 per cent in comparison with the previous year, and in 1993 it went down by another 30 per cent. While Serbia and Montenegro had a respectable $3300 per capita social product in 1990, in 1993 it was only $700 and in 1994 $1100.[13] Despite a sudden drop in inflation and a significant degree of economic stabilisation in 1994, due to the programme of economic reforms of the Governor of the National Bank, Dragoslav Avramović, industrial production in 1995 was only 3.8 per cent above the low level of 1994.[14] Unemployment has in the meantime grown considerably, too: out of the 10.5m inhabitants of Serbia and Montenegro, 720,000 are unemployed and the number is still rising; in addition, 1m out of 2.3m officially employed do not in fact work; they are on paid leave and receive only a fraction of their wages.

---

[9] The falseness of these expectations is analysed in Susan Woodward (1993) Yugoslavia: divide and fall, *The Bulletin of the Atomic Scientists*, autumn, p. 25.

[10] More about this in Vesna Bojičić and David Dyker (1993) Sanctions on Serbia: sledgehammer or scalpel?, *SEI Working Paper*, no. 1, Sussex European Institute.

[11] Federal Statistical Office, Belgrade, various reports.

[12] More or less GDP.

[13] Aleksandra Pošarac Pauperizacija stanovništva u Srbiji: jedan od osnovnih uzroka potisnutosti civilnog društva (Pauperisation of the population of Serbia: one of the basic reasons for the squeezing-out of civil society). In Pavlović (ed.) 1995: 333. See also Dinkić, 1995. The figures cited are at exchange-rate parities. Corresponding figures at purchasing power parity, as calculated by the London Economist Intelligence Unit, are: 1990: $4750; 1993: $2300; 1994:$2500.

[14] *Ekonomska Politika*, 25 March 1996, p. 52.

In spring 1994, two years after the imposition of sanctions, the Belgrade government calculated that the total cumulative damage already inflicted by sanctions amounted to more than $45bn – and that by the time the country once again achieves the economic results achieved before sanctions (in the year 2011), the cost of sanctions will have cumulated to $150bn.[15] The $45bn figure can be broken down into the following main items: GDP losses ($38.136bn); lost income from abroad ($1.136bn), and humanitarian aid to refugees and Serbs in Croatia and Bosnia ($5.13bn).

Serbia and Montenegro have also suffered from a serious brain drain: hundreds of top scientists, and probably as many as 200,000 educated young people, have left the country since 1991.[16] The worst consequences of sanctions, however, have been felt by the most vulnerable: children, old people, those sick with chronic diseases, and refugees. According to data released by UNICEF, the mortality of newborns in Serbia and Montenegro drastically increased during the first year of embargo, to stand at 21.7 per cent more than in the previous year. In underdeveloped parts of Serbia (Kosovo) as many as 33 out of 1000 newborn babies die, which is the highest infant mortality rate in Europe today.[17] In just two pediatric hospitals in Belgrade, 141 patients died in the course of 1993 because of shortage of medicines and surgical materials, which is 80 more than in 1991. The mortality rate of the elderly was five times higher in 1993 than it had been in 1986. Twice as many people died in Serbia from infectious diseases and diabetes between 1991 and 1993 than in the previous two years.[18]

In the first half of 1994, 2.1m people, more than one-third of the Serbian population, were officially below the poverty line, as compared to 1990, when only 360,000 people, or 6.23 per cent of the Serbian population, were officially classed as poor.[19] The new poor come mainly from groups employed by the state and from the middle classes. Sanctions also further widened the gap between the small number of privileged people who have managed to maintain their living standards or even to get rich from the crisis and the majority of the population.[20]

Ineffective economic policy-making by the federal government, and by the Serbian and the Montenegrin governments, have contributed abundantly to the economic crisis. Instead of embarking on the structural reform of the economy – always an option, however bad the conditions – federal and republican governments have remained preoccupied with the preservation and strengthening of their

[15] See Miso Jandrić (1994) Gubici u SR Jugoslaviji nastali uvedenim sankcijama (Losses to the FRY caused by sanctions). In Kosta Mihailović (ed.) *Sankcije* (Sanctions) (Belgrade: Serbian Academy of Sciences and Arts).

[16] Vladimir Grečić (1993) Brain Drain in Yugoslavia. In Susan Biggin and Vladimir Kouzminov (eds) *Proceedings of the International Seminar on Brain Drain Issue in Europe* (Venice: UNESCO-ROSTE).

[17] *Politika ekspres*, 8 December 1994.

[18] *NIN*, 27 May 1994.

[19] Pošarac, *ibid.*, p. 338.

[20] See Mladen Lazić Preobrazaj ekonomske elite (The transformation of the economic elite). In Lazić and Višnjic (eds) (1994).

monopoly control over the economy. Serbia has been especially consistent in this. Its stubborn rejection of privatisation culminated in July 1994 with the passage by the Serbian Assembly of a law on the revaluation of privatised assets. Although state (formerly socialised-sector) enterprises (with 77 per cent of the capital stock and 45 per cent of the workforce in Serbia) had already begun privatising in 1990, this law reduced the share of private assets within the paid-up capital of most enterprises to less than 1 per cent (in some cases it had previously been over 50 per cent) – on the pretext that enterprises were being sold off too cheaply. In this way the whole privatisation process was effectively annulled.

In 1995 Montenegro chose the opposite way, and embarked on mass privatisation at a rapid pace.[21] The Montenegrin Government Agency for Economic Restructuring reported on 3 January 1996 that nearly 80 per cent of the enterprises in Montenegro had been privatised by the end of 1995. By the time the process is completed, at the end of 1996, the category of 'social ownership' (abolished in principle with the introduction of Montenegro's new constitution in 1992) will finally disappear, leaving only private and state ownership.

The dominant model of privatisation in Montenegro (one of four originally envisaged) features the following main elements:

1   In the course of 1995 all employees received free shares, to the aggregate value of 10 per cent of the enterprise in question, with the total value of shares going to any one individual, subject to a ceiling of ECU 3000.
2   In addition, employees are entitled to buy up to 30 per cent of the total value of the shares of their enterprise on concessionary terms, with each year of service at the enterprises generating a 10 per cent discount, and ten years to pay, plus a two-year grace period. There is an upper limit of ECU 10,000 on share purchases by any individual under this scheme.
3   The rest of the shares of companies under privatisation is transferred to the republic's Development Fund (60 per cent), Pension Fund (30 per cent) and Employment Fund (10 per cent).

A number of independent economists and opposition politicians have criticised the Montenegrin government, alleging that, in giving 60 per cent of enterprise capital to state-run funds, the government is actually nationalising rather than privatising, and claiming that in reality there is very little difference between the Serbian and Montenegrin approaches to privatisation: in both cases the aim is monopoly control on the part of the ruling elite over the entire economy. In fairness, however, the Montengrin approach, with all its weaknesses, is different from the Serbian. And it is creating strains within the federation and putting pressure on Serbia to adopt a more liberal approach.

---

[21] See a series of papers on this issue in *Obnova i Razvoj Tržišnog Sistema u Jugoslaviji* (*Renewal and Development of the Market System in Yugoslavia*), Naučno društvo ekonomista Jugoslavije i Savez ekonomista Jugoslavije, Beograd, 1995.

Neither war nor peace

Let us now briefly examine the internal political scenes in Serbia and Montenegro, and at the level of the federation, from the introduction of multipartyism until the present time. Each has evolved in the last five years and each has specificities, but they all share two key features: the absence of any regime change and domination by one politician – Serbian president Slobodan Milošević – over the whole political space of the new Serb-Montenegrin federation.

While there has really been no radical change in Serbia and Montenegro similar to the changes in other East European countries, it would be grossly misleading to say that the communist system has simply survived untouched. At republic and federal level, there are institutions familiar in other post-communist and democratic countries. The big surviving difference is a disproportionately strong ruling party and correspondingly weak opposition. Following G. Sartori's classification, the system can be labelled a 'system of one predominant party'.[22] This kind of political party concentrates power to a much greater extent than is reflected in the share of seats it holds in the parliament. The most important reason for that is that ruling parties in Serbia and in Montenegro have never abandoned the hard core of monopoly power over the state, which they acquired in classical communist times, back in 1987 and 1989 – a monopoly over the police and the army, over the most influential media, and over key economic sectors and enterprises. A peculiar 'personal union' of party and state survives, irrespective of later changes.

In any case, all the moves towards democracy have been made reluctantly, in response to serious protests by the opposition parties, but still under the control of the 'predominant parties'. Those latter were able to make these moves without feeling threatened, because of the charismatic leadership they possessed, and because the whole transition in Serbia and Montenegro was being conducted under the very special conditions of war, sanctions and economic austerity. Frightened, disoriented and impoverished people, especially in societies that are ostracised and punished by the rest of the world, people under constant bombardment from carefully controlled media, very rarely organise themselves to a sufficient degree to be able to overthrow the government.

Serbia did witness radical anti-regime protests, but only in the first part of the half-decade under consideration. These protests were mainly a consequence of a 'highly polarised pluralism' that did not exist in Montenegro.[23] The ruling Socialist Party of Serbia (SPS) was at one and the same time in sharp conflict with most Serbian opposition parties, and with the Kosovo Albanians who, unlike the Serbian opposition, have boycotted all multiparty elections so far. The Serbian opposition certainly did not go as far as the Albanians, who consider Serbia an occupier in Kosovo. Nevertheless the SPS-opposition conflict does centre on the very foundation of the political organisation of the republic of Serbia. In the aftermath of the

---

[22] Vasović and Goati (1993) p. 199.

[23] *Ibid.*, p. 202. See also Vladimir Goati Pecularities of the Serbian political scene. In V. Goati (ed.) (1995).

first parliamentary elections (held in December 1990), Belgrade witnessed two large anti-regime protests: in March 1991 and at the end of June 1992. In the first of these, the Serbian opposition were demanding more democracy and free media, and the intensity of clashes with the police was so great that JNA tanks were sent on to the streets of Belgrade to restore/preserve order (see Chapter 7). The June 1992 protests, known as the 'Vidovdanski sabor' (St Vitus's Day rally), called for the resignation of Serbia's president (who had just been awarded UN sanctions for his policies) and for a total restructuring of the political system, through the mechanism of a roundtable and a Constituent Assembly. Both these protests showed that most of the opposition did not consider the Serbian constitutional order to be legitimate.

The boycott of all elections by the Kosovo Albanians is an equally difficult problem for the consolidation of democracy in Serbia, since Albanians account for 17.1 per cent (1,674,353) of Serbia's population, and 82.6 per cent of the population in Kosovo (1,596,072 out of a total of 1,956,196).[24] The Albanian 12–13 per cent of the Serbian electorate makes a big difference to electoral results in Serbia. In their absence, the SPS easily won virtually all the seats in the Serbian Assembly from the Kosovo electoral constituencies – with an extremely small number of Serbian electors' votes. Thus the SPS profited greatly, at least in the short run, from the behaviour of its 'arch-enemy'.

In the long run, however, there can be no real democracy in Serbia without a 'grand consensus' of the Serbian and the Albanian nations, and of their political representatives. For the time being, such consensus is almost impossible to conceive. Serbs and Albanians live in the same country, but in complete isolation from each other. Through a heavy police and army presence in Kosovo, Serbia is trying to prevent Albanians from establishing their own state and any kind of self-rule. It can only do this by violating the rights of the Albanian population. Passive Albanian resistance to complete Serbian domination over Kosovo has been, over the last few years, transformed into a genuine parallel Albanian state in Kosovo, with shadow political organisations, economy, education and fiscal system … This 'state' is run by quasi-state bodies, the main political party being the Democratic League of Kosovo, headed by Ibrahim Rugova, who is also the unofficial elected president of Kosovo. Such a situation cannot last long. But as long as it does last, it will hinder the consolidation of democracy in Serbia (see Chapter 8).

Conciliation is equally urgent with the other national minorities, who have felt uneasy with the new wave of Serbian nationalism and who have suffered discrimination in recent times. One out of three citizens of Serbia belongs to a nationality other than Serbian (Hungarians account for 3.5 per cent of the total population and 16.9 per cent of the Vojvodina population, Serbo-Croat-speaking Muslims for 2.5 per cent of the total population). This percentage can only grow in the future, because of the exceptionally high birth rate among the Albanian population.

With a very similar pattern of non-titular nationalities (61.8 per cent Montenegrins, 13.9 per cent Muslims, 6.2 per cent Albanians, 3.5 per cent Serbs …) Montenegro has, through a more conciliatory policy, succeeded in building, rather

---

[24] Zoran Lutovac *National Minorities and Elections*, p. 141. In Goati (ed.) (1995).

than burning, bridges with its national minorities. The minorities in Montenegro do not boycott elections, which is why the electoral victories of the ruling Democratic Party of Socialists (DPS) look that much more convincing. There have been two multiparty parliamentary elections so far in Montenegro. In December 1990 the DPS secured 56.16 per cent of the votes and 66.4 per cent of the Assembly seats (83 out of a total of 125). In December 1992 the DPS, led by President Momir Bulatović and Prime Minister Milo Djukanović, received fewer votes (42.6 per cent of votes to give them 46 out of 85 seats). The second time, it experienced stronger competition from both ends of the Montenegrin political spectrum. Pro-Serbian parties won 14 + 8 seats in the Assembly (the People's Party of Novak Kilibarda and the Serbian Radical Party of Vojislav Šešelj, respectively). The Liberal Union of Slavko Perović won 13 seats on a platform of full sovereignty for Montenegro, and the Social Democratic Party of Reformists, with a similar programme, won 4 seats. Through 1993 and part of 1994 Montenegro had a coalition government, with all parliamentary parties participating in the government, except for the Serbian Radical Party. But the DPS kept key ministerial posts to itself and maintained total control, which alienated the other parties. As a result, they gradually deserted the government.

Montenegrins have had one crucial additional possibility to express themselves through a ballot-box vote which the electorate in Serbia have not had. In the aftermath of the formal dissolution of the former Yugoslavia, a referendum was held on 1 March 1992 in Montenegro, to decide on whether its citizens wished to remain in a common state with Serbia. With Muslims, Albanians and some opposition parties boycotting the referendum, only 66.04 per cent of the electorate voted. But 95.94 per cent of those cast their votes in favour of the new Serbian-Montenegrin federation: the Federal Republic of Yugoslavia.

The Serbian regime simply disregarded demands for an analogous referendum in Serbia, and on 27 February 1992 a decision on the acceptance of the new federation was simply passed in the Serbian Assembly, in which the SPS had a safe majority. The Federal Republic of Yugoslavia was formally created in an equally irregular way, when the rump Federal Assembly of the former SFRY passed the new FRY Constitution on 27 April 1992. The Serbian and Montenegrin leaderships were in a hurry, trying to get international recognition for the new state, and the tactic here was to get the FRY recognised as the legitimate successor of the SFRY. It did not work, because of a very firm rejection by the most influential states on the international scene. The FRY instead got UN sanctions only one month later, and remains unrecognised to this day.

On 31 May 1992 elections for the Assembly of the new federation were organised, but they were boycotted by most opposition parties from Serbia and Montenegro. That is why they were rerun in December 1992. In the meantime, in order to improve the image of the internationally isolated FRY, the Serbian and Montenegrin ruling parties elected, within the framework of the Federal Assembly, two prominent personalities to lead the new federation. One was the famous Serbian writer, Dobrica Ćosić, who became president of the federation; the other was the American businessman of Serbian origin, Milan Panić, who became Federal Prime

Minister.[25] Within six months they had come into conflict with Milošević, because of independent attitudes and rapidly growing popularity. Panić ran for the post of the Serbian president against Milošević in December 1992. He lost the election but won a respectable 1.5m votes (34 per cent). His political career in Serbia finished soon after the elections, while Ćosić was sacked not much later, in May 1993. He was replaced by a colourless and powerless SPS party official, Zoran Lilić. The Federal Assembly elected in December 1992, had no real power either. It was ruled by a coalition of the SPS and DPS, but all important decisions were taken by the republican leaderships, within which the presidents of the two republics had the final say.

SPS rule in Serbia has been uninterrupted through the 1990s, but the only time the party won an absolute majority of seats was in the first elections for the Serbian Assembly, in December 1990. That produced a convincing victory for the SPS, which got 46.1 per cent of votes and – because of the majoritarian electoral system – 77.6 per cent of seats (194 out of total 250). Two years later, in the December 1992 parliamentary elections, they got 28.8 per cent of votes, and 40.4 per cent of seats in the Assembly (101 out of 250). Their vote split on that occasion into two. The more moderate voters stood by the SPS, while the more militant gave their mandate to the most chauvinist political organisation in Serbia, the Serbian Radical Party (SRS) of Vojislav Šešelj. The SRS's striking success (seventy-three MPs) was achieved mostly with the help of the SPS-controlled propaganda mouthpiece, the state-owned TV channel. The SPS kept all ministerial posts in the government, but worked through an informal coalition with the Radicals.

This coalition was abandoned by the SPS only a few months later. Trying to get himself out of the war in Bosnia and Hercegovina, Milošević accepted the Vance–Owen peace plan in Spring 1993, and continued to push the peace line. In August of that year Milošević and his party launched a fierce campaign against the SRS, accusing it of warmongering, war crimes and militant chauvinism. On the eve of a motion of no confidence in the SPS government, in October 1993, Milošević dissolved the Serbian Assembly, upon the motion of the Serbian government, as provided for in the constitution of Serbia.

New elections for the Serbian Assembly were held in December 1993. The SPS improved its results, as compared with previous elections, but was still three seats short of an absolute majority (it obtained 123 out of 250 seats). Four Serbian opposition parties, the coalition DEPOS of Vuk Drašković (with the Civic Alliance of Vesna Pešić and the New Democracy of Dušan Mihajlović), the SRS, the Democratic Party of Zoran Djindjić and the Democratic Party of Serbia of Vojislav Kostunica, together won three seats fewer than the socialists, although they won many more votes than the SPS (2,026,669 as against 1,576,287). The peculiarities of the electoral system contributed to this, the same as for the previous election, as did the Albanian boycott, not to mention irregularities during the electoral campaign. The Radicals were the main losers in the election (they went down to

---

[25] See Jovan Teokarević (1992) How to get in and out of War Communism, *East European Reporter*, vol. 5, no. 5, September–October, pp. 60–2.

thirty-nine MPs) and the Democratic Party the main winners (they raised their number of MPs from seven in 1992 to twenty-nine in 1993). This was a clear sign that voters in Serbia were turning their backs on extremism (leftist extremists from the Yugoslav United Left – JUL – did not manage to pass the 5 per cent threshold), and were beginning to prefer parties of the political centre. Another encouraging consequence was the stabilization of the party system: small parties, which had done well in earlier elections were squeezed out; Serbian political life was coming more and more to depend on a small number of big parties.[26]

After many tensions and conflicts, a new Serbian government was formed on the basis of a completely unexpected coalition of the SPS and New Democracy, a tiny party from within the coalition DEPOS. This destroyed the hard-won unity of the opposition. The trend was only intensified when Milošević's party resolutely opted for peace in Bosnia during 1994, accepting the 'Contact Group's' peace plan and imposing sanctions on the Bosnian Serbs in August 1994. This led to a radically regrouping on the Serbian political scene, with the SPS, the Serbian Renewal Movement of Vuk Drašković, the Civic Alliance and New Democracy on one side (the 'peace lobby') and the SRS, Democratic Party[27] and Democratic Party of Serbia on the other (the 'war lobby', supporting the Bosnian Serb leadership). These new formations have still not been formally constituted, but Milošević has succeeded in making a radical policy turn, without losing critical mass among the voters.

Milošević's popularity received a big fillip at the end of 1995, with the signing of the Dayton peace accord ending the war in Bosnia and Hercegovina, and the concomitant suspension of UN sanctions on Serbia and Montenegro (Security Council Resolution 1022, 23 November 1995). If this impetus is to maintained, however, Milošević will have to obtain a permanent lifting of sanctions, and engineer a rapid and sustained economic recovery, with the former likely to be a critical condition of the latter.

The UN Security Council has promised that sanctions will be finally lifted ten days after elections have been held in Bosnia and Hercegovina, provided that Serbia/Montenegro/FR Yugoslavia fulfils all its other obligations under the Dayton agreement, in terms of respecting human rights, cooperating with the War Crimes Tribunal in the Hague, etc. The USA and the EU are also putting pressure on Belgrade to grant 'a large measure of autonomy' to Kosovo. Meanwhile the unofficial 'outer wall of sanctions' continues to stand, preventing Serbia/Montenegro from joining international organisations.

Judging from the experience of the first few months since Dayton, Milošević is going to find it extremely difficult to achieve the goals of full normalisation of relations with the rest of the world and rapid economic recovery. While continuing to appear conciliatory in foreign affairs, he has opted for a more severe dictatorship on the domestic front, disregarding demands from the opposition and tightening his

---

[26] For more about this see Jovan Teokarević (1995) Kontinuitet uprkos promenama: politicka dinamika u Srbiji i Crnoj Gori u 1994. godini (Continuity in the face of change: political trends in Serbia and Montenegro in 1994). In Kovačević and Dajić, 1995.

[27] Joining the 'war lobby' was an odd political tactic for a basically centrist party.

control over the key media. Islands of independence in Serbian public life which managed to survive the war are now sinking under the repressive pressure of the regime. The latter seems to understand that peace in the region and an end to isolation are not, in the long run, to its advantage. As long as Milošević remains in power, Serbia and Montengro will continue to live in a state of 'neither war nor peace'.

References

Čavoski, K. (1991) *Slobodan Protiv Slobode (Slobodan against Freedom)* (Beograd: Dosije).

Dinkić, M. (1995) *Ekonomija Destrukcije. Velika Pljačka Naroda (The Economics of Destruction. The Plundering of a Nation)* (Beograd: VIN).

Goati, V. (ed.) (1995) *Challenges of Parliamentarism. The Case of Serbia in the Early Nineties* (Belgrade: Institute of Social Science).

Inter-ethnic Conflict and War in Former Yugoslavia (1992) (Belgrade: Institute of European Studies).

Kovačević, S. and Dajić, P. (1994) *Chronology of the Yugoslav Crisis 1942–1993* (Belgrade: Institute of European Studies).

Kovačević, S. and Dajić, P. (1995) *Hronologija Jugoslovenske Krize 1994* (Beograd: Institut za evropske studije).

Lazić, M. and Višnjić, F. (eds) (1994) *Razaranje Društva. Jugoslovensko Društvo u Krizi 90-ih (The Destruction of a Society. Yugoslav Society in the Crisis of the 90s)* (Beograd: Institut za evropske studije).

Nakarada, R., Basta-Posavec, L. and Samardžić, S. (eds) (1991) *Raspad Jugoslavije – Produžetak ili Kraj Agonije? (The Break-up of Yugoslavia – Continuation or End of the Agony?)* (Beograd: Institut za evropske studije).

Pavlović, V. (ed.) (1995) *Potisnuto Civilno Društvo (Civil Society Squeezed out)* (Beograd: Eko Centar).

Vasović, V. and Goati, V. (1993) *Izbori i Izborni Sistemi (Elections and Electoral Systems)* (Beograd: IBN Centar i NIP Radnička štampa).

Chapter 11

Croatia

CHRISTOPHER CVIIĆ

Introduction

Croatia's bid for independence from Yugoslavia in 1991 was contested, and it was costly, in terms both of material destruction and human casualties. Croatia suffered casualties to the extent of 6829 people killed and 25,951 wounded in the seven-month-long war fought on its territory from July 1991 till January 1992. Its opponents were the Yugoslav People's Army (JNA), Serb paramilitaries recruited from the ranks of the Serb minority in Croatia, and Serb volunteers from Bosnia and Serbia proper. Of those killed, 2296 were civilians. Of the wounded, 7298 were civilians. At 1993, 12,751 people were still officially missing, including 416 children.

Croatia also suffered substantial material damage and significant loss of territory. According to official Croat estimates, the war destroyed about 30 per cent of the country's industrial potential. Total material damage is variously estimated at between $22bn and $25bn. About 7800 miles of roads, or 38 per cent of the total road network, was badly damaged. Dozens of important bridges were wrecked, including the bridge at Maslenica near the port of Zadar on the Adriatic coast, which carries the bulk of the tourist traffic to and from Dalmatia, Croatia's most important tourist region. Severe damage was inflicted on other port facilities and airports. Thousands of factories, schools, hospitals and churches were deliberately targeted for artillery and aerial attacks.

Nearly one-third of Croatia's territory – including, in the east, some of the richest agricultural land as well as Croatia's oil wells – remained under Serb control at the end of the war in early 1992. So did part of the Zagreb-Split railway that links Dalmatia with the rest of the country. The Serbs also retained control of a section of the old Zagreb-Belgrade highway, built after 1945, thus cutting off Zagreb, the capital, from eastern Croatia. Refugees from the occupied Croat territories presented a serious problem. There were a quarter of a million of them at the end of the war. The outbreak of war in neighbouring Bosnia and Hercegovina in May 1992 produced around another 400,000 refugees. Approximately 20 per cent of those were Bosnian Croats and about 80 per cent Bosnian Muslims. The refugee burden, alleviated by humanitarian aid right from the start, has eased since then. Some of the Muslim refugees have gone on to other countries in Europe and beyond. A small number have returned to Bosnia since the end of fighting in November 1995. But many remain in Croatia.[1]

The birth of independent Croatia in 1991 was thus violent: far more so than that of neighbouring Slovenia in the same year, though less violent than that of Bosnia and Hercegovina a year later. It was an outcome far removed from the peaceful parting, modelled on that of Norway and Sweden in 1905, that many Croats had hoped for. We might expect that transition from communism to post-communism would be more difficult in a multinational state like Yugoslavia than in a nationally homogenous one like, for example, Poland. But why did a peaceful parting prove possible in the (also multinational) Soviet Union in 1991 and in Czechoslovakia in 1993, but not in Yugoslavia?

The circumstances of Yugoslavia's violent demise and Croatia's role in that demise clearly raise important questions that need to be answered *because the answers contain clues to the future of the whole region.* In search of answers, this chapter first notes and describes – after a brief look at Croatia's early history — the country's constantly shifting position *vis-à-vis* the old regional power centres (notably Budapest and Vienna, but also Venice and Constantinople) and then, in our own time, the Croats' complex relationship with Yugoslavia and its largest ethnic group, the Serbs. This essentially historical part is followed by a second section which traces Croatia's road to independence and war in 1991. The chapter concludes with a brief look at the main features of contemporary, post-independence Croatia.

In and out of empires

Croatia is one of the newest members of the United Nations – it became a member in May 1992 – but its recorded history goes back to the second quarter of the seventh century when the Croats, a people whose name and origin have not to this day been satisfactorily explained,[2] came to the Adriatic Sea from what is now Central Europe. In cooperation with the Byzantine Empire and the local Slavs who had migrated to the region earlier, the Croats managed to defeat the Avars and secure for

---

[1] These and other figures about the 1991 war quoted in the text have been culled from a variety of Croatian government sources. For the best study so far of the war in Croatia, see Cigar, 1993.

[2] Early Croat history, a subject scarcely known outside Croatia but for decades a political battlefield in Croatia, fiercely fought over by scholarly cliques with different political agendas – e.g. the 'Yugo-integralists' promoting the primacy of the Croats' Slav dimension versus the 'independentist' anti-Yugoslavs who stress the (non-Slav) Gothic-Iranian one – is dealt with in a refreshingly detached manner in Goldstein, 1995.

A comprehensive scholarly account of the political background to historical controversies about the status of the Croatian language is provided by Banac, 1990. His paper is accompanied by an extensive bibliography of books, longer studies and articles in various languages about Croatian language questions, prepared by the volume's editor, Professor Slobodan Prosperov-Novak. Banac is also the author (1984) of an authoritative monograph on the nationality question in pre-1941 monarchist Yugoslavia.

themselves the territory along the coast and inland towards the north. The Slavs further north gravitated towards the new Croat state, which inherited the political and social traditions of the ancient world from those settled there before – the Romans, Romanized Illyrians and Celts – along with their more advanced economy and culture.

By the later Middle Ages, the more numerous Croats had assimilated almost all of the previous settlers, and had also united with the northern Croatian state situated in the region between the Sava and Drava rivers. Branches of the Croat nation also existed in Istria, to the south-east of the Neretva (so-called Red Croatia), and also within the emerging Bosnian state. Croatia became a kingdom under Tomislav (910–928), who united the northern and southern Croatian principalities and created a state capable of resisting the Hungarian drive towards the sea from the north. He also defeated the Bulgarians in what is today north-eastern Bosnia. Under Tomislav, Croatia established full control over the coastal towns of Dalmatia, and supported the founding of an integral system of ecclesiastical jurisdiction over a territory stretching from the Rasa River in Istria in the west to the Bay of Kotor in the east, and from the Adriatic Sea in the south to the Drava River on the edge of the Pannonian plain in the north.

Under Tomislav's successors, Croatia's position *vis-à-vis* both the Byzantine Empire and Venice weakened considerably. Its fortunes were restored under King Petar Krešimir IV (1058–74), who ruled over the Dalmatian towns and islands, Bosnia, Slavonia and the principality of the Neretva River. However, a rapid decline set in under his squabbling successors. King Petar (1093–97) was defeated by the Hungarians, and in 1102 the Croatian nobility accepted the suzerainty of the Hungarian Arpad dynasty. Croatia and Hungary remained separate states, connected only by personal union. This was reflected in the practice of the separate coronation of the Hungarian ruler as Croatian king (who had the right to appoint a governor (*ban*)), and in the retention by Croatia of a separate diet, tax system, currency and army.

First under the Arpads, and then under the Anjou dynasty, the joint Croat-Hungarian kingdom lost most of the Adriatic coast to Venice and most of its possessions in Bosnia to local rulers. Bosnia finally fell to the advancing Ottoman Empire in 1463. After the Ottoman victory over the Croatian-Hungarian army at Mohács in 1527 and the death of the king, the Croatian nobility elected Ferdinand Habsburg as their king in the hope that he would ensure the defence of the country. However, as a result of the struggle for the throne in Hungary, where the election of Ferdinand was fiercely resisted by another candidate, the Ottoman advance continued. Croatia, which had a territory of 50,000 sq km in 1526, was reduced to 20,000 sq km by the middle of the century and 16,800 sq km by the end of the sixteenth century. It became popularly known as the 'relics of relics' (*reliquiae reliquiarum*) of the old Croatian kingdom. Croatia was never completely conquered – the Turks stopped just short of Zagreb, the capital – but the wars led to both considerable loss of life and to mass migrations. It is estimated that, by the end of the eighteenth century when the Turkish wars ended, about 1.6m Croats had emigrated, been killed in battle or captured. (As a result of the migrations, there are about 180,000 Croats living in Austria, Hungary, Italy, Romania and Slovakia today.)

Under Habsburg rule, which lasted just short of four centuries, most of the old Croatian lands were reconquered from the Ottoman Empire and Venice. However, Croatia remained divided. Dalmatia, with the city of Dubrovnik and Istria, was administered within the Austrian half of the Empire, and central and northern Croatia within the Hungarian part. In 1881, after much pressure from Zagreb, the region of the *Vojna Krajina* (Military Frontier) was reintegrated into Croatia. The *Vojna Krajina,* which had been set up by the Habsburgs in the sixteenth century as a string of army-run districts along the border with the Ottoman Empire, stretched from eastern Slavonia along Bosnia's northern border down into central and southern Croatia. Christian (mostly Orthodox) refugees from the Turkish Empire had been settled there and given land by the Habsburg authorities in return for military service.

The political class in Croatia was forced, from the end of the eighteenth century right up to the Empire's defeat and dissolution in 1918, to manoeuvre – usually from a position of palpable weakness – between the centres of power: Budapest and Vienna and, until the end of the eighteenth century, also Venice. (Napoleon took over the Venetian possessions, including Dalmatia, in 1805; after his defeat in 1814 they went to the Habsburgs.) For the Croats, the overriding issue remained that of the unification of the Croat lands into a single unit within the Empire. Despite a series of disappointments with the Habsburgs, the bulk of the Croat political class went on believing that the Croat *raison d'état* could best be promoted within the Empire, by playing alternately the Vienna and the Budapest 'cards'.

From the middle of the nineteenth century, however, 'Magyarisation' emerged as an increasingly dominant theme in the eastern half of the Empire, of which Croatia proper formed part. Magyarisation was perceived as a serious threat by a growing part of the political class in Croatia and much of the (small) intelligentsia. This perception acted as a spur to those elements to look for a different solution, one within the framework of a state comprising all Southern Slavs ('Yugoslavs'), to include those (like the Bulgarians and the Serbs of the then Kingdom of Serbia) who were outside the Habsburg Monarchy. The conversion of more and more Croat politicians, intellectuals and churchmen to the Yugoslav idea meant that by the time Austria-Hungary's military defeat and collapse in 1918 had become a reality, public opinion in Croatia was mentally and emotionally prepared to exchange for a new Southern Slav union their centuries-old, but increasingly uncomfortable, association with an ever more aggressively nationalist Hungary.

As events started to unfold towards the end of the First World War, what had for many Croats been no more than a political and cultural 'Yugo-enthusiasm' turned into a geopolitical imperative. At the end of 1918, with Austria–Hungary unravelling, a serious danger to Croatia's national territory loomed from the south. The Entente Powers had promised Italy, under the 1915 Treaty of London, most of Croatia's northern Adriatic coast (including the offshore islands), as an inducement to it to drop its erstwhile alliance partners, Germany and Austria–Hungary, and join the war on the Entente's side. Italy accepted the offer and entered the war. When the war terminated, it proceeded with the occupation of the specified territories, adding here and there others (like the important port of Rijeka/Fiume) which had not been assigned to it under the Treaty of London. For the Croats, union in a new Southern

Slav state with Serbia, a member of the victorious Entente coalition, seemed the best protection against the Italian advance.

The Croats and Yugoslavia

Post-1918 Yugoslavia (called, until 1929, 'The State of the Serbs, the Croats and the Slovenes' (*Država Srba, Hrvata i Slovenaca*, or *SHS* for short), proved a severe disappointment for the Croats. This was partly because the government in Belgrade proved unable to stop Italy from acquiring much of the territory promised to it under the Treaty of London. Some Croats were even suspicious that the predominantly Serb administration in Belgrade was plotting with Italy a future carve-up of Croatia that would leave a Greater Italy on the one side and a Greater Serbia on the other. This surmise was based on the well-known antipathy of Nikola Pašić, Serbia's Prime Minister during the First World War and again after it, towards the idea of a South Slav state. Pašić favoured the outright annexation by Serbia of lands he considered as Serb: Bosnia, large parts of southern Croatia with the Adriatic coast (including Dubrovnik), most of northern Croatia right up to Zagreb, Macedonia and Montenegro. He accepted the idea of a Yugoslav state only very reluctantly. Perceptions of Italy were, therefore, very different in Croatia ('a dangerous predator') and in Serbia ('a friendly country and, at the very least, a country Serbia can do business with').

Even more important for the Croats, they not only failed, within the new state, to achieve equality with the Serbs, but actually ended worse off, both *de jure* and *de facto*, than they had been within Austria-Hungary. For under the Habsburgs, the Croats had always enjoyed a well-defined autonomy as one of the Empire's 'historic nations'. In that sense, the Croats had been in a privileged position compared with, for example, the Slovenes and the Slovaks, who were not recognised as 'historic nations', and did not enjoy any legally guaranteed autonomy. Croatia's autonomous status had, indeed, been given a modern form in an agreement (*Nagodba*) reached with Hungary in 1868, a year after a similar Austro-Hungarian compromise (*Ausgleich*). Although politically dependent on Hungary, the Croats had kept the main features of statehood and preserved their pre-eminent position among the Slav peoples of the dual monarchy. The Kingdom of Croatia had retained autonomy in its internal administration, judiciary, religious affairs and education. Under the dual monarchy Croatian was the official language in the Croatian civil service and in the offices of the imperial administration located on Croatian soil (post offices, railways, banks and the forestry service). Croatian deputies could use Croatian when speaking in the common parliament in Budapest. Defence, finance, trade and transport were declared joint affairs under the administration in Budapest. The army remained under the control of the Emperor in Vienna, but in certain regiments the language of command was Croatian. Croatia's administration was headed by a governor (*ban*) appointed at the recommendation of the prime minister of the Hungarian half of the dual monarchy. Croatia retained 44 per cent of its tax income; the rest went to the joint treasury in Budapest. The port of Rijeka remained a *corpus separatum* (separate unit) under direct Hungarian control until 1918.

It must be said that the *Nagodba* was seen as deeply unsatisfactory, even humiliating, by most Croats – at the time of its conclusion and afterwards. In retrospect, seen against the background of Croatia's total loss of autonomy and lack of any separate status within the new South Slav state after 1918, it looked a lot more attractive. The new South Slav state adopted the centralist French model in 1921. In 1929 it became a personal dictatorship under King Alexander Karadjordjević, who divided the state into eight units (*banovine*) named after the country's main rivers, and paying no attention to historic identities. Not surprisingly, many Croats felt that their country had fallen from the Austro-Hungarian frying-pan into the Serbian fire.

After the assassination of King Alexander in 1934 by a Macedonian terrorist acting together with Croatian terrorists, a political thaw set in. In August 1939, on the eve of the outbreak of war, prospects for Croat-Serb accommodation improved. A separate Croat unit called the *Banovina Hrvatska* was created under an agreement negotiated by the government of Dragiša Cvetković acting on behalf of Prince Paul Karadjordjević, Yugoslavia's Regent, and Vladko Maček, leader of the Croatian Peasant Party. Croatia's new status was supported by its Serb population, the so-called *prečani* ('people from the other side', as the Serbs from Serbia proper called their fellow-Serbs in Croatia and Bosnia). The *prečani* had come to mistrust the rapacious and corrupt central government in Belgrade and to see their interests as better protected by Zagreb.

However, the Cvetković-Maček agreement was undermined by the vehement reaction by the Serb public in Belgrade and elsewhere in Serbia. The democratic opposition in Serbia came out against it, as well as the Serbian Orthodox Church which had, two years before, successfully torpedoed a proposed concordat with the Vatican that would have given the Roman Catholic Church equal status with the Serbian Orthodox Church within Yugoslavia.

Behind the Croats' persistent quest for territorial autonomy and the formal recognition of traditional Croat identity lay their sense of insecurity about the Serbs, particularly what they saw as the threat of assimilation disguised as campaigns for unity ('Yugoslavism'). It is in this light that the Croats viewed King Alexander's ban after 1929 of all national symbols (including flags). Some commentators talk of a 'narcissism of small differences' or, even, of a Croat 'paranoia'. But in Yugoslavia before 1941 there *did* exist the ideological basis for an assimilationist Yugoslav 'unitarism'. It was the theory that the Croats, the Serbs and the Slovenes (the Macedonians and the Bosnian Muslims were at that time not recognised as separate entities) were three sections, or 'tribes' (*plemena*), of one 'Yugoslav' people. In reality, the very linguistic closeness of the southern Slavs, which had been seen as a good basis for harmony, turned out to be a divisive factor because it brought the prospect (or threat) of assimilation closer.

That threat was perceived as only too real by Croatian eyes. The Croats noted the widespread acceptance among the Serbs of the views of the nineteenth-century linguistic reformer, Vuk Stefanović Karadžić, who defined as Serbs all those who speak the central-south (*štokavian*) Slavic dialect – among them the vast majority of Catholic Croats and Bosnian Muslims. Vuk's ideas, which before 1918 and for a while afterwards had also been accepted by many prominent pro-Yugoslav Croat linguists, served to reinforce the official concept promoted after 1918 of a single

Yugoslav nation made up of three 'tribes'. But an ever-increasing number of Croats began to see Vuk's ideology as a back door to the 'Serbianisation' of the country's non-Serb Slavs. In the end, Yugoslavia broke up in 1941 not because of internal discords, but because of a foreign invasion. But by then the South Slav unity project had already clearly failed. Few Croats, not to mention the other non-Serbs of Yugoslavia, were sorry to see the kingdom founder – though the horrors that followed came as an unpleasant shock to all.

The communist corset

In 1945 Croatia became one of the republics of the Yugoslav communist federation set up by Marshal Tito. Equality was what the Tito regime offered, at least on paper, to the non-Serbs, in contrast to the Serb supremacy which is all the pre-1941 monarchist regime had been able to offer. The promise of national equality had helped Tito's Partisans gain extra support during the Second World War, but the reality after their victory in 1945 proved different. Yugoslavia was in practice to be a centralised state run by the Communist Party and its leader, Tito. Elements of Serb supremacism did, indeed, reappear in the new, supposedly internationalist-minded, Yugoslav regime. Tito needed to appease the Serbs in the immediate post-1945 period. As part of that policy, Tito deliberately avoided any forthright denunciations of pre-1941 Serb 'hegemonism'. The reasons for Tito's tactics were clear. During Germany's wartime occupation of Serbia, the majority of Serbs backed General Draža Mihailović, leader of the royalist Chetniks. The Chetniks hoped to restore Yugoslavia, once it had been liberated from the Germans, to the prewar, strongly Serbian-flavoured kingdom. They opposed the idea of a Yugoslav federation propagated by Tito's communists. Tito never won the allegiance of the Serbs in Serbia during the war (in contrast to the mainly rural Serbs in Croatia and Bosnia who joined the Partisans to escape the murderous quisling Ustasha regime of Ante Pavelić that the Germans and the Italians had installed in Croatia in 1941). Belgrade and the rest of Serbia, it should be added, were liberated from the Germans in October 1944 by the Red Army aided by Tito's Partisans – not the other way round.

Tito badly needed to build a power base in a largely hostile Serbia once he had come to power. The Serbs of Serbia held against Tito the fact that he, half-Croat, half-Slovene, had not only dethroned the Serbian Karadjordjević dynasty in 1945, but had also had Draža Mihailović tried and shot as a Nazi collaborator in 1946. To appease the Serbs, Tito espoused Yugoslav 'unitarism', which both directly and indirectly favoured the revival of Serb influence – especially in the army, the police, the diplomatic service and the federal government in Belgrade, the capital of Serbia as well as of Yugoslavia. This policy was also reflected in superficially minor but significant decisions, e.g. to publish the official party daily *Borba* in the *ekavian* (Serbian) version of the official Serbo-Croat language (though in the traditionally Croatian Latin, rather than the traditionally Serbian Cyrillic script). In the same vein, in 1945 the Serbian variant of Serbo-Croat was made the official language of command in the Yugoslav People's Army. (During the war, the Partisans had encouraged the use in Croatia of the Croat variant of Serbo-Croat and, in Slovenia, of Slovene.)

But this bargain did not last. Isolated from the Soviet bloc after the Stalin–Tito split of 1948, Yugoslavia was obliged in the 1950s and early 1960s to look for alternatives to its own earlier version of Soviet-style centralism in all spheres of public life. The fight against centralism in the economic sphere and also in the political was led by Croatia and Slovenia, the industrialised Western republics. The struggle eventually widened to take in the extremely sensitive issue of national equality, and from 1966 the post-1945 'unitarism' began to come under increasingly strong attack from most of Yugoslavia's non-Serbs. The Croats tended to take the lead in all this. However, in its fight against 'Belgrade centralism', Croatia was politically handicapped by the appalling heritage of the wartime Pavelić regime. There was an element of irony in this, in view of the Croats' massive participation in the wartime anti-Fascist struggle on the Partisan side (Pavelić's Ustasha movement was minuscule before it was put in power by the Axis in 1941, and only a minority of Croats sided with the Ustashas). But the embattled centralists (as well as those among the Serbian non-communist nationalist opposition who hoped for the restoration of pre-1941 Serb supremacy) found it politically convenient to undermine the position of the Croats by harping on and, indeed, exaggerating, the numbers of the Pavelić regime's victims. For example, the notorious Ustasha death camp in Jasenovac, where some 60,000–70,000 people (not all of them Serbs) were killed between 1941 and 1945, was said to have claimed the lives of 700,000 Serbs alone. These exaggerations had a political purpose: to prove that Pavelić and his Ustasha movement had enjoyed mass support among the Croats.[3]

The strength of this tactic was that it made it possible to characterise the various anti-centralist *démarches* from Zagreb – whether political, economic or even cultural – as 'separatism' and 'nationalist extremism'. This was demonstrated in 1967 by the case of the so-called 'Language Declaration', signed on behalf of eighteen Croat cultural institutions by 140 prominent scholars, writers and other intellectuals. The Declaration demanded the return to the language position as of the wartime Partisan period and immediately after 1945, when full constitutional recognition was given (even on Yugoslav banknotes) to four languages: Croatian, Macedonian, Serbian and Slovene. It also demanded the use in schools and in the mass media throughout the republic of standard Croatian instead of Serbo-Croat, which was rejected by many Croats as a 'political' language and, as such, another manifestation of Yugoslav 'unitarism'. The 'Declaration' caused a bitter public row. Many of its signatories were expelled from the Communist Party and lost their jobs. The

---

[3] The official Titoist figure for Yugoslavia's Second World War population losses, frequently quoted over a period of many years, was 1.7m. According to two remarkably objective studies, one by Bogoljub Kočović, a Serb author living in the West, and the other by Vladimir Zerjavić, a Croat population expert living in Croatia, the actual figures were very different. According to Kočović's calculations, which tally very closely with Zerjavić's, Yugoslavia lost 1,014,000 people (5.9 per cent of the total population) from all sides in the 1941–45 period. Serb losses were 487,000 (6.9 per cent of the total Serb population), Croat 207,000 (5.4 per cent), Bosnian Muslim 86,000 (6.9 per cent), Jewish 60,000 (77.9 per cent) and Gypsy 27,000 (31.4 per cent). See Kočović, 1985, and Zerjavić, 1989.

entire printing of 40,000 copies of an orthographic handbook produced by three Croat linguists in 1971 was banned as 'chauvinist' and 'separatist' the following year, and ordered to be burnt.

The book burning formed part of a purge in Croatia which President Tito had ordered at the end of 1971, and which formed part of a broader crackdown on 'liberals' and 'technocrats' throughout Yugoslavia. The purge was harshest in Croatia. The new leaders installed by Tito crushed the 'Croatian Spring', a political and national revival which had been going on since 1966. Its protagonists had been leaders like Miko Tripalo and Savka Dabčević-Kučar from the liberal-reformist wing of the Communist Party; a group of intellectuals centred around *Hrvatski Tjednik*, the popular cultural weekly edited by poet and journalist Vlado Gotovac and published by *Matica Hrvatska*, founded in the nineteenth century and the oldest Croatian cultural association; and a group of Zagreb University students led by Dražen Budiša and Zvonimir Čičak. It was not a coordinated movement – all the three elements worked independently of each other – but Tito was sufficiently alarmed to want to put the whole thing down.

The purge had a stultifying effect on political and cultural life in Croatia – similar to that of the crushing of the 'Prague Spring' after 1968 in Czechoslovakia. The prolonged, systematic repression that followed earned Croatia the soubriquet of the 'silent republic'. The Western media, which had taken up with vigour the case of persecuted 'Prague Spring' activists, played down both the extent and the harshness of Tito's purge in Croatia. In that, they were quietly encouraged by Western governments anxious to maintain Tito's ties with the West.

As part of the purge, thousands of Croats were expelled from the party and lost their posts, with only a handful of matching losses among the (admittedly few) Serb supporters of the 'Croatian Spring'. Anti-Serbian feeling in Croatia was further fuelled by the fact that the deeply unpopular and insecure leaders Tito installed in Croatia after his crackdown were obliged to rely heavily on 'faithful' Serbian party cadres in the implementation of their repressive policy. One of the most important long-term effects of Tito's purge was, therefore, to deepen mistrust between the majority Croat population and the Serb minority, which also cut off the possibility of reviving the pre-1941 anti-Belgrade alliance between Croats and *prečani* Serbs. Perhaps inevitably, the Croats' instinctive response to Tito's purge, which they saw as a full-scale attack on their basic national identity, was to concentrate on defending those things that seemed to be in particular danger – such as the national symbols and the Croat language and culture. Unfortunately, there was nothing there for Croatia's Serbs to identify with. They felt left out of that particular struggle and, with memories of Pavelić's extremist brand of Croatian nationalism still fresh in their minds, apprehensive about the future.

This Croat-Serb rift, set against the background of an increasing tendency for Croats to reject Yugoslavia, was the main reason why there was no joint Croat-Serb struggle for democracy and civil rights in Croatia, or indeed in Yugoslavia. The apparent inability of Croats and Serbs – except for a few small groups – to cooperate in joint projects (including 'neutral' ones supported by human rights' organisations from the West), or even to sign joint petitions to the authorities, puzzled outsiders. But there was no mystery: the reasons were clear. While more and more

Croats were coming to reject Yugoslavia, the vast majority of Serbs (including supporters of democratic change) continued to take its existence for granted – whatever their own particular criticisms of Yugoslavia's current political and economic system from the Serbian national point of view.

Among the Croats, the increasing emphasis on the purely 'national' aspects of the anti-regime struggle and the need for the broadest possible Croat unity led to a de-emphasis of democracy, pluralism and civil rights as the struggle's principal aims. This echoed the attitudes prevalent among the Kosovo Albanians, but was in marked contrast to the situation in nationally homogenous Slovenia. There, a broad national consensus in favour of ever-greater autonomy for Slovenia within Yugoslavia was from quite early on matched by well-supported 'non-national' initiatives arising from concerns with the environment, anti-militarism, sexual freedom and other 'civil' issues. In other words, the Slovenes' fight for national autonomy went hand-in-hand with that for democracy, while in Croatia the two were separated, with the national struggle being given 'for the time being' absolute pre-eminence over that for democracy.

'Croatia firstism' triumphs

The Croats' growing absorption – in the wake of the 1971–72 purge and to the exclusion of almost everything else – with the 'national question', accompanied by the steady growth of anti-Yugoslavia and pro-independence sentiment, found delayed expression in Croatia's first multiparty election since the Second World War in April–May 1990. The election was won overwhelmingly by the Croatian Democratic Union (*Hrvatska Demokratska Zajednica* or HDZ), a heterogenous movement which emphasised the 'national issue' and presented itself to the electorate as 'the most Croat party'. Its leader, Dr Franjo Tudjman, a former general in the JNA and a historian, had been sacked in 1967 from the post of head of the party history institute in Zagreb for his attempts to correct what he saw as anti-Croat bias in official communist pronouncements about the Second World War. Tudjman was later twice arrested; he was sentenced in 1972 to two years' imprisonment for 'counter-revolutionary nationalism' (though he played no active role in the 'Croatian Spring'); and in 1981 to three years' imprisonment and a five-year ban on all public activity for giving 'hostile' interviews to the Western media about the situation in Croatia. His appeal to the Croats in 1990 was to look on him as the true champion of Croatia in her struggle to refute the various anti-Croat 'black legends' of recent history, notably the one about the Croats as a 'genocidal nation' promoted by certain Serb churchmen and intellectuals.

The election in Croatia took place a week after the conclusion of Slovenia's first multiparty election. Under the moderate, reformist communist leadership of Milan Kučan, Slovenia had been experimenting for several years with political pluralism and already had a quasi-party system. Croatia, by contrast, had only had a short time to prepare for democracy. There was little political talent available, thanks to the communist policy of 'negative selection', which operated particularly effectively in Croatia. The unpopular party leaders installed by Tito in the wake of the

1971–72 purge had been replaced in the late 1980s. But by that time it was too late for their more reform- and 'Croat'-minded successors to produce a new image – except for changing the party's name. This meant that any opposition party able and willing to challenge the communists' dismal record in Croatia and offer itself as an effective alternative trustee of Croatia's national interest stood a good chance of winning.

Tudjman's HDZ proved to be the largest and best-organised of those opposition parties. The HDZ had been operating illegally for about a year and had branches in all the municipalities – not only in Croatia but also among the Croats in Bosnia and Vojvodina as well as among the large Croat diaspora in Australia, Canada and the United States. By being first in the field and presenting himself to the exiled Croats as the spokesman of true Croat national interests, Tudjman managed to secure considerable hard-currency financial support, which gave his HDZ a major advantage over the other parties.

Many of the overseas Croats who contributed to Tudjman's party especially generously came from those who had emigrated to Australia, Canada and the United States from the poor but strongly nationalist region of Hercegovina in the south of the republic of Bosnia and Hercegovina. The Hercegovina Croats were strong supporters of the idea of joining Croatia and hoped that Tudjman might help them achieve that aim. When the war broke out in Croatia in 1991, many Croats living in Hercegovina crossed over into Croatia to enlist in the new Croatian army, where they were joined by many Croat Hercegovinians living abroad. Here, in this close relationship between Tudjman and his Hercegovina backers, some of whom have returned permanently from their new homes across the seas and even joined the government (e.g. Gojko Šušak, the long-serving minister of defence, who is reputed to be the second most powerful man in Croatia) lies the basis of the power of the 'Hercegovina lobby' in Croat politics. The Croats from Hercegovina have also used their influence in Croatia to promote their economic interests and have become powerful and highly influential in business.

Given everything that had happened before – especially since the 'Croatian Spring' – it was not surprising that the question of Croatia's relationship to the Yugoslav state dominated the 1990 election. All other issues – including that of the introduction of the market economy – took second place. Without explicitly calling for independence and the immediate dismantling of Yugoslavia, as some others in the election campaign did, Tudjman made it clear that, if he were elected, Croatia would operate on an independent basis within a radically reorganised Yugoslavia. The most controversial features of the campaign were Tudjman's statements criticising the preponderance of Serbs in administrative positions in Croatia and, even more controversially, hints at a possible partition of Bosnia between Croatia and Serbia along the lines of the 1939 Cvetković-Maček agreement. Any idea of border changes among Yugoslavia's six republics was rejected by most other parties, including the HDZ's main rival, the *Koalicija Narodnog Sporazuma* (Coalition for National Accord), whose prominent figures included the former popular Croat party leaders sacked by Tito in 1971, Miko Tripalo and Savka Dabčević-Kučar.

The election, a cross between an anti-communist plebiscite and a Croat national rally, was a triumph for Tudjman's HDZ, with the reformed communists coming second and the Coalition far behind in third place. Helped by an electoral law drafted by the communists, who had hoped to win the election (see Chapter 2), the HDZ won 205 out of 356 seats in the tricameral Croatian parliament, with a majority in each of the three chambers. Croatia's Serbs (12 per cent of the total population) voted either for the reformed communists or for the small Serbian Democratic Party led by Dr Jovan Rašković, a Zadar psychiatrist. Opinion polls held during the campaign showed that the majority of Croatian Serbs strongly opposed plans for converting Yugoslavia into a loose confederation, and that they rejected the very idea of Croatia's independence. Among the Croat voters, an important factor militating in favour of the idea of a loose confederation was resentment at the Serbian political and propaganda offensive, then in full swing, initiated by Serbia's President, Slobodan Milošević. That resentment grew rapidly into an overwhelming desire to break loose from Belgrade for ever – a desire that found expression in the massively pro-independence referendum result in Croatia in May 1991, which closely matched a similar Slovene referendum held the previous December.

In January 1991, the JNA, which had at the time of the 1990 election in Croatia managed quietly to disarm the republic's territorial defence forces, moved to prevent the self-arming of Croatia. This heralded the beginning of a process that gradually escalated towards a full-scale crisis of state, declarations of independence by Croatia and Slovenia on 25 June 1991 and, eventually, war, first in Slovenia and then in Croatia. Serious fighting began in Croatia in July 1991, as the JNA was withdrawing its soldiers and heavy equipment from Slovenia to Croatia and Bosnia. From its many bases throughout continental Croatia and on the Adriatic coast, the JNA guided, supplied and backed Serb paramilitary units (both local ones and those brought over from Serbia) in a number of regions in southern, central and eastern Croatia, occupying the territory staked out by them until nearly one-third of Croatia was under Serbian control.[4]

Was the war in Croatia sparked off by a spontaneous uprising by Croatian Serbs, fearful for their future on account of Tudjman's nationalist rhetoric? It is certainly true that many Croat Serbs were apprehensive, confused and worried – especially for their jobs, which was not surprising in view of their disproportionate representation among the *nomenklatura* in Croatia. However, all the available evidence tends to support the view that what happened was not spontaneous, but highly organised. The war in Croatia was not an uprising by Serbs afraid of the Croats, but an offensive prepared long before 1991 in Belgrade and carefully coordinated from there right from the first open Serb challenge to the Croat government in August 1990. It was then that the so-called *revolucija balvana* ('tree-trunk revolution') was

---

[4] The background to the complex political and military manoeuvres in Croatia conducted from Belgrade in the late 1980s and early 1990s is provided in two important books by prominent Serb protagonists. They are: *Poslednji Dani SFRJ* (*The Last Days of Yugoslavia*), a 1989–92 diary by Borisav Jović, a close ally of Slobodan Milošević who was in the critical twelve months after May 1990 President of Yugoslavia's collective eight-member state presidency as well as chairman of the little-known but influential Council for the Protection of the Constitutional Order; and *Moje Vidjenje Raspada* (*My View of the Breakup*) by General Veljko Kadijević (1993), Yugoslavia's Minister of Defence from 1988 to 1992.

unleashed, with the Serbs placing obstructions on all roads leading to Knin, in southern Croatia, close to the port of Zadar, and a strategic Chetnik stronghold under the Italian occupation during the Second World War. Mass rallies attended by Serbs from all over Yugoslavia had, in fact, been held in the Knin region as early as June 1989, to coincide with on-going pro-Milošević rallies held in Serbia. The secret arming of local Serbs began at the same time. The blockade in Knin in August 1990 was accompanied by a referendum on the question of autonomy, in which the Serbs of eleven predominantly Serb districts proclaimed themselves collectively an autonomous region to be called *Krajina* (from the name *Vojna Krajina* or Military Frontier – see page 199). The Knin irregulars repeatedly cut rail and road links between Zagreb and the Adriatic coast. Another armed Serb uprising began in Slavonia in eastern Croatia in February 1991. Supported openly by the Milošević regime in Belgrade, and, more discreetly, by senior JNA commanders in Croatia, the *Krajina* Serbs proclaimed themselves on 1 April 1991 a part of Serbia, a step which Serbia's National Assembly in Belgrade took note of but did not formally acknowledge.

The Croatian authorities tried to quell the rebellion, but each time Croatian police went in, the JNA moved in as well, claiming that it was stopping ethnic clashes. In reality, the JNA was at no time a neutral force. This might seem surprising, in view of the fact that it was a conscript army, drawn from all the nations and national minorities of Yugoslavia. But an estimated 70 per cent of its officers and non-commissioned officers (NCOs) were Serbs. By that time, too, many Croat, Slovene and other non-Serb conscripts had either left the army or been sent to Serbia and Montenegro.

Could major political concessions by Tudjman to Croatia's Serbs have, nevertheless, averted the ultimate tragedy of war? Any answer must remain speculative but, on the available evidence, it seems that Milošević and the JNA were not prepared to let Croatia go, whatever they might have thought of Slovenia's secession. Croatia's Serbs, for their part, were divided. Many urban Serbs were probably prepared to accept Croatia, but a radical minority in control of strongholds such as Knin rejected any concept of Croatia at all and, moreover, believed themselves strong enough (with Milošević's and the JNA's help) to confront Zagreb.

None of this excuses the triumphalist insensitivity shown by Tudjman and his party towards the Serbs at the time of the former's electoral triumph in the spring of 1990 and afterwards. That helped Milošević and the JNA gain initial credibility in the eyes of the outside world for their claim that they were acting to protect the Croat Serbs from another round of genocide like the one back in 1941. But the reality was quite different: the Serb minority in Croatia – just like that in Bosnia later on – was, in fact, being used as a tool of a policy aimed at creating a Greater Serbia. The pessimistic conclusion must be that, even if Tudjman had showered Croat Serbs with all manner of offers of wide autonomy, backed by international guarantees, it might have helped his image but would not have changed the situation. There was probably nothing – short of total surrender – the Croats could have done to appease Milošević and the JNA.

Ironically, Tudjman did in fact try to appease Milošević and the JNA in 1991. In Croatia he continues to this day to be criticised for his passive, accommodating attitude towards the JNA during their campaign in Slovenia and afterwards. Croatia, for example, cooperated in the JNA's withdrawal – with its heavy weapons – from Slovenia, rather than going over on to the attack with a view to seizing the JNA's weaponry. That was the advice proffered in vain at the time to Tudjman by General Martin Špegelj, who was until 1988 commander of the JNA region taking in Croatia and Slovenia, and who in May 1990 became Croatia's minister of defence (Rat ili mir …, 1993). Tudjman's critics in Croatia allege – though they cannot (yet?) prove it – that the Croatian president rather naïvely believed that he had a deal with Milošević whereby the latter (and the JNA) would give him a free hand in Croatia in return for his promise not to assist the Kosovo Albanians, and for his cooperation with the Serbs against the Bosnian Muslims in a carve-up of Bosnia. It was in that hope, the critics go on, that Tudjman postponed national mobilisation in Croatia until well into the autumn of 1991. By that time the 'dirty war', which had begun in the summer of 1990, had developed into a full-scale war.

The full-scale war ended with a ceasefire in January 1992. But under the so-called Vance Plan, just under a third of Croatia's national territory remained under the nominal protection of the United Nations (UNPROFOR), although actually under the control of the authorities of an entity calling itself *Republika Srpska Krajina* (Republic of Serb Krajina, or RSK) with its centre in Knin.

Unfinished business

For several years Croatia, internationally recognised since 1992 as a sovereign state within its pre-1991 borders, remained too weak diplomatically to mobilise sufficient international pressure on the government in Belgrade, the ultimate controlling factor in the RSK, to return those territories. Even offers of extremely wide autonomy guaranteed by the international community failed to persuade the leaders of the Croat Serbs to come back under Croat sovereignty. But by 1995 Croatia had built up a strong army, with discreet American help inspired by Washington's desire to establish a better regional balance of power and thus contain Serbia. In a series of lighting military operations, the Croat army recaptured, first, Western Slavonia (UNPA West) in May (Operation *Bljesak*, or Flash) and then, in August, as part of Operation *Oluja*, or Storm, the Serb-held territory in central and southern Croatia, including Knin (UNPAs North and South). The second operation – like the first one, a military success – left a bad aftertaste, not only because of the mass exodus, ordered by the Serb RSK leaders, of virtually the entire Serb population of some 120,000 people, but even more because of the widespread looting and burning of abandoned Serb houses and farms and the maltreatment (including a number of killings) of the (mainly elderly) Serb civilians who had stayed behind.

Milošević's passivity during those Croatian offensives was attributed by some to a secret deal with Tudjman. More likely, the Serbian president sacrificed the Croatian Serbs, his former clients whom he had latterly vainly pressed to reach an accommodation with Zagreb, in order further to bolster his international position as a peacemaker and secure the lifting of the UN sanctions imposed on Serbia in 1992 for its involvement in the war in Bosnia. Under an agreeement negotiated on the eve of the Dayton agreement in November 1995, the remaining Serb-held territories (4.5 per cent of Croatia's total territory) in the east – eastern Slavonia, western Srijem and Baranja – are scheduled to go back under Croat sovereignty after a year-long transition period which could be extended. But the accelerated relocation in the area of Serb refugees from other parts of Croatia, and also from Bosnia, places a question-mark over this settlement. Though less and less likely, Croat military action to recapture the territories in the east some time in the future cannot be ruled out.

Leaving aside the east, the recapture from the Serbs of the bulk of the Serb-occupied territories in 1995 represents the fulfilment of one of the major aims of Croat policy, and thus a success for Tudjman – though the Croatian president's critics, like General Špegelj, continue to argue that it was Tudjman's poor generalship and political judgment that led to unnecessary territorial losses in 1991. The real complication for Croatia still arises from the government's policy towards the war in Bosnia.

It is in Bosnia that Tudjman has thoroughly compromised Croatia by backing the shady, deeply unattractive regime running Herceg-Bosna, the Croat territorial unit set up in 1992 in the solidly Croat region of Hercegovina in the south-western part of Bosnia. Nay more, Tudjman has *de facto* allowed the annexationist 'Hercegovina lobby', represented in Zagreb by Gojko Šušak, the minister of defence, to dictate Croatia's Bosnia policy. Behind this essentially anti-Muslim policy has lain (some say, still lies) Tudjman's stubborn belief that only a division of Bosnia between Croatia and Serbia along the lines of the 1939 Cvetković-Maček agreement will ensure peace and stability in the region. (See Chapter 6 on Bosnia in this volume.)

The pro-Herceg-Bosna policy, which has caused deep distrust among Bosnian Muslims towards Croatia, was one of the key factors in the bitter Croat-Muslim war of 1993, which almost handed the Bosnian Serb leaders victory on a plate. Stimulated by an initiative on the part of a group of Bosnian Croats opposed to the Herceg-Bosna group to end the Croat-Muslim war, Washington (aided by the Vatican) mediated a cessation to the conflict, and the setting up of a Croat-Muslim Federation under the so-called Washington Agreements of February 1994. Croat-Muslim military cooperation based on those agreements radically altered the military situation in Bosnia to the Serbs' disadvantage, and thus paved the way for the Dayton agreements which ended the war in December 1995. Under those latter agreements, a dismantling of Herceg-Bosna is envisaged – which is why, unsurprisingly, the Dayton provisions are being undermined by, among others, leading Herceg-Bosna officials, seemingly with the connivance of Zagreb. Under great international pressure – not least from the United States and Germany, the two states most friendly towards Croatia – President Tudjman, it seems, is gradually being forced to rein in the 'Herecegovina lobby', to the delight of most of Croatia's population, which has now become deeply hostile to the Hercegovinians. But steps towards consolidating the Federation and, ultimately, Bosnia as a unit, are anathema to Herceg-Bosna's powerful backers in the Zagreb HDZ establishment. It hardly needs saying that an outbreak of Croat-Muslim hostilities, threatening the Dayton agreements, could have extremely grave consequences in Bosnia, but could also seriously damage Croatia in the West – just at a time when she has started to come out of the international isolation, even ostracism, she had earned on account of Tudjman's devious and opportunistic policy towards Bosnia.

For the foreseeable future Croatia will remain an important geopolitical factor in south-eastern Europe. Once peace becomes better established in the region, she will also become an attractive proposition for international business. Despite the fact that the privatisation process has been going very slowly, there are signs of quickening international interest in Croatia's economy as an important factor in the region's reconstruction. In some ways, the economic outlook has already started to brighten. The normalisation of diplomatic relations with ex-Yugoslav partners accompanied by the resumption of trade links could be an important factor in the acceleration of Croatia's economic recovery.

But under President Tudjman Croatia has amassed a large (and still growing) 'democratic deficit', which could impede progress in various fields, including the economic. The 'democratic deficit' includes:

1 State interference in the workings of the judiciary at all levels;
2 Violations of human rights – not only *vis-à-vis* the Serb community (much smaller now and estimated at 3 per cent to 4 per cent of the total population of Croatia, compared with 12 per cent before the 1991 war) but also in relation to the majority Croat population;
3 Manipulation of state-controlled television, which has become the main instrument of President Tudjman's 'personality cult';
4 Attempts to muzzle the printed media, often with the use of state money;
5 Persistent abuse of the HDZ majority in the Croatian parliament to push through important new laws without proper scrutiny or even debate; and so on.

The authoritarian tone is set by President Tudjman himself, who is in practice constantly expanding his already-wide constitutional powers. This was clearly demonstrated in his recent refusal to approve an opposition deputy as Mayor of Zagreb, despite the fact that at the general election in October 1995 an opposition party alignment won a majority in the capital. The President's increasingly autocratic behaviour has prompted Ivo Škrabalo, a former member of parliament and now vice-president of the Croatian Social-Liberal Party (HSLS), the main opposition party, to describe the present system as one of 'multiparty autocracy' (Škrabalo, 1995; see also *Civil and Political Rights … , 1995*).

Neverthless, change is in the air and it will be accelerated by the arrival of peace. Croatia needs a thorough shakedown, if it is to become a functioning, viable, democratic state. It is unlikely to get it as long as President Tudjman stays in power. But Tudjman has already served two terms as president and, under the Croat constitution of 1990, may not run for a third. The constitution could be changed to enable him to stand again in 1997. But such a constitutional change would require a two-thirds majority in both houses of Croatia's parliament, which the HDZ does not command on the basis of the October 1995 elections. Those elections saw a comeback on the part of former reformed communists, who are now one of the key elements in a new opposition alignment which is unlikely to allow Tudjman to have his own way.

Croatia's 'democratic deficit' is one of the factors stopping Croatia from entering even the Council of Europe, let alone NATO or the European Union. A presidential change would remove this blockage. Certainly President Tudjman, who has modelled himself on Tito, the man he served as a general, will not go easily. Nevertheless, the end of the war and the onset of peace may help Croatia make the transition to a more normal type of politics in which at long last the rule of law, democracy and civil rights will come to mean at least as much as a hard-won national independence.

References

Antoljak, Stjepan (1994) *Pregled Hrvatske Povijesti* (*A Survey of Croatian History*) (Split: Orbis/Laus).

Baletić, Milan (ed.) (1994) *Croatia 1994* (Zagreb: INA-KONZALTING).

Banac, Ivo (1984) *The National Question in Yugoslavia. Origins, History, Politics* (Ithaca and London: Cornell University Press).

Banac, Ivo (1990) Main trends in the Croatian national question, *Most,* Croatian Literature Series, vol. 1, pp. 7–96.

Cigar, Norman (1993) The Serbo-Croatian war, 1991: political and military dimension, *Journal of Strategic Studies*, September, pp. 297–338.

Civil and Political Rights in Croatia (1995) (Helsinki and New York: Human Rights Watch).

Gazi, Stephen (1973) *A History of Croatia* (New York: Philosophical Library Inc.).

Goldstein, Ivo (1995) *Hrvatski Rani Srednji Vijek* (*The Croatian Early Middle Ages*) (Zagreb: Novi Liber).

Jović, Borisav (1995) *Poslednji Dani SFRJ* (*The Last Days of Yugoslavia*) (Belgrade: Politika).

Kadijević, Veljko (1993) *Moje Vidjenje Raspada* (*My View of the Breakup*) (Belgrade: Politika).

Kočović, B. (1985) *Žrtve Drugog Svetskog Rata u Jugoslaviji* (*Victims of the Second World War in Yugoslavia*) (London: Naše Delo).

Macan, Trpimir and Sentija, Josip (1992) *A Short History of Croatia* (Zagreb: Croatian P.E.N. Centre).

Rat ili mir u Hrvatskoj (War or peace in Croatia) (1993) discussion by Karl Gorinšek, Martin Špegelj, Miko Trpalo and Ozren Zunec, *Erasmus* (Zagreb), no. 4, pp. 11–27.

Sidak, Jaroslav, Gros, Mirjana, Karaman, Igor and Sepić, Dragovan (1968) *Povijest Hrvatskog Naroda g.1860–1914* (*History of the Croatian People 1860–1914*) (Zagreb: Školska Knjiga).

Škrabalo, Ivo (1995) Političke slobode (Political freedoms). In Ljubo Čučić (ed.) *Demokratske Slobode u Hrvatskoj* (*Democratic Freedoms in Croatia*) (Zagreb: Croatian European Movement).

Zerjavić, V. (1989) *Gubici Stanovništva Jugoslavije u Drugom Svjetskom Ratu* (*Population Losses of Yugoslavia in the Second World War*) (Zagreb: Yugoslav Victimological Society).

Chapter 12

Slovenia: a Success Story – or Facing an Uncertain Future? *

FRANE ADAM

In the view of two American social scientists who recently edited a book on Slovenia, that country was able to avoid the tragic fate of wars and violence in ex-Yugoslavia thanks to three circumstances: ethnic homogeneity, a (relatively) high level of economic development and a developed civil society. At the same time, they point out that 'Slovenia is a forgotten survivor of Yugoslav wars, even for many academics who work on south-eastern Europe' (Benderly and Kraft 1994, in editors' introduction). A case in point is the book published in 1994 and edited by Bryant and Mokrycki dealing with the 'transitology' of East-Central Europe, where the editors claim that Albania and (all) the former Yugoslav republics are 'special cases' which cannot be compared with dynamic states like the Czech Republic, Slovakia, Hungary and Poland. The truth is that Slovenia – despite its problems and contradictions – is indeed comparable with the Visegrad countries and is, on some indicators (GNP, standard of living), actually far ahead of them.

The aim of this chapter is to outline the main processes and trends in the political, economic and societal spheres in Slovenia. I have tried to build my analysis on a broad data basis, using a wide variety of sources.

Political system: on the way to stability

Stage of elementary consolidation accomplished

If we consider the indicators of consolidation – the marginalisation of political violence and groups backing a return to an authoritarian regime, the adoption of a new constitution and the creation of fundamental institutions for resolving conflicts, the 'double exchange of power', the fostering of a political culture embracing the fundamental principles of democracy – we may conclude that the Slovenian political

* I would like to thank my colleagues, Gregor Tomc, Miroslav Stanojević, Martina Trbanc and Aleksandra Kanjuo-Mrčela (all from the Institute of Social Sciencies) for their help with the collection of data and/or useful suggestions.

system has completed that initial stage of consolidation, meaning that the preconditions for stabilisation are fulfilled.[1]

As far as political viewpoints, values, or (essentially) the political culture of the populace are concerned, a certain ambivalence can be observed. Indisputably – as demonstrated in annual opinion polls and a relatively high voter turn-out – Slovene citizens evaluate positively the multiparty system, freedom of speech and the existence of parliament and other democratic institutions, at least in principle. At the same time, there is a relatively high level of mistrust of democratic institutions, especially of the political parties, but also of the unions and, to some extent, the parliament. Furthermore, public opinion survey findings show that Slovenes are less proud of their democratic institutions than Austrians, for instance (as demonstrated by a recent Slovene-Austrian survey of value-orientation). It is also striking that many people value the opinions of experts and prominent personalities more than those expressed in parliamentary debates (Adam, 1993; Toš, 1994a).

These surveys of public opinion create an impression of 'partyphophia', a widespread phenomenon from which not even mature Western democracies are immune. It therefore comes as no surprise to find that the level of identification with political parties is strikingly low, and the behaviour of voters unstable. A well-known US political analyst explains expressions of mistrust and intense criticism levelled at democratic institutions in the former socialist countries as a result of the illusions and exaggerated expectations which accompanied the process of democratisation in these societies. Disillusion is a precondition for consolidation, the argument goes on; people must realise that democracy cannot provide definite answers to all questions, but rather provides a way of learning and a basis for the gradual solution of problems (Huntington, 1991). This is not the only possible explanation. The fact is that increasing mistrust and loss of credibility could lead to apathy, which from the viewpoint of the development of young democracies would certainly be harmful.

Inclusiveness or policy community: experiments in semi-consociative democracy and neocorporatism

Although the formation of a policy community in the sense of structuring a network of actors who participate in the conceptualisation and implementation of policies has not yet been achieved in Slovenia, foundations are being laid. The process has not gone far enough for the actors (parties, interest groups, the state administration) to have formed and crystallised to a degree where they could collaborate in the political process as reliable partners. Procedural rules defining the relations and competences of these various groups are at a similar stage of development, and the pattern of decision-making is still largely indistinct. Despite all this, certain tendencies can be discerned, although it is not altogether clear whether they represent

---

[1] In my opinion we should draw a distinction between consolidation and stability: a consolidated political system is not necessarily a stable one. Political stability in the analytical-heuristic sense can be defined as including two necessary components, besides consolidation: inclusiveness, in the sense of a formed policy community, and effectiveness (see Adam, 1994).

short-term experiments or more permanent structures. Here I refer to the establishment of a grand coalition after the second election, and the founding of a *tripartite socioeconomic council,* bringing together representatives of government, business and organised labour.

Let us start by specifying the characteristics of the (semi-)consociational model. According to Lijphart (1991: 487), the possibility of development towards this model is the greater to the extent that the following conditions have been fulfilled: (1) the cabinet contains members of several parties; (2) the ratio of power between the government and the parliament is balanced; (3) the parliament has two houses (bicameral legislature); (4) the structure is federal or decentralised; (5) the constitution can only be altered by a qualified majority of votes; (6) a 'judicial review' institution exists which enables the constitutional court to test laws suspected of being at odds with the constitution; (7) the system is multiparty, rather than two-party; (8) there are several, criss-crossing lines of division within the given society – not only the socioeconomic one – mediated by 'multidimensional' parties; (9) the voting system is proportional.

As far as the Slovene political system is concerned, we can confirm that it meets all these conditions, with the partial exception of (4). On (3) and (8) additional clarification is required. With regard to bicameral legislature, it should be noted that the new Slovenian constitution envisages a special body resembling a senate (the National Council), which is not, however, a second (equal) house of the parliament (the National Assembly), but rather a corrective body for the parliament, in a sense playing the role of 'judicial reviewer' in that a law to which it does not consent must be re-deliberated by the parliament. Even more interesting is its structure, since it is a corporative institution (similar to the senates of Bavaria and the Republic of Ireland), based on the functional representation of organised interest groups (unions, university and professional associations) and regional interests. The National Council has not yet asserted itself in its operation as a functional part in political decision-making and the policy community, so it is unclear how its future form and role will evolve.

It is probably fair to say that the consensual basis provided by the grand coalition has not been sufficiently exploited in the interests of greater efficiency. One of the main reasons for this is to be found in its distributive orientation and – on the other side of the coin – in an incomplete overall reform strategy, unconvincing to the public. But there have been a few positive effects, primarily in terms of a procedural decision-making capacity (legislation) and a temporary assuagement of political tensions (these would have been far more serious without the grand coalition).

Neocorporatism is still in an embryonic form in Slovenia. We noted that a tripartite socioeconomic council was founded in 1994, after long negotiations between the government, the unions and employers on incomes policy and collective agreements, though it has not yet begun to perform its designated tasks. It is worth pausing to point out some of the special circumstances that led to the emergence of this pattern:

1   The union scene is pluralistic and fragmented. There is still a division
    between old and new unions, which increases mutual competitiveness and

      intensifies rivalry over membership. The two union structures find great difficulty in formulating common positions when negotiating with the other two groups.

2   Strictly speaking, the employers' delegation has not been properly convened. The Chamber of Commerce acts as its functional equivalent, in conjunction with the recently founded Employers' Association. But the two institutions represent the managers, rather than the owners, this reflecting the fact that the privatisation process is far from complete.

3   The privatisation model applied in Slovenia is designed to create a proprietary structure containing essential elements of 'folk' and worker's capitalism, where workers will become co-proprietors or shareholders in their companies. (Individual cases already exist.) The question arises of how this will affect the unions' operating strategies and approach to social partnership.

4   Neocorporatism usually prospers in times of boom and prosperity and a strong welfare state, while Slovenia – although in the process of economic recovery – is still going through a period of crisis and unemployment . A neocorporatist arrangement in this context is only realistic if the unions exchange their classically 'economist' (in the Leninist sense) strategy (advocating higher salaries and social benefits), which in conditions of crisis is effectively just a protest action, for a participative strategy. If they are to do this, the government must provide them with certain guarantees (e.g. active employment policy; guarantees that they will be treated as partners in political decision-making and that they will play an active role in the privatisation process).

5   Neocorporatism, as a rule, plays a bigger role when social democratic parties hold the majority, but other combinations are possible. It appears in the form of 'neoconservative corporatism' in the Czech Republic (Bruszt, 1993: 73) – and also in Slovenia.

Although macro-neocorporatism is no longer the most important factor in political decision-making in the West, it is useful in new democracies and also in post-socialist societies (Schmitter, 1992). It may be especially appropriate for Slovenia as a small social system, if we accept the argument that the main justification for the neocorporatist arrangement is the dependence of small countries' national economies on their presence in the international market and on export-led development (Steiner, 1991: 259). Macro-neocorporatism would also facilitate the structuring of a policy community and the disencumbrance of the government, with more use being made of the negotiation pattern of regulation. This in turn would aid crisis management (Marin, 1987: 48).

Efficiency: 'survival' management or crisis management

On the basis of what has been said, especially in terms of a partly structured policy community and the assumption of a distributive character within the grand coalition, it becomes evident that the efficiency of the political system is not at the optimum. As far as the process of decision-making is concerned, time-wasting and delays to important decisions and laws have been common. The most glaring deficiency is that there are no clear priorities. Regarding the implementation of decisions and the choice of regulatory regime, it appears that the government is often uncertain as to what regulatory (intervention) pattern would be the most appropriate for the solution of given problems. The government's liberal position often predisposes it to inappropriate deregulation. It also occasionally follows the technocratic-decisionist pattern of regulation, primarily in the form of emergency intervention, but avoids this if possible, on grounds of resistance and lack of organisational resources. Negotiation has had priority in discussions with the unions regarding incomes policy – the technocratic approach has simply not worked on this dimension. These contradictions and inconsistencies in policy style can largely be put down to the top-heavy system of political decision-making, and the fact that Slovenia is a young country still in the process of setting up the infrastructure required for the operation of state institutions and the political decision-making system as such. Qualitative elements affecting efficiency – human resources, the organisational infrastructure and the programme of the government – also leave much to be desired.

The crucial problem to my mind is the third element – the absence of a comprehensive strategic framework within which to implement reforms and policies. This influences the style of the government's political decisions, which tend to be improvised and pragmatic to a fault, while specific measures are often inconsistent and ill-balanced. The government operates on the basis of 'survival' management, rather than on that of strategy for crisis, which is what the circumstances definitely require. Obviously it is not possible to programme every event and decision in politics. But it is helpful for a society to have a reasonably consensual strategic plan, a frame of reference to reassure its members that they are not in a leaking boat.

Political crisis management presupposes a strong, competent government, which is likely to emerge on one of three possible scenarios. The first is the majoritarian-competitive model, where the winning party takes over the responsibility for solving the crisis with the party chief or prime minister acting as the 'emergency leader': Margaret Thatcher was an example (Ranney, 1990). The second possible framework is that of an authoritarian, but developmentally successful regime (e.g. the four Asian Tigers during certain periods) that is able to implement a technocratic-decisionist pattern of regulation without scruples. The third option is the consociational-corporatist model, based on the formation of a *strong and competent government based on large-scale consensus*. In the special circumstances of Slovenia, faced with very specific transformation priorities but with no single dominant political party, this last formula is clearly the key one.

Economic performance and problems

Government spokespersons and experts alike have been praising the economic success of Slovenia. In early 1995, the Minister of Economic Relations and Development quoted 1994 data as evidence of revitalised economic growth. According to the minister (*Delo*, 25 January 1995), we really can talk about a 'success story'. True, growing social differentiation and the rise in the number of people with income below the national average gives cause for concern. But 5.5 per cent growth in GNP and an 18.5 per cent increase in exports in 1994 (the corresponding figures for 1995 were 5 per cent and 24.5 per cent) clearly prove that 'Slovenia is the most dynamic society in Europe'. Positive trends are noted in the public finances. Public debt stood at 30 per cent of GNP at the beginning of 1995. (With the completion of negotiations on the assumption of part of the former Yugoslav debt at the beginning of 1996, the ratio rose to 35 per cent – still within acceptable limits.) Slovenia, the minister claimed, is a monetarily stable country, with its balance of payments in equilibrium and foreign currency reserves currently standing at US$2.8bn and expected to rise further. The 1994 inflation rate of 19.8 per cent was expected to be cut by half in 1995. (In the event, the rate of inflation in 1995 was down to just 12.6 per cent.)

It is certainly beyond dispute that in terms of international comparisons, Slovenia – despite having only two million inhabitants – occupies a relatively high position. On per capita exports it stands in 21st place in the world, ahead of Spain, Portugal and Greece. Slovenia's per capita exports are, indeed, just US$266 lower than those of Japan. And GDP per capita of US$6000 puts it in 26th spot on that indicator. It is a similar story with the standard of living (Svetličič, 1994: 53). In comparison to other post-socialist economies or economies in transition of Central and Eastern Europe, Slovenia is far better off than average (Ferfila, 1994). In summary, Slovenia is a medium-developed industrial society bidding farewell to the socialist, self-managed and Fordist economy which was characterised by two elements in particular – attempts to exploit economies of scale and soft budget constraints – and preparing itself to enter the post-Fordist phase (Križanič, 1994).

In the last few years successes have been undeniably recorded and the economy is now slowly recovering. But it is still in order to discount somewhat the optimistic statements and forecasts of government spokespersons. Transition to a developmentally successful market economy is a complex process which involves a number of factors and assumptions. If we focus first on the economic (or political economy) perspective, we have to distinguish analytically between the following dimension and parameters:

Macroeconomic stabilisation policy

Soon after the first democratic elections (April 1990), and particularly after independence was gained, anti-inflationary and monetary policies recorded some impressive results. The government and the National Bank managed to control the quantity of money in circulation, keeping the growth rate of prices down through classical restrictive monetary methods – supplemented between 1990 and 1992 by the application of a restrictive incomes policy (Kraft, Vodopivec and Cvikl, 1994) – and managed to reduce the inflation rate significantly. Lately the government's success rate at controlling salaries and public sector spending has slipped a little. High interest rates remain a huge burden on the economy. Export-oriented companies complain of an overvalued domestic currency and consequently unfavourable exchange rates. But overall the short-term macro-stabilisation record is extremely good.

Restructuring

This refers in the first place to the organisational and technological modernisation of companies and production programmes aimed at more profitable and competitive operation. It also includes modernisation and reform of the financial system and infrastructure. At the macro-level, it means establishing more suitable (post-industrial and post-Fordist) relations among sectors of the economy (primary, secondary and tertiary). Slovenia's economy can be described as being in a phase of restructuring which is far from nearing its conclusion. Many unprofitable companies have gone bankrupt and there are many – this particularly applies to the large 'systems' – hanging on by the skin of their teeth. The three key causes for bankruptcy or the shutting down of individual production lines are: loss of the former Yugoslav market (in the case of companies that were focused on this market and were unable to redirect to other markets); overindebtedness; and cuts in state subsidies. The result has been a relatively high unemployment rate. In contrast to, for example, the Czech Republic – which has a very low rate of unemployment (3.2 per cent in 1994) indicating that large-scale restructuring is not yet on the agenda – restructuring in Slovenia began before privatisation. Despite the huge social shake-ups triggered by this process of restructuring, policy-makers have always been clear that there is no other way of putting the economy to rights. Unwanted social consequences can be alleviated by an active employment policy and the transition to a new development cycle, which will foster stable economic growth. Some of the active employment policy measures actually taken have worked, preventing the unemployment rate from climbing even higher, but this instrument has not been fully developed. Steady economic growth 1994–95 has, nevertheless, led to a steady fall in the unemployment rate.

We can distinguish between negative restructuring, which ends in bankruptcy, and positive restructuring (Jaklič, 1994), which is the result of enterprising management increasing productivity and the competitiveness of products by reorganising and introducing innovative changes. Or, as Schumpeter has put it, 'competition based on new goods, new technology, new supply resources and new forms of organisation of work is what determines the wealth of the nation' (Schumpeter, 1947: 84). If a company passes the test of competitiveness on foreign markets – this applies especially to small economies – we can conclude that factors of production have been efficiently allocated (Jaklič, 1994: 125). Some Slovenian companies have already been restructured in this sense and many more are in principle suitable for such treatment (according to some estimates, 25 to 30 per cent of companies). But most experts agree that Slovenia's restructuring programme is still far from matching her macroeconomic stabilisation programme (Kraft, Vodopivec and Cvikl, 1994; Sočan, 1994). One economist warns:

> As harsh as it might sound, if Slovenia fails to improve its position within the coming decade, improve technology and develop or introduce new products or services to the extent of at least one-half to two-thirds of its total range, then it will start to drop down into lower price categories, and will lose its current partners to countries with significantly lower prices.
>
> (Sočan, 1994: 31)

Slovenian society can tackle these tasks only by mobilising and utilising all its production potential and supplementing it with 'injections' of foreign capital and technology. On this latter point, despite the fact that in terms of FDI per capita Slovenia is at the top of the list of former socialist countries, the absolute level of FDI remains 'extremely modest, falling into a more or less marginal economic category' (Rojec, 1994:2).

Newly emerging, small private companies and new entrants into traditional crafts can be included as forms of positive privatisation. The number of private companies, crafts excluded, grew from about 1000 in 1989 to almost 40,000 in 1993 (according to some estimates, to as many as 46,000 in 1994). Of all registered companies, 89 per cent are privately owned, small businesses (up to 50 employees), but the majority of these are very small, with only a few employed persons. They include a lot of companies that do not actually operate (40 per cent in 1993), or were founded purely for the purpose of self-employment (Prašnikar, 1994). We do not have detailed and updated information on how many employees the private companies have, but it has been claimed that in the first half of 1993 the figure was 37,000 (Prašnikar, 1994). According to Statistical Office data, there were in 1994, 50,000 independent enterpreneurs and craftsmen (manufacturing), employing 44,000 people. If we add in farmers, we obtain a figure for total private-sector employment of 125,000 (which amounts to approximately 15 per cent of all persons in employment).

A separate question, and one which cannot yet be answered, is how many of these new companies are actually capable of developmental and technological breakthroughs (so-called gazelles) and have the potential to become a major factor in the revitalisation of the economy.

Privatisation

The objective of ownership transformation is to convert socially owned property into three major forms: individual, joint-stock and worker-owned (cooperative) property. A number of companies will remain state or publicly owned even after the privatisation programme is complete. In Slovenia, two draft proposals for the Law on Privatisation were drawn up, neither of which received sufficient support. The first was based on the concept of internal privatisation on the basis of worker/management buy-out. The second favoured the distribution of shares among the citizens of the country (i.e. voucher privatisation) similar to that implemented in the Czech Republic, Slovakia and Russia. In the end, the National Assembly adopted in November 1992 a third, compromise draft, which is a combination of the internal and external approaches (Kraft, Vodopivec and Cvikl, 1994; for more detailed information see Mencinger, 1994).

A total of SIT 950bn of socially-owned capital (approximately DM 12bn) is to be privatised under the programme. By early 1995 the Privatisation Agency had received 1359 privatisation programmes (the privatisation programmes chosen by the companies must be approved by the Agency), and most companies (80 to 90 per cent) had already opted for one of the privatisation models. A total of 541 privatisation programmes, from companies employing a total of 117,000 people and with a total socially owned capital value of SIT 313bn (around DM 3.9bn), had been approved, with 91 per cent opting for mainly internal buy-out, and the remaining 9 per cent for public share offer, although this latter group included a number of large, capital-intensive companies (all information from *Delo*, 15 February 1995, and *Agens*, January 1995). By early 1995 SIT 550bn worth of privatisation certificates had been issued, with investment companies buying up around SIT 325bn (around DM 4.3bn) worth. The privatisation process continued slowly but steadily through 1995, and by mid-February 1996 a total of 1075 programmes had been approved by the Privatisation Agency.

Let us repeat and stress what we said at the beginning of this chapter: that at least in the first phase the main mode of privatisation will be worker/management buy-out. This means that in most cases employees will become the majority, or at least the principal owners (shareholders) of their companies. The question is whether the property distribution will remain like this in the future. Some forecasts suggest that internal shareholding will prevail in small and medium-sized companies in the more successful areas of the economy. On this prognosis, the first companies to open up to external, more concentrated capital (domestic and foreign) will be the successful sizeable domestic companies in which the majority or controlling share (package) cannot be secured by internal purchase, and large unsuccessful companies that cannot survive without fresh capital. (In the event, some of these latter companies would probably remain state-owned for a while.) Other analysts believe that employee ownership is of a transitional character, and that a general concentration of capital in the hands of managers or external capital will soon follow. If 'internal ownership' does prevail, this could have both positive consequences (stronger employee identification with the company) and negative consequences (preventing new, fresh capital from entering, and with an unclear division of roles within the company). Even if there is a fall in the incidence of internal ownership and an increase in ownership concentration, the employees will surely retain a quite significant ownership stake, substantially greater than in any other capitalist or post-socialist society. For the time being, then, Slovenia is following the path of 'folk', or to be more precise, workers' capitalism. What is interesting is that the public does not necessarily see the process purely in this light. Many see it as crude capitalism, pointing to so-called *wild privatisation*, i.e. the use of illegal or at least morally dubious privatisation procedures, usually by members of the old *nomenklatura*. (See the findings of the inspectors of the Agency for Payments Transactions reported in *Delo*, 13 February 1995, and *Mladina,* 31 January 1995, which tend to confirm that this really is a burning issue.) It comes down to a belief that the managerial elite is the main winner in the ownership-transformation game.

Incorporation into the international division of labour and the international market

This is the most demanding task facing all post-socialist economies. For an economy as small as Slovenia's, it is essential to be export-oriented. Slovenia has lost the former Yugoslav markets and is now trying to redirect to West European markets. It has already achieved some good results in this. In 1993, exports were equivalent to 63 per cent and imports to 62 per cent of GDP (Križanič, 1994). Slovenia now trades mostly with West European countries, particularly with the countries of the EU (with which Slovenia has signed a cooperation agreement and is trying to get an association agreement). Almost 70 per cent of foreign trade is currently directed towards that market.

The problem lies with the composition and quality of exports. There are two types of exporters. The first enters the international market on an equal footing with other major exporters, which means that their goods and services are competitive and profitable. The second group participates in an inferior, marginal way, which is reflected in the fact that they normally perform work requiring fewer qualifications or routine work on behalf of others, or build their export capacity on underpriced products and underpaid labour. There are some indications that a significant proportion of Slovenian exports fall into the second group, and it is clear that a policy of forcing exports at any cost cannot be used as a long-term strategy for Slovenia's incorporation into more developed markets. The solution for Slovenia is neither in the currently very dispersed and in many ways traditional (Yugoslav) export range, nor in winning a large market share through the exploitation of economies of scale. Most suitable and realistic seems to be the market-niche strategy based on comparative advantage. Within these niches Slovenia could launch 'specific high-skill, intensively differentiated products with a not-too-high R&D component which could be complementary to the large-scale efforts of world high-tech leaders' (Svetličič, 1994: 59).

Economic growth

Economic reforms make sense when they result in growing industrial output and higher GDP. As we have already said, Slovenia's economy has recently displayed an impressive degree of dynamism and achieved a solid growth rate, after years of recession and depression. The government and certain economists are proud of this fact (which is understandable). But we must ask the question: Is this sustained growth, or only a temporary constellation of favourable circumstances (internal demand grew because salaries went up, and exports to developed markets grew because the recession in the countries that are Slovenia's most important partners ended)? In other words: Has a new development cycle begun, or is the economy merely riding the ephemeral wave of economic contingency? This is not an easy question to answer, but our findings on privatisation, restructuring and export orientation provide only sparse evidence to back up the thesis of a new development cycle. This brings us back to the key issue of a lack of development strategy.

Strategic regulation of the economy

From the analysis of the process of restructuring and export expansion, we learn that a qualitative shift is possible only if based on industrial policy as a constituent part of an overall development strategy (Jaklič, 1994; Messner and Meyer-Stammer, 1994). In our section on the political system we established that the government functions more on the principle of 'survival' management – which it portrays as a neo-liberal, non-interference stance – than on that of any notion of crisis and strategic management. This is also true for other post-socialist governments (Agh, 1994). A Slovenian study on economic strategy was carried out in 1994, but it was generally limited to the macroeconomic parameters and the problem of how to move closer to the EU. It did not lay sufficient emphasis on industrial policy and its role in the identification of and support for (potentially) internationally competitive companies and production programmes (Kovač, 1994).

The function of a development strategy is to define the development options, to encourage social discourse on the relations between politics, science and the public, and to search for avenues of consensus. The concept of development strategy is therefore the exact opposite of the old, communist ideas of fixed (planned) development and tight state regulation. But the concept of development strategy has still not been 'naturalised' in Slovenian politics.

We began our review of the economic situation by quoting the optimistic statements of the government. We then proceeded to question, and ultimately to qualify, these statements. We finish by reporting a recent study that casts the future of the economy and society of Slovenia in an even more pessimistic light. A well-informed university teacher who is also active in politics has been talking about 'black scenarios', warning of possible 'reruns of the Yugoslav disaster' if the same mistakes and patterns that destabilised the economy of the former Yugoslavia keep on being repeated (Glavič, 1995). He is referring to high salaries, overspending in the public sector and high social transfers, which lead to the impoverishment of the economy, lower retained profits and therefore lower investment and decapitalisation. He presents figures confirming that the share of salaries in GDP is growing while savings and investment is falling. He quotes one of the most prominent Slovenian economists, who in an earlier macroeconomic analysis had already warned of the danger of 'squeezing the purchasing power out of the economy' (Bole, 1993: 33), of a 'rapid deterioration of the balance of the economy's resources' (Bole, 1993: 31), and of the heavy strain that the high total cost of labour is putting on the economy (Bole, 1993: 20), consequent on rapid growth in salaries and related social transfers (pension funds in particular), and on the 'relentless pressure' by the unions, political parties, the media and some of the professions for the immediate introduction of a living standard on a par with that in neighbouring countries, or at least the preservation of the living standard enjoyed in the old Yugoslav days. These warnings suggest that the foundations of economic and social development are standing on rather unstable and treacherous ground, and that excessive private and public spending could be 'eating away its own flesh', which could prove fatal within a couple of years. The line from the government (from the prime minister, for example) on this is that established social rights cannot be revoked and that continued economic growth will neutralise the negative effects of overspending. But what government economic policy has to face up to is the vital need, over the next few years, to restrict salaries and public spending, at least to the extent of keeping them within the limits of productivity growth. This can realistically be achieved only with a social pact and a functioning social partnership.

The new social portrait: winners and losers

Economic trends, however we may choose to evaluate them, have an undeniably huge influence on the social structure and social development. In the Slovenian case, amidst all the abundance of statistical and public opinion survey data, it is no easy task to draw a convincing and unbiased picture of trends in the sphere that Parsons calls the 'societal community', Habermas the 'Lebenswelt' (as opposed to the political and economic systems), others the sphere of social integration (and thus distinguishable from the domain of system integration) and still others generalise as 'civil society'. We are only interested here in particular aspects of this sphere, especially changes in the social structure and the impact those changes have on patterns of social integration or disorganisation and anomie.

The modernisation of the social structure could result in a new social balance, but it could also exert a destabilising influence and lead to the emergence of the so-called dual society. The relationship between the social costs of transformation and the level of tolerance among social groups for these costs is clearly critical here (Bruszt, 1993). This is what the pace and success rate of political and economic reforms ultimately largely depend on. In terms of the 'compatibility thesis' of A. Przeworski (1991; see also Bruszt, 1993; Rus, 1994), economic reforms impose social costs which the population (particularly the workers) are not prepared to accept. They therefore use democratic institutions to stop the marketisation process. This in turn places democracy under threat, since it can only strengthen and develop if the marketisation process continues. The way out is to install either an authoritarian regime which will neutralise the resistance, or a form of political decision-making based on consensual and inclusive policy which will be capable of guaranteeing the mobilisation of social support or at least passive tolerance for the economic reforms (Bruszt, 1993; Offe, 1991).

In this section we are interested principally in the question of the social costs of the transition in Slovenia, how the population perceives those costs and whether the data supports the compatibility thesis. This question is clearly linked in turn to the changes in the social structure of Slovenian society.

We can say with certainty that *unemployment and growing social inequalities (increased differentiation between social strata)* are two key phenomena, structuring social relations anew, and changing established patterns in the organisation of everyday life for a large proportion of the population. Unemployment, for most of those who have lost their jobs or cannot find one, is an unwanted, even painful, but to a certain degree unavoidable consequence of the economic reforms (restructuring, privatisation). Growing social inequalities are the result of a new distribution of political power and social wealth, and are connected to the shifts in social structure and the emergence of new social categories (entrepreneurs, the self-employed, those working in the growing service sector).

There was hardly any unemployment in Slovenia up until 1990. Then it swelled quickly, and by the end of 1994 stood at 14.5 per cent of the active population, i.e. of those registered with the Employment Office (but only 9 per cent according to ILO methodology). Although the upward trend was brought to a halt in 1994, and the unemployment rate (13 per cent in 1995) is now no higher than the EU average by the ILO methodology, unemployment remains one of the most severe problems in Slovenian society. Particularly worrying is the fact that the time spent out of work is getting longer each year. In 1994, 50 per cent of unemployed people had been looking for work for over twelve months (Labour Statistics, December 1994). Unemployment not only affects the unemployed themselves (mainly people with poor or incomplete qualifications and older people), but also has wider social and psychological repercussions. People fear for their jobs. Insecurity is growing with the restructuring process only just begun and the new development cycle still in its infancy. This is confirmed by the results of an opinion poll in which 13 per cent of the sample of employed people said they were very worried about losing their job, 23 per cent that they were worried to some degree, and just 20 per cent that they were not at all worried (Toš, 1994a). Two reactions can be distinguished: some fall into depression and resignation; in others self-initiative and entrepreneurial spirit become stronger, and this is reflected not only in the growth of new (small) businesses, but also in the incidence of involvement in the grey economy. Competition is playing an increasingly significant role in our everyday lives; but there is a growing realisation that people are unevenly equipped for participating in this competition (Bernik, 1994). In principle, people accept the view that competition is healthy, but what is interesting is that the relative incidence of positive attitudes is falling (Toš, 1994b).

The process of changing structure by social stratum, accompanied by growing social inequalities, is not particularly dramatic – we cannot talk, as we shall see later, about a sharp division between winners and losers. There is, nevertheless, a slow but discernible and persistent tendency for income inequality to rise. In 1983 the poorest 20 per cent of households disposed of 9.3 per cent of all income; in 1988 the position was the same. But by 1993 the figure had fallen to 8.6 per cent. By contrast, the richest 20 per cent of households disposed of 33 per cent of all income in 1983, 35.5 per cent in 1988, and in 1993, 39.2 per cent (Stanovnik, 1994). People's perceptions of their own class (stratum) position give another dimension to this picture: in four opinion polls carried out between 1992 and 1994, 4 to 10 per cent described themselves as 'absolutely the lowest' class, between 34 and 43 per cent as working class, between 37 and 48 per cent as middle class, between 4 and 6 per cent as upper middle class and between 0.2 and 1 per cent as upper class (Toš, 1994a, 1994b). It would be difficult to draw the conclusion on this basis that the bulk of the population sees itself as being relatively well-off. But there are indications of a certain stability in the social structure, or at least the absence of sharp class divisions. We should note that a large section of the population – the working class and in particular the unemployed – do live right on the poverty line

We said earlier that the growth in social inequality is not particularly dramatic. By the same token, a clear-cut increase in the proportion of the population with income so low that they live below the poverty line has not yet taken place in Slovenia (which does not mean it could not happen in the future). If we define the poverty line as 50 per cent of the average equivalent household expenditure on the OECD modified scale, we find that in 1993, 13.6 per cent of households in Slovenia were poor (Ružič, 1994). Comparisons with the EU countries (not including Austria, Finland and Sweden) based on data from the period 1987 to 1989 put

Slovenia among the countries with the lowest poverty rates (Belgium, Luxembourg, The Netherlands, Germany). All the other countries have a larger proportion of poor households. The list is headed by Portugal with 26.5 per cent.

Public opinion polls reveal that people describe the time before the transition as a time when everyone had a better standard of living. Also relevant in this connection is the finding of the Statistical Office that the average household income has not yet regained the levels of the 'prosperity' years of the communist period. The comparison is in many ways a superficial one, as that 'prosperity' was only possible on the basis of the foreign loans to the former Yugoslavia in the 1970s. Average household income in 1993 was only 73 per cent of its 1978 level (Stanovnik, 1994). But the comparison is thrown into a different light if we consider the fact that in this period (1978–93) the number of consumer durables (colour TVs, fridges, washing machines, dishwashers, cars) in the average household shot up; 83.5 per cent of households now own a colour TV (63 per cent in 1988), 68 per cent have a car (against 66.6 per cent in 1988), and the average apartment size is 76 m^2 (75 m^2 in 1988). The structure of ownership reveals that most housing is privately owned (87 per cent against 64 per cent in 1988). This shows that the standard of living is improving, at least in some areas, despite the fall in average income. The pattern is confirmed by another public opinion poll (Toš, 1994a), which shows that people were somehow more satisfied with their financial circumstances in 1994 than they had been in 1992 (in 1994, 50 per cent found the situation satisfactory, 43 per cent described it as not very satisfactory, and 6 per cent as very unsatisfactory; average monthly income per family was SIT 92,000 or around DM 1300). Surveys on the quality of life (Novak, 1994) reveal similar tendencies and point to the 'ambivalence of the whole perception of quality of life'; some indicators have improved, others worsened; and half of those surveyed assessed living conditions as very good or good (as they had done in a similar survey in 1984) and the impoverishment process as less clear-cut than in 1991. We must assume that 'invisible' and unregistered income, coming mainly from the hidden economy – in addition to the drawing-down of savings or reserves from previous years – plays an important role in the maintenance of a tolerable standard of living. The share of privately owned housing, which is one of the highest in Europe, is a result of the privatisation (selling-off) of the housing fund.

Another interesting comparison is that between Slovenian gross monthly salary, and salaries in other Central and East European transition economies. The average monthly salary in Slovenia in 1993 (US$729) was more than three times the average for Hungary, the Czech Republic and Poland (US$210), three countries that are seen as the most successful in the implementation of economic reforms. The difference between this group of countries and Slovenia is greater than between Slovenia and Austria, where the average monthly salary amounts to US$1495 (Svetličič, 1994). To make a more detailed comparison we would need information on net salaries (in Slovenia around US$550 in 1994) and purchasing power.[2] We should

---

[2] According to the calculations of the Statistical Office and the Ministry of Employment, Family and Social Affairs, the minimum monthly living costs (expenditures) for a family composed of three members amounted in August 1994 to SIT 110.000 (app. DM 1450), and for a family composed of four members to SIT 131.000 (app. DM 1700). Some experts argue that these figures are too high and the methodology used is inappropriate.

mention, however, that relatively high salaries are a problem for Slovenia's economy, as most comparable countries competing with Slovenia on international markets have lower salary levels.

In the opinion of experts the *hidden economy* is growing, and incomes from this sector are an important element in family budgets. According to preliminary assessments, some 239,000 people, or 28 per cent of the active population, were engaged in (part-time) hidden economy activities in 1993 which, converted into full-time equivalent, amounts to 80,000, or almost 10 per cent of the active population. Almost 10 per cent of real GDP is generated in this manner, i.e. official estimates of GDP have to be adjusted in an upwards direction by around 10 per cent (in 1961 by 3 per cent, in 1981 by 4.4 per cent and in 1991 by 7 per cent) (Kukar, 1994). This means that the hidden economy has an important impact on the distribution of income and helps to improve the financial situation of many who would otherwise live in poverty – but also further improves the financial situation of those groups that already live in more favourable circumstances.

When discussing ways to alleviate poverty and social tension we should not forget social policy and the active role of the (welfare) state in areas such as health, education, social security and disability insurance. The prevailing opinion, even though not everyone will agree, is that in Slovenia we have succeeded in preserving the functioning of these systems at an appropriate level. Public spending on social care as a percentage of GDP is similar to that in other European countries, on health comparatively higher, while pension costs are among the highest (Kidrič, 1994). It must be stressed that all economic projections and scenarios, including the 1995 budget memorandum, forecast lower public spending on social security (see Strmšnik, 1994). It will be interesting to see whether shareholding on the part of workers will help to alleviate social differences and uncontrolled social differentiation. Any forecasts would be very hazardous at the present time.

Using this data, which is still incomplete, we can draw a rough sketch of the emerging social and strata structure. There are two factors we should draw attention to: the hypothetical character of the sketch; and the fact that it is a dynamic, processional portrait of strata (class) structure (rising or falling social groups). Strata or even classes can be discussed only in a conditional sense, as the process of differentiation and stabilisation of class structure has not yet worked itself out fully. But we can identify:

1 An *upwardly-mobile stratum*, characterised by a tendency towards social advancement, and showing a clear-cut improvement in its financial situation (not necessarily the wealthiest people, and not necessarily those with inherited wealth). We can include here some of the new entrepreneurs, the managers who managed to acquire a substantial share in the ownership of companies, some highly qualified professionals and experts and a section of the (new) political elite. When – and if – this stratum becomes consolidated it will become the upper stratum or class.

2 *The stratum that managed to preserve or slightly improve their old position and resources (status, financial situation).* Essentially this is a middle

stratum, including some professionals and intellectuals, officials, freelancers, some of the small business people and traders, and some farmers.

3   *The stratum which is finding it very difficult to provide conditions for even a minimum quality of life.* In simple terms, this is mainly the working class (and probably a section of the lower middle class), including some of the unemployed and a large proportion of pensioners who, at the bottom of the scale, are already touching the poverty line.

4   *The stratum living in poverty or below the poverty line*: marginalised groups, some of the unemployed, workers' families with a large number of children, some pensioners, and a section of the population that have moved to Slovenia from elsewhere in the former Yugoslavia during the last few decades.

Although this sketch of trends in stratification provides no basis for any talk of a sharp division between winners and losers, the fact is that the second and third strata are by far the most numerous (between 70 and 80 per cent of the population). Thus it does seem that the tolerance for social costs (and for the given pattern of the distribution of those costs) is declining and may have reached its limit. This is apparent from the fact that 71 per cent of the sample in a 1994 poll considered the differences in incomes to be too high and agreed that they needed to be reduced (Toš, 1994a). It is true that lately there has been no major outbreak of dissatisfaction and conflict on a social basis. The question is how long it will be before the restrictive incomes policy and the falling level of social security start affecting the social climate and the social peace, given that it is the third and the fourth strata that will be mainly affected.

Latent forms or symptoms of social tension and anomie can, certainly, be found.[3] An opinion poll carried out in Slovenia and Austria shows that the number of people who see everything around them as chaotic, and who do not understand their surroundings, is twice as high in Slovenia as in Austria (Ogris, Lay and Toš, 1994). Slovenes on the one hand trust in the future, and believe that the political and economic situation will improve within five years (Toš, 1994b), while at the same time – at least as of 1992 – saying that they are looking to the future with fear as well as hope (34 per cent), with quite a few (28 per cent) being even more pessimistic and looking to the future with fear and anxiety (Toš, quoted in Bernik, 1994).

---

[3] For example, the high Slovenian suicide rate (one of the highest in Europe over several decades) which shows no sign of falling (despite hopes in some quarters that independence and a new social climate would help to bring it down), or the growing number of traffic accidents, suggesting the presence of destructive and anomic potentials. One of the indicators of distrust in the future is the constantly falling birth rate (the current birth rate is only 65 per cent of what would be required just to keep the population constant), with the result that the population is getting older and, consequently, the ratio between the retired and active population is becoming increasingly unfavourable (currently 1:1.7). We must stress that all these phenomena are multifaceted, and have their own dynamics (not to mention inertia), which are only indirectly related to patterns of change in social relations.

Conclusion

Proceeding from this analysis, we can conclude that Slovenia is a typical 'transition' society, characterised by *fluid configuration* and ambivalent processes in the political, economic and societal spheres. There is no guarantee that articulated final goals (profound societal modernisation, integration into the EU) will be attained – at least in the form and to the timetable which the political actors and public would prefer.

It is true, especially for small states, that the building of national identity, not to mention the process of endogenous modernisation, depends to a significant extent on the capacity to rise to challenges and adapt to impulses coming from the international environment. Slovenia has three options in this connection. The first is *autocentric development with association*, which means the preservation of national identity, with a simultaneous opening-up to world markets and international cooperation. The second one is *peripheral development* (and peripheral integration into the EU), where all important levers of decision-making are in the hands of exogenous actors. The third option is a kind of (relatively) *autarkic (self-sufficient) development*. It is quite a realistic assumption that Slovenia will oscillate over the next decade between first and second options. In so far as attempts to implement the autocentric development with association option demonstrate that this is not a feasible solution, the voices in favour of the third option will become that much stronger.

References

Adam, F. (1993) 'Strukturiranje političnega prostora po drugih volitvah in vprašanje politične stabilnosti (The structuring of political space after the second elections and the question of political stability). In Adam, F. (ed.) *Volitve in Politika po Slovensko (Elections and Politics Slovenian Style)* (Ljubljana: ZPS).

Adam, F. (1994) After four years of democracy: stability and fragility, special issue of *Družboslovne Razprave (Small Societies in Transition – The Case of Slovenia)*, no. 15–16, Ljubljana.

Agh, A. (1994) The social and political actors of democratic transition. In A. Agh (ed.) *The Emergence of East Central European Parliaments: The First Steps* (Budapest: Hungarian Centre of Democracy Studies).

Benderly, J. and Kraft, E. (1994) Editor's introduction. In J. Benderly and E. Kraft (eds) *Independent Slovenia* (New York: St Martin's Press).

Bernik, I. (1994) Der Übergang von der heroischen in die prosaische Etappe: Slowenien. In A. Pradetto (ed.) *Die Rekonstruktion Ostmitteleuropas* (Opladen: Westdeutscher Verlag).

Bole, V. (1993) 'Proračunski' in 'transferni' problem ter ekonomskopolitične alternative (The 'budget' and 'transfer' problem and economico-political alternatives), II and III, *Gospodarska Gibanja (Economic Fluctuations)* (Ljubljana: EIPF), November and December.

Bruszt, L. (1993) Transformative Politics: Social Costs and Social Peace in East Central Europe. In R. Schönfeld (ed.) *Transforming Economic Systems in East Central Europe* (München: Suedosteuropa Gesellschaft).

Bryant, C. and Mokrycki, E. (1994) Introduction. In C. Bryant and E. Mokrycki (eds) *The New Great Transformation?* (London: Routledge).

Ferfila, B. (1994) Slovenia and the world – statistical comparison, special issue of *Družboslovne Razprave* (*Small Societies in Transition – The Case of Slovenia*), no. 15–16, Ljubljana.

Glavič, P. (1995) Pojedli smo semenski krompir in zdaj smo ostali brez novega pridelka (We eat up our seed potatoes and end up without a harvest next year), *Delo,* 15 February.

Huntington, S. (1991) *The Third Wave. Democratisation in the Late Twentieth Century* (London: Norman).

Jaklič, M. (1994) *Strateško Usmerjanje Gospodarstva* (*Strategic Steering of the Economy*) (Ljubljana: ZPS).

Kidrič, D. (1994) Socialnovarstvena mreza (Social security net). In *Približevanje Evropi. Strategija Gospodarskega Razvoja Slovenije* (*Drawing near Europe. The Strategy of Economic Development of Slovenia*) (Ljubljana: Zavod za makroekonomske analize in razvoj).

Kovač, B. (1994) Slovenska razvojna strategija (Slovenia's development strategy), *Delo,* 24 December (Saturday Supplement).

Kraft, E., Vodopivec, M. and Cvikl, M. (1994) On its Own: The Economy of Independent Slovenia. In J. Benderly and E. Kraft (eds) *Independent Slovenia* (New York: St. Martin's Press).

Križanič, F. (1994) Slovenska gospodarska razglednica (Slovenian economic prospects), *Družboslovne Razprave,* no. 17–18, Ljubljana.

Kukar, S. (1994) Siva ekonomija v Sloveniji v obdobju tranzicije (The Grey economy in Slovenia in the Period of Transition). In S. Marn and A. Kramberger (eds) *Slovenija, Statistika, Evropska Unija* (*Slovenia, Statistics, the European Union*) (Ljubljana: Zavod Republike Slovenije za statistiko).

Lijphart, A. (1991) Majority rule in theory and practice: the tenacity of a flawed paradigm, *International Social Science Journal,* no. 129, August.

Marin, B. (1987) From consociationalism to technocorporatism: The Austrian case as a model-generator. In I. Scholten (ed.) *Political Stability and Neocorporatism* (London: Sage).

Mencinger, J. (1994) From socialism to market: The case of Slovenia. In A. Bibič and G. Graziano (eds) *Civil Society, Political Society, Democracy* (Ljubljana: Slovenian Political Association).

Messner, D. and Meyer-Stammer, J. (1994) System competitiveness: lessons from Latin America and beyond – perspectives for Eastern Europe, *The European Journal of Development Research,* vol. 6, no. 1.

Novak, M. (1994), *Kvaliteta Življenja, 1984–1994* (*Quality of Life, 1984–1994*) (Ljubljana (Research Report): Inštitut za družbene vede).

Offe, K. (1991) Capitalism by democratic design? Democratic theory facing the triple transition in East Central Europe, *Social Research,* vol. 58, no. 4.

Ogris, G., Lay, M. and Toš, N. (1994) Novi nacionalizem na vzhodu in zahodu, Slovenija in Avstrija (The new nationalism in East and in West, Slovenia and Austria). In Toš, N. (ed.) *Slovenski Izziv II* (*Slovenian Challenge II*) (Ljubljana: Fakulteta za druzbene vede).

Prašnikar, J. (1994) *Drobno Gospodarstvo v Sloveniji* (*Small Business in Slovenia*) (Ljubljana (Research Report): Ekonomska fakulteta).

Przeworski, A. (1991) *Democracy and the Market: Political and Economic Reforms in Eastern Europe and Latin America* (Cambridge: Cambridge University Press).

Ranney, A. (1990) *Governing. An Introduction to Political Science* (New York: Prentice Hall).

Rojec, M. (1994) *Tuja Vlaganja v Slovenski Razvoj (Foreign Investment in Slovenian Development)* (Ljubljana: ZPS).

Rus, Andrej (1994) Quasi privatisation: from class struggle to scuffle of small particularisms. In Benderly, J. and Kraft, E. (eds) *Independent Slovenia: Origins, Movements, Prospects* (New York: St Martin's Press).

Ružič, G. (1994) Anketa o porabi gospodinjstev kot vir za analizo revščine v Sloveniji (Survey on household consumption as a data source for research on poverty in Slovenia). In *Slovenija, Statistika, Evropska Unija (Slovenia, Statistics, European Union)* (Ljubljana: Zavod Republike Slovenije za Statistiko).

Schmitter, P. (1992) Consolidation and interest system, *American Behavioral Scientist*, No. 4–5.

Schumpeter, J. (1947) *Capitalism, Socialism and Democracy* (New York: Harper & Row).

Sočan, L. (1994) Biti ali ne biti – zraven (To be there or not to be there), *Delo*, 19 November (Saturday Supplement).

Stanovnik, T. (1994) Revščina in življenski standard v Sloveniji (Poverty and living standards in Slovenia), *Razgledi*, 25 November.

Steiner, J. (1991) *European Democracies* (New York and London: Longman).

Strmšnik, I. (1994) Scenariji gospodarskega razvoja Slovenije (Scenario for the economic development of Slovenia). In *Približevanje Evropi. Strategija Gospodarskega Razvoja Slovenije (Drawing Near Europe. The Strategy of Economic Development of Slovenia)* (Ljubljana: Zavod za makroekonomska analize in razvoj).

Svetličič, M. (1994) Contemporary development strategy options of small countries: the case of Slovenia. In B. Bucar and S. Künhle (eds) *Small States Compared: Politics of Norway and Slovenia* (Bergen: Alma Mater).

Toš, N. (1994a) *Slovensko Javno Mnenje in Slovensko-Avstrijska Raziskava Vrednot (Slovenian Public Opinion and Slovene-Austrian Research on Values)* (Ljubljana (Research Report): Fakulteta za družbene vede).

Toš, N. (1994b) *Slovensko Javno Mnenje in Mednarodna Raziskava Narodne Identitete (Slovenian Public Opinion and International Research on National Identitity)* (Ljubljana (Research Report): Fakulteta za družbene vede).

Chapter 13

Macedonia – an Island on the Balkan Mainland

FERID MUHIĆ

Introduction

In one of his lectures on British history,[1] Edward Gibbon began with the statement
'Gentlemen, Britain is an island!' He had good reason to open his discourse in this
way. The famous historian proceeded to show how this one fact had fixed the key
characteristics of the whole region. The history, culture and psychological and
anthropological characteristics of Britain had all been formed under the influence of
this single factor, and it had played a critical role in forming the reaction and behav-
ioural patterns of the British. So obvious as to be generally neglected, this fact, in
Gibbon's interpretation, took its proper place as a central principle of interpretation
and a key methodological proposition.

We could begin our chapter on Macedonia in the same style, with the statement
'Gentlemen, Macedonia is no island!' This statement is as useful as it is accurate.
Macedonia is certainly no island. It has been subjected – continuously, through millennia – to the most varied influences. It has hardly had the chance to draw breath,
never mind to form, in its own time, a clearly defined, independent profile. At the
mercy of everyone and without the protective cordon of the sea, Macedonia has
been shaped by foreign pressures in relation to all key variables. Those pressures
have frequently pulled in different directions, and have not always had a favourable
impact on domestic culture.

On the other hand, no one of those pressures, nor indeed their sum total, have
managed to efface the deep lines of the specific profile of Macedonia. Thus the
country has to be understood in a conflictual perspective. It is an integral part of the
geographical, historical, cultural and political mainland. It is, indeed, the centre of
gravity for the three main parts of the Old World – Europe, Asia and Africa. For that
reason it was vouchsafed the epithet 'hub of the world' (*catena mundi*) by the
ancients. But there is a key sense in which Macedonia *has* remained an island. The
waves of history have dashed upon it and sometimes – even for long periods – submerged it. But Macedonia's character and uniqueness have never been washed

---

[1] Professor Muhić is referring to Gibbon's 'An Address &c' (1793). It should be noted that
Gibbon does not use the precise words here attributed to him. (eds)

away. In a methodological context, it is clear that the more uncompromising interpretations of the 'Macedonian Question' are precisely the most critical consequences of a failure to take account of this paradoxical historical configuration, and
of the absolutisation of one moment in history. Like a man who swims in a stormy
sea, whose head is now lost from view, now visible amidst the spume of the break-
ers, Macedonia has been proclaimed 'non-existent' or 'existing', depending on the
moment when the judgment was made. Those who would dispute its existence point
to the moments when the drowning man was really not visible above the water. But
is not the fact that this 'drowning man' not only emerges each time from the break-
ers but is *even now* swimming and calling for help, sufficient to resolve the academic dispute about his status, and the practical question of his rescue?

If we want to understand Macedonia and its current situation, to assess its positions, its real possibilities and its strategic orientations, we should, indeed must,
bear this contradictoriness in its situation, these sinewy contours of identity, constantly in mind. Macedonia is, to paraphrase Gibbon again, 'Britain without the
sea'. But it has never ceased to be 'Britain' in ideas and aspirations, in its continual
struggle to 'hold its head above water', to escape drowning, to survive as an island
and to retain its identity and multifacetedness. With all the implications of its paradoxical situation, Macedonia is best understood as an 'island on the mainland'. This
approach also has the advantage that it is consistent with the factual evidence in
relation to relevant historical specificities, with a kind of static reconstruction of
Macedonia. At the same time it can serve as a reliable base for a methodologically
coherent assessment of the present, and of the dynamic elements necessary for an
understanding of Macedonia's aspirations and the attitudes of the world towards
her. We propose, therefore, to interpret all facts relevant to Macedonia in the light
of, or at least in the context of, two factors: a pattern of history that was not always
well-disposed towards Macedonia; and the constant efforts of Macedonia to retain
her integrity.

The trials of history and the imperative of identity

The social life of any community flows in a single stream in all spheres and at all
levels. But some segments flow faster than others. The more slow-moving, slow-
changing area of general characteristics and basic assumptions – in short, the *static
dimension of society* – is frequently, often by force of inertia, treated as simply the
setting for the more fast-moving sphere of direct social action which we describe as
the *dynamic dimension of society*. There is obviously a danger here that we make an
uncritical identification between the concepts of *static* and *passive*. The slow pace
of evolution of the underlying patterns of social life makes it more difficult to trace
the trends immanent in them. Hardly any single human life is long enough to obtain
a perspective on these trends. But the underlying patterns, however *incrementally*
they may evolve, are never really passive. To assess the main features of the static
premises of Macedonia, as a politically, culturally and ethnically constituted community, and through this to reconstruct the basic tendencies contained in their slow
but measured rhythm, is the key task of the first part of this chapter.

In the filigree-rich and varied history of the Balkans, Macedonia stands out. The Balkans, the cultural cradle of Europe for more than 2500 years, the hub of the Old World, has its centrepoint on the territory of Macedonia. All the cultural influences, the political events, the artistic and linguistic processes, and all the ethnic mixing to which the Balkans has been subjected and through which the region has had such a powerful impact on Europe, have sedimented and often finally crystallised on the territory of Macedonia. This concentration of historical and socio-anthropological heritage has marked off, but also greatly complicated, political relations in Macedonia, through history and today. In some respects, and at particular historical moments, these layers of sediment (static but never passive) have more directly and decisively affected the social reality of Macedonia and the attitudes of its inhabitants than a whole range of factors of direct, material importance, which operate at a particular moment and which impose the pattern of direct action.

The relief of Macedonia is to a great exent constituted as a kind of geographical anticipation of history. Like the island in the *Utopia* of Sir Thomas More (1516), Macedonia is surrounded by a rim of mountains which opens only to the south, at Gevgelia – more or less as in More's mythical island. This geographical profile, which expresses the desire for isolation and peace, is in total contradiction to the stormy activity which has characterised the dynamic social sphere in Macedonia. The concentration of historical events in Macedonia has greatly outweighed the size of its territory (about 160 km across, with an almost perfectly circular shape), and has severely tested the psychological capacity of people to react rationally and to act in an autonomous way. Nowhere on the surface of the globe have so many historical dramas been played out as on these 20,000 square km. More than any other place on earth, Macedonia is a Shakespearian stage, on which the theatrical productions have changed so frequently, and with such regularity, that virtually all its citizens are descendents of famous actors, in some cases stretching back for 2500 years, in no case less than 600 years. Take, for example, the Turks, who have played a great role in the history of Macedonia, and some of whom still live in Macedonia, although they were the last to arrive – as much as two centuries before the first white man set foot on the American continent! One could look on them as 'immigrants', though they themselves certainly do not look on themselves as that. And why should they?[2]

Be that as it may, the human mental substance has been subjected in Macedonia to a degree of pressure such as is rarely encountered. Even the faintest echo of some old historical 'earthquake' is amplified on the sensitive oscillograph of the Macedonian to the scale of a new tremor. The tension between the need to cope with the almost unbearable sense that one is the legatee, the descendent, of this or that ancient people, which played this or that role, at this time or that time, and the immediate imperative to build one's own identity, with clearly delineated contours of historical continuity, poses a question of the greatest practical and above all moral significance. We must bear in mind that in Macedonia there are really no

---

[2] For a more detailed discussion of Macedonia as a geographical, historical, anthropological and cultural entity, see Muhić, 1994. For a discussion of political conditions in Macedonia see Muhić, 1992a, 1992b.

'weak players'; we cannot dismiss as an outsider someone who has lived on a given territory, without a break, for more than six centuries. On the other hand, differences in the degree of participation in the building-up of the capital stock of history do not produce reciprocal effects, such as might to a degree clear up these dense and complex relationships. To have a rich past may be a big plus when we are talking about history. But we should not forget that a long history means a reduction in our intrinsic vitality, and a weakening of the capacity to formulate prospects for the future. Those who do not have a long history may have a handicap when looking backwards, but are at an advantage when looking ahead. Nations that have no past have a future. So also in Macedonia, through the millennia and the centuries, there have lived people carrying greater or lesser burdens from the past, and who therefore have widely differing attitudes to the future and unequal capacities to cope with change. On the one hand, this heightens the feeling of tolerance, which is, indeed, second to none in Macedonia. But at the same time it increases the degree of social, cultural and intercommunity tension, with a corresponding increase in the risk of conflict. This situation, so complex as to appear almost ungraspable, represents the main form of psychological, cultural and political disharmony among the inhabitants of Macedonia. However, ''Where there is an illness, there is a cure.' The given situation has formed a kind of mental and intellectual structure which has a high capacity for cooperation and tolerance. The problems of Macedonia can be solved perfectly efficiently by the inhabitants of Macedonia, as long as the international community is prepared to guarantee that there will be no interference (in the first instance military intervention) from abroad.

Historical disputes

One thing must be emphasised: the political rivalries which exist within Macedonia are not a matter of *actual* tensions. Their main stimulative force lies in the area of potentiality. The great swathe of historical conflicts have been largely neutralised by the millennia of living together. Only when people start to ask 'If this, then what?', does this huge historical accumulation began to come through as a real force. In these games and reasonings, historical arguments are brought into play which may, indeed, not be resolvable, even from the most objective position conceivable. In Macedonia there is no ethnic group or nation, irrespective of size, which cannot, by the legal standards accepted in the world at large, be considered autochthonous. The Turks, the most recent arrivals and the smallest ethnic group (about 80,000 people, representing 4 per cent of the total population), have lived for 600 years on Macedonian soil. Beyond that, they have a very powerful psychological argument on their side. The Turks exercised sovereignty over Macedonia for many years, as indeed they did over every state in the Balkans. The territory of Macedonia was, in fact, an integral part of the Turkish Empire for more than 500 years. This fact, this simple historical datum, takes on enormous importance in the context of polemics, the nub of which comes down to the very real threat that circumstances may precipitate some kind of settling of accounts, and division of assets, or indeed of territory.

The Albanians, the second most numerous group, have nothing like such a long tradition of continuous statehood. But they can point to the fact that they have been in the Balkans, including Macedonia, longer than any of the Slav nations, or indeed than any of the other nations of the Balkans. Historical evidence links present-day Albanians directly with the Illyrians, Trojans, Thracians, Dalmatians and the ancient tribes of Epirus. Despite all the efforts of politically committed researchers over the past few decades, it is difficult to dispute this proposition. The fact is that the intensity of the scientific and pseudoscientific polemic about the Illyrian (or other) origin of the present-day Albanians, from the viewpoint of the current rivalry and political confrontation between Slav and Albanian, is pointless, if understandable. Leaving the Illyrians to one side, even if the Albanians came into the Balkans later, they must have done so much earlier than the generally accepted date for the arrival of the Slavs in the Balkans – about the fifth century AD. Thus from the viewpoint of the Albanians, the truly authochthonous inhabitants of Macedonia (and indeed of the Balkans as a whole), with more historically valid arguments than any other nation currently living on these lands, are precisely themselves.

There have been recent attempts to refute this conclusion, by reference to Turkish censuses from the seventeenth and eighteenth centuries. According to these, there were virtually no 'Arnauts' ('Arnaut' is the Turkish word for Albanian) living in the Macedonian lands at that time. But this cannot be taken as firm evidence that the Albanians are not autochthonous, because forced resettlement was very common at the time of these censuses. Moreover, if we look at the problem in terms of the arrival of the Slavs, it is again incontrovertible that there were Albanians, or their direct ancestors, virtually throughout the Balkans, including Macedonia, at that time.

If the Turks in Macedonia can lay claim to the longest tradition of statehood, but on the other hand suffer the handicap of small numbers, and if the Albanians can amortise the fact that they have never had their own state on the territory of Macedonia by reference to their long, continuous habitation of the Balkans and Macedonia, the Macedonians themselves can lay claim to some advantages *vis-à-vis* both groups – but also some weaknesses. Formed mainly from the stock of Slavonic tribes, in the earliest phase of Slav colonisation of the Balkans (probably not earlier than the fifth century AD), the Macedonians are now incontrovertibly the most numerous nation on the territory of Macedonia. They have been here significantly longer than the Turks, and have had their own state, which the Albanians in Macedonia have not. On the other hand, that state has existed for a much shorter time than did the Turkish state in Macedonia and, in addition, the Macedonians have not been here for as long as the Albanians. But psychologically and morally – especially when we talk about the state called 'Macedonia' – the key argument of the Macedonians is that only they lay claim to be the legatees of the ancient inhabitants of this territory – only *they* call themselves Macedonians! And this appellation *has never in the past been disputed by any interested party.* The first vehement objections on the part of Greece came only with the break-up of Yugoslavia – i.e. barely three years ago! The fact that the Macedonians legally and legitimately, and without opposition from any party at any international level, formed their own state just before the end of the Second World War (by decision of ASNOM in 1944: see *ASNOM 1944–1994*, 1994), which they then brought into the federal community of

Yugoslavia, in combination with the values of tradition, numerousness and cultural distinctiveness, gives weight to the claim of undisputed legitimacy over a period of more than five decades. The deeply rooted aspirations, which eventually led to that constitutive act, reach back to the nineteenth, if not the eighteenth century, and have without doubt contributed to the consolidation of national consciousness, and of belief in Macedonian rights and primacy, on this territory.

The Serbian and Bulgarian factors come into a secondary category as far as numbers involved and historical significance are concerned. But the strength of Serbian pretensions to Macedonian territory, the clever propaganda, and the historical presence and effective ascendancy from the end of the nineteenth century to the end of the Second World War, promoted them to the status of potentially first-rank factors in the conceptualisation and development of the situation in Macedonia, and concerning Macedonia.

Numerically weak (about 38,000, under 2.5 per cent of the population), the Serbs manage to come up with impressive arguments. In the early thirteenth century and especially in the first half of the fourteenth century, they exercised complete domination in this area. In the age of Tsar Dušan, who was indeed crowned in Skopje, Macedonia, as an integral part of the Serbian Empire, was under the strong cultural, religious and political influence of Serbia. Traces of this era can be found in the many monastries built by the Serbian gentry and preserved through the centuries of Turkish rule. The period from the end of the Balkan Wars to the beginning of the Second World War was marked by a sustained propaganda campaign on the part of the Serbs. It included linguistic, educational and cultural assimilation, and also severe police repression. Of more than 20,000 policemen (*žandar*) in the Kingdom of Yugoslavia, more than half were stationed on Macedonian soil. Officially described as a 'floating mass',[3] the Macedonians found their ethnic identity and consciousness subjected, in this period, to systematic pressure to assimilate to the Serbs. The concepts 'Southern Serbs' and 'Southern Serbia' were imposed, within the framework of the Vardar Banovina, right up to the beginning of the Second World War.

To the sum of influences, and indeed claims to the status of legitimate owners and original inhabitants of Macedonia, we must, finally, add the strenuous efforts of the Bulgarians. From the time of the founding of the modern Bulgarian state, immediately after the Balkan Wars, but even earlier, during the second half of the nineteenth century, Bulgaria sought to apply assimilatory pressure on Macedonia. A good proportion of the historical facts, and the majority of the key figures in the chronicles of Macedonia, Bulgaria simply interpreted as elements in her own history. In the short periods when Bulgaria managed to occupy Macedonia, she treated the terrritory as an integral part of Bulgaria and the population as straight Bulgarians. Church and educational centres in Macedonia were, in those periods, turned into centres for demacedonisation. The similarity between the Bulgarian and Macedonian languages, and the indisputable cultural and traditional links from the period of the decline of the Turkish Empire, facilitated this policy, especially in

---

[3] The term was invented and popularised by Jovan Cvijić. See Cvijić, 1987.

areas where there was no organised competition from rivals (in the first instance the Serbs).

The other groups, in particular the Vlachs (who have been in the area for a very long time), advance their own cases, but they are too few in numbers to have any serious influence. At the same time these small groups are a potential factor of cohesion and could reduce tension between the three main groups.

Resolution of the dispute about the interpretation of history, in the context of national rights to constitute a state on all or part of the territory of Macedonia, has been greatly complicated by the fact that the history of Macedonia encourages pretenders to believe that no solution of the Macedonian question is ever final! We only have to wait a little, and our time will come: that is the lesson that can be drawn – all too plausibly – by the regimes of all four of Macedonia's neighbours. Against that background, the manipulation of national passions, which was shown to be such an effective method in the break-up of Yugoslavia, comes through as objectively the greatest danger for the future of Macedonia and its stability and independence. And the main pillar of Macedonia's political existence – the Macedonians – have no trustworthy counsellor among neighbouring states, who are all, without exception, awaiting 'their hour', and thinking in terms of their own ethnic factor. And in no case is that factor the Macedonians!

The long tradition of intervention on the part of these countries, which have never missed an opportunity to 'mark', in various ways, the territory of Macedonia with signs of their own ownership, has meant that one model or another of linguistic, cultural, religious, economic or military pressure was always being imposed. Any attempt to organise a Macedonian national consciousness was always brutally suppressed, by whatever means. At different times, and in different parts of Macedonia, Greek, Serbian and Bulgarian security forces have all tried to suppress this consciousness.

We can mark the beginning of a politically clearly defined struggle for Macedonian national consciousness with the Ilinden Uprising of 2 August 1903 (see Perry, 1988). The suppression of this uprising, also known as the 'Kruševo Republic', did not extinguish the ambition of the Macedonians to form their own national state. However, their dependence on Bulgaria, not only in financial terms, but also for people and, later on, even ideas, put Turkey off the idea of creating an autonomous Macedonia, as an independent political unit within the Turkish Empire – to Macedonia's great loss.

As Turkey retreated and lost virtually all its Balkan territories, the opportunity for a legally grounded demand for the foundation of an independent Macedonia passed. The complicated relations between the new states – all with a pronounced appetite for the annexation of Macedonia – became even more complicated after the signing of the Peace of Bucharest (1913). By this treaty, Macedonia was partitioned between three rival states – Serbia, Bulgaria and Greece – none of which missed the opportunity to label their occupation of parts of Macedonia as 'liberation from Turkish power'.

In this way, parallel with the age-old ambitions of the Serbs, Bulgarians, Greeks and Albanians to annex Macedonia to their own states, there developed a determination on the part of the Macedonians to create their own state, and to ensure that the dispute between their neighbours should be resolved in *their* favour. With the decision of ASNOM (see *ASNOM 1944–1994*, 1994) to take Macedonia into Yugoslavia as an equal, constituent element, the struggle entered a new phase. With the securing of official political legitimacy, Macedonia became a key factor in the decision of its own fate.

The break-up of Yugoslavia, of which Macedonia was a constitutive part, opened up an opportunity to take that phase to its logical conclusion and create a fully sovereign state. With the removal of the instance to which all the constitutive elements had owed loyalty, Macedonia ceased to have any reason to owe fealty to a state which did, in truth, no longer exist.

Factors in the break-up of Yugoslavia

The erasing of Yugoslavia from the geopolitical map of the world came precisely at the moment when the federal powers in Belgrade renounced jurisdiction over one particular federal unit. Up until that decision, all the members of the federal state had been under a legal obligation to respect the laws governing the whole territory. One of those key laws, embodied in the constitution of the Socialist Federal Republic of Yugoslavia (clause 5, *Concluding Provisions*), made secession from the federal state strictly conditional on a *unanimous* vote of the members of the federation. In failing to consult the members of the federation, and in arbitrarily and unconstitutionally giving Slovenia the all-clear to leave the federal state, the government in Belgrade destroyed the legal basis for the existence of Yugoslavia – at the same time proclaiming its intention of refusing the same right to the other members of the federation and compelling them to remain in the reduced federation by force of arms. Objectively, psychologically and in terms of legal logic, each republic, and also the two autonomous provinces of Vojvodina and Kosovo, found themselves in a position where any loyalty to each other, or to the former Yugoslavia, had been rendered null and void. That legal phantom, that politically non-existent state did, however, hang on to its insignia and, what is more, its pretensions, including its name. If it is absolutely clear that the chemical compound H_2O is water only when it is compounded, and that two molecules of H and one of O are no longer water when they are separated, and should not properly be referred to as such, it is even clearer that a political unit formed under the name 'Yugoslavia' by acts of accession of given constitutive units ceases to exist as such the moment there is any radical change in its 'molecular structure' – for instance, the secession of four out of a total of six members.

The fact that one of the 'molecules' of the old compound has arrogated to itself, and keeps to this day, the name 'water', i.e. that one-third of the old territory now calls itself 'Yugoslavia', must be understood in the present context in terms of one simple factor – the monopolisation of the enormous military machinery of the former JNA. This *argumentum baculinum* ('argument by the stick') was brought to bear when the constitutional requirement for unanimity in relation to Slovenia's desire to quit the federation was violated, and it was also made clear that it would be used equally as a means of forcing others to stay within the 'community'.

Thus, in the lead-up to the break-up of Yugoslavia, a situation arose whereby Serbia, the most powerful republic, deeply dissatisfied with its situation, acquired monopoly control over the instruments of coercion, which were strong enough to give the Serbs a good chance of bringing all the territories of the old federal state back under their rule. There had to be an excuse. Given that no such excuse could be dreamed up in relation to Slovenia, whether on historical, political or demographic grounds, it had to be allowed to go. The same went for a part of Croatia. For the rest, a logically incoherent system of 'explanation' was introduced, which rested on demographic arguments where there was no historical pretext (parts of the territory of Croatia), stressing, for example, the fact that Serbs are the majority population in the area around Knin, while ignoring historical and political factors which clearly show that there has never been a Serbian state in this area. And in the opposite cases, where the demographic argument was overwhelmingly to the advantage of the non-Serbian population (Kosovo, parts of Vojvodina, the Sandjak), its force was simply ignored and historical and political arguments were brought to the fore. That the problem of interpretation is not an important one for them, and that the logic of arguments is as nothing against the logic of the premeditated use of raw military force, the authorities in Belgrade demonstrated with maximum clarity in the case of Bosnia and Hercegovina. The republic of Bosnia and Hercegovina as a whole covers a region in which Serbs were never in the majority – so the demographic argument has no strength here. Nor has there ever been a Serbian state on the territory of Bosnia, so the political and historical argument for incorporating even a part of it into Serbian territory is similarly invalid. To paraphrase Lord Acton, whose position on power is well known, 'Unjustified actions require force; absolutely unjustified actions require absolute force.'

A good example of this is the slogan with which Belgrade condemned the outcome of the democratic referendum conducted in Bosnia and Hercegovina: 'No one can impose their will on the Serbian people!' Given that that 'no one' represented, in the given case, more than 67 per cent of the citizenry, it is clear that a more accurate rendition of the underlying thinking would be: 'The Serbian people will impose its will on anybody it likes, whether they are in a majority or minority.'

How has this issue of the imposition of wills turned out in the case of Macedonia? In a situation in which the precedent of Slovenia had received the official approval of the central authorities of the former federal state, the citizens of Macedonia were faced with two options:

- to remain in the reduced federation;
- to secede from a community already to a great extent broken up, and to finally realise the age-old dream of an independent state.

In favour of the first option stood the indisputable comparative advantages of life under the old system, the economic links and the real integration of all important aspects of social life, and also the psychological routine of virtually an entire generation. In favour of the second stood the clear-cut nationalist profile of the key players in the new structure, unequivocally unprepared to tolerate anyone's national programme except their own. At the same time, it rapidly became clear, as soon as the troops of the supposedly joint army were pulled back from the territory of

Slovenia and regrouped in the areas of vital interest for the realisation of the programme of the centre, that this was the best moment to break with an ally to whom
no loyalty was owed – because he himself had violated every obligation of loyalty.
There can be no doubt that the Serbian programme was not 'the unification of all
Serbs within one state', but rather the destruction of a federation based on the principles of national equality and its substitution by a state dominated by Serbs. The
fact is that in Yugoslavia the Serbs *were* objectively united in one state – to a greater
degree and on a greater terrritory than is envisaged in their most radical national
programmes. The problem was that that state was not a *Serbian* state, certainly not
to the extent that would have satisfied the authors of the centre's programme for the
creation of such a state.

All this notwithstanding, the weight of inertia of the common Yugoslav life in
Macedonia was so strong, that a year after the attack of the JNA on Croatia, and six
months after the aggression against the officially recognised, independent state of
Bosnia and Hercegovina, the Macedonian government, in fear and trembling that it
might share the same fate, was still in alliance with the government in Belgrade.
The army of the Belgrade regime, which was still installed on Macedonian territory,
gave an unambiguously realistic cast to these fears and trembling. And after the referendum of 8 September 1991 showed that the majority preferred the independence
option, and Macedonia was proclaimed an independent state, that army demonstrated that the anxieties had not been groundless. Although defined as 'Yugoslav',
it retreated – under pressure of international circumstances – more or less as if it
had been retreating from an occupied country. All its arms, its movable military
stocks, its equipment, it took with it, this 'joint army of all the peoples and national
groups of Yugoslavia'.

Macedonia found herself in an unusual situation: finally herself and free, but
practically without resources or assets and without a single genuine ally. She did not
have the capacity to defend her independence from within, and she was faced with
four immediate neighbours, all prepared to use any weakness on the part of
Macedonia to their advantage. Psychologically, this could hardly be a factor of
unity among Macedonians as they assessed the situation. Joy at the attainment of
sovereignty (predominant among younger people) was mixed with fears about the
price that might have to be paid (predominant among the older generation). In addition to this generational polarisation, there began gradually, under the pressure of
uncertainty about future events, to crystallise elements of internal stratification on
the basis of ethnic (linguistic, cultural, religious) identity. The thesis that it was
worth becoming 'smaller, weaker and more isolated', as the price of becoming
freer, began to be undermined by a growing feeling of mutual distrust, and a sense
of the very real threat to the newly acquired independence posed by possible intervention from outside.

The 'Sinking of the Titanic' as a social and political paradigm

Treatments of the situation in Macedonia, even when they appear in the most rep-
utable journals and emanate from the most distinguised pens of Britain, France,

Germany and the USA, reduce, without exception to schematic ideologising and empty phrases. This extends to a kind of anamnesis, when the arrant nonsense about Tito and Stalin as the 'creators of the Macedonian nation' is repeated, with a total lack of any evidence or even the most elementary knowledge of the history of the 'Macedonian Question'; and in relation to possible future scenarios, when the problem is simplifed to the level of political machinations, or of some 'historical animosity' among the citizens of Macedonia.

The long-term political interests of the most powerful states, and the more concrete implications of those interests for Macedonia (which are difficult to analyse expect *ex post* because they are conceived outside the sphere of domestic debate) apart, the situation in Macedonia is determined to a considerable degree – by its citizens! The key problem for Macedonia today is how to define, preserve and strengthen its critically threatened cultural and psychological identity. *Contrary to the dominant interpretation, the problem is not how to integrate Macedonia, as a multiethnic community, but how to prevent its disintegration.* The tradition of different cultures living together goes back centuries, even millennia, in Macedonia. The problem is how to preserve that tradition and that cohesion. It is under greater threat now than at any time previously, in great part because of the opening-up to a variety of influences, institutions and factors, so numerous that control over their operation is practically impossible, and which justify their presence by seeking *to create something which already exists.*

To take the matter into one's own hands, to constitute one's own axiological model on the basis of the distinctive characteristics of one's own life situation – that is the imperative that faces every social unit, and faces Macedonia with exceptional and dramatic clarity at the present time. At a time when others are deciding about crucial aspects of your cultural life, economics, politics and strategy – and that really is the situation in Macedonia today – the very bases of society are undermined, its vitality drains away, and self-respect and moral orientation are gravely threatened. The conditions for an immediate stabilisation of Macedonia, combined with a rapid implementation of the declared aims of the international community in relation to Macedonia, are two-fold:

- strong guarantees from Europe and the UN against *armed interference from outside*;
- restriction of all foreign missions and representations to an advisory capacity, to be activated only on the express demand of the social and state organs of Macedonia, to allow full freedom of decision-making and action in relation to domestic matters to domestic actors!

If 'the road to Hell is paved with good intentions' (Dante), then the domestic aspects of the Macedonian Question cannot be solved by deferring to the suggestions of advisers from other countries, however good their intentions. The urgency of the issue of regaining the initiative, and full sovereignty in all decisions of a domestic character, as an imperative condition for the effective handling of fractured social relations and the establishment of a strong social identity for Macedonia, can be illustrated by an analysis of human behaviour in situations of real, direct threat to life. If we take the Titanic disaster as a case study, we will be able to map out some universal characteristics and make some sensible predictions about the behaviour of the actors in such situations.

As is well known, the Titanic was sailing across the Atlantic with around 2000 people on board. It was a magnificent ship, irreproachably well-organised and ordered. There were three classes of passenger, plus a microclass: the crew. Respect, tolerance and decorum were, by all accounts, maintained at an impressive level throughout the voyage, so that 'class' differences were barely noticeable, regardless of the nuances with respect to cabins and service. If they had not met with disaster, it would have remained thus until the end of the voyage. Hitting the iceberg, and the introduction of the danger of sinking, radically changed the pattern of behaviour and dramatically pointed up the latent differences. First-class passengers received (or demanded) absolute priority on the lifeboats; and second-class were given priority over third-class. They all realised at that same moment that, quite apart from questions of fairness and morality, they were really not equal – and that this lack of equality could mean that *you* would lose your life. Certainly, the strong had to defer to the weak, the young to the old, men to women and the healthy to the sick; but within each category an atmosphere of fierce rivalry and competition developed. While a man might be obliged, by some social logic, to give up his place to a woman, a given woman would see in another woman only a rival in the struggle of life and death; the irreproachable harmony that the ship had sailed in was shattered in a cacophony of shouting and screaming.

The situation in Macedonia is very similar, though more complex, and in terms of the consequences of internal strife, *under the impact of foreign threats,* significantly more risky. Macedonia is a part of a continent which has grown into an island, a mountain surrounded not by inanimate icebergs, but by 'smart' icebergs, which think and watch for the best moment to hit the side of the ship and sink it. And there is not one iceberg, but four, and the ship is steered amidst continual interference from a multitude of advisers, who bear no consequences if there is a catastrophe (they were, so to speak, lowered on to the deck by helicopter, do not live here, nor intend to stay here). And on this ship there is none of the abundance, the comfort of the Titanic, but rather a crisis of existence, and nothing more than an abyss where social status, authority and real possibilities of salvation ought to be, should things come to the worst ...

A referential analytical approach clearly demonstrates that the highest levels of harmony and integration, of social and cultural tolerance of cohesion, cannot survive long under the pressure of a real threat which would, if realised, impinge unequally, i.e. would privilege some and disadvantage others. This is precisely the situation in Macedonia. The objective dangers come from all four sides (the 'icebergs'). If there were armed intervention from the side of Serbia, it would greatly favour the Serbs of Macedonia, might bring some advantage to a section of the Macedonian population – and would place the Albanians in great peril, possibly signalling the start of genocide against the Muslim population. The big question in this context is the following: How do the different groups reckon the odds in relation to these possibilities? Could they rely for help on groups that were not threatened in the given situation? More concretely, could the average Macedonian Albanian count on unstinted help and a readiness to fight shoulder-to-shoulder from all the citizens of Macedonia in the case of military aggression from Serbia, which would, undoubtedly, target him as the main victim? Or if the 'iceberg' came from Bulgaria, the situation would be similar, except that it would be one section of the Macedonian population that would be favoured, while things would not be so good for the Serbs. How would the different groups behave if events fell out thus? Who could we trust? Who would we have to be wary of? On the scenario of Greek intervention: again the same dilemma. Military intervention from Albania would reverse the order of privileged and threatened in relation to the first two possibilities. What all four scenarios have in common is that they are all quite realistic, on the basis of what has happened over the past three years. All deepen and directly feed the growing distrust among people who grew up in conditions of a high level of coexistence and mutual tolerance. If this had not been so, Macedonia would not have been able to survive as long as she has under the pressure of threats, propaganda, emissaries, rumours … It is no wonder that intercommunity relations have cooled. The real wonder and feat of cohabitation is the fact that relations within Macedonia *are still quite bearable*.

The sense in which all the ethnic groups of Macedonia are in the same situation is in terms of extreme uncertainty about their future, and the critically acute feeling that they need to seek support from 'kith and kin from outside', not to mention the anomic effects of power struggles, a difficult economic situation, pressures about the very name of the country, conditionality, even brutal blackmail and the adoption of models from alien cultural matrices. (Now the very kindergartens are under systematic pressure from American 'educators'.) All this raises the degree of mutual distrust dramatically and with it the risk of conflict. Actions aimed at removing the very substance of cultural, linguistic and national identity, common to Macedonia as a whole, are being systematically imported from the centres of global political and economic power. They affect all our citizens in equal measure. The objectively competitive status of historical, political and demographic disputes could be solved through the introduction, by emergency procedure, of a temporary 'sole bearer of sovereignty',[4] accompanied by the suspension of particularist demands – also temporary but no less urgent. This compromise solution (with recognition of the full equality of all ethnic, religious and cultural groups), which is logically best and feasible, and through which everyone would be simultaneously defined on the basis of belonging to the state of Macedonia in the primary and dominant sense of being citizens and subjects, is in practice greatly hindered, if not deliberately blocked, by the continued manipulation of the 'Titanic' situation by one or other of the four sides. For if any of the sectarian variants was implemented, it would simply destroy the very idea of a community based on equal rights; each one would involve relationships of inequality, conflict and unremitting discrimination.

At this moment, it is realistic to consider that the basic goal of the majority of the citizens of Macedonia is the same: to create an independent and sovereign state, an equal member of the European Community. How big that majority is in percentage terms is impossible to say, nor is it very important. The desire to maintain the sovereignty that has been asserted, and to remain at the helm of Macedonia's destiny,

---

[4] *jedinstveni nosilac suvereniteta.*

dominates everything. But 'Gentlemen, Macedonia is no island!' Many roads lead to Macedonia and it is easy to get in to it, whether your intentions are good or bad. Macedonia is susceptible and vulnerable. At the same time, 'Gentlemen, Macedonia is a kind of island' – with its unmistakable features, priceless on the palette of the cultural and anthropological wealth of the world, which it is our duty to cherish and protect. Macedonia is not strong enough to survive, if it comes to an internal confrontation of its citizens on the basis of nationality, any more than any other state in the world. But at the same time, like every other state, Macedonia is capable of surviving any ordeal, on condition that all external violations of the cohesion and solidarity of its inhabitants cease. If that condition is fulfilled, Macedonia will continue to be what she has been through more than two thousand years: an island of harmony and moderation in the heart of the tempestuous Balkan peninsula.

A beleaguered economic transition

Macedonian transition has been slow. While a privatisation programme was drawn up as early as 1992, it remained largely unimplemented through the years of uncertainty, and at March 1996 only 604 companies had been privatised, with an additional twenty-five post-socialist giants under a special, World Bank-sponsored pre-privatisation restructuring regime. But the really extraordinary thing is that there has been any Macedonian transition at all. In conditions of double embargo 1994–95 – with the UN sanctions on Serbia cutting the southern republic off from its traditional, Yugoslav markets, and the Greek embargo denying it access to its traditional port, Thessaloniki – Macedonia made a better show of maintaining budgetary balance and keeping prices stable than most transition economies in this period. The inflation rate fell from 335 per cent in 1993 to 57 per cent in 1994 and 10 per cent in 1995. The price of relative stability, in terms of production levels, has been high. Officially reported real GDP fell 16 per cent in 1993, 7 per cent in 1994 and 3 per cent in 1995, and GDP per head now stands at just $700. But average monthly personal income is still around $140, reflecting the fact that the second economy now makes up more than one-half the aggregate real economy.

This predominance of the second economy is at once the greatest strength and the greatest weakness of the Macedonian economy. It was the second economy, in particular the smuggling and boot-legging economy, that kept the country going through the years of double embargo. But now that there are, once again, real prospects of a sharp increase in legitimate trade, the mafia-vested interests, the drug barons and the corrupt politicians that play their game could emerge as major obstacles to sustained recovery. On the more technical side, the banking system remains weak. The government has followed a policy of reorganisation, aimed at breaking the communist-era dominance of Stopanska Banka, still Macedonia's biggest bank, and recapitalisation. The programme has the support of the World Bank, and has shown some positive results. But it is unlikely, in the immediate future, to provide the kind of mobiliser of investible funds that Macedonia desperately needs. That means that foreign investment will be crucial. Slovenian investors are already active in Macedonia, but Skopje must hope for a full-scale commercial rapprochement with Greece, economically her strongest neighbour, and ultimately a flow of FDI from that country. There are also prospects for international investment in Macedonia's tobacco industry.

Prospects for social peace

Bringing the gangsters under control and following sensible restructuring policies will come to nothing if Macedonia's fragile ethnic and social balance is disrupted. As we have seen, the Macedonian record on keeping the tension between its two main ethnic groups under control has, up to now, been as impressive, and as untypically Balkan, as its record on inflation. The main political party representing the Albanian minority, the Albanian Party for Democratic Prosperity, continues to work with the social-democratic (i.e. former communist) government, holding five ministerial portfolios at early 1996. But the difficult issue of the Albanian university remains unresolved. And the 'ethnic timebomb' still worries the Macedonian majority, with Albanian birthrates likely to continue to be two to three times higher than Macedonian. The Albanians continue, too, to complain – with some justification – about discrimination in employment. The worry is that as restructuring gathers pace, and unemployment soars, probably to around 50 per cent, the mixture of ethnic and social tension may become explosive. Some of that tension will be neutralised by the continued development of the small enterprise sector (there were more than 70,000 registered companies at mid-1995). But the statesmanship of the Macedonian leadership is likely to face at least as many challenges in the future as it has in the past.

Leadership and security

President Kiro Gligorov, by common consent one of the outstanding political figures to emerge from the ruins of Yugoslavia, made a remarkable, if not absolutely complete, recovery from the assassination attempt of October 1995. At early 1996 he was in a position to review Macedonia's progress since independence with some satisfaction. The Serbian threat has receded, at least for the time being; economic cooperation with Albania and Bulgaria is burgeoning (having started to develop as a response to the Greek embargo); and the September 1995 agreement with Greece has provided a basis for the normalisation of external relations to the south. Macedonia's small army is well-organised, if lightly armed. Together with the 1200 UN troops still stationed on Macedonia's border with Serbia, it represents a 'minimum sufficiency' deterrent to a would-be aggressor. But the accord with Greece did not resolve all points of disagreement between the two states. And trouble could still come from Serbia, especially if Kosovo ignites. Perhaps more than in the case of any other transition state, Macedonia's prospects are critically dependent on *good government* and on the willingness of the international community, and especially the EU, to support good government at home with realistic prospects of international integration abroad.

References

ASNOM 1944–1994 (1994) (Skopje: Dokumenti, Arhiv na Makedonija, Matica Makedonska).

Cvijić, Jovan (1987) *Sabrana Dela* (Belgrade: Srpska Adademija Nauka i Umetnosti).

Muhić, Ferid (1992a) Makedonien im Spannungsfeld zwischen Serbien, Bulgarien und Griechenland. In *Dokumentation einer Veranstaltungsreihe über die Zukunft der Ehemaligen Jugoslawischen Republiken,* Graz, April–July, pp. 37–46.

Muhić, Ferid (1992b) Der Dominoeffekt in Jugoslawien – eine Untersuchung zur Genese des politischen Zerfalls und der Konflikte. In Johann Gaisbacher (ed.) *Krieg in Europa* (Linz: Sandkom), pp. 49–58.

Muhić, Ferid (1994) *Macedonia. Catena Mundi* (English edn) (Skopje: Tabernakul).

Perry, Duncan (1988) *The Politics of Terror – the Macedonian Revolutionary Movements 1893–1903* (Durham and London: Duke University Press).

Chapter 14

By Way of Conclusion
to Avoid the Extremes of Suffering ...

IVAN VEJVODA

> I hate these absolute systems which make all events of history depend on great first causes by a chain of fatality, and which as it were exclude man from the history of mankind ... I believe ... that many important historical facts can only be accounted for by accidental circumstances and that many others remain inexplicable; that finally chance, or rather this intertwining of secondary causes which we call chance because we cannot disentangle them, plays an important role in what we see as the theatre of the world; but I believe firmly that chance only does what has already been prepared in advance. Previous facts, the nature of institutions, the condition of the spirit, the state of mores are materials with which it composes these impromptus which so astonish and scare us.
>
> Alexis de Tocqueville

The best counter-example to the former Yugoslavia is Switzerland. At the peace of Westphalia in 1648 Switzerland's neutrality and security were guaranteed. With 'minor' hiccups (including a brief civil war in the nineteenth century and, most notably in the present century, a long-running dispute over the Jura canton) this Alpine country had 350 years to work out, stabilise and consolidate a multinational, multilingual and multireligious state. The former Yugoslavia was on an historic fault-line with a short-lived history in two parts (of twenty-three and forty-six years respectively) from 1918 to 1991, during which a centralised monarchic authority and later a communist-totalitarian regime in turn failed to sow the seeds of a possible democratic community, but rather engaged in power-preserving strategies. Even with such an 'unfinished state' (Djindjić, 1988), such an 'improbable survivor' (Pavlowitch, 1988), there still seemed to exist the 'possibility of a pluralist [re]constitution of Yugoslavia' (Puhovski, 1989), predicated on 'social change ... democratisation [as an] imperative for [it's] survival as an independent and integral community' (Golubović, 1987: 446). The pluralist reconstitution, the democratisation, finally came with the first free elections in 1990 at the republic level. But that spelt the end of Yugoslavia.

State formation theory has identified:

> two large processes ... The first is the extension of power and range of a more or less autonomous political unit by conquest, alliance, bargaining, chicanery, argument, and administrative encroachment, until the territory, population, goods, and activities claimed by the particular center extended either to the areas claimed by other strong centers or to a point where the costs of communication and control exceeded the returns from the periphery. [The second consists] of the more or less deliberate *creation* of new states by existing states. The carving up of Yugoslavia and Czechoslovakia out of the trunk of the Austro-Hungarian Empire is a relatively pure case.
>
> (Tilly, 1975: 636)

Yugoslavia was a country that had been imagined in the nineteenth century by Croat, Serb and Slovene cultural elites alike – a dream (the unification of the South Slavs) that their respective politicians espoused and endeavoured to turn into reality. This internal political and cultural dynamic was forcefully thrust forth by the Versailles-Trianon Wilsonian chemistry made possible by the defeat of empires after the First World War. A unification project had come to fruition at a time when the development of the identities of the South Slav ethnic groups was already well-advanced (Pavlowitch, 1994: 205). The ideal of creating a nation-state, composed of Yugoslavs, to be created – in the manner of the Italian Conte Massimo d'Azeglio ('We have made Italy, now we have to make the Italians')[1] – out of the South Slav subgroupings, proved to be a Herculean and ultimately impossible task, in view of the completely inadequate, non-democratic political dynamics that were used in running the newly created (1918) and then (in 1945) revived state.

Yugoslavia was thus seen by many as an artificial construct. On the other hand, its seventy-two-year-long, often stormy, existence created a territorial reality which, especially after the Yalta settlement, cried out for political legitimisation. That legitimisation was provided in the postwar period by a communist ideology that thrust Yugoslavia on to centre stage, as a buffer country between the two Cold War blocs – but without changing its essentially peripheral position. The territorial reality was coupled by the experiential reality of generations being born and socialised in a country that, notwithstanding its communist garb and largely because of its growing international prestige, gave its citizens a sense of belonging to a stable European country. It was a country in which people were brought up to believe – like other Europeans – that war was a phenomenom of the past. *Never again ...* This lulled many into the illusion that, for belligerence to be buried once and for all, it was enough to be geographically on European soil and that somehow the invisible hand of progress would do the job, irrespective of the institutional and political realities.

There were others who dreamed of a break-up and partitioning of the country into a series of new states. They have been particularly prominent among the various diasporas. The phenomenon of the 'long-distance nationalism' (Anderson, 1992), of those who invoke the need for partition from several thousand miles away while peacefully living with their multinational neighbours in the United States, Canada or elsewhere, has been one of the elements fuelling the wars and divisions in the former Yugoslavia. Internally, within Yugoslavia, there were those who did not believe in its viability or its longevity, viewing it only as a transitory construct. Interestingly enough, Edvard Kardelj, the main party ideologue in the communist period, stated in private in 1957 to the carefully selected small working group writing the Communist Party programme:

> Yugoslavia is an historically temporary creation. It is a phenomenon and result of the imperialist epoch and the ensuing constellation of international relations in that epoch. With the development of world integrational processes and the withering away of the imperialist epoch its peoples will be able to go and join new associations and integrations following civilisational and spiritual affinities, and Yugoslavia will thus inevitably be recomposed as a state. In that sense we Slovenes will understandably be with the Italians

---

[1] The words were spoken at the time of the unification of Italy in 1861.

and Austrians, and the Serbs with the Bulgarians or with other historically close Orthodox peoples.

(Ćosić, 1987: 7)

Some thirty years later his co-national, Milan Kučan, now President of independent Slovenia, then member of the highest body of the Communist Party of Yugoslavia, wrote an article in the main party paper entitled 'In search of a new identity for Yugoslavia' (Kučan, 1988). He evoked a possible future for the country based on constitutional reform, but argued that this was only possible 'on the basis of a 1974 constitution which is still valid today when it comes to the founding principles of the relations within the federation, i.e. the relations between our nations and nationalities and their national states'. Competing visions of how the federation was to be recast, and more importantly how the spoils of communist power were to be shared or snatched, defined the contours of conflict over constitutional reform and later over territories and borders.

Identity crisis, political crisis

The continuously 'unsettled state of Yugoslav society and politics' (Shoup, 1968: 265) produced a unique feature in Yugoslav politics, in that the question of the 'sense and justification of its existence' (Samardžić, 1994: 93) was constantly being raised. After Tito's death in 1980, it seemed, in this connection, that a watershed had been passed. The death of the man who had ruled singlehandedly for more than thirty-five years was seen in the West as a possible breaking point, and a cue for the collapse of the federation. This opinion hinged on the simplistic idea that Tito had held the whole country together like a keystone in an arch, and that after the disappearance of the keystone the structure would simply fall down. The fact that Yugoslavia survived for another eleven years laid to rest the worst nightmares of Western foreign policy-makers, but unfortunately it also lulled them into the false belief that Yugoslavia as a problem had been solved, and that the danger had passed. This 'unpreparedness' (Pavlowitch, 1994: 203) on the part of the West, caught by surprise as the edifice began to crumble, proved to be fatal for the form and content of Western intervention – it came late and clumsily, and simply intensified the endogenous dynamic of conflict (Rupnik, 1992; Rieff, 1995; Danchev and Halverson, 1996; see also Chapter 9 in this volume).

The profound crisis into which the country was sinking had been diagnosed by many an actor and analyst. Milovan Djilas's break with the party and the consequent formulation of his critique in *The New Class* in the mid-1950s presaged what was to follow. In 1971 the critical journal *Praxis* (later banned) devoted a whole issue to a critique of the current state of society (*Praxis*, 1971). But it was only with the ever-worsening economic situation after 1980, with the debt crisis and the ensuing stagnation and decline, that it became apparent once again that a major overhaul of the whole political and economic system was necessary. In a closed meeting of a largely symbolic body, the Council of the Federation, in 1984, a liberally minded representative of the old party guard charged that the party leadership and hierarchy was turning a blind eye to the crisis, in fact denying its existence, turning it to personal profit, and only deepening it by seeking to preserve the status quo (Todorović, 1984).

It was clear by the mid-1980s that the chickens of the 'crisis of identity of contemporary Yugoslav society' (Golubović, 1987) had come home to roost. Many authors (Bolčić, 1983; Mirić, 1984; Golubović, 1987; Goati, 1989; and others) produced analyses of the causes of the crisis. But the 'system' (i.e. the top political elite) was unwilling to admit at first that there was anything seriously the matter. Accordingly it was unable to come to terms with the situation, and when it did finally recognise and accept that there was a crisis, it showed itself incapable of reforming itself at the federal level and breaking the permanent stalemate that had developed there. It was hardly surprising, then, that the pressure for change built up and broke through at the level of the republics.

The fact that so many occasions and opportunities for fundamental reform were missed or only very partially pursued, simply produced an accumulation of problems, systematically neglected and therefore running increasingly out of control. Because of its 'independent' stance in international politics, Yugoslavia was flooded with Western financial support. This support artificially bolstered the economic prosperity of the individual Yugoslav, but more importantly 'made it regrettably easy for [successive] Yugoslav governments to postpone decisive action' (Dyker, 1992: 281).

There had been secret offers after the conflict with Stalin and the USSR for Yugoslavia to join NATO (1953–54); there had been advances from the Council of Europe in 1967. But Tito's communist 'reflex', and his continued deference to the 'big brother' (the USSR) meant that any move by Yugoslavia into the Western sphere was simply outside the feasible area. Yugoslavia remained within the 'totalitarian logic' (Lefort, 1979) and within the communist bloc, although independent of it in many respects. Yugoslavia's advantages over other East-Central European countries – the endogenous character of its communism, its uniqueness and 'socialist-market' originality, proved, after 1989, to be simply ingredients of a violent demise, thwarting any attempt to come to terms with its complexities and communist heritage in a peaceful manner.

The many intellectual debates in postwar Yugoslavia over its future are indicative of the trials and tribulations of Yugoslavia itself and are an important facet of the complex, and often confusing, dynamic leading to the Yugoslav breakdown. We can mention just one such debate – between the Slovene Dušan Pirjavec and the Serb Dobrica Ćosić in 1961 – as a cultural disputation over Yugoslavism, 'unitarism' of the country versus the 'fullest development of the republic or national traditions' (Shoup, 1968: 197–8). The central issue here was whether or not to seek to develop a unitary, national (Yugoslav) identity. The controversy resurfaced repeatedly through the 1970s and 1980s (Milosavljević, 1996: 1), ending finally in a meeting in Ljubljana in 1990. Thus intellectuals *were* meeting and communicating on these crucial issues across republican borders. But notwithstanding often successful join cultural endeavours, they, too (with notable exceptions), were tending to be driven back behind national-republican boundaries and compelled to answer the call of the nationalist sirens.

Yugoslavia's unsuccessful 'revolt against Yalta'

Eastern Europe's 'long revolution against Yalta' (Fehér, 1991) led gradually but decisively to a successful shedding of the communist ideology and the espousal of the principle of peaceful regime change. The fact that Yugoslavia had already found a way to free itself of the Yalta dictate and 'float freely' between the two blocs during the Cold War period – benefitting greatly from Western financial support while remaining communist and even constructing a Utopian 'third way' that would be better than anything yet seen in the way of socialism – in practice simply produced over-experimentation and an overheated polity, society and economy. Most notably, 'the constant tension between center and region in Yugoslav politics ... the continuing destructive potential of allowing interregional conflicts to persist long enough to acquire ethnic meaning' (Burg, 1983: 347, 349) had produced, by the end of the 1980s, a situation whereby every issue, however trivial, had 'acquired ethnic/national meaning', as increasingly strong links were forged between the communist elites, intent on preserving power, and the nationalist intelligentsias. In the words of one journalist, spoken in 1989, one could not say in communist Yugoslavia that a given individual was politically inclined to the right or the left; the only meaningful political label was Slovene, Croat, Serb, Albanian, etc. Allowing nationalist sentiments to substitute for political arguments, allowing the refraction and reduction of all conflicts to national grievances, facilitated the formulation and appearance of a 'logic of final solutions' (Vejvoda, 1992).

As nationalist intellectuals and *nomenklatura* circles drew closer, a new consensus began to emerge that the time had come to 'finally iron out' all inherited problems, to 'resolve once and for all' the Yugoslav tangle, to grasp the opportunity presented by the fall of the Berlin Wall and the end of communism to 'sort out' interethnic grievances. There was much talk of the impossibility of continuing to live together in one country, in a Yugoslavia which seemed increasingly to have been an 'illusion'. This kind of talk helped foster processes of ethnic homogenisation and tended to marginalise those who were not only advocating a possible institutional recasting of Yugoslavia in a democratic, multinational image, but were also warning against the possible escalation of ethnic conflict.[2]

The economic and social crisis, the rising rate of unemployment, the prevalent sense of economic hopelessness, all played into the hands of the exponents of this expansive nationalist rhetoric of the 'us' (our ethnic/national group) being 'exploited by them' (all other ethnic/national groups). *Everybody* had a grudge against Yugoslavia and against each other.

---

[2] One notable attempt to prevent the spread of war was the 'Pre-Parliament of Yugoslavia and Round-Table of the Authorities and Opposition Parties', held in the autumn of 1991. It published its findings (September 1991) under the ominous title 'How to prevent total war'.

The Great Fear

This profound economic and social crisis and depression, compounded by the agenda of unsettled scores between the poltical leaderships of the republics, the endless high-level Communist Party meetings where the future of the country was supposedly being sorted out, but out of which nothing ever resulted, led progressively but insidiously to the appearance of a 'Great Fear' among the population of the whole country. Although emanating from a quite different historical setting, the 'Great Fear' of 1789, and the vivid analysis of that phenomoneon provided by Georges Lefebvre (1971) can help us understand the state of mind of authorities and citizens alike in the Yugoslavia of *c.* 1990.

What were the leaderships afraid of? They were all afraid of the new post-communist world of pluralistic politics they were headed for. They feared each other and each others' secret goals. The leadership of Serbia under Slobodan Milošević had, in addressing the very real problem of relations within Serbia, thrown off balance the federal architecture of 1974, 'provok[ing] resistence and strengthen[ing] the aspirations for independence of the other peoples of Yugoslavia' (Perović, 1993: 63). Indeed, when Serbia, territorially the biggest unit, with the most numerous population and also the greatest number of nationals living in other republics, decided to move on the constitutional issue, it sent a veritable shockwave through the country.[3] The repressive actions against the Albanians living in Kosovo were perceived, rightly or wrongly (it makes no difference in terms of the Great Fear) as the model of future behaviour of the Serbian leadership toward the other republics. And so the Great Fear spread to the population as a whole. The Albanians in Kosovo were in fear of the Serb leadership, but the Serb minority living within Kosovo had similarly been in fear of the Albanian majority with which they were sharing Kosovo. Once Croatia, the second largest republic, started to make clear moves towards putting forward its own independent agenda, fear started to spread among the Serbs living on its territory. Pronouncements by the newly elected President, Franjo Tudjman, to the effect that he was happy that his wife was neither a Serb nor a Jew (Rieff, 1995: 65) did nothing to dispel this fear.

This cascade of fear, uncertainty, and utter insecurity spread into Bosnia, where three of the six constitutionally (1974 constitution) defined 'constituent nations' of Yugoslavia were sharing one republic in a communist 'consociationalism' (Lijphart, 1977) of sorts, with no group having a majority. The fear in Bosnia and Hercegovina was heightened when it was reported that the meeting between

---

[3] Here is a view from Slovenia of Yugoslavia as a communitarian construct, framed by Serbian policies:

Yugoslavia fell apart 'because of intolerance, and even more so of Serbian incapacity to accept Yugoslavia's ethnic and cultural diversity as a reality and a benefit. In terms of the latter factor, one can say without exaggeration that from the Slovenian perspective the Serbs' equation of Yugoslavia with Serbia contributed substantially to the Slovene shift from Herder to Hegel, a move that ultimately led to the emergence of an independent Slovenian state. Serbia had tried since 1918 to turn Yugoslavia into an association of individuals, although it was in reality a community of collective personalities' (Vodopivec, 1994: 44).

Presidents Tudjman and Milošević on 17 March 1991 in Karadjordjevo had focused on plans for the partition of Bosnia (Glenny, 1993: 149; Silber and Little, 1995: 143–4). Against this background, relations between the three communities of Bosnia and Heregovina, always delicately poised (see Chapter 6), became increasingly precarious and vulnerable to the destabilising effect of rumour and hearsay.

The fear thus born was accompanied by and exacerbated by the revival of the bad memories of the period of the Second World War. And 'where the images of the past and the affections which attach to these (and around which action is organised) … are pulled apart, where human beings have forgotten or no longer agree on … "the first and last things", there is "opened up a great vacuum in the public mind, yawning to be filled", and men rush in only to exhaust themselves' (Smith, 1985: 4). This vacuum is filled with a multiplicity of narratives: historical, real or invented, constructed or imagined, based on experience or heard from ancestors, practical political, instrumental and manipulative, all joining one main current, feeding apprehensions and purveying black and white interpretations in which the majority of the positive sides of the past are pushed aside and obliterated.

One could make a hypothetical journey through all of the former Yugoslavia and its republics, spelling out the political, social, economic and existential fear that was slowly building up under the pressure of the acceleration of the dynamics of the crisis. In such a situation, when all is uncertain *and there is no outlook for the future*, the identity haven of ethnos/nation seems an ideal harbour for those stricken by stifling fear and discontent. 'Nationalism was the most important such collectivity, promising a happy and healthy world protected against the rush of time' (Mosse, 1987: 1).

Individuals feared the exit from communism and the protective cocoon it offered. They struggled to come to terms with the risks involved in that exit. They were led by the loss of certainty into a pattern of homogenisation which gave no scope whatsoever for alternative action. The role of the media in the build-up of the Great Fear was at all times crucial. There had been a gradual 'republicanisation of the press' (Ramet, 1992: 61), a raising-up of media walls inside which each *nomenklatura* could closely control the messages it was sending out to its constituency. The content of these messages became increasingly hostile to the 'others' as the war approached.

The consequences and costs of war and the 'high price of peace'

The consequences of war, more specifically of 'new wars' (Kaldor and Vashee, 1996), are seldom what those who engage in them anticipate at the outset. Rarely do wars lead to improvement and, even where the public or hidden aims of war are attained, it is generally through the unmeasurable suffering of civilian populations.

The Yugoslav wars have been fought by overlapping ethnic/national groups over conflicting claims to territory, against a background of confusion as to who has the right to self-determination – the former Yugoslav republics or the nations of the former Yugoslavia. The outcome has in the event brought independence and sovereignty to the former republics without changes of border, a higher degree of ethnic homogeneity in certain republics (Croatia and Bosnia) and a difficult multiethnicity in others (Serbia/Montenegro/FR Yugoslavia and Macedonia). The Yugoslavia that in 1991 had a population of around 24m has been broken down in to five smaller states: Slovenia (2m population); Croatia (4.4m); Bosnia and Hercegovina (composed, for the moment, of two entities: the Bosnian(Muslim)-Croat Federation and the Serbian Republic) (4m), the Federal Republic of Yugoslavia (Serbia and Montenegro) (10.5m) and Macedonia (2m).

There have been enormous losses to set against the gains. All the new states, with the exception of Slovenia, have been severely set back in economic and social terms. The war has perverted the course of economic restructuring and transition to the market economy. It has indeed led to a widespread criminalisation of the economies at the focal point of the war. War profiteers, in league with corrupt politicians, have made immense fortunes, while the lot of the majority of the population has been that of loss and despair. Much of the population of the new states now lives below the poverty line and people are forced into the grey economy to survive. The wages from official jobs simply cannot provide even for bare essentials. Brain drain has been the personal solution for many highly qualified individuals, but this does not bode well for rapid recovery in the economies concerned, because much-needed expertise will simply not be there. Those who have stayed behind will continue to be hampered for years to come by the deficiencies of a run-down, vandalised transport and energy infrastructure.

The most serious damage, however, has been psychological. Individuals have been, in various ways, some more, some less severely, knocked out of their everyday private and professional routines. When asked by a journalist what was the greatest problem for his business in postwar conditions, a small private entrepreneur in Lebanon answered that it was the fact that his workers had simply lost the habit of working eight hours a day at a machine.

There has also been a political cost. While the formerly hardline communist eastern neighbours of the former Yugoslavia have already embarked on the road to accession to the European Union, with six years of consolidation of democratic institutions behind them and a successful record of alternation in power, in the war-struck states that have emerged out of former Yugoslavia the political dynamic has been wholly distorted. Those who were and remain in power have managed to throw off balance and marginalise their oppositions. The latter will only now, in postwar conditions, be able to begin to recover.

The fact that the Yugoslav wars coincided with the move towards democracy, that democratisation seemed to have opened them up to war-prone behaviour (Mansfield and Snyder, 1995), will also have relevance to future political developments (Puhovski, 1989: 218–19). Majoritarian democracy has proved fatal in the case of Bosnia and Hercegovina. This former Yugoslav republic, which had functioned politically in terms of a three-way power-sharing relationship, should not have been forced by the EU Robert Badinter Commission into majoritarian democratic decision-making (29 February–1 March 1992). It would have been much better to develop a consociational democratic model (McRae, 1974; Lijphart, 1977). As in the case of other similar, if not identical conflicts, as in Northern Ireland, Israel–Palestine and South Africa, inventiveness and imagination are an indispensable element in the quest for a satisfactory solution for all parties involved. The 'high price of peace' (Crick, 1990: 269) becomes evident with the realisation that there can be no ultimate victory for any one of the parties, that the 'other' (as co-national or as neighbour) will always be there, and that therefore accommodation is *unavoidably necessary*.

As 'the elusive search for peace' continues, the new states are increasingly in a situation where they can articulate their interests, and thus find common ground with neighbouring new states in the pursuit of stability and prosperity. And although 'national states are not the only possible form of human government, nor necessarily the best' (Crick, 1990: 275), new institutional solutions will have to be sought within the framework of the newly formed national states on the territories of the former Yugoslavia. It is clear to even the most nostaligic of former Yugoslavs that Yugoslavia will not be reconstituted in its previous form, as a common state, in any forseeable future. The Yugoslav idea may have only gone into hibernation. But its reawakening is so distant a possibility that it is frankly not even worth contemplating. The stark fact is that five new states, some of them in a precarious condition, will have to fend for themselves in a globalised world.

Of the role of individuals and states

We can legitimately ask questions as to the role of individuals in the breakdown, of elements that go beyond societal and political structures, institutions, 'habits of the heart', customs, norms. The positive or negative contribution of individual actors to the whole dynamic cannot and should not be discounted. The preponderance of politics from above, not only under communism but also under preceding regimes, has given immense power to the power-holders in the region. It has been noted for the nineteenth and early twentieth century period of East-Central European history that 'in each of the countries ... certain individuals emerged who had an enormous impact on the outcomes' (Stokes, 1989: 243). In such a context it is possible to imagine different outcomes with different key political actors in the leading roles. Further, what was true of the nineteenth century, namely that 'in the Balkans ... [the] introduction of a state on a European model occurred in a social situation that was almost completely unprepared for it' (Stokes, 1989: 245) is equally true of the introduction of democratic institutions, rules and procedures at the present time. The state continues to be used by the main political protagonists in most of the former republics as a tool of monopoly, rather than of rational governance. 'It is not surprising, therefore, that they constantly interfere in the day to day operation of politics, [seeking] to create personal regimes' (Stokes, 1989: 244).

The individuals that were elected as heads of the republics at the time of break-up are all still in power, in their presidential roles, six years and several wars later. It can be said that Slovenia and Macedonia, the northernmost and southernmost republics, have had the benefit of the more moderate politicians. Irrespective of how we judge the role of Milan Kučan in the lead-up to the unilateral declaration of Slovenian independence and the ensuing ignition (via Slovenia) of the Yugoslav wars, Slovenia is one of the success stories of East-Central Europe in transition, while Macedonia, under Kiro Gligorov, is the only former Yugoslav republic to have made an exit from the federation (and secured the retreat of the JNA from its territory) without a shot fired or a citizen of Macedonia killed. And Gligorov is now seeking to play a difficult internal political balancing act between the competing political parties on the one hand, and between Macedonians and the large indigenous Albanian population on the other, rather than to establish any kind of personality cult of his own. Presidents Franjo Tudjman, Slobodan Milošević and Alija Izetbegović, by contrast, have been heavy-handed in the conduct of internal politics, using all the means at their disposal to maintain their positions, and largely sidelining legislative and other executive bodies by concentrating all power in their own hands. They have largely worked with very narrow inner circles of advisers, in the context of which key decisions have been made without consultation with their legislatures.[4]

The relevance of all this to the question of whether there could have been a peaceful parting of the ways for the Yugoslav republics and the Yugoslav peoples is brought out by an episode – one among many such, in varying instances and circumstances – illustrating the way in which the chemistry of the political dynamics of post-Yugoslavia has worked and the intended or unintended consequences it has brought. The episode in question is the agreement *manqué* between Slobodan Milošević and Alija Izetbegović in 1991. Adil Zulfikarpašić, a liberal of the Bosnian (Muslim) diaspora, brokered the deal and awaited the final go-ahead from Izetbegović. But the Bosnian president backed out at the last moment (Djilas and Gaće, 1995: 203–26). Zulfikarpašić offers valuable insights into the background to this vitally important series of developments, and seeks to explain the breakdown of the deal in terms of the peculiar post-Yugoslav pattern of interaction between individuals and political groupings. 'However catastrophic it may seem, it was rejected out of consideration of petty party and personal interests' (Djilas and Gaće, 1995: 221). Izetbegović may have been unwilling for Zulfikarpašić to take all the credit for an agreement (although the latter disclaimed in advance any desire to make political capital out of the matter). Milovan Djilas, in his book-length debate with Zulfikarpašić, is inclined to lay most of the blame at the door of the Serbs, and secondarily at that of the Croats (Djilas and Gaće, 1995: 223). But Djilas and Zulfikarpašić are agreed that the three 'nationalist, totalitarian parties' in Bosnia 'paved the way for the conflict; they live by it and draw their strength from it' (Djilas and Gaće, 1995: 223 and 226).

Pax Daytoniana – ceasefire or peace?

Four-and-a-half years after the eruption of the first armed conflicts in 1991 the war(s) in former Yugoslavia have come to an end, or at least to a durable truce. After violence, destruction and looting, with 200,000 dead and 2.7m displaced

---

[4] The character, features and method of Milošević's rule is well-documented in a recent book by one of his acolytes, who, after the publication of the book, lost his high-ranking position in the ruling party in Serbia (Jović, 1995; see also Djilas, 1993).

persons, the war stopped, not because one side had won, but through a peace which had been brokered/negotiated/imposed from outside. *The warring parties were unable to sort it out themselves.* In the end, they had to seek intermediaries to lead them out of the chaos they had, with varying degrees of responsibility, plunged themselves into. This plea for intervention was, in fact, very much in line with the nineteenth and twentieth century history of these territories. They have always been fenced around in one way or another by the great powers, never left to themselves, always dependent on the broader constellation of the state system prevailing at the given point in time.

It is easy to be cynical and pessimistic about the Dayton peace agreement (initialled on 21 November 1995 and signed in Paris on 14 December 1995). And, perhaps, we should be: a peace achieved through 'proximity talks' involving three intra-Bosnian actors, two key actors on Bosnia's outer perimeter (Croatia, Serbia) and five of the major world powers (the US, Russia, the United Kingdom, France and Germany), with three multilateral organisations (NATO, EU, OSCE) also in attendance; an internally contradictory constitution written for one country/state composed of two independent entities, although *de facto* made up of three entities, written by US State Department legal experts, a document which embodies probably the most generous human rights provisions known to date in any constitution, but gives no indications as to how the military is to be controlled, to be upheld for one year by a 60,000-strong multinational military force under NATO command, after which a plethora of appointed civilian foreign experts are to oversee the proper functioning of the new institutional framework – need we do more than quote the local proverb that says: Too many midwives make a feeble child?

The ceasefire is precarious, the outcome of the talks reprehensible, unjust and unrealistic to many of the people affected.

But cynicism leads up a blind alley. There was no velvet divorce, no peaceful parting of the ways between the former Yugoslav republics, and it is no use expecting a good outcome after a violent separation. There can only be more or less bad solutions, and the longevity of any given solution will depend on the sincerity and will of the signing parties (internal and external) to implement them. The Dayton agreement is what exists and the players involved have to work with it. It is, like all similar agreements, a compromise to which all parties have adhered in an attempt to save what they can of what they have left – a power game in which all those who were in the leading roles at the beginning of the war are still in power now. Those in whose name this war has been fought – the countless civilians – are the losers and victims, in the worst case, that of Bosnia, virtually wholly dependent on aid, without work, plunged back into darkness, having attained a relatively prosperous standard of living before the war in the 'old' country.

The Dayton agreement has stopped the killing. This is its greatest achievement, critically important in the short term. The construction of peace, through an infinity of small steps at the everyday as well as at the macropolitical level, will be a long, painstaking, precarious process, strewn with as many pitfalls as the countryside is with landmines. The violent interruption in the Northern Ireland peace process occasioned by the IRA's bomb in central London on 8 February 1996 exemplifies the kind of obstacles that stand in the path of any search for the stable settlement of large-scale community strife. We must expect similar interruptions to the peace process in the former Yugoslavia.

The physical reconstruction of Bosnia will require an enormous effort. International commitments have already been made, although not all the money from the main contributors is yet forthcoming. Even more important, it will take repeated concrete and successful examples of freedom of movement, of returned refugees, of freedom of speech and assembly, of chances for work and employment, of media openness, of war criminals brought to trial, of the de-ethnification of politics, before the still pervasive fear, insecurity and uncertainty among individuals passes. Trust and confidence in people and institutions have to be rebuilt just like the infrastructure and the economy – only this is a much more intricate and complex process.

The top-down nature of politics in post-communist territories means that the rhetoric and signals from the respective leaderships to each other, and to their populations, will have a profound influence on the overall political atmosphere, and therefore on the prospects for change. The leverage that the United States and other foreign countries have over the internal actors (who have accepted that leverage) is a key tool in the furthering of the search for a lasting peace. The conditionalisation of economic and financial aid on compliance with the spirit and letter of the Dayton agreement is a key factor in the quest for a permanent solution.

But the agreement is only a stepping stone. *Whatever happens further down the road, peace, trust, confidence, normality require that those definitely committed to abandoning violence prevail over those who secretly still cherish it and want to bring it back.* A tired, war-weary, disillusioned population must be allowed to recover its energies and recover its capacity to voice its needs and interests. The first condition of all this is guarantees for human rights strong enough to start to rebuild the feeling of security.

The recovery and rediscovery of the political in a postwar situation, the process of re-establishing the social fabric and social bonds, of forging plurality and legality, are as important as jobs and social security, once the bare essentials have been satisfied. This is as true of Croatia and the Federal Republic of Yugoslavia (Serbia/Montenegro) as it is of Bosnia. Quite simply, without a return to a normal political dynamic, without the fostering and strengthening of democratic practices in all these countries, there will be no stability in the region and no 'creeping normalisation', such as can lead the new states from ceasefire to peace. The dangers loom large; a return to violent conflict is still possible. All the more reason to enforce the Dayton agreement rigorously on those who have agreed to act on behalf of the populations concerned and the international community.

In 1946 István Bibó wrote:

the peoples of Central and Eastern Europe must be prevented from constantly upsetting the tranquillity of Europe, with their territorial disputes … This means that in every area where some kind of consensus is yet feasible – not a mere political agreement, but a clarification of principles – we should implement this with all our force within the framework of the present [1945] peace construct, because unsettled territorial issues represent a grave threat.

(Bibó, 1991: 80)

Fifty years later, we must simply register the fact that Bibó's warning was not heeded. The creation of new nation-states has provoked havoc for more than four years in one former country of South-East Europe. The pattern produced by the exit from totalitarianism coupled with the emergence of democratic institutions has again demonstrated the truth of Tocqueville's adage that societies are most vulnerable and prone to collapse when they embark on a change of regime. That syndrome has led, in the area of the former Yugoslavia, to a return to conceptions of organic society and ethnic homogeneity. The consequent haemorrhaging of pluralism has made it that much more important that the distinct, multiple identities of the individual (all of which are tending to be submerged by the ethnic element) be brought forcefully to the fore. In the end, the 'struggles for recognition' (Habermas, 1994) will have to reconcile all these various identities.

That collective identities exist in this region of Europe is a given. But something must be done to blunt their edge and lessen their grip on the citizenry, through the rooting and guaranteeing of individual rights The problem is that communism, and before that traditional, patriarchal societies, stifled the development of any counter-balancing individualism based on an awareness on the part of individuals of their *right to have rights,* as the 'basic principle of all political modernity' (Arato and Benhabib, 1994: 31). Any awakening to rights and to solutions that do not necessitate a nation state ('Why should we be a minority in your state when you can be a minority in ours?': Gligorov, 1994: 87) will demand vision, much institutional imagination, and the will of (emerging) democratically minded leaders and active citizens to begin the ascent from 'self-imposed immaturity' (Kant, 1991: 54). Is the fact that this time, and for the first time, the war came from within the former Yugoslavia, a guarantee of calmer historical waters in the future?

> The first public obligation is to avoid the extremes of suffering ... The best that can be done as a general rule is to maintain a precarious equilibrium that will prevent the occurrence of desperate situations, of intolerable choices – that is the first requirement for a decent society to which we can always aspire in the light of the limited range of our knowledge and even of our imperfect understanding of individuals and societies. A certain humility in these matters is very necessary.
>
> (Berlin, 1990: 17–18)

References

Anderson, B. (1992) The new world disorder, *New Left Review*, no. 193, May–June, pp. 3–13.

Arato, A. and Benhabib, S. (1994) The Yugoslav tragedy, *Praxis International*, vol. 13, no. 4, January, pp. 325–38.

Berlin, I. (1990) The Pursuit of the ideal. In *The Crooked Timber of Humanity* (London: John Murray).

Bibó, I. (1991) The distress of East European small states. In I. Bibó, *Democracy, Revolution, Self-Determination. Selected Writings*, edited by Károly Nagy (Highland Lakes: Atlantic Research and Publications).

Biserko, S. (ed.) (1993) *Yugoslavia: Collapse, War, Crimes* (Belgrade: Centre for Anti-War Action & Belgrade Circle).

Bolčić, S. (1983) *Razvoj i Kriza Jugoslovenskog Društva u Sociološkoj Perspektivi* (*The Development and Crisis of Yugoslav Society in Sociological Perspective*) (Beograd: SIC).

Bougarel, X. (1996) *Bosnie: Anatomie d'un Conflit* (Paris: La Découverte).

Brown, C. (ed.) (1994) *Political Restructuring in Europe: Ethical Perspectives* (London: Routledge).

Burg, Steven L. (1983) *Conflict and Cohesion in Socialist Yugoslavia: Political Decision-making since 1966* (Princeton NJ: Princeton University Press).

Burke, A. and MacDonald, G. (1994) The former Yugoslav conflict (1991–). In M. Cranna (ed.) *The Time Cost of Conflict* (London: Earthscan Publications).

Chirot, D. (1989) (ed.) *The Origins of the Backwardness in Eastern Europe* (Berkeley, Los Angeles, Oxford: University of California Press).

Čolović, I. and Mimica, A. (eds) (1992) *Druga Srbija* (*The Second Serbia*) (Belgrade: Plato, Beogradski krug, Borba).

Ćosić, D. (1987) Uslovi demokratske budućnosti, *Književne Novine*, 15 December, pp. 7–8.

Cranna, M. (ed.) (1994) *The True Cost of Conflict* (London: Earthscan Publications).

Crick, B. (1990) The high price of peace. In H. Giliomee and J. Gagiano (eds) *The Elusive Search for Peace: South Africa, Israel and Northern Ireland* (Cape Town: Oxford University Press with IDASA), pp. 261–75.

Danchev, A. and Halverson, T. (eds) (1996) *International Perspectives on the Yugoslav Conflict* (London: Macmillan).

Djilas, A. (1993) A profile of Slobodan Milošević, *Foreign Affairs*, vol. 72, Summer, pp. 81–96.

Djilas, M. and Gaće, N. (1995) *Bošnjak Adil Zulfikarpašić* (Zurich: Bošnjački Institut).

Djindjić, Z. (1988) *Jugoslavija kao Nedovršena Država* (*Yugoslavia as an Incomplete State*) (Novi Sad: Književna Zajednica).

Dyker, D. (1990) *Yugoslavia. Socialism, Development and Debt* (London: Routledge).

Dyker, D. (1992) Yugoslavia – a peripheral tragedy, *Journal of Interdisciplinary Economics*, vol. 4, pp. 281–93.

Elias, N. (1982) *The Civilising Process* (vol. 1 *The History of Manners*; vol. 2 *State Formation and Civilisation*) (Oxford: Basil Blackwell).

Fehér, F. (1991) Eastern Europe's long revolution against Yalta. In F. Feher and A. Arato, *Crisis and Reform in Eastern Europe* (New Brunswick, New Jersey: Transaction Publishers), pp. 481–512.

Fehér, F. and Arato, A. (1991) *Crisis and Reform in Eastern Europe* (New Brunswick, New Jersey: Transaction Publishers).

Glenny, M. (1993) *The Fall of Yugoslavia* (Harmondsworth: Penguin Books).

Gligorov, V. (1994) *Why do Countries Break Up? The Case of Yugoslavia* (Uppsala: Acta University).

Goati, Vladimir (1989) *Politička Anatomija Jugoslovenskog Društra* (Zagreb: Naprijed).

Golubović, Z. (1987) *Kriza Identiteta Savremenog Jugoslovenskog Društva* (*The Crisis of Identity in Contemporary Yugoslav Society*) (Beograd: Filip Višnjić).

Habermas, J. (1994) Struggles for recognition in a democratic constitutional state. In C. Taylor and A. Gutman (eds) *Multiculturalism: Examining the Politics of Recognition* (Princeton, New Jersey: Princeton University Press).

Hayden, R. M. (1995) The Bosnian 'constitution' as a formula for partition, *East European Constitutional Review*, vol. 4, no. 4, autumn, pp. 59–68.

Janjić, D. (1994) *Conflict or Dialogue: Serbian-Albanian Relations and Integration in the Balkans* (Subotica: Open University, European Civic Centre for Conflict Resolution).

Jović, B. (1995) *Poslednji dani SFRJ* (Belgrade: Politika).

Kaldor, M. and Vashee, B. (1996) *New Wars – Part I of the Changing Global Military Paradigm* (London: United Nations University, Cassell Academic).

Kant, I. (1991) *Political Writings* (Cambridge: Cambridge University Press).

Kučan, M. (1988) Traganje za novim identitetom Jugoslavije (In search of a new identity for Yugoslavia) *Komunist*, 16 December, p. 2.

Lefebvre, G. (1971) *The Great Fear of 1789. Rural Panic in Revolutionary France* (London: New Left Books).

Lefort, C. (1979) *Eléments d' une Critique de la Bureaucratie* (Paris: Gallimard).

Lerotić, Z. (1987) *Jugoslovenska Politička Klasa i Federalizam* (*The Yugoslav Political Class and Federalism*) (Zagreb: Globus).

Lijphart, A. (1977) *Democracy in Plural Societies: A Comparative Exploration* (New Haven CT: Yale University Press).

McRae, K. D. (1974) *Consociational Democracy: Political Accommodation in Segmented Societies* (Toronto: McClelland).

Mansfield, E. and Snyder, J. (1995) Democratization and war, *Foreign Affairs*, vol. 74, no. 3, May–June, pp. 79–97.

Milanović, B. (1992) *Protiv Fašizma* (*Against Fascism*) (Belgrade: Radio B92).

Milosavljević, O. (1996) Jugoslavija kao zabluda – Odnos intelektualinih i političkih elita prema zajedničkoj državi (Yugoslavia as an illusion – the attitude of the intellectual and political elites to the common state) *Republika*, vol. 8, no. 135–6, pp. I–XVI.

Mirić, J. (1984) *Sistem i Kriza* (*System and Crisis*) (Zagreb: CKD).

Mosse, G. L. (1987) *Masses and Man: Nationalist and Fascist Perceptions of Reality* (Detroit: Wayne State University Press).

Mostov, J. (1995) Explaining ethnocracy in the former Yugoslavia, *East European Constitutional Review*, vol. 4, no. 4, autumn, pp. 69–73.

Pavlowitch, S. K. (1988) *The Improbable Survivor: Yugoslavia and its Problems 1918–1988* (London: Hurst).

Pavlowitch, S. K. (1994) Who is 'Balkanising' whom? The misunderstandings between the debris of Yugoslavia and an unprepared West, *Daedalus*, vol. 123, no. 2, Spring.

Perović, L. (1993) Yugoslavia was defeated from inside. In S. Biserko (ed.) *Yugoslavia: Collapse, War, Crimes* (Belgrade: Centre for Anti-War Action & Belgrade Circle).

Popović, O. (1991) Problem državnog ustrojstva Jugoslavije kao fundamentalno pitanje njenog opstanka i uzrok oba njena sloma 1941 i 1991 (The problem of the state construct of Yugoslavia as a fundamental issue in its formation and a reason for both its collapses (1941 and 1991)), manuscript.

Praxis (1971) Special issue: *Trenutak Jugoslovenskog Socijalizma* (*The State of Yugoslav Socialism*), no. 3–4.

Puhovski, Z. (1989) Mogućnost pluralističke konstitucije Jugoslavije (The feasibility of a pluralist constitution for Yugoslavia) *Theoria*, vol. 32, no. 1, Belgrade.

Puhovski, Z. (1994) The Moral basis of political restructuring. In Brown, C. (ed.) *Political Restructuring in Europe: Ethical Perspectives* (London: Routledge).

Ramet, S. P. (1992) *Balkan Babel: Politics, Culture and Religion in Yugoslavia* (Boulder, San Francisco, Oxford: Westview Press).

Rieff, D. (1995) *Slaughterhouse: Bosnia and the Failure of the West* (London: Vintage, Random House).

Rosandić, R. and Pesić, V. (eds) (1994) *Warfare, Patriotism, Patriarchy: The Analysis of Elementary School Textbooks* (Belgrade: Centre for Anti-War Action, Association MOST).

Rupnik, J. (1992) Lees enjeux internationaux. In *De Sarajevo à Sarajevo: L'Échec Yougoslave* (Paris: Editions Complexe).

Samardžić, S. (1994) *Prinudna Zajednica i Demokratija. Prilozi o Krizi, Slomu i Upotrebi Države* (*Enforced Union and Democracy. Essays on Crisis, Break-up and the Purpose of the State*) (Belgrade: Institut za evropske studije, Akademija Nova).

Shoup, P. (1968) *Communism and the Yugoslav National Question* (New York and London: Columbia University Press).

Silber, L. and Little, A. (1995) *The Death of Yugoslavia* (Harmondsworth and London: Penguin Books, BBC Books).

Smith, B. J. (1985) *Politics and Remembrance: Republican Themes in Machiavelli, Burke, and Tocqueville* (Princeton, New Jersey: Princeton University Press).

Stokes, G. (1989) The social origins of East European politics. In D. Chirot (ed.) *The Origins of the Backwardness in Eastern Europe* (Berkeley, Los Angeles, Oxford: University of California Press).

Tilly, C. (1975) Western state-making and theories of political transformation. In C. Tilly (ed.) *The Formation of National States in Western Europe* (Princeton, New Jersey: Princeton University Press).

Todorović, M. (1984) Izlaganje na sednici Saveta federacije u Beogradu 15. novembra 1984 (Speech at the meeting of the Council of the Federation, Belgrade, 15 November 1984), manuscript.

Vejvoda, I. (1992) The logic of final solutions. In I. Čolović and A. Mimica (eds) *Druga Srbija* (*The Second Serbia*) (Belgrade: Plato, Beogradski krug, Bouba).

Vodopivec, P. (1994) Seven decades of unconfronted incongruities: The Slovenes and Yugoslavia. In J. Benderly and E. Kraft (eds) *Independent Slovenia: Origins, Movements, Prospects* (New York: St Martin's Press).

Index

Abdić, Fikret 95, 96, 106–7, 108, 112, 133
Adžić, General Blagoje 126, 129, 130
Agrokomerc 95, 96, 162
Albanians
  Kosovo 53, 94, 138–54, 180, 190–1, 253
  Macedonia 146, 235–6, 238, 243–4, 246
  Montenegro 191
apparatchiki 48, 49–50, 58
Austro-Hungarian Empire 89–90, 198–9, 200

Badinter Commission 101, 168, 169, 255
Baker, James 168–9
Banja Luka 107, 111, 112
banks 32, 54, 56, 57, 58–9, 67, 162
Boban, Mate 101, 102, 105, 107, 110
Bosanska Krajina 105
Bosnia and Hercegovina 87–115
  Army of 103, 109, 135–7
  Bosnian Serb Army 104, 107, 130–1, 132, 133, 136
  Croat/Muslim clashes 105–6, 110, 210
  elections 89–91, 94, 96–7, 98–9, 255
  ethnic cleansing 104, 110–11
  international intervention 155, 169–70, 172, 174, 176
  JNA 131–2, 132
  League of Communists 94–5
  nationalism 77, 89, 95, 97, 98
  partition 91, 99–103, 254
  population 88n, 255
  pre Yugoslav break-up 18, 53
  reconstruction 108–9, 259
  Second World War 11, 91–2, 119
  Serb/Croat cooperation 102, 105
  Serbia and Montenegro 179, 185, 240
  Serbian Autonomous Regions 100, 112
  see also Croat-Muslim Federation; Croats;
    Muslims; Serbs

Bosnian-Croat Federation *see* Croat-Muslim
  Federation
Brezhnev, Leonid 51–2
Brioni declaration 167
Bulgaria 237, 238, 244, 246

Cazinska Krajina 95, 96, 105, 106, 107
Cold War 157–8, 162, 172–3, 249, 252
Communist Party of Yugoslavia
  1974 constitution 16–17, 18
  disbanded 118, 122
  federalisation 54
  history 11–12, 53–60, 119
  JNA 116, 117–18, 120–1, 124
  Kosovo 145–6
  Muslims 92
  opposition 21–2
Conference on Security and Cooperation in
  Europe (CSCE) 161, 164, 165, 167, 173
Contact Group 111, 112, 113, 174, 186
Ćosić, Dobrica 192–3, 251
Council of Europe 164, 211
Council on Mutual Economic Assistance (CMEA)
  160, 161–2
Croat-Muslim Federation 110–11, 113, 135, 137,
  172, 176, 210, 255
Croatia 196–212
  arms imports 122–4
  Bosnia partition 102, 113
  Brioni declaration 167
  Communist Party 12, 94–5, 183
  Croatian Army 133, 134–5
  democratisation 162–3
  economy 160, 162
  elections 22–3, 94, 205–7
  Herceg-Bosna 110, 210
  international relations 155, 163, 164, 165, 170,
    172, 175

Croatia (*continued*)
  JNA 116, 127, 128–30, 132, 207–9
  Kingdom of Yugoslavia 10
  nationalism 54
  population 255
  pre Yugoslav break-up 53
  privatisation 62, 74, 211
  recovery 259
  secession 43, 166–9
  Second World War 11, 202, 203
  Serbia and Montenegro 122–5, 128–30, 179,
    185, 207–9
  see also Krajina
Croats
  Bosnia and Herzegovina 18, 89–113
  ethnic cleansing 104
  Herceg-Bosna 101, 103, 107, 109, 110, 113,
    210
  JNA purge 130
  Muslim clashes 105–6, 110
  nationalism 135
  Owen-Stoltenberg plan 107
  Ustashas 91, 107, 108, 122, 202, 203
  see also Croat-Muslim Federation
Czechoslovakia 28, 60–1

Dayton peace agreement 112–13, 172, 173, 175,
    186, 210, 257–9
debt-service crisis 21, 33, 34–5, 56, 57, 159, 162
Delić, General Rasim 109, 136, 172
Demaci, Adem 140, 142, 148
Djilas, Milovan 12, 14, 250, 257
Duraković, N. 95–6, 108

education 13–14, 17, 71–2
ethnic cleansing 104, 110–11, 133–4, 136, 149,
    155
European Union
  association agreements 164
  Bosnia and Herzegovina 103, 169, 176, 255
  Croatia 163–4, 165–6, 167, 175, 211
  economic integration 160, 161
  International Conference on Former Yugoslavia
    170–1, 172, 173
  Kosovo 152
  Macedonia 244
  mediation 168
  recognition of republics 168–9
  sanctions 134
  Slovenia 163, 164, 165–6, 167

gangsters 66, 104–5, 108, 111
Germany 173, 174, 210
Gligorov, Kiro 48, 60, 100, 246, 257
Gorbachev, Mikhail 52, 60

Goulding, Marrack 169
Great Britain 158, 166
'Great Serb Bank Robbery' 59–60, 74
Greater Serbia 128, 130, 132, 135, 144, 184–5, 208
Greece 2, 168, 174–5, 236, 238, 244, 245–6

Herceg-Bosna 101, 103, 107, 109, 110, 113, 210
Hercegovina *see* Bosnia and Hercegovina
Holbrooke, Richard 112, 113
Hungary 56, 198–9, 200

International Conference on Former Yugoslavia
    (ICFY) 170–1, 172, 173
International Monetary Fund 34–5, 159, 160, 176
Italy 199–200
Izetbegović, Alija 104, 169, 257
  Bosnia partition 102–3
  elections 96, 98, 99
  international negotiations 106–7, 172
  reintegration 108–9

Jews 11, 88n, 90, 203n
JNA *see* Yugoslav People's Army
Jorvić, Dr Borisav 125–6
Jurjević, General Zvonko 129

Kadijević, General Velijko 103, 126, 127, 129,
    130, 137, 207n
Karadžić, Radovan 100, 102, 105, 111, 112, 131–2
Kardelj, Edvard 12, 15, 16, 18, 249
Khrushchev, Nikita 51
Kljujić, S. 101, 104, 105, 108
Komšić, I. 108, 109
Kosovo 138–54, 239
  1974 constitution 15
  1981 crisis 121
  Albanians 94, 138–54, 190–1
  autonomy suspension 182
  Bosnian Serbs 95
  brown-coal deposits 58
  elections 151–2
  international monitoring 164, 166, 168, 173
  Macedonia 175
  performance indicators 32, 40–1
  pre Yugoslav break-up 53
  Serbs 94, 180–1, 253
Krajina
  international intervention 168
  mutiny 107
  pre Yugoslav break-up 53
  see also Republic of Serb Krajina
Krajišnik, M. 99, 100
Kučan, Milan 48, 60, 205, 250, 256

Lazić, M. 104, 108

Macedonia 232–47
Albanians 146
Gligorov 257
Greece 2, 168, 174–5, 236, 238, 244, 245–6
inflation 245
Kosovo 175
League of Communists 94
population 255
Macedonians 53, 92, 236–7, 238–9, 246
Marković, Ante 59–60, 73, 79, 122, 163–4, 166, 184
Milošević, Slobodan
Bosnia and Hercegovina 102, 106, 131–2, 185, 254
coup attempt March 1991 124–6
Croatia 122–3, 126–7, 185, 207, 209–10
elections 23
'Great Bank Robbery' 59–60
international intervention 163, 171, 193
JNA 116, 117, 121–2, 130, 131, 184
Kosovo 141, 150, 153
League of Communists 94, 180
nationalism 180–2
police force 134
Slovenia 127–8
transition 48
Yugoslav Army 118
Mladić, General Ratko 111–12, 132
Montenegro 179–95
leadership change 182, 183
League of Communists 94
national minorities 191–2
privatisation 62, 189
see also Serbia and Montenegro
Muslims
Bosnia-Hercegovina 18, 88–113, 153, 169–70
Cazinska Krajina 96, 107
Croat clashes 105–6, 110, 210
internal conflicts 106–7
JNA 130
Kosovo 138–54
Macedonia 243–4
nationalism 96, 98–9
Partisan Movement 91–2
pre Yugoslav break-up 53, 92, 93
refugees 196–7
Sandjak 101
Serbia 191
Turkey 174
see also Croat-Muslim Federation

nationalism
Bosnia 89, 95–7, 98
Croats 54, 135
identity 66, 77–9, 81

JNA 130
Kosovo 94, 145
market economy 53–4
Milošević 180–2
Muslims 96, 98–9
nomenklatura 48–9, 60–1
pre Yugoslav break-up 18–20
Serbs 80, 132, 145, 184–5
Soviet Union 51
transition 49
NATO
Bosnia and Hercegovina 110, 111, 170, 172, 173, 174
Croatia 211
Dayton 258
I-For 172, 173
non-intervention 164, 167
pre Yugoslav break-up 157, 162, 251
nomenklatura 48–9, 50–1, 55, 57–61, 62–3, 221

Ottoman Empire, Bosnia 87, 88–9
Owen, Lord David 171
Owen-Stoltenberg plan 106–7, 109

Panić, General života 130, 131
Panić, Milan 192–3
Pavelić, Ante 202, 203, 204
Pavlović, Dragiša 180
Pelivan, J. 99, 104
P,rez de Cu,llar, Javier 167, 168
Poland 48, 56, 62, 159

Ranković, Aleksandar 12, 14, 93, 140
Rugova, Dr Ibrahim 144, 147, 151, 191
Russia 2, 173

Sandjak 101, 105, 108, 153
Sarajevo 106, 135–6
Dayton agreements 113
international intervention 170
paramilitary gangs 108, 136
population 92n
Serbs 101, 110, 112
Second World War 11
Bosnia 91–2
Communist Party 12
Croatia 202, 203
Kosovo 139
Partisans 91–2, 108–9, 118–19, 202
Serb Republic of Bosnia-Hercegovina 100, 103, 107, 109, 111–13, 150, 255
Serb Republic of Krajina (RSK)
defeat by Croats 79, 112–13, 131, 132–3, 134–5, 209
Serbia 127, 150, 208

Serbia and Montenegro 179–95
  Bosnia and Hercegovina 102, 113, 185, 240
  Communist Party 12, 15, 94, 180, 182–3, 184
  Croatian war 128–30
  elections 22–3, 183–4, 192–4
  Federal Republic of 185, 192, 255, 259
  'Great Bank Robbery' 59–60, 74
  inflation 179, 187
  Italy 200
  JNA 116–17, 239–40
  Kosovo 142–3, 147–51, 180–1, 253
  Macedonia 237, 238, 243–4, 246
  monetary policy 61
  nationalism 80, 184–5
  opposition 190–1
  Owen-Stoltenberg plan 107
  police force 116–17, 134
  population 255
  pre Yugoslav break-up 15, 53, 202, 253
  privatisation 62, 74, 189
  recovery 259
  sanctions against 111, 185–8, 209
  Sandjak 101
  Second World War 11, 119, 202
  Serb Republic 111, 186
  Slovenia 185
  unemployment 187
  US 169–70
  Yugoslav Army 117–18, 130, 134
Serbs
  Bosnia and Hercegovina 18, 88–113, 130–1
  Chetniks 91, 108, 119, 202
  Croatia 122–3, 127, 201–2, 207–8
  Kosovo 94, 138–54, 180–1
  nationalism 80, 132, 145, 184–5
  Second World War 11, 91, 107
  socialist elites 92
  Tito 143, 202
Serbs, Croats and Slovenes, Kingdom of the 10, 72, 90, 200–1
Šešelj, Vojislav 103, 131, 193
Silajdžić, Haris 108, 109, 110, 111, 136
Slovenia 213–31
  arms imports 123
  Brioni declaration 167
  Communist Party 12, 94
  economy 32, 162, 216–23
  elections 205, 214
  federalism 160, 161
  international relations 163, 164, 165
  JNA 116, 121–2, 130, 132, 209
  labour market 221–2
  political system 214–17
  population 255
  privatisation 62–3, 219, 220–1, 226

road-building crisis (1969) 15
secession 43, 127–8, 166–8, 205, 239
Serbia 185
transition 2, 48, 256
unemployment 218, 219, 224–5
Soviet Union
  break-up 52, 60
  Communist Party evolution 50–3
  coup attempt 126, 128
  military aid to Yugoslavia 120
  nationalism 49, 51
  Tito split 12, 53, 251
  Yugoslav break-up 164
Špegelj, General Martin 123, 209, 210
Stalin, Joseph 12, 14, 50, 53
Stambolić, Ivan 180
Surroi, Veton 146

Tito, Josip Broz
  1974 constitution 15, 18
  Bosnia 91
  Communist Party evolution 53–4
  Croatia 54, 202–4
  death 94, 250
  Kosovo 140
  nationalism 54–5
  purges 14, 54
  Second World War 11, 12, 91–2, 108–9, 119
  Serbia 143, 202
  Stalin 12, 14
  success 157
totalinarianism 13–14, 23, 65, 116–17
Trifunović, General Vlado 129
Tudjman, Franjo 257
  arms imports 122, 123
  autocracy 211–12
  Bosnia and Hercegovina 102, 106, 254
  elections 23, 122, 205–7, 208
  Herceg-Bosna 210
  international intervention 171
  nationalism 253
  transition 48
Tumanov, General Simeon 130
Turkey 174, 238
Turks, Macedonia 234, 235, 236

United Nations
  arms embargo 167–8
  Bosnia 170, 171
  Croatia 169, 172
  International Conference on Former Yugoslavia 170–1
  Krajina 168
  sanctions 110, 111, 134, 179, 185–8, 209, 245
  UNPROFOR 112, 170, 172, 173, 174, 209

United States of America
  Bosnia and Hercegovina 169, 171–2, 176
  Cold War 158
  Croatia 171–2, 175
  Kosovo 163, 164, 166
  military aid to Yugoslavia 120
  Serbia 169–70

Vance, Cyrus 168, 169, 171
Vance Plan 168, 209
Vance-Owen peace plan 105, 106, 131, 134, 186,
  193
Vatican 160, 163, 174, 201
VJ see Yugoslav Army
Vlachs 238
Vllasi, Azem 141, 144, 145
Vojvodina 15, 29, 53, 180, 182, 206, 239

Washington Agreement 106, 171, 210
West European Union 167, 173
World Bank 176, 245

Yugoslav Army (VJ) 117–18, 130, 134
Yugoslav People's Army (JNA) 116–30
  Bosnia 102–3
  Communist Party 120–1, 124
  Croatia 122–4, 196, 207–9
  Kosovo 141, 146, 182
  Macedonia 241, 257
  Milošević 116, 117, 121–2, 130, 131, 184
  power pre-break up 17–18

Serbia 202, 239–40
Slovenia 209
Territorial Defence Forces 18, 159, 160
Yugoslavia, Federal Republic of see Serbia and
  Montenegro
Yugoslavia, Federative Republic of
  1974 constitution 15–17, 18, 19, 22, 33, 55, 250
  corruption 55–6, 59–60
  decentralisation 15–16, 32, 33, 44–5, 70, 75, 93
  economy 67–74
  elections 18–19, 22
  growth 29–34, 35–6, 40–1, 57, 69, 71
  inflation 32, 34, 58–60, 61, 159–60
  investment 31, 32, 33, 35–40, 41
  labour 32, 34, 70, 221–2
  market economy 14, 28, 30–1, 33, 53–4, 67
  Muslims 92, 93
  nationalism 18–20
  privatisation 74, 76
  regional development policy 40–4
  self-management 18, 30–1, 33, 44, 54,
    70–1, 75
  social structures 21–2
  standard index of structural change 68–9
  trade 72–3
  unemployment 32, 159, 162
Yugoslavia, Kingdom of 10–12, 90–1, 119,
  201–2, 237

Zejnullahu, Jusuf 147
Zubak, Krešimir 110